First published in 2011 by Priory Publishing

Priory Publishing, 113 Rodney Drive, Christchurch, Dorset BH23 3LL

ISBN 978-0-9565260-1-4

Copyright © K. Cook 2011. The right of Kenneth Cook to be identified as the author of this work has been asserted in accordance with the Copyright & Designs and Patents Act 1988.

All rights reserved.

A CIP catalogue record for this book is available from the British Library.

Justice Denied

How to steal intellectual property helped by the
Intellectual Property Office and the British Police.

Ken Cook

Priory Publishing

Bournemouth, England

CONTENTS

Chapters		Page
1.	Introduction	14
2.	My Background Story	17
3.	The Beginning of My Kitcar Business	19
4.	The Start of Growth	23
5.	The Start of All the Problems with the Busbridges	32
6.	Nineteen Years of Battles Commence	44
7.	Robert Busbridge Tries to put Me Into Jail	52
8.	The Finalising of the Chrysler Saga	58
9.	The Actions of the IPO from 1992-2004	59
10.	A Breakdown in My Health	61
11.	My Battle of Words with the IPO Continues	63
12.	My 2003 Complaint to the Parliamentary Ombudsman Re The IPO	70
13.	My Opposition to Busbridges Application to Register My Mark	75
14.	The Hearing of My Opposition to the Registration Application	131
15.	The Hearing Held By Mr Landau into Irregularities	192
16.	The Events After Landau, 2005-2008	203
17.	My Complaint of Maladministration to the CEO of IPO	206
18.	Transcript of What Hobbs QC Said at Appeal Hearing 2005	211
19.	My Complaint to the Parliamentray Ombudsman About the Ipo	220
20.	The Rectification Application	223
21.	The Foley Rectification Decision	232
22.	Statement of Grounds for Appealing the Decision of Foley	246

Chapters	Page
23. The Appeal Hearing Before the Appointed Person Prof Annand	255
24. Transcript of the Annand Hearing	258
25. The Annand Decision Document	262
26. What is My Position Now?	268
27. The Application for Invalidity Against My Registration	273
28. The Sudden Appearance of Martin Busbridge	290
29. My Second Letter of Complaint to the CEO of the IPO, Mr Marchant.	295
30. The Statements of Martin Busbridge	302
31. The Invalidity/Rectification Heard in London 2010	310
32. The Decision of the Invalidity Hearing	321
33. My Thoughts on Where I Am Now	327
34. My Lawyer and Did He Do a Good Job?	332
35. Justice British Style	335
36. My Efforts to Try and Get Other Government Departments to Act and Dispense Some Justice	339
37. Complete List of All the Failings of the IPO 1992-2010	355
38. My Continuing Efforts to Get Somewhere	362
39. Trying to Get the Police to Act	367
40. Continuing Efforts to Get Justice	383
41. Showing How Incompetent/Corrupt Hearing Officers Are	390
42. Conclusion	407

The following individuals and government departments completely failed to deal with the injustices I suffered:

1: David Cameron, MP
2: Ken Clarke, MP—Justice Minister
3: Dominic Grieve, MP & Attorney General
4: Chris Chope, MP—my local MP, Christchurch
5: Tobias Ellwood, MP—my local MP, West Bournemouth
6: David Atkinson, MP (ex)—my local MP, West Bournemouth
7: Ministry of Justice
8: Office for Judicial Complaints
9: Judicial Appointments and Conduct Ombudsman
10: The Parliamentary Ombudsman
11: The Intellectual Property Office
12: The Insolvency Service
13: The Department of Trade and Industry
14: Companies House
15: Local Government Ombudsman
16: Trading Standards at Sutton, Bournemouth and Dorset County Councils
17: Office of Fair Trading
18: The Dorset and Metropolitan Police Forces
19: The Independent Police Complaints Commission
20: The Information Commissioners Office
21: The Victims Commissioners Office
22: The Treasury Solicitor Office
23: Sutton Council Planning Department
24: HRMC—re tax affairs

Forward

First of all I have to say right out front, that if you are of a sensitive nature, do not like people speaking their minds, occasionally swearing, ranting about injustices they think have been heaped upon them, talking in a very forthright and no nonsense way about what they think... ***do not read this book!*** You may wonder why I say that. Well it is my opinion which has been formed by years of observing the British character, I have come to see that we have grown into a nation of wimps, people who are so left wing, people mostly under 40 who think that anyone who complains is a psychotic nutter and if your old to boot, you should be locked up. In other words they have not an ounce of experience in life yet they know all about people and they are willing to trash you with absolutely vile language and even threats of violence against you, just because you are complaining in a forthright way. To hell with whether you are justified or not, for *justice* is not a word they recognise. If you rise above this type of vacuous rabble, have an ability to show empathy for others and their problems, can recognise injustices and be concerned for the implications for others, have morals and empathy... ***read on...*** but do not expect to get a story impeccably written in Classic English grammar. I reckon my grammar is not so bad, but I am not a trained journalist or writer. So this book is written in colloquial English and its prime purpose is to get a story across and not win some literary award. So all you smart Alecs who will want to jump in and rubbish the way it is written... take a hike and do not bother reading it.

Whilst this is a story about Intellectual Property (IP) it is also a story about humans and the way they behave. You will see the example of the willingness to commit crimes against others by the main character who is responsible for this story, for reasons of greed and a whole host of other negative aspects that humans suffer from. You will also see how indifferent people can be to the plight of others and this can be seen coming from no less than 18 different government departments, several members of the media fraternity in the form of newspapers and magazines and so on. All were totally disinterested. In the case of some of the government entities, the Ombudsmen, that are set up so people like me who are suffering from the inaction and misdemeanour's of government departments, can go to get redress, turn out to be no better than those you complain about. For they do absolutely nothing when you turn to them with complaints. They always have a bundle of excuses as to why they cannot help you gain redress. They are just another politicians con trick on the Public!

All this banging your head against the brick wall of indifference by all you turn to, can have a very negative effect upon the person in the position of trying to get justice. Some will very quickly give in, others will carry on for some while and then give in. The very few who like me are obstinate and determined that as they are in the right, they will never give in, can in the end be capable of suffering a breakdown when years of deliberate obstruction by forces who have powers that you do not and who are also determined never to give in and who use those powers to that end absolutely ruthlessly.

So even the hardest can in the end be broken in some way or other. Some will suffer mentally and have a mental breakdown. Those who suffer a mental breakdown that could mean they will wreak revenge against those they see as their tormentors. So we see with this latter type the episodes of mass killings. These people who carry out those mass killings nearly all seem to have suffered in some way at the hands of people who they feel have wrecked their lives and the only way to get revenge, for that is what they want, is to kill those they think are responsible or even people who are not even remotely connected. For to some, it is just people they want to get back at.

I am not the type of person to reach that kind of position, but one has to take into account what could happen to some. Intellectual property is something that is being stolen all the time by all sorts of people and I would say that it is highly probable that most who own IP do not even realise this, let alone think it could happen to them. If you have IP that gets stolen, then you can see how resorting to trying to get help from the Intellectual Property Office (IPO) can end up with you experiencing a situation like mine.

So if you do end up trying to use the IPO, this is a story that you should read. You will see in this story the incompetence of the government and their departments which are filled with civil servants. Of course the department that deals with Intellectual Property which is central to this sad, sorry and outrageous story, is the IPO, formerly known as the Patent Office. In my opinion they should have left it called by the the former name as anything to do with this department cannot fall under the description of Intellectual. I doubt if there is one person in that edifice of a building that has any Intellect. But then that is Great Britain today, with it's broken society and broken useless government departments filled with lazy incompetent people. So this story is also about the general malaise of government and the way nothing works any more in this once GREAT country. For I have not found one governmental department that actually works, as you will see, and I only deal with the departments connected with this case. I have had to suffer similarly from all manner of other government departments, like the DWP, DVLA, Passport Office etc ad nauseam.

It is not an easy story for the layman to follow and this is because of the actions of the principal players within it, namely one Robert Busbridge (RB), culprit number one and the IPO, culprit number two.

It will be reasonably easy for anyone in the justice system and especially in IP, to follow. However anyone who has created IP should try to get to grips with the story, because it is a story of immense significance to anyone trying to protect their IP.

Now in this country we hear many times on TV and other parts of the media, the Intelligentsia, Government Officials of every sort and from every corner of the huge machinery of government, about how awful it is that crooks in this country and from around the World, steal well known entities I.P by copying their designs. However you will see that what they are talking about is mostly IP being stolen from the big companies of the world and not from the little man. The individual one man businesses or the small companies are ignored in all this. We hear endless drivel about how awful it is that these crooks are copying films and the like onto DVD's and songs stolen from mega rich pop stars, and put onto CD's. How big time clothes and fashion accessory manufacturers who sell the real stuff at huge over inflated prices, just because their name has become well known, have had their stuff copied. How well known brands of watches and the like have also been copied and sold for £20 each.

What they do not go on about is we small folk who have had our designs stolen and our businesses trashed as well as our lives. We are not big enough to be bothered about. Because these politicians who go on about this copying of other peoples designs, epidemic, are only saying what they do because they want to get credibility for their own careers. It makes me sick when I see Trading Standards Officers on TV crowing about a bunch of crooks they have caught with thousands of copied CD's and DVD's and they are putting a Road Roller over the lot. Why do I feel that way? Because when I tried to get these same Trading Standards fraudsters (for that is what they really are) to investigate the crook copying my product and making misleading advertising on a grand scale, they told me "So what, if he copied your product, it will be of the same quality if he copied it exactly as you say" That says it all, I think.

On this day as I write this into this book, I have done so because in the Sunday Telegraph there was an article written by the chief of the Metropolitan Police, Sir Paul Stephenson. He was giving his street cred a boost by writing this article (and no doubt being handsomely paid for it too) by discussing the way criminals are getting into peoples bank accounts and stealing millions. He as an aside also mentioned the case of the Chief Executive of a large company (he did not identify this company and I wonder why) who came to him (something I find hard to believe he would be able to easily do) and complained about criminals copying his line of jewellery and flogging it on websites.

To such a loss of business, that he would have to lay off 8,000 workers if it carried on. I find that hard to believe that any company making jewellery in this country is that big.

However why I tell you this is because that is exactly what has happened to me with the conman in my story who has been selling his copy of my car online, on his website since 2001. Even showing cars that I built and saying they were cars he had built. He comes within a whisker of even claiming he designed the car and when I die, if he is still going, I know he will then go to claim outright that he did design the car. Yet when I complain to the correct authorities that this is going on, I am told it is OK and in any case they cannot spend tax payers money on chasing him. This is what you designers and producers of IP in this country will be up against and you will see by reading this story just how horrific it can all become and just how helpless you will become to stop it. You could like me, even end up in jail, accused by your tormentor of being a crook, and because our warped Establishment seem to like believing what criminals say and not believing victims, you could be doomed. For if you are like me, with limited resources, you will not be able to mount legal attacks on your tormentor, by going to the Courts to sort him out.

It is disgusting what goes on in this country, the way our government behaves.

Endless bullshit and lies from them about protecting the Public, but it is just smoke and mirrors, plus lies.

A layman does not need to digest every minutiae of information, especially with regards to all the documentation involved in all the hearings. You could lightly skim through those, so as to just get a feel for the skeleton story of what was involved, documents wise. It is the balance of the story and the details of the grinding battles I have had with the shiny arses in power that you can pick up on. (we called pen pushers in the Forces by this name, as by sitting on them all day long the seats of their serge uniforms got worn and shiny and you could always pick out a useless clerk who did nothing but sit around all day, doing nowt by the shiny patches on the arse of their trousers) so I have tried to make it as easy as possible to understand. If I had included absolutely every bit of information in full, this book will have been twice as long. Also it is not possible for me to show exhibits or to recreate each document as it appeared in evidence at the various hearings. So I have cut everything down as much as possible without losing the plot of the story. Some of the hearings are reproduced on IPO websites, so for instance if you search for 'Cobretti Engineering' or 'Viper' you will see them pop up. Also they can be seen on the IPO's own website under various search terms. However beware of what you do read, for anything said by the IPO has to be viewed with suspicion as they have a vested interest in putting everything in ways that do not cast a bad light on themselves.

I talk in colloquial English and not high brow, exactly spot on English, with impeccable grammar.

I also do not beat around the bush either, being a straight talking Northerner who has spent much time in the Merchant Navy, then the RAF and long periods of my life in Australia and elsewhere. For in these areas, being a typical effete upper class Brit, doesn't go down well. So if you are of a sensitive nature, tough. For you will see me swearing when I get worked up over something I am passionate about. Of course these days Brits like me are a dying race as so many Brit men are so soppy and spineless and when they experience Brits like me, they hate me. Maybe this explains why some in the IPO have treated me the way they have. A back lash to my out-spoken character which will come through in hearings and written evidence (see forward in this story when I call all the pen pushers in the Tribunal Section, "tossers" and the reaction I got from the Head of that section the effete Mr James, he of the corrupt Hobbs hearing, which you will also read about). If this is the case, and you act in an outspoken manner, it will not speak well for anyone trying to get justice. One should not be trashed for the way they put things across. What should matter only, are the facts of a case and not the character presenting the evidence. But of course this is yet another character of the Brits in that they do practice this business of judging people by the way they talk and present themselves. Anyone outspoken with opinions is a dead duck, especially one who takes no crap from some government jobsworth, but I am afraid with me, I am a product of my upbringing and I am not going to change for anyone. I tell you this so that if you are like me, maybe you should put on an act when dealing with the IPO, for if you do not you will experience what I experienced. (You should practice what is known arse licking and making the jumped up little twerps feel good by pandering to their overblown feelings of power over people.)

Some will comment to themselves that I constantly call a lot people and groups of people thick or stupid etc. I do this as this is how I find them to be. I find these days so many people in Britain seem to be thick and they get thicker by the year. I put this down to the hordes of kids that come off the production lines of our useless 'Eduction' system with their uneducated left wing, brainwashed and useless teachers, and this has been going on since about the 70's. Anyway I make no apologies for this.

I should also point out that in order to keep down costs, I have had to edit my own contents of this book. I have done that three times and yet I know I will have missed mistakes as it is hard to edit your own ramblings. Please forgive me for my mistakes, but you will get the gist even with my mistakes. No publisher would touch this book as it hasn't been written my some well known 'A' list person, so it has to be a self publishing job. They would be all scared rigid about being sued anyway. Me I don't care as they have put me into penury so I have nowt to sue. It will mainly go out free of charge to all those I feel should get to know about the story.

For those who are not in the legal services, this book will help you to realise that protecting your IP is a must and without delay. For those in the legal services maybe it will also teach you something, as the story is from someone on the other side! My opinion of the legal services is not high, because in part I would not have had to suffer what I did if the legal profession were not full of people who seem to only be concerned with their pockets rather than in protecting those who are not rich and so cannot help to fill their pockets. Who knows there may even be someone with a conscience and morals who could come forward and help me gain justice? Not just for me but also to help others who may benefit from the exposure which this story could get, which will in turn maybe help reform the IPO, for one. For it is there supposedly to protect peoples IP, just like Social Services are supposed to protect abused and vulnerable kids and people, but who are as abject as the IPO at doing their job.

Chapter One

Introduction

I decided to write my story as a warning to others who create intellectual property (IP) and who like me did not take timely steps to protect their assets. I think that many people do not even realise what intellectual property is, even when they are in business and create it. There is a lot of ignorance on the subject. I was further prompted by the behaviour over the past 20 years, of the very institution who should be there to help protect peoples IP, namely the Intellectual Property Office (IPO).

So this story will not be one that will be of interest to everyone as it will only interest certain people. These could include lawyers and especially those who specialise in IP law and their issues, business people who create IP in the course of their work or business, and those who are interested in the incompetence and divisiveness of government departments and the civil service.

Because of its very nature, the story is long and complicated by actions and by the IP law. The actions of the person responsible for the theft of my IP meant that the IPO became involved and they added to my frustration by being slow, incompetent, prone to making mistakes and telling lies, and showing bias. Because of their actions I was forced to endure no less than EIGHT separate hearings when in my opinion I should not have had to put up with SEVEN of them. The actions that started some 20 years ago should not have even been allowed to start, had the IPO acted within the law, right at the beginning.

As a consequence, this story contains much evidence by way of statements, which by their necessity have to be laid out in full, so that the reader can see what was being said and claimed. Similarly with the various decisions. In both cases I have tried to set them out in brief form and to include all the statements and decisions in their full form, on a blog I have run on this subject for some time. This way any reader who does not have access to the IPO website where the documents can be seen, can at least see those documents in full if they wish. So the necessity of laying out pages and pages of the documents as they were said, could be for some, somewhat boring. However when you deal with such issues, you are telling a story not for titillation of some sort, but trying to tackle a serious issue. Of course underlying the whole legal side of the story, is a story which highlights many personal character issues, such as greed, criminal tendencies, forgery, perjury, sibling problems, fraud, perverting the course of justice, revenge, IP theft, misleading advertising, passing off and so on. In fact some of what went on, you couldn't make it up. So maybe some readers who can look beyond the legal side will be able to see the other story within it, which is interesting.

The behaviour and incompetence of such governmental organisations, and in this case the IPO, resulted in the theft of my trademark by persons who firstly attempted to make £500,000 by selling my trademark to a third party, namely the Chrysler Motor Corporation, posing as the legal owners of it. Because I intervened I was able to put a stop to that, but not to the continuing theft and use of my mark over 20 years. So in a nutshell it is a story which shows you can initiate the use of a trademark legally and above board, use it for years and then have it all stolen from you by a determined conman who is aided by a weak, believing and compliant IPO, who may even have behaved illegally, in order to hide mistakes.

The IPO even though warned of the illegal acts of the thief, ignored my warnings and because of the length of time it took me to deal with this situation, I ended up losing hundreds of thousands of pounds in profits, over 20 years. The thief managed to get me charged with forgery, with his lies and I could have ended up in jail for up to four years. I also ended up with a virtually worthless business at the point when I had to retire early through ill health. The stress of all this gave me a heart attack which needless to say has had a large effect on my continuing health problems. Maybe even shortening my life.

So the IPO could honestly be said to be yet another civil service department that is 'not fit for purpose' and as I am sure most of you will agree, that trying to get retribution and compensation for failings of government departments, borders on the scandalous. This because civil servants will never admit to failings unless the press bring their failings out into the open. It is very difficult for any one person to be able to get the press to do this as they are only interested in the rich and famous and anything to do with *sex!*

Then they, the civil servants know, that should legal action be taken against them, they have the taxpayer paying their costs. They can string it out forever thus costing the private litigant hugely. As legal aid is no longer available for such cases, a litigant has to pay a minimum of £150 and hour for an IP lawyer. So you end up getting horrible vacuous civil servants like those in the Parliamentary Ombudsman's office saying "well you have the right to appeal before a Court so we will not intervene". This when they know full well that today any ordinary person just cannot afford to take things to the High Court because they cannot get legal aid. They are therefore being duplicitous, lying hypocrites.

Even if you could and you win, it is not certain you will get all your expenses back. So this book hopefully will show anyone who has created IP during the course of starting and building up their fledgling business, that it is imperative to take steps to protect your IP from crooks and sharks, and to do it right from the very beginning. So to my story...

Chapter Two
My Background Story

I could write a book on my life up to the time I decided to build a Cobra Replica sportscar, which I would sell as a kit or fully built. However I will leave out most of my personal history prior to 1985 as it does not have a direct impact on this story. My decision to become involved with kitcars was made whilst I was in business in Australia making fibreglass power boats, from 1980 to 1985.

Since leaving the RAF in 1965 I had been self employed with various manufacturing businesses, as I was a person who thrived on creating products for which I thought there was a good market. I had always been good with my hands and loved making anything, especially if it were of a technical nature. For some years I had a business in the UK and the USA restoring classic British sportscars, before moving to Australia in 1979, from the US.

So the eighties saw me with a boat building business that I bought in a run down condition. However my boat building business was not making enough money and I found trying to break into the Aussie market as a Pommy, was fraught with disadvantages. Previous to the boat business, having been in the car industry, I decided that I should look to getting back into that, if I could sell the boat business.

By using my experience in engineering and fibreglass and my love of British classic sportscars, I decided that it would be a better move, to go down the road of making kitcars. However Australia was not the place to do it as getting type approval for such a car was difficult. Not unobtainable, but expensive and long winded due to the bureaucracy of the Aussies. On top of this, due to the immense size of the country it meant when trying to sell your product, you were faced with the problem of the distance that your customers faced, in being able to see your product. Also the transporting of your goods to them if you made a sale, was very expensive, and the market was too small.

It made sense to look at returning to the UK for I knew there would be no trouble selling my kitcar, from a government approval angle. The market in the UK was four times the size of Australia and there was the possibility of being able to sell to Continental customers, not to mention to the USA.

It was in April 1985 that I moved back to the UK after selling the boat business and within months I had found a suitable cheap workshop to start up my business involving kitcars. Prior to moving back to the UK I had decided that should I make a Cobra replica that I would call 'Viper'. At that stage no one in the UK who was making Cobra replicas, and there were about half a dozen companies, called their Cobra by this name. Certainly no one was advertising any Cobra replica by this name.

I decided to first of all test the market potential of this car by trying to get the agency for an existing Cobra Replica manufacturer. I did a deal with a company based in Birmingham called Sheldonhurst who were making what I thought was a credible Cobra kit, to act as their Southern agent. I purchased a kit and said I would build it up as a demonstrator to sell off.

I had been joined by my eldest son Chris and we got the car finished in three months, but not long after that, Sheldonhurst went bankrupt. I had a couple of orders in the pipeline and I felt that the only way forward, now I had built a car and seen that there was a market, was to build my own version of a Cobra Replica. The Sheldonhurst replica was based on Ford Granada mechanics and whilst the chassis was generally well engineered, it had inherent design faults. The body which was generally of a more pleasing shape than others as it had nice wide wheel arches, which others did not have, was not up to my standards.

So I set about doing three things. One was to re-engineer the Granada chassis completely, two was to design a new Jaguar based chassis, and three was to re profile the whole body and make body moulds, and make panels for the boot floor, dash, interior panels and inner wheel arches, all panels that were missing on the Sheldonhurst. We started to advertise in early 1986, that we were in the market with our version of the Cobra which I was calling 'Viper'. The Granada version was first off the presses as it were, and by June 1986 my new Jaguar version was also on the market. Both kits used the same body and both used the trademark 'Viper'. The chassis for the Jaguar based car was a completely new chassis designed by myself and my staff and nothing like the Sheldonhurst. It shared the same body as the Granada based car. This is the very kit that I had the design of, stolen from me by a conman along with the Trade Mark 'Viper' by which it was called.

Chapter Three
The Beginning of my Kitcar Business

I believe that an awful lot of people who start up businesses, especially if they are younger and without a depth of experience in the world, and such matters as their creative rights, will know little or nothing about intellectual property laws. They like me will be too busy racking their brains on how to get the businesses off the ground. They will no doubt be operating on a shoe string and so getting the business into profit and selling whatever it is they have to sell, is their number one priority. The furthest thing on their mind is IP, if it is on their mind at all.

I knew about IP and had experience with people pinching my ideas and copying my products. In the past I had dealt with these episodes either by in one case giving the miscreant a good hiding, and with the second in Australia, a good scare with threats of legal holocaust actions.

I also knew I had common law rights and that probably taking legal action to protect my copyright and trademark, could wait until I had more time and spare money to pay someone to do it. My main consideration for some years was to get my company off the ground and get the products sold in a very competitive world. Generally most other car companies would not try to use a trademark that someone else was using, so I thought it would be highly unlikely anyone would be so stupid as to try and pinch the trademark I was obviously using... *how wrong I was!* My main initial efforts was to get into profit as quickly as possible.

I wanted, unlike all the other kit car manufacturers, to build up my business by building our kits into fully built cars. It has to be realised that to sell a kit is quite easy, as all you do is offer a chassis that will take the mechanics from a mass produced mainstream car. Then add a fibreglass body and the customer has the hassle of putting it all together. Actually building up a credible business building up your kit into fully built road going cars, is an entirely different kettle of fish. It takes much more business experience and you need more working capital to do it. My having built boats meant I did have production experience and being highly organised, I felt I could eventually build up a business similar to Morgan and TVR, even if that sounds presumptuous.

What I did lack, was the money for working capital to do it and so, very early on in 1986 I started positive steps to try and find someone with money who could pump in capital, to enable us to do what we wanted to do. We advertised in our local paper for an investor who was interested in cars to join us. As we had a sexy product that would interest any hot blooded man, I thought we may get local businessmen interested. Indeed we did get interested parties, some where the usual dreamers and time wasters, but one guy did come up with a proposition.

I put in a similar advert in the Sunday Times business section and from that I got a visit from an American bloke who said he was looking for start up businesses to invest in. He did not make an offer there and then but said they would stay in touch.

It was at this time I realised that if I did get someone who would be genuinely interested in investing, they would no doubt want certain conditions imposed on the deal. Like them owning 51% of the business or more. Then there was the subject of our design rights and the trademark. With my experience in business and of manufacturing things, I knew that I did not intend for any person or entity to get control of my business, then when it suited them, boot me out. I had seen cases like that and I knew that if I gave up my IP rights, then if I were eased out by an unscrupulous person, as I had let my IP rights go, I would have lost everything.

With this in mind I decided that I would never allow my IP to be part of any deal. I also knew that as my son and I were operating under the arm of a limited company, anybody looking at our circumstances may think that the IP assets would be owned by the company. This even though I financed the start of the kit car business with my own money and separately from our main business which was just the usual garage services business that we relied on for our bread and butter. We decided that we should make it quite clear that the trademark and chassis designs belonged to myself and not the company. It seemed to me to be legal, that if any company wished to divest itself of any asset that it may own, all it had to do was have a board meeting where the directors would pass a motion that the company was giving this asset to a named person or persons. This is exactly what my son, who was a director, and I did. We drew up a document stating that the company wished to make it clear that the assets of the trademark and the chassis design copyright were being given to K. Cook.

In retrospect I believe that in law, the company never even owned these assets, in any case. For I was not in the true sense an employee of the company. I had no employees contract of employment, nor was I paid any wage by the company. I loaned the company sums of money from my bank account as and when it needed to pay for daily running costs, until it was able to generate enough working capital of its own. So as I have said the money that was needed to build the first Cobra demonstrator (which was a Sheldonhurst) came from my pocket. Similarly the monies to set up the chassis jigs and the body mould also came from my pocket. So I believe that these assets were in fact my property and not the companies. So that document was produced just to show that the company Brightwheel Ltd did not in actual fact own any IP rights to the kit car side.

What I did in retrospect now appears clumsy and it certainly muddied the waters as far as all the legal eggheads in the IPO were concerned, but what do those idiots know about running a business and what the practicalities and every day problems are?

In any case I have read that IP can be owned by a company employee if by agreement with that company. If this is the case, then we satisfied that criteria by virtue of the board meeting where it was agreed that IP assets be owned by myself. By my owning them, if any investor came in, we would make it plain that I owned these assets and I was allowing the company to use them. Naturally goodwill would be earned by these IP assets by virtue of the fact that they enabled a product to be built which went on to accrue goodwill if the product sold well and gained a good reputation.

It has to be acknowledged that throughout the UK there are thousands of small limited companies that are only set up by an individual in order for that individual to be safeguarded should the company go into bankruptcy. These companies are set up using the directors own money to get the company up and off the ground. The directors like myself, very often do not even pay themselves, so as to give the company time to get off the ground and into profit. Once the company gets to a level of turnover and hopefully profit, then the director could start paying himself a wage. I would say that at this point he then becomes an employee.

My point in all this is that the life of Brightwheel Ltd, which was my starting company, was very short. During this short span I loaned the company some £25,000 which in the event was never paid back to me. I always paid myself wages from my own savings. This company's life came to end in the following manner.

As I have recounted we were looking to get an investor to invest in our business and the first guy who helped us was a local businessman who owned a large company making boat by marinising Ford engines. He had a small spare factory unit at the back of his factory, which he said he would be prepared to let us have rent free. He would not put in any cash at the beginning, preferring to watch how we went and then see what he wanted to do. In the event after nearly a year in these premises, he suddenly decided that the husband of a friend of his wife wanted a factory unit and it was obvious that he had lost interest in us, or his wife was the boss. So we were given our marching orders.

As it was, we had during this first year of being our own kitcar manufacturers, got off to a great start and this workshop was proving too small anyway. I quite quickly found a bigger factory unit that was twice the size and we moved into that over the Christmas period of 1986/7.

Chapter Four
The Start of Growth

It was at this very time that we were contacted by the American guy who had first contacted us at the end of 1985. He wanted to visit us and see how we had grown in the past year, and this he did in the January of 1987 at our new factory in Christchurch. He was very impressed at the speed of our growth and said that he was so impressed that he now wanted to invest in us.

So it was that we set up a meeting at which their business plan was outlined to us. Basically what they wanted to do was build up a group of small businesses such as ours, that had not been up and running for long, but which had a good product and owners who looked like they knew what they were doing. Companies that were being run competently and who had growth and potential, but who like us needed working capital in order to grow further and faster. They wanted to invest in my company as it had a glitzy product which would enable them to use as a beacon to others to follow and to join with us.

It was envisaged that a group of around five companies would be got together. All these companies would be run on a day to day basis by their respective owners, and the two Americans whose expertise was in accounts and how to raise capital and eventually float companies onto the stock exchange. These two would run the companies accounting sides and thus keep a strong grip on how they behaved monetarily. In other words the owners who had started each company and who had the drive and energy, would continue to run these companies without too much interference from the investing Yanks. The companies would then slowly grow and hopefully they would generate profits.

A holding company would run all these companies and each separate company owner who entered into the scheme, would have their companies taken over by this holding company. The holding company would invest monies into them as needed. Each director of the companies would have shares in this holding company in keeping with the agreed value of their own company. The holding company would own the shares of each respective company. When each company had reached a certain level of profits, it would then be agreed by all that a time had come when it could be shown that the holding company now had reached a level that could enable it to approach the stock exchange and be floated. The shares we all owned in the holding company which were given us at the start at say, a low value of one pence or two pence a share, would rise as the company attracted value on its float. They could rise to a much higher level than their starting value, and this is how people make money on such floats.

It all sounded very feasible and as we were promised an initial input of £75,000 investment in order to kick-start our company into even greater levels of turnover, we had nothing to lose. Without this deal we would have to carry on growing at a slower pace, than with it. Whilst I would have to **give** over my business to them for no payment to me personally, the fact was that the value of the assets of the business at that period, was not huge. I made it plain that I personally owned the IP of the chassis designs and the trademark and as these did not impinge on the company carrying on manufacturing its product, they agreed I would continue to do so.

Let us face it, all they wanted was that my business manufactured its product and who owned the IP did not interfere with that. I was hardly going to withdraw my permission for the company to be able to use the two chassis designs and the trademark Viper. Doing so would mean I would lose out on all the potential that could be gained if I stayed and helped the company to grow. After all I could end up with a huge profit out of a float. Also if necessary I could at a later date assign or sell my IP to the company for a price.

So a deal was agreed to go ahead and a new limited company had to be started from scratch just in case I had saddled Brightwheel Ltd with debts. I agreed to hand over a number of assets in the form of tools, office equipment, company cars, van, and stock in hand. These were listed in an agreement document and it has to be noted that on this document no mention was made of me handing over IP in the form of rights to the trademark 'Viper' or my two chassis designs of the Granada and Jaguar chassis jigs or the Cobra body mould.

A new company was formed by me and was called Brightwheel Replicas Ltd which kept as near to our original name so as not to lose the momentum we had built up in that trading name. I would be a director, my son was another director and my then partner Vivian, was made company secretary as she worked as a bookkeeper for the company. The two Yanks were also made directors. So the voting controls were neutral at that time. Contracts were drawn up by a London firm of solicitors (which I still have) which dealt with a contract of employment for myself, a share agreement contract which dealt with limiting my share control of the holding company, 'Atlantic Capital' . This was because I was the first company taken on, I naturally had the biggest number of shares in that company. The two Yanks had a lesser number of Atlantic shares. My initial position of holding the most shares would get diluted as more companies were added in to the holding company. The third contract dealt with contractual details of the new company but did not deal in any way with the IP that I owned. You may wonder why I have taken time to outline all this detail, however you will see in time just how important all these details are with regards to my IP issues in the future.

At this stage I had still done nothing to register any of my IP and especially my trademark, Viper. It has to be remembered that at this stage my business activities were only 18 months old and in that time I had packed in one hell of a lot of work. Designing two chassis and making moulds, getting the fledgling company off the ground, attending many kit car shows to show the car to the public, dealing with advertising, building a number of fully built cars we had been able to sell. And of course making chassis and bodies for those cars and the kits we also had sold. Marketing the cars also took up much time as exposure to the public in the form of car magazine articles was a big must, if the public were to get to know we had a winner for sale. It was a hectic time and I worked seven days a week almost every week.

The subject of IP was furthest from my mind all this time and I was not unduly worried on this score, as I believed that it was highly unlikely that anyone in the car world, be they in mainstream car manufacturing or in the kitcar world, would try to use my trademark Viper. This because by now our car was getting quite well known and we had even had exposure in the mainstream car magazine press. In any case I knew that I at least enjoyed Common Law rights. It would have to wait until I had the time and money to spend on such a matter.

I am sure that this state of affairs re the IP was a state which many people in businesses of all sorts, will recognise in their own business lives. Many will not even know that in fact they have Intellectual Property, let alone its worth. I aim to show you with this long and painful tale, that this is a state of affairs that could be a disaster for you if you like me, ignore it.

So here we are at the beginning of 1987 with a new company, Brightwheel Replicas Ltd (BRL), new partners in the form of these two Yanks, and in a now prominent position in the kitcar industry, in relationship to Cobra Replicas. There were two companies bigger than us and both had started some two years before we did. Most of the other companies that had been going when we started 18 months previous had disappeared. So in terms of kits sold we were at about number three in size and importance and we were the only one who were selling fully built Cobras and going for export sales.

During the years of 1987, 1988 and 1989, BRL grew rapidly and by 1989 we were at that time the biggest Cobra Replica manufacturer in the UK in terms of the number of kits sold and the fact that we were the only company selling completed cars as well, at the rate of around 20/25 a year. Now I could write a great deal about how the company grew and all the details to do with that. However I will only stick with the facts of that three years growth, that appertain to facts to do with the eventual IP matters that came out of those three years.

During these three years BRL added a Lamborghini Countach Replica kit to the Cobras which I designed, and later on at the beginning of 1989, a cheaper Viper Cobra based on the Ford Cortina mechanics was also added, which I again designed. The IP that accrued to these two kits, of course belonged to the company as did their tooling and all the extra hand tools and other equipment and stock.

Initially this input of extra working capital was used to fund the addition of this Lamborghini which I felt we needed to as to expand our product base. It was also used to promote further exposure in the market place by way of a much better brochure to send out, and in August 1987 to attend the big yearly London Motor Show at Earls Court. We had a terrific promo video made which we could use at shows. We attended more shows all that year and always had well made demo cars to show. We correspondingly started to get much more notice taken of us, as a company, and this resulted in more exposure in national newspapers and mainstream car magazines. Our sales correspondingly went up with all this extra exposure.

So it was that in late 1987 we got a visit from a Japanese company who had seen our exposure and had seen us exhibit at Earls Court, where we had quite a big and impressive stand. Eventually we obtained a very lucrative order from them to build and supply 100 fully built cars a year. We were understandably overjoyed at this as it really meant that we had arrived and all our hard work had now paid of. We received more good exposure by the press, writing articles on how a small Dorset company had gained such an order from of all places…Japan. We were featured one evening on both ITV and BBC Nationwide news. Then a slot on Radio 4, so what more could we ask for?

Of course for our investors, the two Yanks, it was manna from heaven for it meant we, as a company now presented in such a way as to make it easier for them to say to other intending or potential companies, just how their stewardship could expand their own companies. Also to verify how well they could do if they joined up in our scheme.

This was all well and good, but things were not to pan out how we all expected or believed it would. For all the cash they had put in at the beginning of the year was now spent and what it meant was if we were to build this order at the rate of two cars a week, we would need much working capital. To cut a long story short these two Yanks proved to be totally inept at obtaining capital and I found out facts about them that made me very angry.

True to all Yanks and certainly all Yanks I have ever met and I spent two years in business in the States, they are all big on talk and bluster, and little on substance. Many are downright dishonest in business and so it was to prove with these two. They gave me the impression at the beginning that they owned an investment venture capital business which was based in Lichtenstein called Zinlic Anstalt. They gave the impression that they had in this company large funds or at least access to large funds. When the time came to put up, of course it all began to unravel and the truth came out. Sure they had this Lichtenstein company, but it had only had around £100,000 in it and that represented the two guys total money that they had. In fact it actually belonged to only one of them and was the proceeds of a house he had sold in London.

They had believed that when my company got to a certain stage they would be able to use this to impress sources of capital in London and elsewhere and they would get capital this way. They were singularly unable to make this work and I found out that as they were Yanks, no one in the city would touch them with a barge pole. So to be brief, we never raised a zack from anywhere and this wonderful order eventually, after us supplying 15 cars, was cancelled as the Japs realised we could not make the cars fast enough for them. It was not economically feasible if we did not make 2 cars a week. What a blow and now I was faced with hopeless situation.

I will now relate to you a story that personifies the abject failings of the British banking system and especially in relation to how they treat small British businesses. Our bank had been from day one, the Natwest. We had never been in the black nor asked for an overdraft, yet when we did approach them after getting the Japanese order, we got the brush off. As the Yank who worked in the city knew someone high up in the Natwest he got hold of this bloke and complained that even after our high profile on the TV News and the local papers, our local bank manager had not even got in contact. Let alone offered to help. This manager got some sort of message from on high and I got a request for him to come and see us and a date was set.

When that day duly arrived, he with his secretary (why he brought her beats me) arrived at our factory. He turned out to be one of those posh gits with a Public school accent. Arrogance was written all over him. I took him around our crowded and extremely busy workshop, showing him how we made the cars and what the order was all about. To me this was what I needed to show him. That we had a viable product, we knew what we were doing and we had a huge order, but as he could see we simply did not have a set up, that at the moment could cope. We needed investment and a lot of it, some £1.5M in fact.

Of course all this talk went on, on the shop floor. Our office was minute and full of office equipment and office staff. I had no managers office as this was out of the question. This was what real business was all about, not your poncy bank set up he was used to. We heard not a squeak from him after his visit but we heard from our contact in London that he had complained that I had not even had the decency to offer him and his secretary a seat in the office, or a drink! Doesn't that say it all? So I will not comment further, as I may come out with inappropriate language!

Today in 2010, things for small businesses do not seem to have advanced much, as banks are as remote from their small business customers as they have ever been and as it was for me on that managers visit in 1987. Loans are as hard to get as ever. It all amounts to the upper class twits of Britain who have never got their hands dirty on a shop floor, so they had no comprehension of manufacturing and that is why the decline in British manufacturing has been so dramatic since the war. The toffs have concentrated on the city and the banks and look at where those ****** have got us!

How could I get rid of these Yank tossers, for that is really what they were. They were bleeding the company dry by paying themselves wages and they were unproductive. The scheme was never going to go anywhere without them having access to lots of dosh. I could not even go after big orders as they did not have the access to the capital a bigger order would require. I could not vote them off as I now lacked voting power as Viv and I had parted. I was well and truly stuck.

It was about mid 1988 that this situation was reached and I just had to get on with it until such time it reached a zenith. I did manage to get them to cease taking wages and we struggled on seeing where it would lead us. We were selling enough kits and fully built cars to keep going at a lower level, and this is how we went on for the rest of 1988.

I then had the idea that if we brought in a cheaper to build, Cortina based Viper, we could at least up our kit sales. So I and my staff designed this new Cortina based chassis and the necessary additions to the body kit. It was finished in record time and a demo car was built and the whole thing was launched in April 1989. (Note the villain in this story has got the cheek to have a picture of this car on his website as one of his cars!!)

It was a staggering instant success and orders came flooding in. I priced the kit at £950 for the body/chassis and this was giving us a £100 profit margin. I did this as a lead in price to get it off to a flying start. After a couple of months I would higher the price and then later on higher it to a level where we made a better profit. This was not to go down well with my immediate competitor, a company called Pilgrim who was the only other kitcar Cobra manufacturer making a cheaper Cortina based Cobra. He accused me of selling it at a loss. Well if I was, it had nothing to do with him, but I later found out what a little vindictive bastard this bloke would turn out to be. We sold 90 kits in four months and this meant we took deposits on each kit sale of £500. Taking a deposit in the kit car scene is normal.

In fact this huge success was, as is the case with many small companies, our undoing. The more you sell the more working capital you need as with our Japanese order. Bigger outputs mean more staff, more purchasing raw materials for stock, and your factory suddenly becomes far too small to handle the extra output needed.

Of course our Yanks once again failed to come up with more capital, thus making it twice that this had happened. Needless to say I was now hopping mad with them and feeling very impotent in being able to find a solution. Our bank still did not want to know about lending to us and this just shows you how hopeless British banks are at helping British businesses. What do you have to do in this country to get help. Now the pollies are falling over themselves to try and get back some of the manufacturing base they have allowed to be lost as they now realise that it provides much needed employment.

We did take on some more staff, but we simply could not build fast enough and in such a situation a position will inevitably be reached. This simply put, is that money coming in from weekly completed sales are unable to keep pace with overheads. (Even though you have a huge backlog of orders.) You enter a downwards spiral.

Your only way out is to put in cash that enables you to pump up your output. We had the orders, but simply needed a bigger factory, two sets of moulds to make the bodies and the extra staff. We needed to stock bigger levels of raw materials. No investment money coming in meant that eventually we would be in a bankruptcy situation.

I gave those Yanks an earful and told them what would happen if their efforts to obtain investment did not succeed. They were still trying and they always were upbeat and I was told about various entities and individuals they were talking to who they always painted as a big possibilities. However even though I lived in hope, I was always let down in the end, by these two incompetents. All this reached a zenith in August 1989 when I issued an ultimatum, either get within a month, £30,000, or something would happen that would finish it all off.

What I meant was that I had worked out that the only way I could get out of this nightmare was to resign if no money was forthcoming. As you can see, I still owned the IP rights and I could take the IP and the tools I owned and the one body mould which I owned and we now did not use as a new set had been made during BRL. I could start up on my own if I wanted to.

Needless to say no money was forthcoming so in early September I resigned. One of the Yanks a Max Suite, by now had scarpered to Italy and he was the one who had most of the business acumen. The other one a Jim Bachmann who worked for American express in London and who was quite hopeless, was still in London. It turned out that the one in Italy had never had a visa to work in the UK and he had had to leave as the authorities had been chasing him. So it just goes to show you how the Yanks are dishonest, for just how did he think he could run one company, let alone the four or five? For if their dream had come true, that number would have been required.

They could not get a replacement for me and in any case as they had no money they could not even run the company, in any way. So they did what they could only do, and that was to close the company down. I was asked if I would physically do this for them. They wanted to sell off the assets to at least realise some of their original investment, which they were entitled to do as Zinlic or Atlantic had a debenture on the assets. I said I would but what were they going to do with all the stock and tools and jigs and moulds that BRL did own? I told them that I was going to continue to make the Viper and even though I had a chassis jig and a body mould there were assets I would like to buy off them. They agreed to sell me what I wanted. I was asked to draw up a list of the assets and what I thought they were worth and this I did. They agreed to my valuations and to selling me the items I had asked to purchase.

Now at this point it has to be realised that had they thought they owned the IP assets of the company, they would have insisted that as I intended to continue manufacturing the Viper, then I would have to pay them for the asset of that trademark. Also to pay them for taking over the asset of the Jaguar based chassis design and the body shape. Anyone with half a brain would have done so, but the cold hard fact is that neither they, nor BRL ***owned those IP assets, as I did!*** You will see how others would challenge this later on, so it is a core issue.

I bought the Lamborghini mould and chassis patterns, the Cortina based body moulds and the chassis patterns and jig. So I now owned all the IP rights to these. As the Jaguar chassis jigs and the body mould that was in daily use, had been made and paid for by BRL money they technically owned them even though I owned the IP rights to their designs. I allowed them to sell them and other equipment that I did not want, to a Swiss guy who our Swiss agent had lined up to buy all this equipment so he could set himself up as a Cobra manufacturer in Switzerland. All this is documented in the list I drew up of all the assets and where they went.

Chapter Five
The Start of all the Problems with the Busbridges

Who are these guys, the Busbridges? Here I need to go back to the end of 1987, to around September.

All through the three year life of BRL, I had looked to get agents around the UK. This because we found that the great British Public, being lazy, were too tired to come to Christchurch to visit us (just how these types thought they had the massive amount of get up and go required to actually build a kitcar I just don't know) and see what we had to offer. It made sense to take on agents dotted around the UK so that lazy potential customers could take a shorter journey to see our product. We put in our adverts that we were looking for agents and because of this, one day in September 1987 we were visited by a pair of brothers at our factory. They were from Sutton in Surrey and they were interested in becoming an agent for BRL.

For me this day became an infamous day and put me to never ending problems that lasted to the time of writing this. The unfolding story of what happened in relation to these two will show you just how important it is for anyone who creates IP, to take immediate steps to protect that IP. It will also show you that the very governmental department that is charged with the protection of peoples intellectual property, would turn out to be an absolute nightmare, and to use the now famous phrase coined I believe by Labours Mr John Reid, that they are 'not fit for purpose'.

Back to the Busbridges. I told them that if they bought a kit and built it up into a fully built car to show me that they had the technical ability to do this and thus show that they could advise customers how to do the same, if the car was of high quality, I would take them on.

By late February they had done this and the car was built to a high enough standard. So a 'verbal' agency agreement was entered into and as they were in the South east corner of the UK, this meant that they were in the most populated area and among people whose incomes were probably the highest in the country. So they were able to sell a reasonable number of kits and also they got a few orders to build up kits into fully built cars, for customers too busy or too incompetent to do so.

Now all went well from February 1988 to the point where BRL had to close down in Sept 1989. They proved to be fairly competent agents and I had no problems whatsoever. Once I got to the situation where BRL was closing and I intended to set up and to continuing the manufacturing of the Viper kit, seeing as these guys had proved so far to be OK as agents, it made complete sense for me to continue using them. Why wouldn't I?

Bearing all this in mind, I phoned them *immediately* I knew that the company was to close.

They were obviously anxious that they could continue, as they had sunk all their efforts into being agents for my product and they obviously wished to continue now, as MY agents. So for the time being it was left there with a verbal agreement for them to continue and I told them it would take some weeks for me to be able to set up production of the bodies and chassis. (You at this point should have it pointed out to you for your future information as the story unfolds, this; they had no big workshop, no experience at building chassis or fibreglass bodies. Nor did they have the money to set up to do that. So they really had no alternative but to continue to have me supplying them as before. You will see how one of the Busbridges lies to the heavens about this and continues to do so to this very date, but you will be able to see why it is lies.)

Also at this point I have to explain what was going through my mind with regards to just how was I going to set up this new Viper manufacturing business. I think anyone with half a brain would be able to see that I had spent all my life savings in setting up BL and BRL, had slaved for four and a half years often seven days a week. Had poured all my efforts and intellect into designing a product and successfully marketing it. Because of the crappy British way of treating aspiring people who want to build up businesses, I had been forced to enter into a situation with none too honest Yanks, (Just like Liverpool Football club!) who effectively stuffed my business and wrecked all my work of those years. Where was I going to head, now?

I thought long and hard about which way and in what direction I should head. My desire to become another TVR or Morgan had proved to be a disaster and for various reasons. Apart from the already mentioned problems of young businesses getting finance, and as car manufacturing is a business that requires huge investment in working capital, you need cash and there are other problems.

Like being able to find suitable premises at an affordable rent, and most important of all, being able to get suitable staff.

I believe the staffing problem is one huge problem in the UK for all businesses, due to the poor quality of the UK work force. Making a hand built car of any sort including the making of the chassis and fibreglass bodies is a very skilled job that requires men of a very high quality. Not to mention the highly skilled job of building up a whole hand built car. I found it almost impossible to find enough suitable staff due to the general slackness of your average Brit worker. This is highlighted by what is happening today where British companies cannot get enough of the well educated and highly motivated European staff with their work ethic.

Bearing all this in mind I came to the conclusion that trying to make fully built cars was a big mistake. You simply couldn't get them made quick enough because of the lazy slow British staff and the whole operation couldn't work because you couldn't get the capital to finance the sales even though they were easy to get, and these sales were 95% ***all export!*** Not only that but even trying to make your own in house chassis and fibreglass bodies, was a trial, mainly because of staff. To cap it all off, there was the fact that even if I tried to maintain in house body/chassis production , I could not afford to pay huge rents for a big factory unit.

My solution now I was on my own again, was to have the chassis and bodies made by outside subcontractors. Let them pay for the factories and have the staff problems. Forget about large scale fully built car production as well. Let the Busbridges and their company Cobretti Engineering handle ALL the retail sales throughout the whole of the UK in their workshop unit and with their staff. I would run the new company which I called Classic Replicas, from a small workshop where I would make a limited number of fully built cars that I personally would build.

The agency agreement that I made with Cobretti whilst managing BRL was as I said, an informal verbal agreement. I saw at that time no need to make it more legal by a written document. Now I was in a different situation as Classic Replicas (CR) now belonged to me 100% and I wanted things to run differently, as it was now my money on the line. So I drew up a written agency agreement and posted it to the Busbridges for them to agree and sign. This they did and sent me back a signed agreement and as I was busy at the time I did not notice it was a photocopy and not the original, which is what they should have sent back with them keeping a copy.

At the end of BRL we were half way through an order for 12 Viper V12's which would eventually go to a Japanese company. They had been ordered by a London firm of luxury car exporters who had many Japanese customers. A Jaguar main dealer in Tokyo had ordered 12 Jaguar based Vipers all with Jag V12 engines in them. We had delivered 8 of them and there were 4 left to be made. The order had to be completed by end of 1990. When I told the owner of this company that BRL were closing down he asked me if I could complete the order myself. I was delighted to do so as it would give me at least a year's work.

I decided that I could only comfortably manage two of these cars throughout 1990 so it made sense to give the Busbridges the balance of the other two cars to make. This way it would give them lucrative build work which would help them to survive. It made sense to do this as making sure they survived meant I continued to have someone retailing my products. BRL had also been part way through a Lamborghini Countach and I had given that back to the London company, 'Wheels Abroad', telling them it was too big for my workshop and that the Busbridges could finish that too, if he wanted. So what I was doing was passing on to Cobretti £60,000 plus, worth of business. Now why would anyone do that if they did not treat the recipient company as their agents? Would a business just give away so much work to just anyone who had no legal ties to you? After all I could have taken on someone local to finish these cars off for *me*. I could have made some money out of them and had their construction under my local control. You will see later on why I say all this about these cars.

So throughout 1990, business between myself and Cobretti continued more or less without too much hassle. I was getting on building my cars and making sure that kits that they sold were made by my two local subcontractors. The chassis were made for me by no less than the bloke who I employed in my BRL factory as the foreman of chassis construction, a Scouse by the name of Mick Frost. When BRL folded and I told him what I now intended to do, he said he would be willing to carry on making the chassis as he had his own little workshop in Poole. That was fine by me for he was a good worker and I had had no problems with his quality of work. As a person that was another matter as he was a difficult little shit who I had to treat with kid gloves as I did not want to sack him and have to find a replacement. None of my other staff liked him either and they were always at me to get rid of him. So it was a case of 'the devil you know' and I decided I may as well continue along those lines at this point. What a mistake that was to turn out to be. My Viper bodies were being made in Southampton by a boat building company.

Martin Busbridge (MB) would drive down to collect the kit orders and to make things easy for both of us he would call firstly into Southampton and pick up the body kit, then proceed onto me to pick up the chassis. Later on I even gave him Frosts workshop address and he would call there and pick up the chassis on his own. Another mistake and my problem is that I was too trusting of people who then turned round and cheated me at the first chance. Now, I do not trust anyone! He of course had to pay me and that meant he would have to call on me to pay me. So in the end he knew where both my subcontractors were situated and this was to turn out to be the big mistake on my part, putting faith in their integrity, of which they had none!

Of the two brothers I always found Martin to be the more intelligent and easier to get on with. I found Robert Busbrisge (RB) to be a dark horse with a character that I did not gel with. There was never any open hostility between he and I, but I did not completely trust him. It was strange, as I could not put a finger on it, what it was with him. I was to find out about his true character later on.

Some of you may remember that in 1991, a quite strong recession set in. Kitcars are a luxury, a hobby that blokes indulge in, in their shed/workshop and when money gets tight, they either stop building it, or sell it part complete. Intending purchasers drop off like dead flies. Just before it started to kick off, I had a discussion with the brothers to try and persuade them to start selling the cheaper Cortina based Viper.

Ever since BRL finished they had said that they really wanted to only sell the higher quality Jaguar based kit. I concurred with that as to get the Cortina chassis made, meant me finding an engineering company who would make it and make it for a very good price. Frost could not handle it as his workshop was too small and anyway I did not want to put all my eggs in one basket. Then I found a company in my home town of Liverpool who were already in the kit car manufacturing business with a Moke replica. They could make it and at the right price, so we could set up production of this cheaper to buy and cheaper to make Viper kit. To make the Del Boy comment of; 'You know it makes sense' because with the looming recession, a cheaper version of the Viper could sell better than the Jaguar Viper which was more expensive to buy as a kit, more difficult and costly to build.

Trouble was, the Busbridges did not have the cash to finance a Cortina Viper demo car, so I thought it would be prudent for me to finance it and to even pay them to build it. They had never built a Cortina Viper so it would give them the experience. So it was all set up and I delivered to them the kit and a lot of the necessary parts. There was a local Kitcar Show at the Epsom racecourse coming up, which it would be a good springboard to launch the rebirth of this kit. They had plenty of time to get it built but imagine to my consternation that with a couple of weeks to go to the show, they were well behind with it. They asked if I could spend a week up in Sutton at their workshop to help them get it finished.

Naturally I said I would and it was arranged that I would stay at Martins house for that week. It turned out to be an eye opener for me, as to how they operated as a company and just how disorganised they were. I saw that their attitude to work was lazy as well as disorganised and it was no wonder they had not finished the car. On top of that I could see how their workshop was so untidy and disorganised and how they would not even turn up for work until 9.30 to 10 am. I could also see that this workshop that they had taken on not long after we carried on in business together and after BRL, was far too expensive for the level of business they were getting. It seemed they had wasted all the profits they had made on the two Viper V12 build ups, and they hadn't even tried to finish off the Lamborghini, saying it 'was too complicated for them'

We did the Epsom Show and I helped them out to man their stand. I cannot remember if any kits were sold at the show or as a result of it. Another way I also helped them out at my expense was to supply them with an A4 colour page of nice photos of the Viper. On the front side there was a beautiful colour photo of a Viper and on the back side there were about 8 shots of different Vipers I had built over the years. The brochure page clearly stated these were 'Vipers' I paid quite a lot to set up this brochure page and I had in total 2,500 copies printed which I kept in stock. I would sell them copies at my cost whenever they needed them. They would use them in their kit brochure which they would post to potential customers and more importantly at shows, where a lot of brochures would get purchased by interested customers.

Both the helping them with the build at my expense, of a Cortina Viper demo car, the supplying of a professionally made colour brochure page and helping them at shows, all showed that our relationship was one of manufacturer and his '*agent*' For why would any sensible business minded businessman behave in this way? It was for my good to help them, so they could continue with a viable business which in turn kept me going in a way that suited me, for the time being.

You could say I was not at all impressed with anything I saw and with this recession, I did not see how they would be able to weather it. *All this would impact on me!* It would mean that there was a possibility that I would end up with no retail outlet for my kits and that would mean me having to think about setting up with a bigger set up than I had at the present. Having to take on a posh workshop, even if small, in order to present an acceptable face to the kitcar public. All this in the face of a recession which no one knew how long it would last.

When I got back to my home I resolved after much thinking to send them a letter outlining all that they were doing wrong and if they did not get their act together they could go under. I stressed it was not a personal thing but comments were to help them and by implication my business too. I said I hoped they took it the right way. They never made any comments either way, but it turned out that Robert was extremely uptight about it and maybe at this point his mind started to formulate his strategies that he would put into effect in due course. Strategies that I now believe he had started to formulate as early as the start of Classic Replicas in 1989 and my taking them on as agents then.

One important point that has to be made at this stage, is how Cobretti and the Busbridges advertised their business in Kit Car magazines. In those days you got 90% of all your business by advertising in all three magazines or at least in two of them. I realised that how they advertised was of prime importance. This because they would effectively be my retail window and if they worded their advert incorrectly, it could appear to the public that they were now the manufacturers of the Viper kits. Of course this was not the case as I was the manufacturer. I agreed with them right at the beginning, that their adverts should read 'These sensational sports cars are now back in production under *new management*" thus showing that the retailing of the advertised Viper was under 'new management' and not under "new ownership". Now even to the most stupid, such a statement can only *mean only one thing!* That now, the selling of the Viper was under new management and management does *not* mean 'under new ownership'. Also that future adverts should be vetted by me. Naturally the trademark 'Viper' would be used, as any trademark would be, by any agent of a UK manufacturer. As they were acting as retail agents for me it was inevitable that this would happen. As an example, a Ford dealer selling cars manufactured by Ford, would obviously use the trademark 'Ford or other trademark model names, of the cars they were advertising. They cannot claim ownership of any trademark owned by Ford, by doing this.

As they had no good pictures of the Viper and I did, all the photos that were used in their adverts, that appeared into mid 1991, were *my* photos. Once again you will see the significance of all this later on.

I did notice a cooling off their attitude from the time that they had received my letter of advice, but nothing I could put my finger on. However I knew that the recession was beginning to bite on their business and that they no doubt were beginning to get short of cash. This manifested itself when a cheque they paid me for a kit and some parts they picked up from me, for some £1,300, bounced. I naturally could not tolerate this happening again and said so. I laid down strict rules which they would have to follow from then on after this payment was made good, which luckily it was. This was; that they would have to pay me by bank draft for all future orders, and they did not like this.

Around the end of 1990 after I had finished the last of two V12 Vipers and it had been delivered, I got an order from a guy in Holland for a Viper. So I started building that straight after Christmas. I had got this order from an advert that I ran in the mainstream car magazine, Classic and Sportscar.

Then shortly after that another guy, a Dr Bechtolsheimer, a Swiss Doctor living in this country, came to see me. He too had seen my advert for fully built cars and had also been to see the Busbridges. He asked me if the two cars were the same and I told him that they were and that Cobretti were my agents. He said he would prefer me to build the car, but he wanted it quickly. I pointed out that I was half way through a car as he could see, but I was sure Cobretti could just as easily build it and could start it immediately.

So because of what I had told him, he on my advice went back to Cobretti and gave them the order. You could say that once again I had facilitated an order for them, for if I had said that I believed he should wait as I believed they were in a shaky state and he should exercise care, he would have had me build it. I felt it better to try and help them get some turnover to help their money problems, and this I believe shows that I was still treating them as an agent of mine.

As for the Cortina car, which had eventually been built, but it was not to a very good standard, so I decided to get back it off them. This due to their obvious poor monetary position, I felt that it was wise to have it with me rather than with them. Also we had not benefited from bringing a cheaper Viper back onto the market, as I had hoped we would. I felt that they were not really trying to promote it in a manner it should be and that their heart was not in it. I picked it up and brought it back to Bournemouth and that, I knew did not go down well, either.

I knew that once this car I was building was finished, it was highly unlikely that I would get any more orders for fully built Vipers. Kit sales had pretty much dried up and the future did not look all that bright. The Busbridges business was shaky and where were they heading?

I had all through the Autumn and Winter of 1990/1991 been in constant touch with my Swiss agent. I thought for one, that the Swiss company that had bought all the necessary moulds and jigs to set up a Cobra business, may like me to come over for a set time and help them get it off the deck. Also Kunzli my Swiss agent, was sure that he could get an order for a fully built Viper.

So by April 1991 my mind was made up, when Kunzli got the order he had hoped for. It was to be an expensive build as the rich Swiss oil guy wanted to race it, so it would have to be built to high and expensive specifications and in Switzerland. The Swiss company who had bought the Viper tooling, wanted to see me as well, but I wasn't too sure what they wanted, if anything.

Throughout May I was making preparations to make a move and I went to see the Busbridges to tell them that as business was now at a low ebb, and that I was not going to get any more full car builds, I was going to Switzerland to build this car. At no time did I say that it was a permanent event.

I told them that things could just continue as before with them getting Viper kits and parts off me. All they had to do was contact me with any order they may get and I would notify my two subcontractors to make the chassis and body. They agreed to this. I later followed that up with written instructions as to how this was

The Start of all the Problems with the Busbridges

to work. I told the subcontractors what was going on and how orders were to work whilst I was away.

I wanted to take the Cortina Viper with me as a demo car in case I and Kunzli could sell more cars or kits. My Father was in the dumps due to my Mother having died at Christmas 1990, so I decided to trailer the Cortina Viper to Kunzli and give my Dad a holiday by coming with me. This I did and on my return I got everything else ready for the return journey back to Switzerland.

I departed for Switzerland at the end of May, taking all my tools and Viper parts, that I would need and I had put all other equipment I did not need to take, into storage. This action shows my intention to return to the UK. Little did I realise what I had set into motion from this point on.

Kunzli had set up the use of a workshop in the outskirts of Winterthur which I would have to share with a bodyworks company. The weeks went by and I never heard a peep from the Busbridges. I knew that business was not going too great, but I thought at least they would sell the odd kit. I would ring them up from time to time and it was always Robert that answered the phone. The story I got was always the same, business was really bad and they had sold nothing and were only surviving by general mechanical work and some classic car restoration. Somehow I did not believe them as it just never sounded genuine. However I just had to get on with my build.

Before the car was finished we got another order and this meant a trip back to the UK to get a chassis and body to make this new car. I phoned through to order a chassis off Frost and a body from BMS the Southampton boat builders.

It was around September that I travelled back to the UK to pick up the kit and on calling into Frost on a day that he was not expecting me, I saw that he was in the process of copying my chassis jigs. On my asking what he thought he was up to, he first of all tried to make excuses that did not wash and on my pressing him, he cheekily admitted it and said he was making a set for the Busbridges. When I pointed out that the designs of that chassis were my property, he said I did not own them as BRL did. I told him in no uncertain terms that I would take legal action against him if he carried on, but he was unconcerned. I took my chassis and I told him I was coming back for all my jigs, which I did later on.

So now the cat was out of the bag and I knew what was going on and what had no doubt been going on behind my back. No doubt kits had been sold and they had persuaded both my contractors to make the chassis and bodies and keeping quite and not notifying me. So much for the total lack of honesty from the Busbridges who I had bent over backwards to help and from my subcontractors, especially the execrable Frost. This a man who I paid more money than any other member of my staff at BRL and who I had kept in employment despite all my other staff hating him and wanting him out. BMS, the boat builders also showed a total lack of honesty and loyalty. Such are people these days, who have no standards and cannot be trusted an inch. Certainly from now on I learnt that I had to treat all people with a great deal of scepticism.

Kunzli and I had, during the summer of 1991, attended a big kitcar show in Germany at Hockenheim and I had sold my Cortina based Cobra to a German. A young man who expressed interest to become an agent for me. So I worked out a deal with him that I would move my operation to his home town of Poppenhausen in central Germany. He knew of a workshop I could rent and that meant I could take the part complete Viper, representing the second Swiss order, with me and finish it off in Germany. So it was that I moved everything up to central Germany.

Once settled in I turned my thoughts back to what the Busbridges had done and how I was to deal with this. Christmas 1991 was coming up and I had to visit my children back in the UK and I thought I would use that trip to check out exactly what they were up to.

After the festivities and a few days into the new year of 1992, I paid an unannounced visit to their new workshop. They had at last seen the light in that their last workshop was too expensive. I knew that if I arrived around 8.30am no doubt the brothers would not yet have turned up. I was in luck that a worker had opened the place and I walked in and asked this bloke when they were expected. He immediately said 'You're Ken Cook, aren't you? I recognise you from the time you used to call at their last workshop'

He introduced himself as Trevor Sangster-Jones, a bloke who had been taken on as far back as mid 1991 to copy the chassis jig of my Cortina Viper 4. He told me that the brothers had decided to snatch my business off me, even when they were still carrying on, acting as my agents. This before I had even set off for Switzerland. He also told me that they had persuaded Mick Frost and the body makers to make chassis and bodies and keeping that quiet, from me. Something

I already had found out. However what he then told me was quite a revelation, for they had approached Chrysler presenting themselves as the legit owners of the trademark Viper.

Chrysler had apparently applied in January 1990 to register the Mark with the IPO and a toe-rag that the Busbridges had got in with, a Colin Bruce, who was renting part of their workshop and who passed himself off as a know all, had found this out. He then advised that they could make a lot of money out of this fact by selling their 'ownership' of the mark to Chrysler.

Sangster-Jones told me that the brothers owed him a lot of money and so I asked him if it came to it, would he be willing to act as a witness and make a witness statement. He assured me he would, and gave me his contact details in London.

Whilst in London I went to see a Patent Agent in order for me to get my trademark registered damn quickly and for him to deal with Chrysler and the Busbridges. Kings Patent Agents were the company I took on before returning to Germany.

I returned to Germany to finish off this car I was building. I sent the Busbridges a letter warning them that I now knew exactly what they were up to and pointed out to them that I owned the copyright of the chassis design they had stolen, and the trademark Viper. I also told them I knew that they were trying to sell the trademark to Chrysler. If they did not immediately desist from all this, I would take legal action. Robert Busbridge replied that they had 'noted' what I had said. In other words 'get lost we do not care a jot what you say'. I think my actions show that as far as I was concerned the trademark belonged to me by right of usage from January 1986 and before Chrysler (Jan 1990) and certainly before the Busbridges illegal usage from June 1991. So I knew that I had a fight on my hands, and from this point on it has been a never ending battle which involved firstly Chrysler and then the Busbridges.

Chapter Six

Nineteen Years of Battles Commence

Kings advised me in January 1992, to put in an application to register the mark Viper. They asked me to send them the money to file an application and I did this straight away. Yet for some unknown reason he did not do this. He contacted Chrysler and told them that the approach by Busbridge was a con and they had no legal rights to that mark as it belonged to me and they had been agents of mine. To back this up he sent a copy of our agency agreement which I had given him before I returned to Germany.

In May 1992 Busbridge put in his application to register what was my trademark (unregistered but still a legal ownership by common law). Of course as soon as I heard this I got onto Kings and asked why he had allowed this to happen when it was he that had told me to get it registered and that I had paid him early on to do exactly this. His excuse was not to worry as it did not matter. I would eventually be able to show after opposing Chrysler and winning against them as they had a weak case, that I had earlier use than Busbridge. I had to take this at face value in my ignorance of IP laws. This turned out to be a *big mistake!*

The negotiations with Chrysler went on very slowly and things wound on into 1993. Kings advised the IPO the application had been made in bad faith as the Busbridges were agents of mine. He supplied them with a copy of the agency agreement. They replied that they were not interested and I would have to deal with that by way of an opposition against his application, if it came to that. His application was put on hold anyway by the IPO and I cannot understand that at all, as he applied to oppose Chrysler before I did. I can quite understand Kings thinking and at the time I was not unduly worried as I thought that when I won against Chrysler, Busbridges application would fall by the wayside anyway. Due to the fact that to win against Chrysler would mean my proving I had legitimate ownership based on usage back to Jan 1986. This line of thinking I thought was common sense, and in any case my expert, Kings were saying this. However I was later on to learn that with the IPO common sense doesn't exist. It is a phrase they have no comprehension of!

Whilst I was in Poppenhausen, Dr Bechtolsheimer got in touch with me. He had seen adverts for my Viper that I was putting in a German kitcar magazine. He told me that he was not satisfied with the car as something was wrong with the steering and as it was a left hand drive car, and as his wife had threatened him with divorce if he did not get shot of it as it was dangerous to drive, he had decided to try and sell it either in Switzerland or Germany. Would I take it on if he got his brother to drive it over? Give it the once over and put it up for sale.

When I got it and gave it a thorough going over, I found a list of around 90 build faults. It looked OK but was a basket case and some of the faults were so bad that I would have to pull the car apart. We settled on my doing as much as I could to get it safe to drive and to tidy up as much as I could without spending too much. The point of my telling you this, will become clear to you much later on in this sordid tale. The car was silver with a nice red interior and obviously I had supplied the body/chassis kit and all the specialised parts including the dash, leather seats and carpets. I never did sell the car and I got Wheels Abroad in London to take it and do a deal with Dr B, where he traded it in against another classic car. This do not forget was the car who's build I passed on to Cobretti. Who did the buyer turn to, to get it sorted... It was not Cobretti.

I returned to the UK from Germany, in Sept 1992 after selling the Viper I had been building, to a local German guy and tidying up the end of my association with Kunzli on the outstanding money matters. Trying to sell many Cobras in Germany had proved a non event due to their bureaucracy. This was in September 1992, and I had now been away from the UK for one year and five months. Things appeared to be picking up money wise in the UK. However when I got back I did not know if I would get back into Cobra kitcars again. I had got pretty disillusioned with people in the kitcar world. The problem was that at the age of 52, it would not be easy to get a job, let alone one I liked. I had been self employed since 1965 and British employers being as they are, ageist and against anyone who has been self employed, it would prove to be difficult to get work. So it did indeed prove impossible and it wasn't long before I started to rethink things.

I still had all the tooling to make kits in storage, but until things really picked up regarding the recession, I did not fancy plunging into the kit car business. I would have to get a workshop suitable for showing members of the public, a demonstrator car and all that. I would have to employ staff, and would it work, would there still be enough business out there? So I decided that caution was what I needed to exercise.

I do not know the exact date it was that I heard that the partnership of the Busbridge brothers had broken up, but it must have been around the end of 1992. But break up it did and I found out that this had happened in June 1992. So little more than a month after the application had gone in for them to apply for registration of the Viper trade mark, in their partnership name, they had broken up and from what I heard it had been a very acrimonious affair, too. That did not surprise me at all and I surmised that maybe Martin had got fed up with the wanton ways his brother ran the company, plus my threatening legal action against both of them. I was to find out the full story later on.

One thing that worked in my favour on the kitcar front, was the fact that just as BRL was closing down, some local low-life bloke, called Findlay, who had a hankering to get into kitcar manufacturing, on seeing the runaway success of the BRL Cortina Viper, decided to copy it. By the time he got into production BRL had ceased to be and I bet he did a dance, thinking that the market would now be open to him without opposition. Unlike the Busbridge thieves he at least called it by another name, of 'Venom'.

Whilst in Switzerland and Germany I watched his progress and decided to take no action as at that time I was not about to get back into the cheaper end of the Cobra market and I would stick to the better Jaguar version. However I did hear that they were getting a poor reputation for making a kit of poor quality and being of dubious honesty. So I thought they would not last long.

Then I heard when I got back to Bournemouth that Findlay, had sold the business to a chap called Barrass. I thought I would go and see this bloke and see what he was about. He turned out to be a nice enough bloke and I quickly found out he knew nothing about kitcars or mechanics. Nor for that matter anything about chassis making or fibreglassing. The more I thought about it the more I thought that here was a way I could slowly get back into kitcars.

I had a meeting with him and put it to him that from what I could see, he needed technical help and marketing help in order for him to progress. I needed a way I could get back into kitcars, but did not want to jump into it straight away. If we joined forces it could be beneficial for both of us. I wanted to keep my trademark alive and I was willing to license him to use it. His Cortina based car was really a Viper anyway and the new name of Venom had a bad reputation due to Findlay's way of business. So if I also licensed him to manufacture my Jag based Viper as well, this would give him a top class kit as well as the cheaper kit and he would be able to call all the kits by the well known and well thought of name of Viper. I would help him in any way necessary, free of charge and when he sold a Jag based kit he could pay me a commission of £500 per kit (the same deal as I had had with the Busbridges). I also asked him to change the name of his business to that of Classic Replicas which I had been using since BRL and to date. He agreed like a shot and we signed an agreement contract to that effect.

Just before leaving Germany I had got an order for a Viper with a Rover V8 engine and I was slowly building that up in my spare time, as time was not of the essence with this order. I had sold it him for a damn good price on the understanding he did not push me to finish it quickly, as I was going to have lots of other things to do. Anyway it got finished about the time Barrass and I did our deal, so it could be used to get a write-up for the new business.

A write-up was duly done around May 1993 and appeared around June in Which Kit magazine, and it gave the full story of our get together and the new names of the business and the trademark usage that would now apply to what had been the Venom. It should be now noted that at this point in time, it was a total of two years since I had been forced into losing the UK usage of my trademark of Viper. This due to the Busbridges stealing it off me. I had used it widely in Europe, but did this count as usage here as well, even though we are all supposed to be the one big happy country of the EU? Now from June 1993 the Viper was back in business here in the UK in a small way selling the odd Jag based kit through Barrass and he once more making sure the name Viper was still in use by me. This is a point that you will see shortly, is of immense importance due to what Robert Busbridge will lie about.

Then I heard the good news about Robert Busbridge going bankrupt in June 1993. Now this did not surprise me one bit as I had forecast it. It only surprised me as to why it had taken so long and how had he been able to afford to carry on after Martin had split with him? I had heard that it was over money and the lack of it. Again I was to find out more on this later.

Imagine how annoyed I was that even though he had gone bankrupt, he was still trading. All he had done was change the name of his business from Cobretti Engineering to Autotrak Ltd. But then this country is a thief's paradise with our slack laws and slack policing of thieves and crooks. I now knew that Busbridge had tried to sell my trademark Viper to Chrysler for £500,000. How is that for cheek? But of course when I stepped into his scam with Chrysler, they dropped all the talks on this, and Busbridge had the cheek to get his solicitor to complain about my interference in 'his negotiations'!

This meant that on his going bankrupt, he had tooling worth quite a bit and an asset with the potential worth of £1/2M in the unregistered trademark (my mark). I notified the Insolvency Service of all this but it turned out they were as slack as the IPO and over the years I banged onto them about it, they never did anything about the goings on of Robert Busbridge and his bankruptcy. I found out much later that they put a lien on his house to stop him selling it but did not make him sell it as they said there wasn't enough equity in it. This even though he had lived there for years and must by then have got to the stage that it had got some money in it. How he worked that I don't know. Of course now it is in his wife's name only, what a crook. He even traded for some time as a director of this new company Autotrak Ltd, when he was a bankrupt and this only stopped when I advised Companies House. I also of course notified the IPO that he was now a bankrupt but it had no effect on their attitude to the legitimacy his application to register my trade mark, Viper. They just ignored that information, but more on that later.

My opposition process against Chrysler rumbled on and on and they were now obviously not really interested in coming to a quick conclusion. The IPO gave them so much slack that helped them prevaricate and pass deadlines. So much so, that I complained time and again to the IPO, but never to any effect. These delays meant that I had to put up with RB using my mark for 10 years as he could say that he had in his application to register the mark so I would just have to wait and in the meantime he could carry on using it and taking business away from me. You cannot imagine how frustrating that was for me.

Regarding the bust up of Martin and Robert, over the years I found out that Martin had borrowed a large sum from his bank on the surety of his house. As he let Robert run the company from an admin point, while he worked mostly on the shop floor, his brother had learnt nothing from the letter of advice I had sent and was merrily wasting all this money, by the incompetent running of the business and slack controls. When the inevitable crunch came it was Martin who lost his house and then his wife as they broke up under the strain of all the business problems. Hence why it was an acrimonious split up. Also my threats of legal action against the two helped Martin to realise that the business was a complete mess and finished. So he left the partnership and I was to find out from gossip and later on from the statements made by Robert to the Police and then the IPO, that he had left the country and had gone walkabout. (Or so he said, but being the liar he is you will see that was just another big lie of his.)

Robert in the meantime, even after running out of money and being now on his own, somehow still managed to cling on in business, and I believe that the belief he had in his crooked head, that maybe he could still elicit a huge sum out of Chrysler, meant that by hook or by crook he would keep going. An example of greed at its best, or worst, whichever way you look at it.

In 1993 I started a legal action against both Busbridges and Mick Frost, for breach of copyright over their copying my chassis. I managed to get legal aid for this as at that date you could still get it, however I really ended up with a solicitor who was out of his depth. That meant three years went by with little progress and he made a meal of every twist and turn of the case and made basic errors in his interpretation of copyright laws. In the end he decided to lie to me by telling me that copyright on a chassis design only lasted 10 years and as my design was now 10 years old, I could not continue. It seemed as if I had no choice, yet now I have found out he was lying and the protection lasts for 70 years. Yet another case of my being done over, but at least I still have copyright and I could still take action, maybe?

So the rest of the nineties wound on. Robert Busbridge continuing to advertise his copy of my kit and still calling it a Viper, meaning I was losing out on sales by a minimum of 50% but probably more like 70%. On my front, at the end of 1995, Tony Barrass told me he had had enough of the kitcar scene even though I was now helping him free of charge on a daily basis. It was too much like hard work for him as he was used to a more laid back life style. Because by this time his business was actually doing OK, I thought, and certainly I thought with a bit more effort I could get more business. So I agreed to his offer to buy the business off him. My Dad who was now in a nursing home and near the end, gave me the money to do this, bless him. After I did that, I was now back in business on my own and able to push the kits in a much bigger way.

My battle against Chrysler came to a head as the hearing to hear my opposition case was now to be heard in 16th February 1998. It was to be attended by Robert Busbridge as well, as 'their witness'.

For what Chrysler had come out with as evidence was that (a) I did not own the trademark as BRL did and (b) that I could not be trusted as a witness as the agency agreement between me and the Busbridges was a forgery, according to Robert Busbridge. Apparently according to him I had forged their signatures. No evidence was put forward to prove any of this and as I was able to prove my assertions by showing the 1986 license from Brightwheel Ltd document, giving ownership of the mark to me and strongly denying any forgery. I also showed reams of evidence of my usage of the Mark from 1986 to the date of the hearing and showing my close involvement with the Mark. That the Mark was not passed onto BRL when they took over BL's business. I won that hearing and it was said by the hearing officer that I had gained registration through concurrent honest use. Quite why it was said to be concurrent as no one else apart from RB was using it and he could not show usage of the trademark back to 1986. The earliest he could prove use in his own right was after 1992. What more can be said? So I am not complaining about this hearing apart from the fact it had taken 8 long years to get to a hearing and this is ***totally unacceptable***. Also I have a sneaking suspicion that some in the IPO may view that decision as wrong. However if it was, Chrysler with access to the best brains in IP Law never went through with an appeal, so if there had been a wrong decision I am sure they would have gone through with an appeal.

It is clear that Busbridge had to do all he could to help Chrysler, for even though a number of years had now passed, they were still interested to buy the rights to the mark 'Viper' They had approached me several times before the hearing and after and offered ludicrously low offers, with the last offer being $60,000 and when I said I would accept £100,000, I heard no more. Later on it will be seen that this desire to still take control of the mark by Chrysler, carried on right up to 2004. Hence why Busbridge hung in for all those years.

Chrylser had said straight after the 1998 decision that they were going to appeal and they set in motion the paperwork to do this in the High Court. The problem was as I have said, they never carried out their threat to appeal and I found it incredible that after lodging papers to start an appeal, apparently the

High Court couldn't be arsed to make them proceed. Does this mean that it is perfectly legal for anyone to start a legal process then sit on it forever, without the Court having deadlines or bothering to force things to move on? So by the end of 2001 I had to take legal steps to force their hand.

Chapter Seven
Robert Busbridge Tries to Put Me out of Circulation

However before my steps against Chrysler proceeded, the execrable Robert Busbridge started a process against me that could have had disastrous consequences for me. Take your mind back to the Chrysler hearing above, in May 1998. I had denied that the agency agreement between me and the Busbridges was a forgery. Had I been able to locate Martin Busbridge I may have been able to get him as a witness to the fact that this document was real. A fact that I think needs answering, is why did it take from May 1998 to November 1999 for Robert Busbridge to go to the Metropolitan Police making a complaint that I had forged this document, and I had committed perjury when I denied the forgery at the Chrysler hearing?

So in December 1999 I got a visit off my local plod who said they were charging me with forgery on two counts, and perverting the course of justice, plus perjury. I could have fallen through the floor. Of course I was taken to the local nick and put in a cell. Quite why the Police do this I have yet to work out. Why can they not just put you in a room and start asking their questions and taking a statement off you should you wish to make one?

Now I have never been a lover of the British Police and this started off my hate of them. As far as I am concerned most are just criminals in uniform. Those who are not, are as thick as two short planks and this goes from the very top right down to the bottom. My thoughts on them are so long I could write a separate book on them and their failings. However at this time even though I disliked them I still thought that telling the truth would mean that in the end 'truth will out' and I had nothing to hide so if they wanted a statement I was happy to oblige. Now I know differently and in the same position they would get nothing from me without a solicitor and my being able to take advice before I opened my mouth. You will see why this is so.

So it was, that eventually we got into a room, and the proceedings started. I was accused of not only forging this agreement but also the agreement of 1986 which passed onto me the rights to the mark Viper. This flabbergasted me as they accused me of forging my own son's signature. Why on earth would anyone need to do this? My son would sign anything I asked him to sign. Also no approach had been made to my son to ask him if he had signed it.

So in my statement I outlined all the history of my involvement with the Busbridges and how Robert was nothing more than a liar and a crook. I outlined why this was and how he had stolen my IP. I told them what's more I have a witness to the facts of what went on in 1990/1991 in the personage of Mr Trevor Sangster-Jones. I told them of the attempt to sell my trademark to Chrysler for £1/2M (*a big motive to have me put in clink... don't you think?*) and I told them that this was Busbridges attempt to have me put out of the way in order for him to make a claim for this trademark and if successful he could them get all this money off Chrysler. I told them I had documentary evidence to back all I said. I told them that they simply could not believe anything Busbridge had said, as he was a serial liar.

I really thought that after detailing all the relevant facts in this statement, they would see that there was more to this accusation by Busbridge than met the eye. I really thought they would drop it, and how wrong I was about this. For not only did they not drop it but they seemed determined to press on come what may. They went on to take on a Home Office handwriting expert to look at my signature and to compare the signatures of the documents in question.

Busbridge was denying that he was ever my agent and that was another reason why this agreement must be a forgery. When I saw his statement it was full of lies and in that regard he committing perjury, yet he was accusing me of lying. Of course Sangster-Jones would have been able to confirm they were my agents.

I told them that I had not been able to locate Sangster-Jones after he had signed the statement. They said not to worry, that they had the means to locate people. Now bear in mind that this person was *my defence witness* and at the time I naively thought that the Police were only interested to find out the truth as this was what the smooth talking copper, who happened to be a Scouse, told me. He assured me they would look into all the facts and if what I had said proved to be correct it could be that it would be dropped. So I was not too worried to tell them of Sangsters last known address in London. What a fool I was and this deepened an already dislike of the Police.

Some weeks later I was told that the charge would go ahead and I would be tried. So much for them checking on whether what I had said was true. They still had not even contacted my son. It was now obvious to me that they had no interest to check anything and it seemed to me that they were determined to press ahead come what may. I found the more I spoke to this Scouse the more he came across as a thoroughly disreputable bum. This was brought home to me when he told me that they had indeed located Sangster to just outside Bideford in Devon and he gave me the address. He had even gone down there and talked to him but that he had declined to give any statement or make any comments. Something about this bastards demeanour told me that there was more to this than met the eye. Why would Sangster suddenly not want to help me?

It simply did not ring true, so I drove down to this address and found after speaking to the landlord of the house, that Sangster had suddenly upped sticks and disappeared. This raised many doubts as to exactly what had gone on when that bastard cop had visited him. I found out where he had worked in Bideford and went there to see if his ex boss could throw any light as to where he had gone. I was told that he had suddenly jacked his job in and had not said where he was off to. All very, very strange. Had the Police put pressure on him? Had they something on him that made him do a runner. Had they threatened him that if he did not do a runner they would have him?

The point is, that in confronting him I believe they had broken the law. He was a defence witness and they should not even have approached him at all. They did not need any evidence off him for their prosecution case, so it was really out of order to go down there and not even tell me about it until after the event.

The firm of solicitors I had taken on to defend me were useless too, and they never made a fuss about this. Then again, the Police did the same thing by contacting my son in Liverpool. He gets a phone call saying they were coming up to Liverpool the coming weekend to interview him. Again he is a **defence witness** and harrying him as well was out of order. I told my solicitor and they told me to tell my son not to talk to them. Being as the cop was a Scouse, of course for him and the mate he took up at taxpayers expense, made it plain that all they wanted was a free weekend away so as he could see all his relatives at no expense. My son being weak, ignored the request by me and my solicitors and thought he could outwit the cops, so he spoke with them. I will never know for sure exactly what went on but I don't think that they got anywhere or to where they may have thought they could get.

But is was another example of the dirty way they were handling this case and it was obvious they were not interested in *justice* but only in getting a **result** for them, no matter what. The most annoying thing was that my solicitors never created a fuss about all this. They should have done so and the accusation that I forged my son's signature should have been dropped due to their interference with defence witnesses. I say this so as to highlight the way British Justice doesn't work. OK you get free legal aid when charged with a criminal offence, but the money that gets paid to any solicitor is peanuts and you do not get a proper or anywhere near good defence. I had many run ins with this bunch of incompetents over the quality of a barrister they took on who I had to tell what I thought of him, refusing to take on our own handwriting expert to refute the prosecutions handwriting expert and the fact that the person handling my case was a learner solicitor. I will not detail all the case in depth, or how we set up our defence, but it does show you what kind of defence you get when the lawyers supposed to defend you are only on legal aid. Also what kind of person Robert Busbridge is, in that he would commit perjury in this case and then go on to commit the exact same perjury in the subsequent hearings before the IPO.

Eventually in 2000 the case opened in the Dorchester County Court. The barrister I eventually ended up opened with a long cross examination of Busbridge and what a squirmy slimeball he presented as. My barrister made the case that he had been an agent of BRL and RB as I shall now on call him, admitted this. He was asked what was the difference when after BRL, he appears to be continuing in exactly the same way? A long time was spent on the subject and no matter what way the question was put to him the more he squirmed and would not answer the question. Quite frankly the Judge in this case was useless as he should have made RB answer the questions. To cut a long story short, eventually through skilful non stop questioning, he had to admit that yes, he was my agent and he bought 'Viper' kits from me up to June 1991.

Now RB was saying that what I had done was to take a set of real signatures off a later document and put them onto a freshly made agreement document, by way of using a copier. Thus making it look like the Busbridges had signed that document when they hadn't. The hand writing expert of course backed this up by saying that is what had undoubtedly happened.

We said that it was perfectly possible that RB had done this himself by actually putting the signatures on the agency agreement onto the second agreement, in an effort to blacken my name, so he could get me out of the way and thus go on to register my mark and eventually con Chrysler out of a lot of money. Indeed it would have been easy for him to do this in 1991 when the demo document agreement was to be signed as by then I now know RB was hatching his plot to steal my business and by setting up a document that had the same signatures as an earlier document, would enable him to in the future accuse me of forgery. He had to show that it wasn't a true document otherwise he had no case and would lose not only his efforts to con Chrysler but would also eventually lose his application to register my trademark. There are also other scenarios by which it could also have been done. What is certain that it was not as he said, a cut and dried case that I definitely did it. In any case had his brother been around in 1993 onwards when RB first claimed I had forged this document, he could not have continued on with his lying assertions and I would never have got into the position that I ended up in. For that agency document would have cut him or anyone else, out of saying that I was a forger and there was never an agency between us. He would have been buried at the first hurdle. So you see how pivotal that document was and why it was so important for RB to lie about it for years to come and to everyone.

On top of this he had in other evidence to back up his claim that he owned the rights to the trade Mark Viper, an alleged document said to have come from Kunzli in April 1990, giving him the rights to the mark Viper and the rights to the Cortina designs. Of course this was yet another forgery as Kunzli would never have done this as we were in constant contact which each other by phone. Also he never owned any such rights himself so could not sell them. I had owned the Cortina rights and had bought the design rights and chassis jigs and body moulds, off the Yanks, as already recounted.

My lawyers had got Kunzli to agree to attend the case to confirm all this was a forgery as he had never sent any such document. Yet because of the hopeless way the case was handled by the court, the day he arrived and he could only stay for the one day, the court was not ready to call him. I made this point to the jury and said that the court had been responsible to messing up my ability to show that RB was a forger and yet he is calling me a forger. The Judge did not like that at all, but then Judges in this country are at their best beyond the pail as some of the things they get up to and say, defy comprehension.

So at the end of the day RB came across as what he is, a squirming, grasping, pathological liar and the jury simply did not believe him. The charge of perverting the course of justice and perjury, was dropped early on, as was the ludicrous charge of forging my son's signature. He was present at the court to shoot this down if needed, and they knew it. That had left only the one charge of forgery and I was found not guilty and the copper who had investigated this looked sick as a parrot which pleased me no end.

As an aside to what a shower the Police are, evidence we had put in defence, for some unknown reason gets passed back to the Police and not my solicitor and of course they contrived, no doubt in their nastiness, to lose some of it. This was evidence that I needed to use in forthcoming IPO hearings. However this is the UK police for you. Crooks in uniform all of them! Mind you in their defence I think all Police around the World are the same! So they are not unique. I guess it takes a certain mentality to want to be a cop and that is why I found my early introduction to policing in the Forces put me off continuing and going myself into the UK civvy police and following my Stepfather. He too was a typical police type, hence why we never got on.

Another mob that are just as bad in my books, are the CPS. The upper class twit who was the prosecution barrister, let it slip that the CPS had allowed this case to continue as he had found this case to be most unusual and concerned a subject he was hot on… namely sexy sportscars. He and the odious Judge even had an inane chat about cars during the case, which made me feel sick. I think that says it all. The complete waste of Public money, seems to have never been an issue those thickos took into consideration.

The question of how this agency agreement document was undoubtedly forged will be dealt with later on. So the first chapter of my long battle for justice against a crook who seems to never want to give up, was over. However I believe it was to have consequences for me over my health.

Chapter Eight
The Finalising of the Chrysler Saga

As I have said I had to take on solicitors to force Chrysler to either continue with the appeal or give it up. Like all things legal, this took forever, with letters going to and fro between my solicitors and theirs. Eventually in early 2002 they said they were going to drop it even though they had to pay all my costs, and when this was finally done, the IPO told me that now this had been done I was now entitled to have registration. You may recall that Kings Patent Agents had not applied for my registration when I paid them to do so in January 1992, but he did get round to it in 1996. So it was that in 2002 I got registration backdated to 1996. I cannot understand why one does not get it from the date you first used it, as I had proved this to be around January 1986.

Five minutes after the IPO told me I now had registration, they told me in their next breath that the application by RB to also register the mark which the IPO had put on hold while my opposition to Chrysler was going through, was now going to be allowed to go ahead. Was I mad,? I expected once I had won on earlier use and he had stolen it in anycase and had been my agent, they would have thrown his application out. So it was that this was the starting point of all my real battles with the IPO and RB.

Chapter Nine
The Actions of the IPO from 1992-2004

The IPO had told me and Kings that they could not throw out the application of the Busbridges when we told them it had been made in bad faith. Preferring to put the onus on us to pursue this at an opposition hearing. Then once I knew Busbridge had gone bankrupt we then told the IPO that now the application which had been made in the name of a partnership that was no longer in existence and on top of that, the remaining partner was bankrupt. As bankruptcy law dictates that no bankrupt can own assets, this meant that this application should be made void (at least to my well ordered common sense mind). The IPO at first ignored us and after, when I kept on to them about this, I was astonishingly told that 'so what, how do we know he is, just because you say he is doesn't mean he is' Here it would seem that the fact that the IPO could easily check as to whether he was bankrupt, completely passed over their heads. Maybe it was too simple for them, or more likely that for some reason best known to them they simply did not want to know about this. More on this later on.

I was to keep on to them throughout the rest of the nineties about this, to no avail. Then to add insult to injury I get notification from them in March 2002 that RB has applied to them to register two assignments. Here he was 10 years after the alleged event, he was claiming that Cobretti (the business name the two Busbridges used) had assigned the assets and trademark from Cobretti to a new company, Autotrak Ltd. This was allegedly done in October 1992. The trouble was that when you looked at the document supposedly doing this, it was obviously a scam. It was not made for a consideration and trademark law states that an unregistered mark cannot be assigned anyway. In any case Robert did not own these assets 100%. Martin owned 50% and he still did. No mention of him being involved in this alleged assignment. Also trademark law (1938 TMA) says that an assignment has to be notified to the IPO within six months and 10 years is a little bit over that, don't you think? On top of that, the assignment paper was not legally done as it should be, as it was just a unprofessional scribbled note.

Soon after in April 2002 I get yet another notification of another alleged assignment this time dated as having been done in March 18, 2002, in which these alleged assets, now allegedly owned by Autotrak Ltd (which by the way had never traded since around 1993, and in any case, *had never even put in any company accounts to Companies House, so it had been struck off) had now assigned them back to RB.* It was obviously a scam made up by Robert because he now knew that soon he would have to show to the IPO that in his application, which even though it was on hold, and which may be soon brought alive again, he could show that he was the legal owner of the trademark asset and not Autotrak Ltd.

I kicked up no end of a stink about this to the IPO, pointing out that whichever way you looked at this business of these alleged assignments, they were obviously a scam. Firstly I pointed out that when the first alleged assignment was made on 22/10/92 it was obviously done, if it was done at all, to take away all the assets from Cobretti and give them to a limited company. However one little point here which the IPO seemed to think wasn't worth taking note of, when I pointed it out to them, is that at this date, Autotrak Ltd was not even owned by RB as he only became a director on the 30/10/92. That RB knew in 1992 that his business was knackered and heading for bankruptcy. His brother had left because of this, so if this ever did take place it was illegal to knowingly transfer assets away from a business going bankrupt.

I also pointed out that by seemingly taking the trademark asset away from Cobretti and then back, not to Cobretti, but to RB, had obviously been done purely because he wanted to show the IPO that he owned the trademark he had applied for. First he takes it away from Cobretti, knowing they would go bankrupt, so that creditors would get nothing, then when that was out of the way, hey presto the asset is back to RB again.

The fact is that all these shady goings on were not legal, as the partnership had not been legally wound up, so Martin still owned half the business and he had not given his blessing for all this.

It seems that the IPO simply had not bothered to ask themselves or anyone else, if any of this was legal. They never asked RB if his brother sanctioned the application or if he sanctioned the alleged assignment, as his signature was not on the alleged assignment. This was completely illegal and against partnership law, but of course the IPO do not care about the law of the land.

Chapter Ten
A Breakdown in My Health

By the end of 2001, quite frankly I was beginning to get tired of the kitcar scene, especially as at least 50% and quite possibly up to 70%, of my potential business was being siphoned off by the illegal goings on of RB. Overall the amount of work and investment for the returns for me, because of Busbridge, was not great. So in January 2002 I began to look for a buyer of my business. 2001 for a change had been reasonable, so I could say legitimately that with someone new who would have more go and enthusiasm, they could take it to higher levels.

I was lucky that locally a kit car build company showed interest. I told them that if they bought, I would back them up with free advice on all they may need to know. It was a Father and son business and they could have done the Viper a great deal of good. I said I would not sell the trade mark with it, but would license them to use it.

It was by that time that I had completed the sale of my business to this local company called Cadini. After that had been done, I decided that I would go to Spain for a break, to wind down from all the madness I was still involved in with the wretched IPO and the infuriating conman Busbridge. So it was early on the 1st April 2002 that my ferry docked into Bilboa and I drove down to the southern Spanish coast to a place called Nerja. I arrived about 8pm and booked into a nice little family owned hotel in the town centre. Then I went for a Chinese and after I settled into my room. I began to feel queasy within about an hour and I thought it was maybe the meal I had just had. However I soon realised something more serious was happening, but what I did not know. Eventually I realised I had to alert the hotel owners who live on the top floor, so I went to the reception area and rang their bell. I was then to suffer the most excruciating heavy chest pain and I then knew what it was... a heart attack.

The owners although they could speak little English knew too I was having a heart attack, so called the ambulance. I had had a massive heart attack and was lucky to be still alive. To cut a long story short I spent nearly a month in the local Alicante Hospital and had a stent inserted in an artery that had become blocked.

What annoys me most about this story, was that this episode had been entirely preventable. I am not overweight and had always been involved in lots of heavy work. I also did lots of walks and cycling and did not eat rubbish fat food. Yet just before I set off on this holiday I had visited my doctor complaining about an unrelated issue and he sent me for a blood check. The result that came back was that I had a cholesterol level of 17 when it should be no more than 5.

What did my ignorant and useless doctor do? All he said was that it was the highest he had ever seen. Now I like many had never even thought about heart attacks, nor about cholesterol. I was entirely ignorant about anything to do with those subjects, so I relied as you would, on my doctor. He said I should have checks done at my local hospital, but there was no sense of urgency coming from him, which I now know there should have been. I said that I had booked a holiday in Spain which should start in a few days. He just shrugged his shoulders as if to say 'well what do you want me to do' The fact is that he did not say 'Do not go as this is serious and you need to get this sorted now, otherwise you could have a heart attack' What he did say was 'see me when you get back'

I tell you all this as an example of just how useless so many aspects of British life is these days and the IPO are just one of many British governmental institutions that are broken and not fit for purpose. The NHS in their incompetence had almost cost me my life, and could that have been down to the actions of them and the execrable Robert Busbridge? I had certainly had to endure years of strain and frustration. So it is entirely feasible that the heart attack was from stress.

On leaving hospital I had to spend at least a month recuperating as I was so weak. My muscles needed exercise to give me enough strength to be able to drive back to the UK. I also had to keep up my trying to deal with the IPO. As I have said I was furious with them for allowing RB to have his application to register my trademark, so I had to complain to the highest person in the IPO.

Once someone has had a heart attack, because the heart muscle gets damaged, it affects you forever. I now have very little strength although I can function fairly normally. In cases where I need real strength, it just isn't there. If I have to run for any distance, I cannot. If I had to swim really strongly say to save my life, I would run out of steam quickly, and so on.

Chapter Eleven
My Battle of Words with the IPO Continues

Before my heart attack, I first wrote on the 16th March 02 to their CEO of that time, a Miss A. Brimelow, setting out my complaints. I got no answer, which once again tells you all about the IPO. Then after my heart attack and on getting out of hospital, I wrote on the 21/4/02 to her once again and complained about the fact that the IPO are always failing to answer letters and have taken ages with every step of the way. Then I made the most important complaint that they were now allowing RB to go ahead with his application when the partnership and company name in which it had been made no longer existed and had gone bankrupt, in any case. So why were they allowing it to proceed? I also pointed out that in any case any asset including the trademark application was or should have been taken over by the Insolvency Service.

I got a reply on the 30th April from her merely telling me that they had sent a reply to Kings Patent re my complaint letter of the 16th March and she was sorry I thought the IPO were slow having taken 6 years to a hearing and a further 4 years to Chrysler dropping out, but my opposition against Chrysler was unusual, which was absolute poppycock. She completely ignored my pointing out all about RB's application that should be voided due to bankruptcy and no longer in partnership etc. It was a scandalous dereliction of her duty.

The letter they sent to Kings that she spoke of was merely a short letter saying they were sending him a copy of my letter of complaint to him. So in effect they were refusing to deal with it and as Kings from then on was out of the picture, because I stopped using them from then, it was a waste of time. I could not afford Kings as they suddenly shot up their hourly cost from quite low to £150 an hour, which was expert solicitors rates and he was not a solicitor. I guessed he just wanted me to disappear and this was a way to do it.

I replied to her letter as I was not going to let go of this. The reply of 3rd May 02 apart from making general complaints of how the actions of the IPO had cost me heaps and now looked it was going to cost heaps more because they were allowing RB to go ahead with an application that should never have been allowed as the IPO laws were being abused. I made a point of stressing that I required her to answer my pertinent questions as to why her organisation was ignoring its own rules and laws?

Of course government organisations like the IPO do not like having to answer questions that query why they are breaking the law. So the answer to that letter was now downgraded to be answered by one of her minions, a Peter Lawrence. He simply used the excuse that the IPO could not discuss RB's application with third parties. This is saying that 'you are only a 'third party what has it got to do with you?' The fact that I already have the registration of the same mark proving use long before this applicant, is irrelevant, as is the fact that I will become relevant, as it is obvious that if they persist in allowing it, I will have to oppose the application of RB.

In any case I was not asking for any discussions about his case but asking why the IPO was breaking its own laws and rules in allowing the application to even start any process. Too subtle for the IPO to understand this distinction, I guess.

I again wrote to Miss Brimelow rather than to her minion, pointing the above out to her. No discussion my dear, just asking you why you are breaking the law. Simple, but apparently too difficult for her to answer! I appear to have got some sort of reply on the 17th May but that letter is lost, but it obviously did not answer my question at all as on the 24th May I wrote back to this Lawrence guy asking him that why he said in his reply of the 17th that the IPO may not have been aware that the applicant was bankrupted. This is a typical example of the vacuous and incompetent nature of the IPO. So I went into detail of all the times since 1993 that I and Kings had told them of the bankruptcy and sent copies of those letters.

His reply of the 30th May was short and terse and simply in a few sentences said it appeared they had not got through to me. (Obviously my brain was too thick to understand what they thought they were saying, when in reality my brain knows full well what they were up to.) Then he staggers me by stating that my telling them he was a bankrupt and no longer had traded under the name that the application had been made in and that in any case the partnership was no longer in existence, may not be factual.

So once again the IPO are saying that it is too much bother for them to lift a phone and call the Insolvency Service or check records that are made public. Nor to contact Martin Busbridge to check if the partnership was still in existence and more importantly to realise that if a partnership dissolves and is no longer in existence, did the partners dissolve that partnership legally, so that a remaining partner could legally own all the assets, such as the application? Not to mention, asking RB why was it is that the application was still in the name of a dissolved partnership and one of the partners was bankrupt.

I replied to this Lawrence oaf on the 25th July 02 and asked him why this application of RB was being allowed to proceed when I had provided the IPO, of my earlier use to him by winning against Chrysler etc etc. His reply of the 8th August defies belief and he comes out with a baffling bit of typical civil service waffle speak; *'There are as I understand it, differences in both the details of who owns this application and some other differences which create different facts'* Sounds like ex president Bush talking, doesn't it? But what does it mean? Again it is another example of just how the IPO does seem not to be able to understand what is going on with the cases it is supposed to be handling. In this case it seems totally incapable of understanding that I, after a 10 year fight, I had *proved* that my use of the mark in question, dating back to *before* the 10th Jan 1990 (the date of Chryslers application) was long before the possible use by the other applicant. They having put in their application in on 10th May 1992. That in my world means that RB cannot lay legitimate claim for the mark over me. If Chrysler were unable to do it, just how can this idiot state that it is not clear as to who has the greater claim, me or RB. Leaving aside that little fact, he completely ignored all the other legal points a to why the application should not be allowed to proceed.

If the two subjects of bankruptcy and partnership were not enough, there is also the subject of 'bad faith' By this I mean that RB's application was made in bad faith. for in law he knew full well that I owned the mark. In fact I think you could not get a more clear cut case of any application, made for any registration, that could be a better example of something applied for in bad faith. I have already told you that I and Kings very early on informed the IPO that RB's application was made in bad faith. We sent them a copy of the agency agreement to show that he had been my agent, which is what I have already told you at the beginning of this chapter.

Their letter dated 16th August 1993 in reply to ours of the 24th June, and that is some seven weeks later, says 'Application 1501909 is still at examination stage and matters of proprietorship cannot be dealt with at this stage' Two points to be made on this are; his application went in, in May 1992 so over a year later and nothing has been done, and we have to deal with it in opposition. It again begs the question as to; is this the way the IPO really work? Why does it have to go through years of waiting and to be only be dealt with, as an opposition case?

In this case it was clear that they had been my agents and there was the proof, and they were attempting to register someone else's trademark. The application should immediately be thrown out. Even if one of the signatories said it was a forgery, the big question was, is the other partner saying that? Had they bothered to get hold of Martin (and he was still in the UK, don't forget) he would have told them that he did sign it and it was not a forgery.

It once more shows that any crook can approach the IPO and apply to register a patent or a design or a copyright or a trademark, when they have no legal right to these IP rights. They simply do not care about this. They cannot be bothered to make any simple checks to make sure that the application is bona fide. (When you think of all the checks one now has to go through, just to be in slight contact with children, then they make you go through so many checks, but if you try to stitch up someone for tens of thousands or even millions of £'s by going through the IPO, you can sail ahead with no checks whatsoever.) Even when they receive information that the application is not bona fide, they are too lazy and uninterested to lift a finger. 'Just give us the money so we can pay ourselves' The fact that innocent members of the public get their IP stolen by these illegal applications and that they are then drawn into long expensive battles to try and prove that the application is crooked, is of no consequence to them. On top of this one runs the risk as I did, that their battle to prove their real ownership is dealt with by idiots and incompetents who then award ***their IP to the crooks!***

I simply was not prepared to be browbeaten down by these lying incompetents and I continued a campaign to expose their lies. So on the 28th October 02, I wrote once again to their Law Section. It was a long letter posing many questions and I once more made a point that the application has been made by a bankrupt and they chose to ignore this. Then I dealt with the two alleged assignments and pointed out all the irregularities of these alleged assignment and asked why it was yet another case of the IPO just accepting paperwork that was obviously false and did not comply with their rules about assignments under the 38 Act?

I then went on to ask why they were ignoring the fact that in any case the partnership no longer existed, so how could the application go ahead? I asked for the application to be thrown out. Which of course they did not do and I then sent emails to their trademarks Examination & Admin section, to a Mr Morgan, bringing up the bankruptcy and broken partnership issues yet again. I cannot trace if I got anywhere with this guy, but I do not think I did.

So I was now racking my brains as to how I could get these lying bastards to admit that they had rules on bankruptcy, I wrote a Jayne Francis in the Law section and posed the same question to her, but not in relation to any one particular case. Just a general question, as it were. Her answer on the 27th November 02 showed me just how the IPO, for reasons best known to them, were simply not going to ever answer my questions on bankruptcy and partnership law. I can imagine by now just how sick of me and my persistence, they will have been. Her answer said:

'Unfortunately in order to preserve our position of impartiality, as there are outstanding proceedings brought by yourself, the registry is unable to comment on these issues.' Then she said if I wanted to know what the laws were I should read text books or pay a lawyer.

Now I had not even mentioned the case in question and I had never talked before to this person, so it is apparent that now the whole of the IPO building in Swansea must have been warned that any legal question that a Mr Ken Cook may ask of the IPO about their own laws, should be ignored. I can picture a 'wanted' type poster on the walls of each department with a mug shot of me and the caption… '*Do not speak to this man… he is trying to get us*'

I now believe that at around this time the IPO probably began to get sick of me and my questioning their actions. What I cannot understand with them is why at no time did they ever try to answer my questions? I was not asking them to help me with a case as I was merely asking them to explain their actions or non actions. I believe it was either an individual or group of individuals that decided to start a process that would eventually deny me my trademark. There is no other credible explanation for what then happened at each hearing and the obvious bias against me and whatever I said and showed in evidence.

We were now up to the date of early 2002 and the application of the Busbridges had been advertised as going ahead, and this is done so anyone can oppose it. However, go back to this business of 'bad faith' You may recall that in 1993 the IPO in a letter had said that they could not deal with it and we had to deal with it at the appropriate time. They said that we should watch out for the advertisement, and then we could apply to oppose any further progress to registration. I find this statement to be vague. Does the writer mean we can only deal with bad faith or bankruptcy or partnership laws, in a full blown opposition case and all the time and expense that entails? Or is he saying that when it is advertised we can bring up the business of bad faith and then that will be dealt with and the application could be voided, without any hearing?

Of course I had been banging on non stop about these three points for years, so the **IPO knew full well I wanted these dealt with**. I was stating my wish to have these dealt with just before the advert and after it, yet they never said they would deal with those aspects… they just ignored my protestations or pooh poohed them and I was then forced to go down the line of fully opposing the application. They knew I was a litigant in person and could not afford to continue using Kings or any other lawyer as I had repeatedly told them this.

Had it been necessary for me to fill in some form and supply reasons why this application should not proceed, I should have been informed of this. I wasn't.

On the 6th November I got a reply from the letter I sent this Morgan guy who I have already mentioned. He was replying to my complaining about this opposition and especially these crooked assignments. Even though I had comprehensively shown that they were crooked and had not followed the IPO's laws about assignments, here was this man telling me he had no authority to question the validity of these alleged assignments or to even ask for any proof that they were legit. This once more if it's true, backs up all I have said about the uselessness of the IPO. Present any crooked, forged or unlawfully composed document and they will rubber stamp it 'OK'… no questions asked.

I obviously replied to this nonsense and asked exactly what trademark law he was relying on to say he had no authority to question or ask for documentary evidence. I also queried why they were ignoring the fact that they had not been notified of these alleged assignment within the required 6 months? The reply I got was more nonsense. First of all, this registration application was made under the 1938 trademark Act, yet I get a whole letter quoting various parts of the 1994 Act, which are different to the 38 Act. So I get rubbish answers to my question of, is the assignment valid at all? as (a) it has not been signed by **both** partners, (b) there is no consideration (c) notification has been made more than six months after the event, contrary to the 38 Act. He says that if I want to apply for a Rectification of the register under section 4 of the 94 TMA, re them accepting the assignments, I can.

I notify him in yet another reply as to why he is quoting 94 when it is all under 38. Also how do I make this rectification? I have to say that I never got an answer to the questions about the assignments and but I was told that I could not apply for Rectification for an unregistered mark. Doesn't this tell you all about the IPO? Time and again when you get them into a corner they will fizzle out their answers as if they have suddenly gone deaf. In this case they send a reply from yet another person. It is obvious this Morgan idiot doesn't even know what he is talking about and now he just throws his hands up and passes it onto some other office clerk and say; 'Here you deal with this difficult persistent bastard'

Chapter Twelve
My 2003 Complaint to the Parliamentary Ombudsman Regarding the IPO

In March 2002 I sent in a complaint about the IPO, to the Ombudsman. Unfortunately I no longer have that letter, but from subsequent letters from my MP and from a letter I sent him, it appears I made the same complaints I had been making to the IPO themselves. Namely why were the IPO allowing an application to go ahead made by a bankrupt person, and why were the IPO constantly ignoring my pointing this out?

Even though I had sent my complaint to the Parliamentary Ombudsman, I got a reply from an MP one Melanie Johnson, whoever she was. She was I think, the minister at that time for the DTI and the IPO are part of that mob. Her reply as all replies you get from politicians and civil servants, did not deal with the core plank of my complaint as to why the IPO were refusing to deal with my complaint, that they have allowed an application from a person who became bankrupt and whose business partnership had collapsed etc, etc.

She had obviously talked to the IPO and got a load of guff off them which was untrue and disingenuous. Her arguments were:-

1: Busbridge had a different version of events to me and this was usually the case in former business associates. My answer to that is we were not 'associates' He had been my ***agent*** and there was a legal document to prove that. Plus had the IPO bothered to ask, Martin Busbridge could have verified that.

2: The IPO simply could not accept one side of events. Again being duplicitous as my complaint was why were the IPO not carrying out there duty to apply their own laws and void the application as it (a) was made in bad faith (b) he was a bankrupt (c) the partnership under which it had been applied in was no longer and RB did not have the authority or legality to apply. Those points should have been dealt ***without*** a hearing having to take place

3: She said it was not true that ***I had won my case against Chrysler***! (So my getting registration was because I had LOST!) She says Busbridge had a rival claim. Excuse me you vacuous Polly (politician) twit, *I won against the claim to the Viper trademark by Chrysler, no other verdict.* Busbridge had put in his application in 1992 *two years after Chrysler.* I had proved first usage from January 1986. My complaints were once again on points of law as to why the IPO were not acting within the law in allowing the application to even proceed.

4: She admits that Chrysler had failed to make the case to claim ownership, so if they could not do so why could Busbridge with his illegal usage of my trademark, do so from a later date?

I put this in my letter to my MP dated 16.10.02, but I got no answer.

So I fired off a second detailed complaint to the Ombudsman on the 28th November 02. I list them:-

1: The question of not voiding his application on his going bankrupt.
2: I sent copies of documents proving I had notified the IPO of his bankruptcy many times and they had ignored me.
3: I showed a document which showed that at last they admitted that they should have got in contact with the Insolvency Service over the application, once I had notified them.
4: I complained about the illegal alleged assignments being accepted into evidence 10 years after the event and against their laws.
5: I complained at their refusal to tell me what their own laws said on bankruptcies.
6: I complained and listed all the numerous times they ignored letters I had sent.

The reply I got on the 19th December from the Ombudsmans Office or should I say one of their minions. I was asked to provide more evidence and information to do with what I had complained about. As if the evidence I had supplied, and which was quite straight forward had not been enough for these numbties. My complaint that they refused to give me the information I asked for, IE "What was the 1938 Law on how they should deal with an applicant who subsequently becomes a bankrupt?" Also information as to why they kept ignoring my letters.

So this meant yet another letter which I fired off on the 24th December 02 . In it I listed the following complaints backed up by 22 copies of letters.

I thought this time I may as well go the whole hog and complain about everything I could, so:-

1: I complained that the IPO had let Chrysler use Busbridge who had been my agent (proved by the agency agreement) and had stolen my trademark, as a witness. Disallowing our complaints about this when he had no bearing on the veracity of my case against Chrysler.
2: I had in that case proved my usage *before* Busbridges use, as well as Chryslers use, yet they allow Busbridges application to proceed.
3: The facts that the IPO knew of his bankruptcy and did nothing.
4: The fact that Mr Morgan when asked to give me facts on why the application was allowed, proceeded to give me facts based on the 1994 Act when the application came under the 1938, thus proving incompetence.
5: Morgan telling me I could take action for a Rectification and this again was incorrect under the 38 Act. Again, incompetence.

I should have also complained about the application having been made in bad faith and the irregularities over partnership law thus also making the application illegal. But I thought it would be too much for these civil service incompetents. The main reason I wanted action on was their refusal to void the application due to his bankruptcy.

They answered on the 11th February 2003 and it is a typical incompetent reply that one expects from yet another civil service mob of incompetents. This Ombudsman's lot are obviously only there to cover the backsides of various other government departments. The reasons they gave for not doing anything are:-

1: They said that the Ombudsman cannot question why the IPO allowed the application and if I was not satisfied I could have appealed this decision. She then quotes the 1994 Act. I ask you what qualifications do these numbties have, that look into these cases? They are absolute useless idiots. Firstly the application was made *before* the ***1994 Act***! Even my opposition to RB, filed in 2002 was heard under the ***1938 Act***!

2: The Ombudsman can look into maladministration. Now if the IPO cannot even comply with it's own laws, wouldn't this be maladministration, plus all the rest of their maladministration?

3: I would have had have suffered an unremedied injustice. If this was not just that, I am a Monkeys Uncle! I had no way which I could remedy it, other than complaining and I had got nowhere. Had there been a way I could have had these cock-ups made good, the IPO should have told me what my remedy could be. They did no such thing, even though they knew that later on I was a litigant in person. Before that when Kings were handling things, you would think that they would have known they could have appealed the decisions of the IPO over the bankruptcy/partnership laws and the application made in bad faith. They as you will know did bring these up with the IPO, only to be knocked back as well.

4: All my complaints about letters ignored and slow responses and the letters I sent which showed the IPO were lying about bankruptcy etc were all pooh poohed. She even said my issues I raised were contentious and have to be dealt with only by an opposition hearing. Thank you very much! It seems that I am quarrelsome, argumentative and even maybe controversial.

It also seems that despite all the evidence in the letters, the IPO were to be classified as good as gold and no cause for concern.

So another wasted exercise, but another MP had warned me a few years back that all Ombudsmen were a waste of time, money and space, and he was so right.

Well amongst all the other things the Establishment seems to think I am, I am a fighter (but nothing like Mandleson, thank God) who will never give in. I was listening on the radio not long ago about a woman who was convicted of killing her Aunt. It appeared yet another cock-up by our wonderful **PC plod police force** and our wonderful, brilliant justice system. No concrete evidence, a shonky so called expert witness, her finger print in a blood spot which was incorrectly seen as proof. Despite two appeals she never got the justice she deserved and despite spending 12 years in jail for that, during which she never stopped proclaiming her innocence, she was released. I always thought that if you were innocent and refused to say you were guilty, they kept you inside forever! So she was lucky. My point is that if a person *knows* they are not guilty or are right and that they have been badly treated by the Establishment, normally they will just never give up. I am in that category, but thankfully I was not done for murder!

I appealed to the Ombudsman and listed all the mistakes they had made in their letter of reply to my complaint. I got nowhere yet again and I went on to try and elicit the help of my MP as you do. I pointed out to him all their mistakes and injustices. I got nowhere with him either. He just was not interested. In fact a lot of my letters were just ignored. Of course I now know that MP's are not there to help us peasants, they are only there to laze around and the only work they want to do is tarting up their two homes bought on taxpayers money or fill in their long expenses claims.

I eventually got a meeting with this little attention seeking twerp (for that was all he was) and I laid it out to him that all he had ever done was act as a post office for all my letters and was useless otherwise. He did not like that and the reply he gave says it all about MP's *'It is not my job to fight your battles'* my reply was 'No, then what are you there for?' I got no reply to that and it was meeting over. Doesn't this tell you all you need to know about MP's and it is a recurring problem that I faced in trying to get one useless bastard MP after another to help me as you will see further on.

Chapter Thirteen
My Opposition to Busbridge's Application to Register My Mark

This hearing took place in the IPO's office in London on 1st June 2004. Prior to it and for approximately 18 months, statements made firstly by me and then in reply by RB, were made over a period of time. In all subsequent hearings up to 2010, the same happened. All the statements made by both sides are too long and the documentary evidence as exhibits are too numerous, and to repeat them word for word in this book as it would be too much. So what I will do is, I will give the reader a simplified breakdown of what was said in each statement and a list of what exhibits accompanied each statement. My first statement was made on the 3rd March 2002 in the form of a 'Statement of Grounds' RB then made a Counter Statement to that, in October 2002.

I should like to point out that from the onset and up to the eventual hearing in 2004, all the following statements are long and tedious. However it is imperative that the reader does try to digest what was being said, especially by Robert Busbridge.

I would have liked to keep things 'to the point' by sticking only to what I felt were relevant facts. However after making my initial Statement of Grounds, which I did keep short and to the point, from thereafter each and every reply statement made by RB went into reams of irrelevant ramblings. He threw in every thing he could possibly think of that would denigrate me. Everything I said was denied and rubbished by a diatribe of lies. As a litigant in person, I was faced with the problem of what were the IPO going to listen to and take actual note of? I had no wealth of experience of what they were like (only experience of how they had behaved from 1992 to 2002 and that wasn't good as they did not listen to anything you said) or what they would ignore. So I had to play on the side of safety. I had to then go into denying every lie and irrelevant piece of rubbish he came out with. In the event I think you will see that the Hearing Officer that heard the case, did take note of many of the lies that Busbridge came out with, and none of what I said in my evidence.

I now know that Procedural Rules on Evidence say that it must be relevant and any statements that are of a personal nature should be made to be taken out. Yet you will see that this was not done and *I have to ask why not?* I say that it was because the IPO wanted the hearing officer to be brainwashed by this tide of invective against my character and my IP rights.

He also threw in so much documentary so called evidence, which was again mostly irrelevant. I am sure that the IPO must have hated this case due to the immense amount of crap it produced. I was then obliged to also counter all the irrelevant documents he produced, thus making it worse. However it is imperative that the reader sticks with it and tries to digest all that was going on, for it shows you what you could be up against if you too get attacked by a determined conman. It will show you what such a conman will do in order to carry on with his con. Make no mistake RB is a very plausible conman, as all conmen are. By muddying the waters with heaps of totally irrelevant lying rubbish they wear down those who have to deal with it. I on the other hand could cope with it and I remembered all the rubbish he came out with. Others who took part in this saga, would have a difficult time in remembering all that was said, or making sense of it. It then becomes all too easy to ignore the relevant bits in order just to get shot of the whole case, and be done with it.

So a bit of patience is required to plough through even what I have tried to simplify.

My grounds for my opposition document:-
A brief list of my grounds:-

1: I pointed out that although I had put in my registration application, after the Busbridges had, I had earlier use back to 1986, **and** I had proved that in my opposition to Chrysler, which I won on that basis. R.Busbridge had never shown evidence of an earlier use to 1991.
2: That Busbridges application was for a trademark that was exactly the same as mine and the goods to which it would apply to were exactly as mine as it had been copied from my product. Thus it would cause confusion.
3: That I had always been the proprietor of the mark and exercised my

control over it. I had made substantial use of the mark up to that relevant time.
4: It should be refused under Section 12(1) a, b & c of TMA 1938. Also the use of the mark was not honest since copying someone's product and mark, was not honest.
5: It should be refused under Sect 17(1) of the Act. That I had advertised the mark extensively, it had featured on Television on the BBC and ITV News and on Radio 4. I also pointed out that the use of the mark by Busbridge was not bona fide and his claim to ownership was false.
6: I pointed out for the umpteenth time that the applicant had gone bankrupt in May 1993 and had not traded since then under the name under which the application was made. I questioned the legality of the alleged assignments and that even if the mark legally belonged to Cobretti, it would be an asset and as Busbridge trading as Cobretti, it should have gone to the Receiver as they were bankrupt.
7: Busbridge had long periods when he did not trade under any name.

The Busbridge counter statement:-

1: He admits I have registration, but says it is not valid and it is not relevant to these proceedings.
2: His application could have protection in a court of justice and is not objectionable under sect 11 of TMA38. Nor does it cause confusion.
3: It is denied that the opponent coined the trademark Viper.
4: He denies that I have been at all times the proprietor of the mark and if I had had rights then I abandoned those rights before he applied in 1992. I had not used the mark exclusively. I had not exercised control over the goods sold in the UK under the mark.
5: I had not made continuous use of the mark or even any use of it prior to 1992 nor had I acquired goodwill or reputation.
6: His use of the mark had always been honest.
7: I had not advertised the mark since 1986.
8: He maintains that the alleged assignment to Autotrak was done before Cobretti 'ceased trading'. No bankrupt company was involved.

9: Busbridge has not abandoned the mark. The applicant RB was not the sole trader of Cobretti Engineering.

My brief comments on above (in their order):-

1: If it was not valid, why did the IPO give it me?
2: Having two identical kit cars on the market both with the same trademark certainly causes confusion and it did so.
3: How can he know that is the truth as he did not even know me in 1986 and before when I coined it. No evidence is ever produced.
4: How can he know what the legal situation was in 1985/86 and onwards as to whether I owned it. I did not abandon the mark at all and he was my agent prior to 1992. I had used it exclusively until he stole it and also used it in late 1991. The evidence shows I did control the use of the mark until he stole it and even after that I continued to use it extensively. Why did the IPO grant me registration based on usage going back to 1986 if I was not deemed to be the rightful proprietor?
5: What was I doing from 1986 through to his stealing it in 1991 and what was I doing in the use of it after 1992 and up to the date of that statement, if I wasn't trading and using the mark?
6: Saying his use was honest when he knew he had stolen my mark and product defies a reply.
7: I do not know how all the advertising I had done for the product under the trademark from 1985 through to 2002, can be said that it was not advertised.
8: No proof was ever shown that the alleged assignment made in 1992 was ever done at that time and that it was legally done. He then cocks up by admitting that Cobretti ceased trading, so the application which when he made that statement, (in 2003) was the still in that name. He says that no bankrupt company was involved when the fact was that Cobretti went bankrupt in 1993 whilst the application was still being made. Cobretti also did not 'cease trading' It stopped when it went bankrupt and that is the truth.
9: Then he says that he, was not the sole trader of Cobretti. So this means

that he was saying is that he was in a partnership, so that by him continuing to be the sole applicant is not legal, as he did not legally take over the assets of the partnership, which would give him 100% ownership of the application. Also this proves perjury as if he says he was in a partnership when in fact that partnership had broken down in 1992, this is a lie.

My first witness statement:-

This was made in June 2002 and I dealt with many points re my history with the Viper. I should point out that I felt it absolutely necessary to set out the history of how the mark came about, how it was used by me and the companies I licensed it to, how I became involved with the Busbridges and how they ripped me off. I reply to all the points made in RB's counter statement:-

1: I gave a detailed history of how I came to make the product.
2: Showed the first use of the name Viper in 1986.
3: I personally paid for the making of the jigs and moulds of the product to which the mark was attached. Thus showing it was myself and not the limited company that paid for this.
4: Detailed how, in case of any doubts who owned the IP rights that a document was drawn up by the company specifying that I owned the rights.
5: Detailed that I was anxious to ensure that all rights to the product, IP, and goodwill was vested in myself and should identify the Viper vehicles as designed by me, was vested in me.
6: I detail the start of trading with my new Viper kit in the beginning of 1986.
7: Detailed the seeking of capital into company and meeting American venture capital people. Also how my IP rights were not part of any deal and their letter of intent to enter into a deal with me did not include those rights.
8: The new company of BRL formed after investors joined me. Zinlic would have a debenture over what assets I passed over and future assets

built up.

9: I controlled BRL's use of my trademark throughout and up to 1989.
10: The Busbridge brothers approach me for agency and are taken on in 1988.
11: I show that in 1989 I resigned and as I was *the* company and owned all the IP rights the investors had to close it down.
12: I show how the assets of BRL that I needed to carry on were bought by me off Zinlic and the rest sold to a Swiss company H&S Replicas.
13: I was then able to start up again on my own with a new company Classic Replicas and I retook on the Busbridges as MY agents. I show all the business I passed onto them, showing I viewed them as my agents otherwise why pass on so much valuable business?
14: This paragraph was empty.
15: I show just how much money I had paid out (£6,000+) to enable me to set up the new business. Thus showing I did not abandon the trademark as claimed by RB. This money was used to set up the manufacturing of the product that had the mark attached to it. Without that mark it had no value.
16: I later on set them up to also promote as agents, a service to supply builders of any make of Cobra replica, with universal Cobra parts.
17: I show that I passed to them a further order for a fully built car which I could not handle, thus further showing that I viewed them as agents, otherwise why would I have done that?
18: I show that further to this I gave them an order at my cost, for them to build a Cortina based version of the Viper so as to build up sales for both of us even.
19: I show that whilst working with them I could see that the way they ran the business was unprofessional and could set them into bankruptcy. How this set the collusion between us on a downwards spiral.
20: I show how their advertising stated the Viper was only under 'new management' and not 'ownership' as they claimed. I point out that their advertising was under my ultimate control as to what they could state.
21: I then show that most of their orders for kits and parts they gave me were subject to orders in writing, as were my invoices. On some of these

documents it is shown they were ordering 'Vipers' Thus this showed they were my agents and I had not abandoned my mark as they claimed.

22: I state that due to the recession and the collapse of UK sales I had to go to Switzerland to build a car and I left the retailing of my Viper to the Busbridges. I show how I set up an ordering system for them whilst I was away, thus showing how I took steps to protect my mark and product.

23: I point out how my Cobra was different from any other Cobra replicas as the wheel arches were wider, and I show that this shows they were selling my version of the Cobra and not any other and their copies were of mine and not of any other.

24: I show how whilst in Switzerland they stole my designs off me and my mark.

25: I show that I took steps to protect my mark and that I sent them a letter warning them I would sue them for breach of copyright and stealing my mark.

26: I show how I continued to make my product on my return to the UK in 1992 by doing a deal with a Mr Tony Barrass to continue making and advertising my product and mark.

27: I show how I met a Trevor Sangster-Jones in their workshop and saw their copying of one of my Cortina based chassis.

28: I show how they approached Chrysler to lie and say they owned the mark, but would sell it to them. I then show how RB had made up five different stories as to how he had been able to take over my business and thus use the mark. I show how RB forges a document supposed to have given him rights to the mark by my Swiss agent Kunzli. I show how RB was trying to get £500,000 from Chrsyler for the mark.

29: I show how from 1993 I carry on selling my product through firstly Barrass and then in my own right when I bought him out. I show that I advertised the mark all this time. I point out that the only break in my UK advertising was between June 1991 and the end of 1992 and that through the actions of the Busbridges. (It should be pointed out here that you have to not trade in a mark for 5 years before you can be accused of abandoning it.)

30: I point out that at all times whilst I traded with kitcars, the trademark was always associated with me. I provide articles and adverts to back this up.

31: I make the point that Section 12 of the TMA's, deal with identical goods, and how his copy of my product has to be identical. So my registration had relevance to his application

32: I point out that Section 11 of the 38 TMA says that it is unlawful to register a trademark that is likely to cause confusion and deceive and I point out why having two Cobra replicas with the same trademark and are identical in shape, will confuse the market.

33: I point out that far from RB saying I did not coin the mark, I certainly did.

34: I point out that RB saying I was not the proprietor of the mark was a gross lie and I show how I have used it since 1986 by listing all the ways I did and steps I took to continue to use it.

35: In reply to their assertion that I had not made continuous use of the mark before the application or after or had acquired goodwill or reputation of the mark, I pointed out that I had dealt with those in my showing that I had been the proprietor since 1986.

36: I reply to the claim that their use of the trademark has always been honest. I point out all the ways he has been dishonest. Show how in May 1991 they made statements to a kitcar magazine, purporting to now be the owners of the product and mark and this when they were still my agents and I had not even left the UK. How they put in a picture of a Viper which was in fact a car made by me. How in sworn statement to the Police RB made claims as to have traded in the mark since 1987, when he was not even an agent of mine let alone the owner of the mark. Then in further statements elsewhere, he makes claims to a different date that he started using the mark. How he, when a bankrupt, was acting as a director of a limited company. I went on to list a catalogue of lies he indulged in, and asked how can this be 'honest use'? I then go on to list a whole list of dishonest actions they committed, too many to all list here. One worth noting, is the fact that their trading name history does not give anyone cause to believe they were honest in any way. I do this by listing 6 different company names RB used. Now why does anyone in business keep changing their trading name? It smacks of them trying to make things confusing for anyone doing business with them, and something to do with the bankruptcy.

37: I make the point that for RB to say I never advertised the mark Viper at all, flies in the face of all the masses of advertising I produced in evidence.

38: I question how they can claim to have 'adopted' my mark and used it continually from 1991. I question how the limited companies he had during some of that time, never gave Companies House trading accounts. Plus in a statement he had made, he stated that those two companies had not traded. Yet he advertised his business using those companies names. What was the truth? I also pointed out he had not shown how he is supposed to have acquired the trademark. Had he been sold it or assigned it, or bought it off me?

39: I point out that an unregistered mark cannot be assigned, so the alleged assignment from Cobretti to Autotrak was not legal on that point alone. I again point out that the partnership was not in existence a month after the application had gone in, and I question as to why the Registry did not when told, insist on a new application. I question why bankruptcy laws were not adhered to by the Registry and I again question the legality of the alleged assignments and why they were said to have happened.

40: I show that the two limited companies he used for part of the time were both struck off for not supplying accounts etc. Hardly the actions of someone whose word can be taken as truthful and honest as he claims he is.

41: I show that in 2002 in a brochure he sent out that he is still using the company Autotrak Cobretti Ltd, the company he never made any accounts for, and is being struck off for that and is at odds with the statement he made previously that those companies were not trading. How in this brochure it is implied that the company owns the trademark. Yet RB tries to have the Registry believe that he has had the trademark assigned to him in 2002. In this brochure it is admitted that the Viper has been in production for 10 years which takes his use of it to 1992, which is correct, (even if illegal) yet elsewhere in his statements, he makes claims that he used it from 1989 and in other places he makes claims he used it from 1987/1988. Which do we believe? I point out claims he makes for a Viper car involved in an accident was in fact a car made from one of my kits and not one of his copies of mine. I show he admits that he copied my product and therefore he is asking for registration of a trademark which he will apply to an identical product to mine, thus causing confusion.

42: I point out his money problems and that he mostly appears not to be in business and yet he says he is still trading and how can this show he is honest?

43: Lastly I make the point that as the partnership has broken up, how can the application be still made in the partnership name?

List of the exhibits I included with the above statement:
(including a brief description of what they show)

EXHIBIT KC 1/1:- Copy of local paper article on my start of producing Viper kits.

EXHIBIT KC 1/2:- Copy of statement from my son showing his involvement in my business and how the Viper name vested in me.

EXHIBIT KC 2:- Document produced in 1986 by Brightwheel Ltd saying rights given to me.

EXHIBIT KC 3/4:- Copies of articles showing the first mention of my Vipers.

EXHIBIT KC 5:- Copy of the 'Letter of intent' from Atlantic re taking over my company and no mention is made of taking over trademark Viper.

EXHIBIT KC 6:- Copy of mortgage debenture on BRL by Zinlic Anstalt.

EXHIBIT KC 7:- Write-up on Cobretti as BRL agents.

EXHIBIT KC 8:- Write-ups on the success of Viper and subsequent goodwill.

EXHIBIT KC 9:- Shows how BRL equipment put into storage by Zinlic.
EXHIBIT KC 10:- Shows how this equipment shipped onto Swiss buyer.
EXHIBIT KC 11/12:- Shows how the equipment breakdown was sold to me and H&S in Switzerland.
EXHIBIT KC 12:- Ditto.
EXHIBIT KC 13:- Invoice to H&S.
EXHIBIT KC 14:- Letter to Kunzli re equipment disposals.
EXHIBIT KC 15:- Statement made by Wheels Abroad re cars I had to make from 1989 on.
EXHIBIT KC 16:- Receipt for Frost making chassis jigs 1989.
EXHIBIT KC 17/1:- Receipt for brochures for Vipers.
EXHIBIT KC 17/2:- Confirmation of an advert I ran for Viper parts during 1990.
EXHIBIT KC 18:- Confirmation from one of my suppliers that he has made parts for me since 1986.
EXHIBIT KC 19:- Advert for fully built cars in Classic Sportscars magazine.
EXHIBIT KC 20:- Bechtolsheimer statement confirms he could have given me the order for his car.
EXHIBIT KC 21:- KC/RB Agreement to build Cortina car.
EXHIBIT KC 22:- Agreement over invoices owed.
EXHIBIT KC 23:- Cobretti Invoice for Cortina build.
EXHIBIT KC 24:- My letter to Cobretti re advice to them.
EXHIBIT KC 25:- 'Under new management' Cobretti advert.
EXHIBIT KC 26:- Copies of orders Cobretti gave me Jan 1990 to May 1991.
EXHIBIT KC 27:- Copies of my Invoices to them, Jan 1990 to May 1991.
EXHIBIT KC 28:- Copy letter ordering chassis.
EXHIBIT KC 29:- Copy of order for body.
EXHIBIT KC 30:- No exhibit.
EXHIBIT KC 31:- Cheque from Cobretti that bounced.
EXHIBIT KC 32-35:- Letters to Cobretti showing how they should order whilst I'm in Suisse.
EXHIBIT KC 36:- Confirmation from BMS Plastics re body.

EXHIBIT KC 37:- Letter sent by Cobretti to customer re arches.
EXHIBIT KC 38:- Letter from Cobretti in 1991 shows they are 'Suppliers of Vipers'.
EXHIBIT KC 39:- Shows my taking back my chassis jigs from Frost due to copying.
EXHIBIT KC 40:- Invoice for one chassis off Frost, at same time.
EXHIBIT KC 41:- Warning letter to Cobretti re using my trademark.
EXHIBIT KC 42:- Invoice for more Viper brochures.
EXHIBIT KC 43:- DMS letter confirming facts.
EXHIBIT KC 44:- Receipt from Frost for Jag chassis, to DMS.
EXHIBIT KC 45:- Statement by Trevor Sangster-Jones.
EXHIBIT KC 46:- Letter from RB's solicitor re who owns Viper.
EXHIBIT KC 47:- Letter from same re lies about Viper ownership.
EXHIBIT KC 48:- Statement made by RB to Police. Another lie re how he obtained Viper.
EXHIBIT KC 49:- Collection of documents re lies of how he copied my Viper & trademark.
EXHIBIT KC 49/1:- Forged document purported from Kunzli selling Viper to RB.
EXHIBIT KC 49/2:- Statement of Kings re above 49/1.
EXHIBIT KC 49/3:- Statement made by Kunzli verifying 49/1 is a forgery.
EXHIBIT KC 49/4:- Witness statement by Kunzli re above forgery.
EXHIBIT KC 50:- Chrysler saying RB 'took over my Mark' Viper in 1988.
EXHIBIT KC 51:- Write-up saying RB 'taken over Viper project.'
EXHIBIT KC 52:- RB says he took over Viper because I owed him money.
EXHIBIT KC 53:- Letter from my solicitor that RB was asking Chrysler £1/2M.
EXHIBIT KC 53/1:- Letter from Isaacs after talking to Chrysler in which Chrysler say they think I abandoned Viper after 1989. (After having been told that by RB)
EXHIBIT KC 54:- Packet of adverts I placed from 1986 to 2004.

EXHIBIT KC 55:- Packet of write-ups in magazines from 1986 to 2004.

EXHIBIT KC 56/1-56/12:- Various photos and articles showing their Viper is a copy of mine.

EXHIBIT KC 57/1 Letter from a Cobretti customer, saying he had been cheated by RB.

EXHIBIT KC 57/2:- Copy of write-up May 1991.

EXHIBIT KC 58:- Letters from my solicitors pointing out to RB's solicitors he is a bankrupt. Yet he is still acting as a director.

EXHIBIT KC 59:- Another page from police statement saying he traded with Viper since 1987.

EXHIBIT KC 60:- Write-up in which he says he used the name since 1988.

EXHIBIT KC 61/1:- Original photo of my Viper taken, with model.

EXHIBIT KC 61/62:- Statement by RB says he transfers assets of Cobretti to Autotrak Ltd.

EXHIBIT KC 63:- Statement by RB's solicitor that partnership ceased.

EXHIBIT KC 64/65:- Companies House records showing history of Autotrak Ltd and Autotrak Cobretti Ltd.

EXHIBIT KC 66:- Cobretti Brochure dated 2002.

EXHIBIT KC 67:- Copies of brochures of mine.

EXHIBIT KC 68:- Photo showing crashed Viper which I took in their workshop in 1990.

Busbridges reply to my statement and made in March 2003.

I should point out that this statement and all future statements Robert Busbridge makes, are full of irrelevant points. This makes them exceedingly long and difficult to follow. I will list the points he makes below, then I will make comments on each paragraphs comments/statements, in italic.

I will list by his paragraph numbers.

2/ He says I claimed to have thought of the name Viper. He shows magazine articles which say in 1984 another company was using the word Cheetah Viper, and another magazine says I pinched it off Cheetah.

What magazines say does not constitute the truth of any matter. I do not remember Cheetah using the name Viper in conjunction with the name Cheetah. However this company only lasted a short time and was out of business by the time I decided to use the name 'Viper' No other company was using it either. Cheetah did not register this mark, nor applied to register. On using the mark no one objected to my use. **End of story!**

3/ He says I admitted to copying the Sheldonhurst Cobra Replica. Nowhere have I done so and it was not copied. I produced an entirely new chassis and body which were both considerably different from the Sheldonhurst. Plus the Jaguar was another entirely new chassis.

He says I did not legally transfer the rights of the mark from Cheetah to myself. Then he asks if I legally transferred the copyright of the Sheldonhurst Chassis to myself. He says I have no rights to the mark as I had sold it to the Americans. They closed down and I disappeared to Switzerland.

Cheetah did not have a registered trademark called Viper and they were long out of business as said above. The Sheldonhurst chassis rights did not vest in Sheldonhurst as their chassis had been designed by another company. In any case my chassis as I have said was different to theirs. Had I used someone else's copyrights I am sure they would have notified me of this. In any case the chassis that Cobretti and RB copied was a Jaguar based chassis whereas the Sheldonhurst was a Granada based chassis, so was **completely** *different. Nowhere is there any evidence that I* **sold** *my rights to BRL, to the contrary, the document 'letter of intent' shows this. Contrary to RB's oft made statement I disappeared to Switzerland, he knew where I was, my address and my telephone number and he spoke on numerous occasions to me whilst there.*

4/ He says that the document I produced showing Brightwheel Ltd gave me the rights is not genuine, indeed he says it is a forgery. He says that they must then have owned it. He says the Jaguar based chassis had not been made by July when the document was produced.

The document in question was dealt with at the forgery court case instigated by RB in 2000 at which he was present, and had also accused me of forging this document. Yet my son had made statements to the Police that it was genuine and he had signed it, contrary to RB saying I forged his signature. Because of that the CPS dropped that accusation, yet here we have RB making the same accusations to denigrate me. The Jaguar based kit was started in early 1986, the Granada based kit was already in production and the Jaguar based chassis was in production by May 1986. Yet RB seems to know my business and the history, better than I do.

The chassis maker CTG's invoice was not made at the same time as the Jaguar based chassis development was finished, but some time after. There is no big gap between late May and mid August. The date of the drawing is irrelevant as it was made well after the chassis was in production. In any case all these comments re the chassis are irrelevant as this case is to do with a trademark, not a copyright! This is what I mean by totally irrelevant, so called evidence.

5/ He says that the same BL document was made so I could cash in on an asset of BRL and he mentions chassis integrity.

He shows an ignorance of facts and this will be shown throughout all his statements and he brings up irrelevant points. Firstly when this document was made in 1986, the company BRL had not even been thought about and quite what chassis integrity has to do with anything, beats me.

6/ He says he has no comment to make on this paragraph as he at this time did not know me.

Yet in all the above paragraphs he did not know me either yet that did not stop him from making statements in paragraph 4 about things he knew nothing about.

7/ He asks questions about the letter of intent to merge with my business, given by Zinlic and asks why they did not include taking over my trademark rights.

Quite what right he has to make such comments about a matter he knew nothing about until I put it into evidence, I do not know. What it has got to do with him, as well? Zinlic did what they wanted to do and the fact is that my IP rights were not up for taking over and that is why they were not mentioned in this letter of intent which listed exactly what they were taking over as assets.

8/ He again lectures about what Zinlic did own.

Is he again privy to all the legal documents that were made on the start of BRL and what legal provisions were made in them. The debenture only gave rights to assets that had to do with assets and property that were built up over the trading period of BRL and not before. They did not include the IP assets I owned before BRL.

9/ Again he is laying down the law over what the legal organisation was of BRL visa vie Zinlic.

Yet another ignorant rant about something he had no knowledge of and provided *no evidence to back up his stupid ideas.*

10/ He says he was an agent of BRL but not of me post 1989. He then says the adverts I designed for BRL were BRL's and not mine.

I had said I controlled the advertising for BRL and that is indisputable. Saying BRL owned them is not the point I was making.

11/ He makes a big issue of the fact that BRL put in an application to register the mark Viper.

He asks why when BRL was wound up by the Inland Revenue, weren't the IP assets made part of the assets of that winding up? He says the assets were listed as an asset of BRL as late as 1991 and he accuses me of removing the application to register, off the records.

Again RB is showing what a fantasist he is who will grasp at any snippet of information which he then turns into FACT to suit his case. The FACTS are, that in early 1989 as I had been faithfully promised by the Yanks that they were about to be able to get substantial investment into the company, I believed the liars and thought that at last the company appeared to be getting a sound future. I then decided that if the future would be rosy I may as well allow the company to take over my trademark Viper. This because if the company was at last going onto a stronger future it mattered not whether I owned it, for if the company owned it and it was properly registered and made safe, I could only benefit. So I took on a Patent Agent to do this in BRL's name. That does not in any way mean that BRL actually owned it. **They would not become the legal owners until such time as it was registered. If circumstances changed, I could always stop the process and resume my ownership.**

Of course the money did not come and soon after the company obviously was going to close. I did not pay the patent agent and he of course stopped the application work. Eventually the application was withdrawn, but not by me. It may have been withdrawn by the agent because of non payment of their bills, but I doubt it. My guess is that the IPO just withdrew it as no action had been taken and it would be apparent that the application had been abandoned. So all of his paragraph is just a figment of his imagination, said to influence the IPO.

12/ His remarks about the customers of BRL being let down etc etc.

These are totally irrelevant to this case, but they are another example of how he tries to blacken my name, and it should not be forgotten that these remarks are coming from a man who himself had gone bankrupt with many creditors, so these comments are hypocritical.

Of course there is a difference. In my case I was a director of a limited company and my rights as such were subjected to various legal agreements, so my hands were tied as to what I could do. So he saying I closed the company is yet another figment of his imagination. It was not in my interests to do so as I lost my job, my original investment of £30,000, and I had to start all over again. **Plus I had no legal ability to do so.** The Lichtenstein investment company (the Yanks) closed the company, not me.

To accuse me without showing a scrap of evidence, that I closed the company and disappeared with all the customers money of course is scurrilous libel. I was not in control of any of the companies monetary side and that was subject to, as I have said, legal agreements. In any case on the closure day, once the staff were all paid off in full, there was little cash left in our bank.

My saying the Yanks had milked the company was the absolute truth, because they put in money and for quite some time took out monies for wages, when they did nothing for the company. I was able to eventually stop that. However all this was completely irrelevant to the application by Busbridge to register someone else's mark, and his remarks just show that his intention was just to denigrate me, which I am sure that the IPO had no interest in... or did they? Knowing as I do now that they should not have allowed this to stay in evidence as it was irrelevant begs some questions as to why the IPO allowed these types of attacks on me to stay in.

13/ Most of this long paragraph again deals in irrelevant rubbish. A diatribe of his imagination.

However he once again trots out lies when he says I eventually contacted them after BRL closed. He again goes on about the alleged forgery of the agency agreement.

The **fact** is they were the first people, within hours of it closing, that I contacted. Also the **fact** is that they did beg me to carry on supplying them as will be seen by his brothers affidavit statement of facts made in 2009.

He denies they had an agency agreement with me and rambles on about this. However once again it will be seen that here he is committing perjury knowing full well that his brother cannot be found to say otherwise. However as I have just said that situation is now much different with the recent appearance of Martin and his statement showing that this is perjury as they did have this agency agreement document. All the facts about the alleged forgery can be seen in the above paragraphs concerning my 2000 *forgery case.*

14/ No such paragraph was made.

15/ RB questions why I did not return money to the creditors instead of spending it on setting up the new company Classic Replicas. Then he talks about a letter I sent a kit car magazine to explain why BRL had closed down. I pointed out that I did not own the company, the investors did, and the creditors should see a solicitor.

Again this is ignorance of Company Law where a director does not have to do this. The money was my own personal savings from my wages over three years. The copy of my letter I believe shows that far from hiding away I took steps to advise all the BRL creditors what they should do. All his other comments are irrelevant.

16/ RB questions the reasons why I set them up to sell on my behalf, Universal Cobra parts.

Then he says I was not able to deal with kitcar magazines. That I never advertised my product under the Viper trademark. He accuses me of stealing the trademark from BRL and its creditors.

*As I have already shown the whole strategy I used after BRL closed was to become only a manufacturer and to leave the retailing under Cobretti. Thus it was not incumbent on me to advertise my product as this was up to them to do, using my trademark under license. Of course I did deal with Which Kit magazine on a number of occasions to do with the adverts for Cobra Parts adverts and a free kit competition and promotion that was run. Of course during this time I was buying from my subcontractors, Viper chassis and bodies and specialised parts. They were then sold to my retailers Cobretti, to retail. I have already shown that the ownership of the mark was **never** invested in BRL from its inception and had it been so, then the Yank investors surely would have taken it and sold it?*

During the period Sept 1989 to June 1991 I did build three Viper cars and subcontracted the Busbridges to build two V12 versions and the Cortina demonstrator for me. So to say I never used my Viper mark during this time is yet another lie, and one car was built as a result of an adverts I ran in Classic & Sportscar magazine and this was for a Dutch bloke.

17/ The Bechtolsheimer car he mentions he built was a car that the customer asked me to build.

The advert KC 19 he says did not say it was a Viper. He refers to my exhibit

KC20 and says that he does not know what I said to Bechtolsheimer, but if I said they were my agents, that was not true.

Bechtolsheimer *knew of me from* **my adverts** *in Classic Sportscar, the very same adverts RB says I never had at all. This car was only made by RB as I could not make it for Mr Bechtolsheimer in the time he wanted it made, so I asked him to get RB to make it. This was confirmed by Bechtolsheimer in his witness statement to Dorchester Court in 2000 in the forgery case brought about by the wretched RB.*

18/ He admits they built a Cortina car for me, but says that doe not mean they were my agents.

What he doesn't of course admit is that I paid for this demo car so that they would have such a car to show potential customers of the cheaper version of my Viper car. Now why on earth would any manufacturer do that, if they... Cobretti, were not my agents?

19/ This is yet another diatribe of irrelevant rubbish and lies. Every statement he makes is a lie and his brother who is now on the scene refutes every one of these statements. He accuses me of making trouble when I had agreed to help them out by finishing off the Cortina Viper at their workshop. He also says at that time they did not really know who I was!!! He mentions the forged letter which Kunzli had supposed to have sent him granting him ownership of the mark Viper.

I was **asked** *by the Busbridges to help them out. No disagreements took place, of course they knew who I was as they had been dealing with me since end 1987. This statement is so preposterous it defies belief he had the gall to make it. They had met me on many occasions and Martin regularly called at my house to pick up orders, throughout 1990/1991. I had not been to Switzerland in 1990 nor had I sent him any letter. He had forged those letters (RB13/13A) as acknowledged by Kunzli in his witness affidavit to Dorchester Court in 2000.*

20/ Robert Busbridge just loved to continually state that I disappeared to Switzerland to avoid the collapse of BRL and apparently the fact that the Inland Revenue were going to make BRL insolvent.

After the closure of BRL in September 1989, I stayed in the UK and they were in constant contact with me right up to June 1991, when I went to my Swiss agent Kunzli to build a car for him. They were fully aware of Kunzlis address and phone number as they too did business with him and I phoned them from there on a regular basis. I was totally unaware that the Revenue were going to make BRL bankrupt, nor did I care. Of course I was fed up with the UK as it was going through a particularly savage recession and business orders had collapsed.

All his other comments are fiction and irrelevant.

21/ He now admits that they indeed did business with me up to 1991, yet denies that this means that there was an agency agreement with me. He then goes off onto another waffle about irrelevant nonsense.

This just shows that what he says cannot be relied on for he has tried firstly to deny they did business, to admitting it. Then he lies yet again by saying the invoices that I sent him never stated that the kits were Viper kits. Some invoices did, many did not and did not need to, for we all knew what the parts and kits were (Vipers).

22/ He questions why I should be bothered about how Cobretti performed. He also states that they were getting tarred by having been BRL agents. He says they were shielding me from BRL creditors. Then he says he saw me at their workshop in 1992.

Yet more lies. If someone is your agent then you ARE going to be very bothered how they perform. They never had any hassle from ex BRL customers and Martin confirms this. In fact they benefited by getting parts business from them. He did not need to shield me from anyone as I never had any hassle from any BRL creditors as we did not owe any money to trade creditors. I helped the Busbridges at various kitcar and this shows I was in the face of the Public! When I visited their workshop in Jan 1992, neither of the Busbridges were there, so another lie.

23/ He says the Viper was a descendent of two other Cobra Replicas and it did not have a defined shape. He asks why shouldn't he copy it? He now admits that he benefited from ex BRL custom, when in the last paragraph he complained that they were disadvantaged. He now blatantly admits he copied my products chassis and body. He says I abandoned the trademark Viper in 1989. Says I was not using it in the UK from 1989. Says I hid behind Cobretti. Says they were doing no wrong in copying the Viper and producing it.

The Viper as sold by me was of my design in both the Granada and certainly the Jaguar and Cortina versions. It had nothing to do with Cheetah and only tenuous links with Sheldonhurst. It was a Cobra Replica that could not be anything but a Viper and no other make of Cobra replica. This because the wheel arches were much wider than any other replica on the market. He then shows just how cheeky he is and what a cool conman he is, by asking why shouldn't he copy it. Obviously he chooses to ignore copyright and IP laws. Of course I was using it in the UK, through him and my own adverts for fully built cars. I have already dealt with this stupid accusation that I had to hide behind them. As for abandoning the mark and not using it, again a total lie. I never abandoned it and so spent £6,000 to get it going again after BRL and set them up as continuing agents to sell it for me! IP law states that it is not possible to use abandonment for 5 years as an excuse to take over a trademark.

24/ He now admits that I phoned him from Switzerland and he accuses me of being abusive to them. He says he told me that they did not want to have anything to do with me. He again admits they copied my chassis. He says that the chassis design belonged to a Mr Palmer who drew up a technical drawing of my chassis. He accuses me of bribing the subcontractor I used to design part of one of my chassis (the Jaguar based chassis which RB copied). He says that Mick Frost who copied my Jag based chassis 'was an innocent person' He again reiterates that I did not own the trademark or the copyright to the chassis and I ran away (presumably to Switzerland) not to been seen since.

Again he says one thing in one paragraph then says the opposite in another. He accuses me of disappearing (when one disappears no one will know where they are) yet now he says I phoned him from Switzerland (so he knew where I was). When I did speak with him, no abuse was ever committed either then and to this date, as this would be totally counter productive to my case. He did not tell me that he did not want to have anything to do with me, but preferred to lie to me by making up stories about how difficult business was due to the recession and that was why no orders had come through.

*Copyright law says that the design vests in the person who pays for anyone to do any design work for them. The technical drawing was done by someone I took on to do this and they were paid like any other employee. Similarly with Mr Maylam who I took on to do some design work for me, in that he designed the relevant part of an existing chassis I had, to be able to take Jaguar suspension and this was done with my help. He too was paid and whilst doing the work he was therefore an employee. I therefore had no need to bribe anyone one. However my copyright action solicitor just asked me to get Maylam to confirm he had done this work. Maylam and Busbridge are two of a kind and Maylam would not do this small deed for me unless I paid him £300. Because Maylam was such an ****** and totally unreliable, I did not keep him for long as a maker* of my Jaguar based chassis. In other words I sacked him and he did not like that at all. Hence the lies from him. It is worth noting here that the solicitor who I took on to go after the Busbridges was absolutely useless and did not know anything about copyright law. He totally messed up my case, but as with a lot of such cases, they the solicitors, get away with it. Firstly he did not understand that I owned the copyright for the reasons I have outlined above, so did not even need to approach Maylam, but after he had milked the Legal Aid Board for nearly three years, during which he achieved nothing, he then told me that I had to drop the case due to the fact that a new EU Law now stated that on copyright such as mine, only lasted 10 years. The fact is that it lasts for 70 years! So be warned on that score, by being very careful on who you take on to represent you. Lawyers are all pretty much legalised highway robbers!

Mick Frost was no innocent party, not only did he completely stitch me up after I had looked after him, but he broke the law in doing so. I will not make any further comment on running away or whether I owned the IP rights to the mark as I have already covered those.

25/ RB now says my taking out action for breach of copyright was not warranted.

Quite what a separate action such as the copyright action has to do with my opposition to him registering my trademark, is a mystery to me, and he is wrong in law. It is irrelevant to these proceedings.

26/ The whole of this quite long paragraph is irrelevant to these proceedings and is yet another example of RB swamping the proceedings with masses of totally irrelevant comments and much muck raking. My trading history is dealt with in detail above and deals with the comments he makes about my trading deal with DMS and Mr Barrass. The rest is not worth commenting on.

27/ His comments on trips I made back to the UK are once again irrelevant and then he makes a comment on the witness statement of Trevor Sangster Jones.

He tries to brush away what this man had to say by trying to cast him as a person whose word should not be taken note of and says his statement is hearsay. Obviously he does not understand exactly what hearsay is. It is worth noting that once again he admits to copying my Cortina based Viper chassis. He has no shame at all, but that is the way with conmen. I listened the other day to an expert on conmen who stated that in the worst cases the conman will tell lies with such regularity that it becomes just a part of normal life. They simply do not understand that lying is an activity that not a normal way of life. They believe all they come out with and they care not that their actions are having very detrimental effects on other people. All they wish to do is convince others that what they say is fact. I thought that this was **exactly** what we have here with this man Robert Busbridge and paragraphs 25/26/27 are manifestations of this type of illness.

28/ This exceedingly long paragraph is so full of lies and fairy tale stories and statements, that to list everything he said is too long a job and they are irrelevant to the facts of this case, so I will just stick to my comments re the main lies he makes.

Once again I have to say I was not hiding abroad. My mark should have continued to be used on license by the Busbridges, but they chose to steal my business and the mark off me, and this was a process they started before I had even left the country. His saying that he only knew that Chrysler were applying for registration in mid 1992 is a complete and utter lie. He knew in 1991 what Chrysler was trying to do and I found out from Sangster Jones this fact, right after New Year 1992. He approached Chrysler with an offer to sell the mark to them between Jan 1992 or earlier, and May 1992 when he applied to register it himself. Of course it was imperative that he also applied to register the mark so as to appear to Chrysler as a credible owner of the mark. He talks in the plural by saying 'we' applied for the mark, yet as you will see further on in this murky story, Martin his brother and partner did not even know that he had applied or even had approached Chrysler.

He says they were aware that BRL owned the mark, yet another lie as he had absolutely no knowledge about who owned what prior to 1989 and whilst he did business with me post 1989 he KNEW I owned it as he signed the agency agreement which pointed out who owned it…ME and they were to use it under license. BRL never owned any of the IP as I have detailed above. FACT; trademark law states that a mark has to be unused for a minimum of 5 years before it can be said to be abandoned. So him saying less than 2 years later he can claim BRL had abandoned it, does not hold water even if it were true that they owned it. What his Patent Agent advises him, does not mean that whatever he had said was solid and true. His Patent Agent could only work on what the Busbridges had told them, which of course was a pack of lies.

RB then lies once again by saying that Martin his brother and he fell out and parted because of my threats of litigation. Yet Martin has now testified that this is a lie and they fell out over the way Robert ran the company, lost huge amounts of the loan that Martin had got on the security of his house, which he had now lost to the bank.

He says that he worked hard to protect their reputation against the backlash of BRL closing. Yet Martin has testified that they had hardly any problems over this and that they gained all the carry on business (which of course they got because I carried on using them as my agents).

RB says they built up substantial goodwill and tries to back this up by saying they had traded with the mark since 1987. You cannot build up any goodwill in regards to a trademark when acting as an agent. They were not made agents until 1988 so saying 1987 is another repeated lie.

He says that during 1989/1990 they were unsure as to where I was, yet they were talking on almost a daily basis with me from the end of BRL in September 1989 and were buying kits and parts off me. The evidence for this is to be seen in all the invoices and orders that were put into evidence and date from the end 1989. So more lies.

Now he tells one of his biggest lies when he says that they were the 'sole producers' of Viper cars. The truth of course is that he actually produced or manufactured **no viper cars or kits until he had finished copying my jigs and moulds**, and that was in early 1992. Prior to that it was I that was manufacturing the kits and parts and supplying him as my agent. Any cars he made from end 1989 to early 1992 was from kits and parts purchased from me.

He says I could not use the mark and made no attempt to advertise the mark (after 1989). Yet the truth once again is that I licensed them to do the retailing and most of the advertising, and yet I did advertise fully built cars as has already been shown above. That even in invoices to RB I denote 'Viper Kits' on some of the invoices.

He states that the equipment to make kits and cars did not belong to me and he says that what equipment there had been was sent to Switzerland. This lie has already been covered in above, paragraphs and chapters, and that the equipment sent to Switzerland was sent by Zinlic. The equipment used to make the kits and parts that RB purchased from me from 1989 to mid 1991 was of course owned by me, either bought by me off Zinlic or already owned by me.

Re the Kunzli forged document, he again states I was in Switzerland when this was allegedly sent and this is yet another lie. He goes on to say he did not know who Kunzli was, another huge lie as they did business with Kunzli over this period when the alleged document was sent and not just from April 1992 as he admits. His other comments about Kunzli are irrelevant as by late 1991 Kunzli and I had parted company.

Now he makes another of his many excuses as to how he could legally thieve my business off me. Apparently now it was because BRL owed him money. **Fact:** BRL never owed him a cent as it was he that bought from BRL parts and kits, not the other way round. Yet another brazen lie.

He now goes into a big spiel about how I was fraudulent over my 1996 statement of how many Viper kits had been sold by me since 1986. Of course some of the periods covered in the list were kits were sold by the Busbridges under license and from early 1993 kits were sold under license by Mr Barrass, firstly under the name of DMS and then under Classic Replicas. No lies there at all. I even show only 4 kits sold in 1992 and this was because this period was mostly when I was in Germany and had lost the sales of my kits in the UK because of the thefts by the Busbridges. I had shown an advert and write-up in early 1993 when I got back selling my kits through Barrass. His statements about me drawing unemployment pay from September 1992, is true and that was as a result of his theft of my business. I continued quite legally to do this as what was being sold under license by Barrass, was only a small amount of money coming in to me and not enough to support me. It is not illegal to draw benefits if ones income falls below a certain level, which mine did. The benefits office knew full well of my situation and even interviewed me about it after being notified by RB. He even questions my getting legal aid to start the copyright action, which due to my unemployment status I was legally able to do. He conveniently doesn't state that he was on legal aid to defend it, and he wasn't unemployed as he was enjoying doing business off the back of my product! Of course after 1995 I had taken over Classic Replicas from Barrass as described in above paragraphs. (It should be noted that I was only able to do this by my Father giving me the money to buy it.)

His protestations that he did not try to sell the mark to Chrysler is just another big lie. We have the evidence from Chrysler themselves on a number of occasions and from RB's own solicitors letters. Again he states he had been using the mark since 1988, yet as I have repeatedly stated, this was another lie due to the fact they were my agents and cannot lay claim to the mark because they sold Vipers as my agent.

I am now accused of trying to cash in on an asset of BRL. I suppose he is referring to the Mark, which as you will know by now, because of the number of times I have pointed out, BRL **never ever** owned it in the first place. So it is not clear what he means by saying I was trying to cash in on an asset. I have **never** approached Chrysler to sell the mark, yet they have approached me on many occasions to sell it them (for buttons).

It must be pointed out that although RB constantly rubs it in to anyone listening, that BRL owned the mark, he has produced not one shred of evidence that they did!

To remind you, I had been using the mark for a year before BRL was even constituted as a company. I have obviously documentary evidence that on the coming together of me and the American investors, the contracts that were drawn up make no mention of my assigning, or selling or anything else, to do with IP. No mention of it at all, not even in their letter of intent drawn up before the contracts were signed.

29/ Here we have him saying that after my deal with Barrass I produced the Vipers myself.

I did not, in this paragraph say anything of the sort re saying that since 1993 I had produced the Viper myself. To quote 'After my deal with DMS I bought out the company'

As I have already quoted this happened at the end of 1995. He poses the question that who was producing it prior to 1993? The question is of course from 1989 after BRL, I was, as he knows, as he was acting as my agent and that only stopped in this country, (I produced it in Switzerland and Germany mid 1991-mid 1992) when he stole my business off me in mid 1991. Of course he lies again by saying that from 1989 to 1994, there were no adverts to be seen anywhere where I advertise the Mark, yet in my documentary evidence I show such adverts and write-ups. Yet again he conveniently ignores the period Sept 1989 to mid 1991 when he was advertising **my mark** as my agent, under license.

It is by twisting the facts and telling lies, that this conman weaves a story which is quite untrue and nowhere better is this illustrated by this continual story he weaves by saying that from 1989 to 1994 there is no evidence that I ever advertised my mark Viper, nor were there any write-ups. He goes on to say that he thinks that this shows I did not take any steps to market my product, and he also berates me for not facing up to my creditors and by implication this is why he says I did not Market or trade in my Mark. If I had wanted to attach the goodwill in my mark to myself I should have done this. It is of course all breath taking lies and innuendo. So what you may say? You will I hope see in due course just how important these immense lies will take this story. So bear with me.

30/ This paragraph is missed by RB

31/ He states that my registration has no relevance to this case, where I am opposing his application to register my mark. He says that as he put in his application before me in 1992 and mine was in 1996, he should therefore have preference. Then he repeats his insistence that from 1991 I was in Switzerland and from 1992 I was unemployed and that I made a false declaration as to how many kits I had sold from 1986.

Well others will disagree about the relevance of my registration which I obtained over and before his. In fact his application was even put on hold until my action against Chrysler was finished. Why was that you may well ask? I have already shown that my use of my mark did not stop after RB stole my business in 1991, for any longer than about 18 months that was forced upon me by RB stealing my business and until I licensed Barrass, and his use is legal and I thus had my mark continue in use.

32/ He says that my registration was granted because I made a false declaration, and I am the one causing deceit and confusion. Then he waffles on about one of his customers who he had swindled out of some money, and which I had highlighted as an example of his lack of honesty.

Once again his slant on the facts is seriously screwed, and he makes up comments and presents them as facts. I have above given an explanation as to what this declaration was about and how the figures in it, for the number of Viper kits that were sold under my ownership (either by me or by others licensed by me, including RB). Does he seriously think that the hearing officer at my opposition to Chrysler only took note of this document? We put in quite a lot of other documents and evidence, of my earlier use to Chryslers application (Jan 1990). Legally I was only obliged to prove my usage of my mark, up to that date, but I included my use up to 1996 when the document was made.

By law, if he thought that he owned the mark, he should have sent me a legal warning not to use it, and this should have been done in 1991 or soon after, when he decided to try and do me out of my mark. However he never did that except one letter in 1992 and none since and up to 2004, the date of his hearing. So by law he gave tacit approval of my use, because he never took legal action to stop me using it.

33/ He refers to an exhibit in a magazine which lists a Cobra Replica which is called the Cheetah Viper. This I suppose is what he thinks proves that I stole the mark of someone else.

As I have already pointed out this company had gone out of business and when I started to use the mark Viper, I had not even known of the company. Certainly it had never applied to register the mark. Thus, even had I known about the company my use was legal and no one objected to my use at any time. It is yet another feeble effort to prove something that was never there and it just muddied the waters, which is exactly what he wanted to do. He of course fails to see that if I could not use it because it belonged elsewhere then that applied to him as well!

34/ For the umpteenth time he states he does not think I owned the mark and this paragraph is yet another repeat of all the fanciful ideas he has thought up to try and convince the IPO that I did not own the mark but that BRL did. Once again he states that BRL abandoned the mark. He also says I did not exercise control over the use of the mark.

Thinking that someone does not own a mark, does not make that a fact. I believe that when one says something like this, you have to back that assertion by producing evidence. At no time has he ever done that. I in the meantime produced in my evidence the letter of intent by Zinlic in which the IP and the mark was never even mentioned. I have pointed out before that the mark was being used by my first company Brightwheel and when BRL was started even if Brightwheel owned it (which it did not), then surely it would have had to pass it over to BRL by way of sale or license. This was never done and BRL therefore never owned the mark. So could not abandon it etc etc.

The point which I now must make, is that throughout this document and those before and after, Busbridge bangs on stating certain points which he makes out are facts. These are:-

1: BRL owned the mark and abandoned it in 1989.
2: I never owned it so RB can legally take it over… just like that, in 1991, without buying it off BRL which he would have to do if they owned it as he states. He would have had to pay the receiver of BRL for it. Also he cannot claim to have taken it over only 18 months after he says BRL abandoned it as trademark law is that 5 years have to pass before that is legal.
3: I abandoned the UK in mid 1991 and fled to Switzerland, thus abandoning any claim, in any case.
4: That he was never an agent of mine and never signed the agency agreement.
5: That I was dishonest and that I closed down BRL and stole creditors

money.
6: That he started to legally trade with the mark in 1988 thus even though he was an agent at that time for BRL, that still gives him rights to the mark.
7: That I never advertised the Viper at any time after 1989.
8: That he and Cobretti were the ones using the mark from 1989 to 1992 when he applied to register the mark.
9: That from 1989 to 1991 I did not use the mark.

None of these statements are true. Each and every one is a deliberate lie.

There are other statements he has constantly reiterated. ***Now my point here is that, what effect did this continual lying and twisting of the real facts have on the IPO?*** Eventually you will see what effect it had, but I want you to see that what may appear to you in all the above paragraphs where I am relating what I have said and what he has said, even though you may think it is repetitive and boring, what I am saying is very important and you will see why in good time.

35/ He now states that he thinks that he has now conclusively 'proved' that I did not make continual use of the mark from 1989 to 1992.

*To prove anything you have to produce conclusive evidence and nowhere has he done this. All he has done is constantly make statements of what he **thinks** was the case.*

This should in law mean that whatever he says has no weight to it and should therefore be ignored by the hearing officer. You will see if this is what happened.

36/ This is yet another long diatribe of repetitive statements of his imagination. Another litany of outright lies. Comments about things that are entirely irrelevant to this case. He denies my assertions and my proof that he himself has been dishonest. He accuses me of a 'vicious' actions against him and caused him extreme difficulties.

He says he continued to developing his product. He was never an agent of mine.

Even though he went bankrupt, his was a whiter than white bankruptcy and he passed various examinations by the Inland Revenue, the Insolvency Service and the DTI, with flying colours.

He makes yet another claim as to the date he started to have rights over the mark, due to him legally using it. This time he goes back to 1987 when he bought a kit off me.

He cheekily claims that as the design of my Viper kit was so good, he stuck with that design 'all these years'

Any goodwill should be vested in Zinlic as they made the Viper what it was.

He relates to a photo taken of a car *I had made myself* and which I let them photo for marketing purposes. He then had this car featured in a magazine article about August 1991.

He states the assets of Cobretti were legally transferred to Autotrak Ltd

He dismisses my list of all the companies that RB used to trade under from 1991 to 2004 to show the shifty nature of his trading standards, as mere 'errors' and not relevant.

During the time from 1989 to 1991 no development as he calls it (copying I prefer to call it) was undertaken by him. This was because I was the person producing the kits and he was selling them.

The agency agreement clearly shows he was my agent and any 'fool' could see that the way I treated them and the trading arrangements we had between us, was as an agent on his part and myself as manufacturer and supplier to him, as my agent.

We have to take his dubious word, saying those government departments passed off all his explanations without a word. No documentary evidence from them was produced by him to back this up.

Stating that because he bought a kit off me in 1987 somehow confers on him the legal right to be able to lay claim to my trademark rights, is so preposterous as to be laughable.

Claiming that my design was so good that after copying it he has not had the need to change it, is the ultimate cheek and this type of behaviour is a classical example of a pathological liar and conman. He cannot see how illegal his action is. To his warped mind it is perfectly legitimate.

The agreement I had with Zinlic was that goodwill was vested in my designs and product that is why I kept the IP rights to it. He has no authority or proof to make such unfounded and lying claims about what went on in BRL. Similarly to say that it was Zinlic that made the Viper what it was. Quite how an investment company in

Leichtenstein can make anything, beats me.

Of course the fact is I made the Viper what it was, and no one else.

The car in question that I made could be also seen on his website right up to the date of writing this (2010). When it appeared in the magazine Which Kit in 1991, I was by then in Switzerland and did not know about it until some years later. Then I could see that he was claiming he had made it and it was a Cobrett Viper, not a Classic Replicas Viper. This in law is known as passing off. More on his website later on.

The assets which he dishonestly transferred into a limited company he set up specifically for this purpose, were not legally transferred. Firstly it is illegal to knowingly transfer assets out of a business you know is going to go into bankruptcy. He knew in October 1992 that Cobretti was finished. When he and his brother split in June 1992 it was because they were broke and Martin had lost his house because of it. No documents that showed a legal assignment of those assets was ever forthcoming. What we did see 10 years on when he notified the IPO of this alleged assignment, it was not a legal assignment. Firstly it was not made for a consideration (money changing hands) secondly he never sought his brothers permission to do so. Martin owned 50% of that business (Cobretti). So once again an illegal action. But for this conman, legality is for idiots.

37/ Here we have RB once again making a statement without any authority. He says that I did not advertise the Viper trademark, BL & BRL did.

Strictly speaking one could say this, if one is ignorant of the facts of how these companies were run and what arrangements they had with me. He has no proof to backup what he says and as he did not work within those companies he can have no knowledge of their working arrangements. In fact, in the case of BL he wasn't in any contact with them, as that company closed down before he appeared on the scene.

As I have repeatedly pointed out I owned the trademark and licensed BL, then BRL to use it. So it was I who advertised the mark physically as Managing Director and my license allowed the mark to be advertised.

38/ Again RB makes lying statements that his use of the trademark is bona fide. Then he says BRL had ceased to trade (once again implying they owned it) and I had 'disappeared', so they could now grab the mark for themselves.

He then refers to my exhibit KC62, a statement he makes that he had started two companies, one, Autotrak Ltd and two, Autotrak Cobretti Ltd, but they were not trading at the time he made the statement in March 1995. I had made the point that RB says that his use of the mark was continuous yet as a bankrupt he could not trade, and the companies he set up never traded legally as no company accounts had ever been produced. My point being, that if the companies through which the mark could only have been used through, were not trading and he admits it, how can he then say he had continuous use? So now he is saying in excuse for my observation that he could have had no continuous use, that in actual fact Autotrak Cobretti Ltd was trading from March 1995 (and using the mark).

He goes on to talking about a visit he had had from the DTI when they wanted to know about why these companies were not sending in returns and accounts as required by law, and he quotes his exhibit RB29.

How can someone say that his pinching of someone else's mark (be it mine or BRL's) when they knew full well when they started to use it in 1991, that it was owned by others, is bona fide? (honest) Also he had with his brother, a legal agreement with me that said that I owned it? Of course this is what conmen do. They make statements over and over again so as to lull the reader into thinking that they must be true.

Once again his trick of repeating the phrase that BRL had ceased to trade and I had disappeared, is used to swamp the reader into thinking it too must be true. Of course by constantly saying I had 'disappeared' makes me look like a fugitive, but he conveniently does not say that I spent 20 months doing business with them before, due to the recession, I had gone to Switzerland to build a car. Again this is trying to cloud the judgement of the hearing officer reading his garbage. You will see whether he was successful when you will see what that hearing officer said in his summing up.

*The visit he had from the DTI, in itself has no relevance to this case. What does have relevance is that my exhibit KC62 shows that in that sworn statement to the High Court he says that these companies were not trading. Yet in this statement made in 2003, he says that in March 1995 it had started trading. This is evidence once more of lies or better described as perjury. Further perjury was committed because in his counter statement made in 2003 in paragraph 8 he states that he had **continous use** of the mark. What is the truth? From 1993 to 1996 he could not trade a director and these companies were being run by his wife. So if any legal use of the mark was being carried out it was not by him. Yet in 2003 it is HE **that is claiming** continuous use of the mark in a sworn statement. He makes up so many different stories that even he cannot remember what he has said previously. Another pit that habitual liars fall into.*

He also conveniently forgets that even if this adoption/stealing/acquiring etc, of the mark by the Busbridges was legal and true, when he formed this Autotrak Ltd to illegally hide assets from his rapidly going down the plughole company, he should have got his brother Martins consent, which he did not do. So his stories about how he was able to take over the mark or adopt and so on, and the many stories as to how he was able to claim continuously whilst being a bankrupt, are all lies and perjury.

39/ He accuses me of making unfounded threats of litigation when I started my copyright action, plus telling him I would act legally over the use of my mark as well.

He says that because the bank (which bank?) withdrew support for him after his brother split with him and this resulted in his bankruptcy in 1993 which was about a year later.

I am accused again of trying to cash in on assets of BRL by taking this legal action re the copyright (a word he always writes as; 'copy writ' thus showing that even an uneducated oaf can be smart enough to be a conman!) and that this made his operating the business, difficult.

He says he is producing his exhibit RB 30, being adverts and editorials from 1991, to date, and he now refers to his exhibit RB31 which is purported to be this assignment of Cobretti's assets to the company, Autotrak Ltd, and then back to him.

Robert Busbridge would have the world believe that he has been hard done by. The cheek of this man knows no bounds. He feels that it is perfectly OK to brazenly steal someone's trademark and Copyright of their chassis and when you take action, that is not fair and is 'unfounded'.

His assertion that his bank withdrew their support is yet another outright lie. Their bank withdrew its support in 1992, over the loan they had given Cobretti and which was backed up by Martins house. The bank foreclosed on the house and that precipitated the breakdown of the partnership. From then on it is hard to see how the bank would carry on loaning money to Robert on his own as he had no collateral, even in his own house. So this is just another lie and in any case is irrelevant to these proceedings. He is merely trying to garner sympathy.

My trying to cash in on BRL's assets is yet another repeat lie and has already been dealt with by me.

Trying to blame me for his trading difficulties takes the cake. All his problems were totally due to his inability to effectively run a company, as forecast by me back in 1991.

It is no more than yet another ploy to garner sympathy and denigrate me.

His exhibit RB30 is a huge bundle of copies of adverts and magazine write-ups and if you analyse what company names he uses, generally up to 1992 it is Cobretti Engineering, (even though there is one advert dating from 1994 in the name of Cobretti Engineering and this is after that business went bankrupt) and from then on it is Autotrak Cobretti right up to 2001. Yet he has said above that that company has not traded, even told the DTI that, and yet here is the evidence put into the arena, by no less than RB himself! What a liar.

Then we have a bundle of 18 copies of letters of enquiry made to Cobretti Engineering from Jan 1989 when he was an agent for BRL and mostly from 1990 when he was an agent for me. So quite what these are supposed to prove, I know not.

These are followed by yet another bundle of various write-ups and editorial comments and mostly refer to the period whilst they were my agents up to June 1991, So proving nothing. He even throws in a copy of some court papers about a case Mr Barrass brought against the owner of Kit Car magazine for breach of copyright. In those papers I am denigrated by the owner Mr Tanner and another person Mr Findlay from whom Mr Barrass bought his company DMS, in 1992. These documents are totally and utterly irrelevant to this case and are only put in the denigrate me. More comments will be made on such goings on a little bit later on.

The assignments he refers to are the same assignments I have pointed out are not legal on a number of counts which I do not intend to repeat again.

40/ He says that he now trades under Cobretti (once more) and admits the two limited companies may be struck off (they were.) *Conveniently he does not say why they were struck off, again another way he blithely dismisses serious failings of his business practices, like not submitting the required accounts and returns of a limited company.*

41/ Here he is giving various reasons as to why he did not behave lawfully re the companies dealt with in the above paragraph. All lies.

Firstly he says he is from 1998, trading under the Cobretti name and now in his next breath he is saying that he sees no reason why he could not trade under the company name of Autotrak Cobretti Ltd. Yet he has admitted that the company was being struck off. Just what goes on in this man's brain I cannot work out. He then once more accuses me of being behind all his trading difficulties.

On the question of RB claiming that a car that was involved in a smash with a Landrover, was one of his cars, thus showing how well engineered it is, he states that it was a BRL kit that it was built from.

All his actions re these two companies are his problem and whilst I as a member of the Public reported him to the DTI for breaking the limited company laws, I make no apology as he deserves all he got.

However here we have yet another of his breathtaking lies (perjury in this case - yet again) He states that he is trading under Cobretti since 1998, and he has not traded under the banner of Autotrak Ltd since December 1994. Since 1995 he traded as Autotrak Cobretti Ltd. He has forgotten that he told us that he told the DTI in 1996 that this company was not trading. The articles he shows us in his exhibit RB30 show clearly that in the main he traded under the name of Autotrak Cobretti Ltd right up to 2001 and maybe a bit longer. Yet he as far as the DTI were concerned was not trading using this company and he never put in the paperwork for this company as required by law. Nor did he ever go through the legal motions to de-register the company. Rather he told the DTI through his wife, who was fronting for him so he could trade illegally due to his bankruptcy, that they were 'going to let both companies die a death' How convenient. To compound his law breaking he even shows us an advert from 1994 where he is still using the bankrupt name of Cobretti Engineering.

Once again his blaming me for his problems with the DTI, shows again what this man is all about. He trades illegally with these companies and has the DTI on his back for that, yet it is all my fault. We never get to see exactly what the DTI did to him, for his not keeping to the rules, and the document he gives us as supposed evidence that they did nothing, is merely page one of a letter to him from the DTI, which does not mention any sanctions on him. But what did they say on other pages? Of course you cannot get the useless DTI to tell you what if anything they did, under 'confidentiality rules'. (This is how civil servants guilty of incompetence hide it.)

Re the car smash car, what he does not admit to, is that this car, even though it was supplied in kit form by BRL, in 1988, the design was done by me and others under my pay, and not as he claimed in the article, a Cobretti Viper (made by him from his kit) Yet another example of his dishonesty and 'passing off'.

42/ Here we go again with another repeat performance just in case the Hearing Officer never got it before. Repeating that all his woes and trading difficulties was all my fault and his partnership with his brother would still be intact, the bank would not have foreclosed etc etc.

He asks why I verbally attacked his wife and son and he accuses me of arrogance and blatant abuse of the process (what process?) plus deceit. Plus of course perjury, forgery, bribery, fraudulently claiming unemployment benefits, false declarations and stealing assets from BRL. (Oh, and stealing their kitchen sink, too) For good measure he then goes on to add some more, by saying I am dishonest and have not exercised control over the mark in the UK.

This paragraph and all the comments in it I will deal with after the next paragraph is covered.

43/ Once again he reiterates that all his problems are down to my actions against him and all he has done is protected the trademark he feels he has legitimately 'adopted' Oh, and he has always been honest about everything. He then chucks in a reference to a magazine writer who made out a letter (inadmissible in law to the case) where he slags me off.

All the blaming of me for all his perceived woes in business and my taking legal actions against him for stealing my IP, show just what a conman this bloke is. This paragraph is the sixth time he has thrown at the hearing officer the litany of blame onto me, in the paragraphs since paragraph 36. This constant drip drip of denigration directed at me is a blatant attempt to play mind games with whoever would be the reader of this and other statements, and who would eventually hear the case.

Now if you have a top, independent hearing officer (HO), he would spend enough time reading through all the statements made by me and RB and deleting all the rubbish that was irrelevant to the case. Similarly with all the documentary evidence. He would not allow himself to be brainwashed by such mind games as played by RB. However if you get a HO who does not show these qualities and more importantly a HO that say, does not like litigants in person, someone is going to find they are on the receiving end of a bum judgement.

As I have said, it is my opinion that RB is a serial liar, indeed a pathological liar and this together with the fact he is a conman, all the behaviour he has shown so far in the lies and perjury etc, only back up my opinion. It is classical conman behaviour. Everyone is at fault except the liar, the lies that are told represent in the liars mind, as the truth. He accuses his opponents of all the actions that in fact he is doing himself and he just cannot see that. So you will eventually see what effect all his claims had on the HO that would hear this case.

44/ He in this last paragraph (thank God) thought that as I had retired in

2002 and sold my business, why did I now need to have a trademark?

Of course I had to retire 5 years too soon because of a heart attack, brought on by stress caused by RB's actions over the years, especially the business of the accusation of forgery, and the subsequent trial. Once again he shows an appalling ignorance of law, because anyone is entitled to sell their business **and** keep control of their IP. They simply license it to the purchaser, which is what I did.

I now list his exhibits with a brief description of what they covered:

RB 1:- A bundle of magazine articles on the company Cheetah, supposedly to show I stole their trademark.

RB 2:- A copy of an invoice from CTG for work they did for me, and a copy of my chassis drawing.

RB 3:- Selected pages of the transcript of my opposition hearing against Chrysler, irrelevant to this action.

RB 4:- A trademark search on IPO website shows that someone abandoned/withdrew the application of BRL to register the trademark.

RB 5:- Copy of a letter I sent a BRL customer returning his money. Plus many copies of BRL Invoices for kits sold. (Irrelevant and what are they supposed to prove?)

RB 6:- Copies of magazine editorials about BRL ceasing business. (Again what these are supposed to prove I do not know, as it is not denied they ceased.)

RB 7:- Copy of our agency agreement/copy of a letter I sent them at a later date which they say I used the signatures off to create the agency document and a letter from their solicitor. (This is been dealt with above on the section dealing with the forgery case.)

RB 8:- Copy of the order for five Vipers from Wheels Abroad, which they asked me to continue making.

RB 9:- Letter I sent to Kitcar International magazine for their records. It is a copy of a letter I sent to all BRL customers who had unfulfilled orders. I point out that as a director I do not own the company as the investors do and as a director I am not liable for the companies debts, and for them to see a solicitor if they wish

RB 10:- Copy of an advert of mine dating to 1994.

RB 11:- Copy of their order to me for the Bechtolsheimer kit.

RB 12:- Copy of a letter from me to Cobretti telling them how to order kits whilst I am in Switzerland.

RB 13:- A letter purported to have come from Kunzli giving them the rights to the Viper 4 (forged by RB and as testified to by Kunzli). Also a letter purported to have been written by me explaining what story they should tell as to how they got the rights to the Viper 4. This too is a forgery and is not even signed by me.

RB 14:- Newsletters printed by Tanner of Pilgrim cars slagging off Cobretti for going bankrupt.

RB 15:- Copies of magazine editorial about another company offering bodies for the BRL kits. Totally irrelevant to this case.

RB 16:- Copy of a statement made by Mr Malem.

RB 17:- Letter to Cobretti from Chrysler saying I had claimed ownership of the Viper mark.

RB 18:- Copy of a court document I made out over someone trying to get money from me for parts he says he sent to me in Germany. Also a court document about a court case I was not involved in. Both are irrelevant to this case.

RB 19:- Copy of a letter from a firm of Patent Agents telling RB that they can accrue any rights to the trademark Viper.

RB 20:- Letter of resignation from Martin.

RB 21:- Letter from Kunzli asking for a quote.

RB 22:- Copy of an article where I say that Chrysler could buy the mark for £100,000.

RB 23:- A Stat Dec made by me to outline my use of the mark since 1986.

RB 24:- Copy of a legal aid certificate for my copyright action.

RB 25:- Court payment slip where he had to pay out money he owed to one of his customers.

RB 26:- Copy of documents that refer to a customer of his.

RB 27:- Copy of the invoice I gave the Busbridges when they bought their kit off me in 1987.

RB 28:- Letters from the Insolvency Service.
RB 29:- Letters from the DTI.
RB 30:- A huge bundle of various copies of adverts and write-ups etc, all post 1992 thus irrelevant to his case.
RB 31:- Copies of alleged assignments to Autotrak Ltd and then to himself.
RB 32:- Letter from one of his customers re the car involved in a crash.
RB 33:- Letter from a kit car magazine writer.
RB 34:- Article about company I sold my business to (Cadini).

The relevance of all the exhibits and the quality of the statement made above.

I must say that the statement made in March 2003 is a disgraceful litany of perjury and totally irrelevant muck, all thrown into the arena in order to swamp the hearing officer with so much nonsense that he would become severely overloaded. Of course this could affect the way he viewed the whole case, including my statements and documentary evidence.

A good hearing officer would as I have said, approach the whole issue of what to digest and what to just throw out immediately and not take note of, with a degree of forgiveness. This because he is dealing with litigants in person who do not know the IP laws and rules and how to stick to only the facts. You will see later on whether the hearing officer who heard this case fell into that category.

Apart from that, the question of perjury is a serious one and this will come up later on in the story, when I deal with it again and again.

At this point I will only say that Robert Busbridge's mind-set obviously thinks that he is safe to tell as many lies as he wishes to, in the belief that it is my word against his and he can get away with it. After reading this statement I could see that it contained lie after lie. What do I do? Do I ignore them in the hope that the HO will see they are lies? How will he know they are lies? So I am drawn into situation where I feel that even though the lies may be about matters that are entirely irrelevant to the case, I am bound to defend myself and to refute each and every lie by statement and by documentary evidence.

For if I do not, then the HO may take it that the lies are in fact true.

I will touch on the perjury in much greater depth later on and what I think is a big failing of the IPO when it comes to how litigants in person are dealt with. *Suffice it to say that the statement contains no less than a total of 163 cases of clear perjury being committed and many of them repeated over and over. This repetitive lying is I believe done so as to create the subliminal effect on the hearing officer's brain. You will see from Reynolds decision whether this has worked or not. I also believe that he was schooled by his Patent Agent to do this as he really did not have the brains or understanding of trademark law to work all that out for himself. All the statements RB made in all the actions right up to 2010 (some SIX hearings all with statements attached to them) contain lies that can be said to be deliberate perjury, and they total well over 200. The above statement just happens to be the worst, with the most number of perjurious statements made.*

My statement in reply to the Busbridge statement made March 2003.

Due to the statement being so long and as I have said so full of lies, this put me in the position that due to not knowing what the HO would take note of or not, I felt that in my reply statement, I would end up having to make it much longer than I wanted it to be. It ended up 15 pages of A4, solid with text. I will not again detail it word for word as that would be too much.

So here is a list of his paragraphs that I comment on in as brief a form as possible;

1/ I point out the comments made by RB about my first use of the mark Viper in Jan 1986, are mostly irrelevant and his telling the reader what I did or did not do regarding my business, before he even knew I existed, had no validity. That magazine articles cannot be taken as bona fide evidence as magazines do not report truthful facts in every case. This is an absolute fact for kit car magazines who mainly have low quality and unprofessional staff.

3/ I deny copying the Sheldonhurst Cobra and as RB was not around at that time how can he know what I did. I point out that during the period 1989 to 1991, the Viper he copied was my Jaguar based car and that was designed well after Sheldonhurst finished and they did not sell a Jaguar based chassis. I point out that this case is not about copyrights to do with chassis designs, in any case. It is about trademarks.

I point out that all his comments on who owned the mark and my relationship with the investors, are not made from first hand knowledge of the real facts. The same for his comments on how BRL was closed and by whom, or for what reasons. I comment on the oft repeated comment of his, that on the closure of BRL 'I disappeared to Switzerland'. (How can you 'disappear to a designated country?)

4/ RB's comment that my exhibit KC2, that being the document drawn up to clarify that I owned the IP rights to the product and not BL, was a forgery. I showed Exhibit 69 which is a statement made by a lady who worked in BL as my company secretary and director and was party to all the negotiations between me and the investors. She verifies that no IP rights were given over to Atlantic Capital as part of the deal. Exhibit 70 is a Companies House document which shows she is a director. My son signed that document and although the stupid police charged me with forging my own son's signature, when my son turned up at Court to refute that I had done that, the equally stupid CPS dropped that charge like a hot potato.

5/ Further comments on KC 2 and the fact that on BRL coming into being, it did not take over my IP rights. He produces no hard evidence to back up all his scurrilous lies about the ownership of the mark etc.

6/ I point out that RB says he will not comment on my paragraph 6 as he did not know me at that time in question. I point out he is quite happy to make accusations about other times when it was also before he knew me and we did business together.

7/ I point out that it is not RB's place to dictate what should have been in my document KC5 (the letter of intent by the investors).

8/ I say that this paragraphs comments are irrelevant and that whether BRL owned the mark has already been dealt with by me.

9/ I admit saying I sold my interest in BL to the investors, but that was a slip of the tongue as no sale was made and no money passed hands.

10/ I point out that even though the Busbridges were agents for BRL as I ran BRL, I was BRL and I interviewed them and took them on. In reality they were 'my agents'. They were also 'my' agents after BRL and all the evidence and documents show they could only have been agents. Similarly it was me that made up all the adverts of BRL and me that controlled the advertising. (Later evidence would show this to be true and it was provided by RB in evidence in a later case, having forgotten his earlier lie on this).

11/ I repeat what the truth really is re the application to register the mark by BRL and why I decided to allow them to apply, but how when it became clear BRL was not going to last, I did not allow the application to go through and the mark stayed with me. I point out that RB can have no bona fide knowledge of what went on in BRL as he was not running it. So all his comments on what happened with this application and whether the mark was 'listed' as an asset of BRL, is all fantasy and not backed up with evidence.

12/ I point out that the collapse of BRL is irrelevant to this case as are all the comments he makes about people losing deposits etc. All the documents he supplies about this closure of BRL are irrelevant.

Note: It should be noted that when my opposition to the Chrysler application was heard, I proved by evidence that my ownership from 1986 to Jan 1990 was bona fide. That is why I gained registration. It must be remembered that Chrysler had the money and access to the best IP lawyers in the UK. If my case was a dodgy one based on sand, why didn't Chrysler bring in the big guns to overturn that decision? So it is ***a fact that my ownership of the mark as of JAN 1990,*** (the date in question) ***cannot be questioned.*** Therefore all this waffle by RB is just that. So when I started the Busbridges off as my agents for my trading business Classic Replicas in October 1989, *I owned the mark.*

13/ I refuted the evidence he states in this paragraph completely. It is either irrelevant or lies, I show copies of a statement (KC 71a & 71b) he makes to the Police where he admits being my agent. I point out that giving RB £110,000 plus, worth of business, proves that they were my agents as I would never give that kind amount of free business to anyone but an agent.

I also point out that his accusation of forging the agency agreement was tested in a court of law and I was found not guilty. This in a court that requires the highest level of proof, not as in some IPO hearing where lies are indulged in and a lower level of evidence will be believed. End of story! However you will see the real truth about this agency agreement later on in this story.

The order for 4 Viper V12 cars given to BRL was passed onto me by the owner of Wheels Abroad, and had nothing to do with this case or the closure of

BRL.

15/ I point out that as a director I had no legal requirement to have to do anything with creditors. The Investors had a legal debenture, so that was that. I show KC72 which is legal advice I got when I tried to see if I could get rid of the two Yank directors. It can be seen I had my hands tied. So I resigned and I show the Companies House document showing my resignation.

16/ I point out the relevance of the Cobra parts scheme I set up with them as this was set up at my considerable cost and helped him make more money selling Universal Cobra parts. Why would I do that if they were not actually agents of mine? I could have easily run that little business myself no problem. His assertions I could not deal with kit car magazines was absolute nonsense as BRL never owed money to any magazines. That was irrelevant yet again, to this case. I was in contact with Which Kit magazine in any case. I advertised the Cobra parts business with Which Kit and paid them for that.

An important point I made was that as they were my agents, there was no reason for me to advertise the Viper kits. They were licensed to do that. You will see later on why this is of huge importance.

I point out that from June 1991 as I was in Switzerland I had reasonably expected them to carry on being my agents and carrying on advertising the mark, 'Viper' So, a gap of only 18 months was forced upon me when my mark was not advertised *by me* or a licensee of mine. They had taken over my mark and went around telling everyone it was theirs.

The huge point here is that I cannot be accused of abandoning it, as the *law* says that it has to be for 5 years before a mark can be said to be abandoned. *This is yet another huge and relevant point...* You will see why later on in Reynolds decision making..

I point out that by early 1993 I had my mark being used once again through my licensee, Mr Barrass.

17/ I reiterate that Dr Bechtolsheimer came to me first *from one of my Viper adverts.*

I had passed him onto the Busbridges. Again, hardly the actions of someone who did not consider the Busbridges to be agents. It also shows I did advertise the Viper. Bechtolsheimer verifies by way of a witness statement that he knew the Busbridges were my agents.

Once again this is a huge point which you will see later on.

18/ I ask why I should give RB the job of building a car for me, when I am fully capable of doing that myself. Once again it shows that I was giving them business on a huge scale so that they could become financially secure and that would be good for me as it would mean that they would be able to continue as agents. I am rewarded by them stealing my business and IP and subjected to 20 years of lies and never ending legal issues.

19/ Once again I am making the same point as above in para 18. I point out the lies that RB is telling the IPO that he was never an agent. The lie when he said I was in Switzerland in 1990 when the forged letter from Kunzli was dated. *The facts* about that forgery, are that I owned the rights to the Viper 4 (I had bought those rights off Zinlic) and during 1990 I was in the UK all the time and in constant contact with them. They bought kits off me and called on me to pick them up at my house. I called on them in Sutton. Most importantly of all, for the last six months of 1990 my Mother was fighting off lung cancer and I was visiting her almost daily (she died on 22nd December 1990). Then there was the forged unsigned letter allegedly from me, which talks about the rights to the Cortina Viper 4. It was said that Kunzli had bought these rights from Zinlic and was now selling them to Cobretti. Kunzli never bought anything off Zinlic he merely handled the sale of the assets of BRL to H&S cars for Zinlic. *All this was verified as a forgery by* Kunzli in his Stat Dec for the Court and him flying in from Switzerland to attend the 2000 Court case to verify all this. Hardly the actions of someone who wasn't telling the truth.

20/ I deal once more with the ridiculous and constant accusations that I fled and disappeared to Switzerland. I point out the wording of the Cobretti advert stating that the Viper was under 'new management' (1989-1991) Then when they stole my business they changed this to 'under new ownership' If that is not clear evidence of the truth of this matter, what is?

21/ I point out that RB, one minute says he wasn't an agent, to saying yes he did business with me and that all the evidence he actually was *an agent* is *overwhelming.*

22/ I show that by sending them clear instructions as to how can continue to get kits and thus continue to act as my agents, it shows that I am doing all I can to continue to 'control' my mark. These letters were ignored and they went on

My Opposition to Busbridges Application to Register My Mark

behind my back to copy my product and steal my mark. RB has more than once admitted he copied my product and this opens up an important point. A trademark can only apply to a product and my product of a distinctive chassis and body shape of a car, could only be called a Viper. If you showed a picture of my Cobra Replica to a knowledgeable kit car person they would say immediately that it was a 'Viper.' So by copying the car chassis and body shape they were also stealing the mark Viper. Of course they could have called it by another name. If they had done that they knew they would lose all the kudos and goodwill I had built up for this product and its mark. So rather than lose out on that they used my mark as well. Also do not forget at this time they were trying to hoodwink Chrysler into believing they owned the mark, so they could make a killing by selling it to them. So that too made it essential to steal the mark.

23/ Again I point out RB is admitting the copying of my product and his statement that BRL abandoned the mark is a lie as he knew full well I owned it. (Later on you will see that this is a true situation and it will be proved to be fact.) I say for the umpteenth time that he is a serial liar. (Would the IPO take note of that especially as I have proved time and again by documentary evidence where he has lied?)

24/ I show more lies are told when I verify that when I spoke with him from Switzerland I was never abusive and had ***never ever*** been abusive even when I had good reason to be so. Then I point out more lies when he said that Mick frost had made a chassis for him to his design. I say that this is borne out by photos I put in as exhibits which show my chassis and his being identical. The statements made by Malem are not worth the paper they were written as he is an unreliable witness, due to the bad blood between us, over his unreliability when supplying me with chassis, which caused me to stop using him.

Then to the charges RB makes about all the crimes he thinks I have committed, and I point out that the only charge that I was tried for was forgery and that was unsuccessful. Evidence rules make these kind of charges unlawful, yet the IPO did nothing to stop them or throw them out of the evidence!

25/ Re the copyright action being stopped. I show that that was the case, because my solicitor told me to drop it (due to his lack of knowledge of copyright laws).

26/ I repeat that the Viper brochures I ordered were obviously not ordered by

BRL as they had ceased business. My printer who had also printed for BRL did not know this and had called them 'BRL brochures' They were in fact newly designed brochures for my use and Cobretti. I reiterate why I was on the dole after 1992 and my rights to be so, and the history of Mr Barrass and Classic Replicas 1993 to 1995. I point out the irrelevance of his evidence shown, re a Mr Hatton, to this case.

27/ I reiterate that I made many visits to the UK from Switzerland and Germany. I point out that if the statement made by Sangster-Jones is hearsay then the statements he put into evidence and made by other people must also be hearsay. That all the magazine articles he puts into evidence were all written by kit car journalists who had never met me and knew nothing about my business.

28/ I point out yet again that the mark was not abandoned and that it was being used by RB under license from me. That advice given to him by a Patent Agent is based on only what they had been told by RB and bore no relationship to the truth. I show that the Busbridges were warned not to use my mark and that the IPO had been warned by my Patent Agent that the Busbridges had no bona fide rights to the mark as they had been my agents.

I then point out that the IPO have erred in law by allowing the application to go ahead by ignoring the facts when they were told of the fact that RB had been my agent. That the application was made in bad faith as they knew full well I owned the mark as that had been pointed out to the IPO.

I deal with the fact that all the goodwill in the mark was down to my endeavours and not by the brothers. I point out that the claim by RB that he was the SOLE producer of the Viper from 1989 onwards was an absolute lie.

I show that in my exhibit KC47, which was a statement made to the Police, and which RB says was a 'mistake' is nothing but yet another lie. It is just one more in a long list of perjurious lies said in this statement.

As this paragraph 28 of RB's statement was a long winded one, I am forced to deal with each and every lie in it. This means that in this statement in reply to his, it too had to be extremely long and I do not intend to repeat here each and every reply I have made, in depth. However here is a list of what topics I dealt with:-

Supplying them with kits after BRL ceased/ sending the assets of BRL to Switzerland/ the Kunzli forged document/ the relationship between Kunzli and

RB/ Kunzli acting as an agent for Zinlic.

The lies by RB as to how he came about to be able to claim the mark/ that what RB did in business, was my business/ evidence of RB trying to sell the mark for £1/2M/ Chrysler approaching me to sell them my interest in the mark/ my list of how many kits bearing my trademark that were sold from 1986 to 1995.

29/ I reiterated my assertion that since 1993 I had advertised the mark either through myself, or through Barrass. Prior to that it was through Cobretti. Due to the number of trading companies RB used from 1992 to 2004, he cannot claim as he did, that *he* used the mark continuously in his own right.

30/ I reiterated that I have advertised my mark through him, through Barrass and then myself. That his claim of continuous use from 1986 is a not backed up by any evidence.

31/ I say that in his paragraph all the comments he makes are legally incorrect. I restate that I have sold kits since 1986 to 2002 and therefore the mark was being used and I point out the evidence I have given shows that to be the case.

32/ I reiterated my use has been honest.

33/ I reiterated that my original paragraph 33 is true and I stand by what I had said and RB has not shown any evidence to the contrary.

34/ Remarks RB makes in his paragraph 34 have all been covered already.

35/ Ditto.

36/ I point out yet again that any use by RB has been dishonest and the application made to register my mark was made knowing full well that I owned it, thus not bona fide.

I point out he has been investigated by many government departments and that RB has kept quiet as to the outcome of those investigations. He did not admit that the two companies had been struck off.

I show that RB claims that by buying a kit and being an agent of mine, somehow gave him a right to just steal the mark

I deal with his oft made claim that Zinlic owned the mark, the facts surrounding his bankruptcy and his saying that the adverts that showed all the different companies he used at various times to trade under, are according to him all 'mistakes' made by the magazines.

37/ I point out that his claim that all his advertising of the mark was made by him personally, was a lie. The fact was that from 1993, *all* of it was made and right up to 2001, by various companies, by a limited companies; Autotrak Ltd then Autotrak Cobretti Ltd both of which he was not a director of, and so trading cannot be said to be, under his own name.

38/ I point out that claiming to have 'adopted' the trademark is a lie as the facts are that he never bought the mark from me, or BRL (if he was right and BRL owned it) nor was it assigned to him or licensed to him.

39/ His claims that I am responsible for his bankruptcy are ludicrous and irrelevant. He omits to say that the real reason his brother Martin broke off with him was because of his prolific wasting of money and the bank foreclosing on Martins house. My legal actions against him were entirely justified and my right to do so.

I then deal with all the copies of adverts he supplies as evidence as to his use of the mark, that all are post 1992 (after he had stolen my mark and then starting his own advertising) most are undated and all show the prolific use of company names and not his own name. I also point out that many feature pictures of Vipers, were made by me under the BRL banner and are not cars made from his copies of my product.

I then go into great detail regarding the alleged assignments he has tried to pass off as bona-fide. I give 8 different reasons that make these not acceptable by the IPO and say that in any case the alleged assignment from Cobretti to Autotrak Ltd, if it did take place, was illegal on several points. These assignments, due to my questioning them, are dealt with in the future as you will shortly see.

I complain that after having been notified that RB had become bankrupt, the IPO should have by law, cancelled the application. Instead they ignored all my letters on this matter.

40/ His claim that he was now trading under the banner once more of Cobretti Engineering, yet I supply proof by way of a recent brochure showing that he is still using the trading name: Autotrak Cobretti Ltd. That this is well after they have been struck off.

41/ I comment on his lies over his not putting in the required accounts for the limited companies and that blaming me for that is evidence of his complete inability to tell the truth.

42/ I say that his saying I am dishonest is not backed up by any evidence and certainly not credible evidence.

43/ I show that a statement he offers as evidence, apart from being hearsay, is by a journalist who has a close relationship with the Busbridges as they gave him a kit to build up in exchange for coverage in a kit car magazine that praised them and 'their' kit (and that journo knew the history of me and my trademark Viper).

I then list in detail by showing the transcripts of my trial in 2000, how RB lied through his back teeth under cross examination by my barrister. Under this examination it is clear he did a lot of business with me through Classic Replicas and that he eventually admits he was an agent of mine. That means that he lied in his last statement made to the IPO for this case. That is perjury. You will see in due course how the HO dealt with my assertion, which has this incontrovertible evidence to back up the truth.

44/ I point out that the IPO are well aware of my licensing Cadini to use my mark.

45/ I say there no evidence that has been shown by RB that can invalidate my registration and the application should be dismissed.

46/ I contend that I have shown many compelling legal reasons, plus documentary evidence as to why his application to register the same mark as mine should be dismissed.

Further documentary evidence put in with the above statement.

> Exhibit KC 69:- A statement made by Vivian Young as to her involvement with the me and my companies and the setting up of the take over by Zinlic.
> Exhibit KC 70:- Companies House document showing Vivian Young is a director of BRL
> Exhibit KC 71:- Copies of two pages of RB's statement to police.
> Exhibit KC 72:- Letter from Ian Fretten solicitors giving me legal advice over getting rid of my co-directors.
> Exhibit KC 73:- My resignation proof.
> Exhibit KC 74:- Letter from my patent agent Kings to IPO telling them he was my agent and sending them a copy of our agreement.
> Exhibit KC 75:- Another letter from Kings showing that Chrysler wanted

to buy my trademark.

Exhibit KC 76:- Copy of an article by Which kit in which it is shown that DMS are acting under License to market my Viper.

Exhibit KC 77:- Letter from Companies House showing that at March 2003 both the limited companies are struck off.

Exhibit KC 78:- Letter from Insolvency Service re the bankruptcy of RB and his asset stripping.

Exhibit KC 79:- Copy of a letter from me to the IPO telling them of the bankruptcy of RB and the Partnership break up.

Exhibit KC 80:- Copy of kit car magazine article by Ian Ayre showing he is an unreliable witness due to the fact he received a free kit to build into a car for himself.

Exhibit KC 81:- Copies of the transcript pages relevant to the perjury of RB saying in his statement he is not an agent of mine.

Before I move onto the next stage of this sorry saga I have to point out the following. In the making of my witness statement shown just above I was given a certain date by which to do this, as is usual. I made up my statement and paid for photocopy pages to be made of the 15 pages and the exhibit documents. I posted them to the IPO.

Some while later I am told by the IPO that Robert Busbridge had applied for further evidence to be allowed to be put into the arena. I got copies of these alleged relevant evidence documents. All of them were totally irrelevant as they were only yet more copies of adverts that RB had offered up to Chrysler as evidence he had a claim to the mark, plus some more adverts he had in magazines all during the period 1989 to 1991 whilst he was my agent.

So I then had to redo my statement to include comments on all these pages of adverts. Thus I had to pay yet more photocopying and postage. I complained to the IPO and asked them to recompense me for what should never have been allowed to happen, as these documents were not *new* and compelling evidence. Needless to say I was ignored and never got a penny for the *extra* expenses I was put to. You will see that this turns out to be a trait that the IPO would repeat over and over. Grab your money under false pretences is really what they do and they break their own rules on how further evidence could only be allowed if it were new relevant and not of the type RB put in. Later on you will see when I tried to put later evidence which was new Prof Annand refused it as she said it was not new. Thus showing the usual IPO double standards and bias for RB.

The next stage just had to be the IPO allowing yet another statement being made in reply to my above statement No2. Thankfully this one was shorter than his others, but just more irrelevant nonsense, denigration of me and more lies.

This latest statement was made in November 2003. You can now see that from the date of July 2002 when I made my first Statement of Grounds for Opposition, to now, a period of time of 1 year and 4 months has gone by. The hearing was held in June 2004 and that makes almost a time scale of two years, before the long winded process was completed. This is what one has to put up with the IPO. They are terribly slow and long winded and any process with them is an exercise in frustration.

The second statement of Robert Busbridge of November 2003.

Comments made to each of his paragraphs;
    1/ He says that new and importance evidence has come to light regarding my alleged dishonesty.
    He produces two statements made in relation to a court case between a Mr Tanner and Mr Barrass.
    You may remember I told you that Mr Tanner is the owner of the magazine 'Kitcar' and he also owned a kit car company called 'Pilgrim' This company copied an Aston Martin look-a-like kitcar that Mr Barrass had bought off Mr Findlay in 1992, when he bought his company, DMS. Mr Findlay was another serial liar and conman, in the same mould as Robert Busbridge. Mr Tanner also produced a Cortina based Cobra Replica with his kit car company and hated me for trouncing him when I brought out my much better designed Cortina Viper, which was also cheaper. So he had an axe to grind.
    Mr Barrass took legal action against Mr Tanner over him copying the Aston kit. I was not involved at all in this matter, yet this reptile Findlay who it must be remembered also copied my Cortina Viper, calling it the 'Venom' so anything he

says has to be ignored as unreliable. However all the contents of these documents should have been ignored by the HO as they were not related to this case and were irrelevant. *The point is, did they?* You will see later on.

I am accused of forgery because I am supposed to have signed a statement made by Findlay which supported Mr Barrass by confirming Mr Barrass had bought this Aston kit off him and he had also passed onto him the copyright. I had visited Findlay on business one day and Barrass's solicitor who was also my solicitor and who I had a meeting with that day over my copyright against RB, asked me to take a witness statement to him as he needed him to sign it straight away. I did that as a favour. Findlay signed it and posted it back to the solicitor. Now he is saying that he never signed it but refused and that I signed it. Quite why I should want to do this as it had nothing to do with me, is not explained.

However there was one big flaw in this lying statement of Findlay. The solicitor concerned rang Findlay back that same afternoon to confirm that he had received it and signed and posted it. Findlay confirmed he had. Naturally that solicitor would have verified that Findlay was lying, if need be.

So it is just another case of how RB will dredge up anything, even if it is a pack of lies and just to sow the seeds of doubt in the mind of the HO as to my honesty or lack of it. ***Once again, was the HO to take notice of all this, even though it was irrelevant and why did the IPO even allow it into evidence?***

2/ RB denies that by reporting me to the police for forgery was an attempt to have me imprisoned and to remove me from being able to claim the mark over Busbridge. Also to get me out of the way so he can then sell it to Chrysler.

He claims he did not ally himself to Chrysler when I was opposing them, yet he appeared as their only witness. He claims *'he was directed to appear by the IPO as a witness'* What rubbish, as the IPO are not a court in the true sense and cannot require or *make* anyone to appear as a witness. Even the High Court cannot do that as this is not the USA. Needless to say he provides no evidence the IPO ordered him to appear.

He rattles on yet again about how I forged the agreement document, how I was a forger, a liar, and of a 'decitful; (sic) nature and how he thinks I should not be allowed to get away with it. (Yet another example of what I was up against with a never ending tirade which one has to ask again… ***"How will the HO's judgement be affected the never ending drip of lies and denigration of my character"?)***

He goes on to say he reported my alleged forgery to the police in November 1993 and says the police refused to act. He gives a crime number of C1148. (in a later statement RB trips himself up on this point as he admits that the Met refused in 1993 to act as they said it was an ongoing civil case) So when the solicitor dealing with my copyright action contacted the Met Police they could find no trace of such a number. Then he says he reported me again after my hearing against Chrysler where I relied on the agreement document and denied it was a forgery. However what he does not say is, why did he take so long this time, as that hearing was in April 1998 and yet he does not go to the police again until November 1999. Why was it that now the police did act on his complaint?

You will see later on in this story how all this pans out re this alleged forgery and why RB mentions it so often.

3/ He then has yet another go regarding the Kunzli forgery by saying that Kunzli had stated in his witness statement where he dismisses the claim of RB that this document was real and not a forgery, by saying that I was with Kunzli in Switzerland in 1990 making a car for nine months. This gave RB an opportunity to slag me off by saying I must have made up this document and sent it to him from Switzerland.

Unfortunately for me Kunzli has got his years mixed up for it was not until June 1992 that I went to Switzerland. However it is obvious that this is a slip of the tongue, as all during 1990 as I have previously pointed out, I had two fully built cars to build in the UK. I was manufacturing Viper kits and parts to supply to RB and was in weekly contact with them. So I must have been able to be present in two countries at once and making cars in both countries at the same time! Also as I have already pointed out above, my Mother was dying of cancer during the last months of 1990 and I saw her daily.

He mentions a letter that my solicitor was supposed to have sent to his solicitor in my copyright action. This letter is supposed to deal with me explaining to RB how to claim the mark Viper and the design rights to the Cortina Viper. Firstly it had absolutely nothing to do with my action against RB for breach of copyright and why would my solicitor be sending his solicitor, copies of any such letter? It is too bizarre for words, as why on earth would I be giving RB help to claim *my mark?* This man will stop at nothing in order to make up stories that he thinks will help his case.

He also says the letter helps me in my efforts to remove the asset of the mark away from the true owners, Zinlic. Again it is another truly bizarre story which does not fit any of the facts. I did not need to think up any such letter as I already owned the mark and Zinlic never owned it and had they owned it, I could have bought it off them along with the other assets I did buy off them! They would have been delighted to be able to raise more money by doing so, don't you think?

4/ Here once again we can see the cunning twisting of facts and claims by RB as to when I did certain business actions. He states he 'believes that I did not start trading with Classic Replicas until late 1990. Yet I have shown documentary evidence where he orders kits and parts from me in the last months of 1989 and into the earlier months of 1990 and from CR as stated on the invoices (Classic Replicas). In fact the agreement he signed for the agency is on Classic Replicas headed notepaper as are other invoices and letters from me to him before this date. In anycase it is entirely irrelevant whether I made it plain that my trading company name was Classic Replicas. When an individual trades without the safety of a limited company, they trade as in my case as K.Cook trading as… If one chooses not to say that you are CR but are KC (Ken Cook) what difference does that make?

All their invoices to me were to KC and my invoices sometimes had KC and sometimes were left blank. It was not necessary every time for me to state C.R or K.C as they knew who they were buying off and as they paid me by cheque and they were to K.Cook.

Then he goes on to repeating himself yet again on another subject that you will see is important, when you will see how the HO came to his decision. That is about my supposedly not advertising my mark after BRL ceased in September 1989. He says he saw no adverts by me from then to 1994. Yet again he ignores the fact that after BRL I did not want to retail kits, that is why I took him on to do this, so it follows that I licensed him to do the advertising for the Vipers. Then from mid 1991 to early 1993, I was forced into a situation where I could not advertise in the UK as I was not in the UK until Sept 1992. Then I licensed Barrass in early 1993 to sell the Viper in the UK, again.

5/ He then waffles on again about the Viper that had the crash with a Landrover, by going into details that are of no matter, but ignores the salient point I made about this episode and the claims that RB then made. That was his claiming that this car was a car made from one of his copied Vipers, when it was made from a kit of mine. He then indulges in another one of his lies when he says that in any case the strength of a car is how it is built. When in fact with kitcars the strength is in the design and quality of the chassis and body. How it is put together is of no consequence whatsoever. All irrelevant to this case.

6/ He then outrageously claims I have shown no evidence of him lying, or forging documents. When my evidence is stiff with documentary evidence of how and when he has lied. Again you will see how the HO does or does not take notice, either of his persistent claims he is an angel, whiter than white, who has never uttered a lie in his life, or takes heed of my evidence that he has committed perjury on a gigantic scale. It will interest the reader that in all the statements he made for this hearing (two) he made a total of 162 outright acts of perjury. All provable by evidence. Many are repeated over and over.

7/ He now claims that even though the jury at the trial against me in 2000, found me not guilty, I was guilty because they did not understand the evidence put before them. What absolute and blatant arrogance. It was because they did understand and because it was blindingly obvious that he was a serial liar and came across as one. Remember this was ***proper court*** with an independent jury and not a corrupt incompetent and biased IPO Hearing. Once again everyone else is at fault, but not him.

He makes stupid threats to have me prosecuted again, but of course even though I have persisted with my actions against him, he never carried out his blustering threats. I even started a blog on him which shows just under his own website for his business, where I lay into him in a no holds barred way and called him all the names I could think of including him being the 'Worlds Biggest Liar' and I am still waiting for this prosecution for libel.

Finally to show just what a rat he is, he then accuses me of using the fact that my Mother had been dying at the end of 1990 and therefore there was no way I could have been in Germany, as being a callous effort to hide my forgeries and lies.

This is yet another example of what one has to put up with when you are unfortunate enough to have your IP stolen by a conman and it is warning enough for anyone who has created IP and who does not take the best steps to protect it and right from the beginning.

The list of exhibits shown with this last statement.

Exhibit 35:- Two affidavits of Derek Findlay.
Exhibit 35a:- Letter from Dennis Tanner to RB.
Exhibit 36:- Letter from Patent Office.

Before I detail the hearing itself and how it was run and what was said, then show you the decision of the Hearing Officer one Mr Reynolds, I must show you the list I have compiled of the most damaging claims made by Robert Busbridge in his statements made for this hearing. I say most damaging, because as I have said above it is my opinion that if one makes constant statements and claims, even if they are completely untrue with no supporting credible evidence, they can have a cumulative and subtle effect on the mind of whoever is reading them. As I have said, any hearing officer should, if they are professional and of high quality, brush aside all these kinds of comments and ignore them completely, especially if they are irrelevant and unsubstantiated. So we must examine what this hearing officer comes up with, minutely. This in order to see if he has been swayed by all the lies and if they have clouded his judgement.

This list is as follows:-

1: Cobretti was never an agent for me after 1989.
2: BRL owned the trademark 'Viper', and abandoned it in Sept 1989.
3: I never advertised my product and trademark 1989-1994.
4: I disappeared after BRL ceased trading in September 1989.
5: I disappeared after June 1991 to Switzerland (apparently again).
6: RB never signed the agency agreement in October 1989.
7: I forged this agreement.
8: From 1989 to mid 1990 they hardly had any contact with me.
9: None of the orders or invoices to or from me to Cobretti mentioned the trademark Viper.
10: Cobretti 'adopted' the trademark. (Really meaning, took control of it—*stole it!*)
11: I had no control over their advertising Jan 1990-1991. (June)

Chapter Fourteen
The Hearing of my Opposition to the Registration Application

The hearing was held on 1st June 2004 in London and I represented myself as did RB. I certainly at that time could not afford to take on an intellectual property lawyer. It could have cost me £10,000 at least and I felt that my case was watertight with overwhelming evidence that I owned the mark and the Busbridges had been my agents and had stolen the mark. So I thought that it should be easy to represent myself. It was mostly, but I now feel that the IPO usually do not try it on with expert lawyers, so self litigants suffer a hard time, especially when the IPO get it into their heads they do not like you, and they want to cover up their own past mistakes. Looking back I am firmly of the opinion that even had I been represented by a lawyer, I would have had the same outcome, so determined are the IPO not to let me win, or at least their actions scream of that.

The first thing that struck me about Reynolds was that he looked a right miserable bastard. His whole demeanour screamed of unhelpfulness. As I do not have the transcript of this hearing I cannot remember the exact way that it went or everything that was said. In any case the main thing is what decision Reynolds would come up with.

Busbridge did a long spiel about matters that were as usual mostly irrelevant and what annoyed me was Reynolds never gave us any advice as to how he wanted this hearing to be conducted and what we were allowed to talk about. This gave Busbridge the green light to do his waffling act. I then replied but tried to keep to relevant subjects. He then gets the chance to ask questions re what I had said and so it goes on.

The one thing that stuck in my throat about this hearing is that as it went on, was the attitude I was getting from Reynolds. That was that he did appear to be anti myself. *Also at some stage he had actually intimated that he did not like hearings where litigants in person are present.* I thought that was a damming indictment of him, as a person I needed to have confidence in, and for him to be able to come out with an independent decision.

The hearing wound on into the afternoon, and I had wanted to cross examine Busbridge over some of the things he had said. Reynolds would not allow me to do this and he looked at his watch and said that the hearing had taken far too long and he had to catch a train. That he had heard enough anyway.

I was appalled and dismayed and wondered exactly what sort job he would do in his summing up and deliberations, and this was the crux of the matter. Well I thought every thing that could possibly be said had been said in all those statements and I decided to leave it and wait and see. I still thought that my case could not possibly fail due to the overwhelming evidence on my side.

The Reynolds decision document.

(To fully understand all of the below comments on what Reynolds says, go to the IPO website and search for this decision document or see it on my blog.)

Before you read the following pages about this document you will see that I make many intemperate and personal remarks about Reynolds. I make no apologies for this and I would invite you to put yourself in my shoes. This case was dealing with my life, my integrity, my ability to design and make things which I had done most of my life. I felt as I had been raped or was being accused of murder that I did not commit. All this was in the hands of a person who I had hoped would be a *professional and independent.* A pillar of the Establishment if you will. Yet the more I read that document when I got it, the more I could see that I was being trashed by a man who was either incredibly stupid, a bumbling buffoon who hadn't a clue about real life in the business world, or I was dealing with a cynical man who had deliberately set out to find as many reasons to find against me and be on the side of the person who I felt was a habitual and pathological liar, and who was no more than a conman... How would you feel in my shoes?

I do not come from the same background as your posh legal people, in the UK. A judicial World made up by the privileged upper class twits who every day of the week give out sentences and judgements that defy belief. So I found it hard to take what I read, which was made up by someone of a class I dislike (and I am no Labourite or Commie, in fact I dislike all the political classes of any persuasion). As I was brought up in a hard world were if you did not swear you were a toffee nosed bastard and got your head kicked in, swearing when I am angry is second nature. Also you do not spend time in the Merchant Navy and 8 years in the

Forces without learning to swear. Not to mention 12 years in Australia. So if you do not like what you read, tough luck mate!

This decision document came within four weeks, and dealt me a crushing blow. I simply could not believe what I was reading, or how anyone could come to that decision . All his points as to how and why he came to the relevant decisions were so stupid and illogical that I had to believe that here was a man with an agenda that was predisposed, even before the hearing. Because of the body language of Reynolds and how he conducted the hearing, it now all screamed of a decision made before the hearing took place. I could not help thinking that for reasons best known to the IPO, they seemed to want to make sure I did not win.

Because this hearing was heard under the 1938 Act, I could only appeal it by going through the **High Court!** This would have cost me up to £25,000 and the IPO knew this full well. They knew I had no money and they therefore knew I would not be able to appeal. I couldn't help thinking that it was a put up job by the IPO with them knowing they were high and dry as I would not be able to take it further. Why would I think this? Well the reasoning of Reynolds was so perverse that you have to come to the decision it was deliberate. So much for British Justice!

Of course after the 1994 act came in, you could now appeal in front of a so called independent person, a lawyer, appointed by the Treasury Solicitor. That would cost you next to nothing. But that did not help me at all. Why didn't the numpties in the IPO make it retrospective when they thought to bring in a more modern trademarks Act of 1994?

So I had to let it slide, and you only have a month to make your mind up as to whether you will appeal. That is simply not long enough to give you time to see if you can find a lawyer who will take it on with some sort of deal.

So that chiselling, lying, perjuring bastard got his way. Words cannot describe my anger at it all and I thought I may have another heart attack through it all. So I decided to bugger off to Australia for a year to cool off and forget things, before I did kick the bucket.

The only glimmer of hope open to me, was that because of all the legal points I had made and the objections I had raised, re the alleged assignments, Reynolds said he could not deal with them and said that the IPO would look into them. You will see in due course what happened there.

I now lay out what he said in this 29 page plus annexes document, in paragraph order (numbered), with my comments on each paragraph, in italic, where necessary.

1-5/ He lays out the background to this case. In other words he briefly mentions my case against Chrylser and that I won that and that Busbridge appeared in that as their witness. Then he points out that I have registration. He then says I raised objections based on Sections 11,12(1),&17(1). *He completely ignores the fact that I also raised other sections of TMA38 as a basis for my case. Also what the hell did the fact that I had opposed Chrysler have to do with this hearing?*

6/ He points out I raised the fact that RB had become a bankrupt and had not traded under the name of Cobretti Engineering as per the application. Also that I raise the issue of the legality on the alleged assignments.

7/ He now points out that RB filed a counter statement where he denied my grounds and denied I had ever been a proprietor of the mark and if I were, that I abandoned it prior to the filing date. That Autotrak Ltd took ownership of the asset of the mark, before the bankruptcy.

8/ Says we both asked for costs.

9/ We both filed evidence for the hearing.

10/ This he heads as 'General observations on the evidence' and he goes on to stating that the evidence was in the form of lengthy statements, two from myself and one from RB. He then states that the evidence was at times accusatory and inflammatory. Other actions were mentioned, notably my trial for forgery where I was found not guilty and my action for breach of copyright which he says 'appears to have petered out'. Then he says that these actions are not of 'direct' assistance '*save insofar as they might shed light on the credibility or reliability of the individuals concerned*' he now goes on to saying that in the light of the outcomes of these cases it would be unsafe to draw conclusions from these, bearing on the integrity of the individuals concerned.

I strongly think that here we have the early signs of what this man Reynolds is going to be all about and his mindset. It also starts to show that he has less of a grasp on all the facts and evidence before him than he should have. For he states that I made two statements and Busbridge only one, when the truth of the matter is that we both made two. If he is incapable of getting such a fact correct, how can one have faith that he will be able to grasp and get right all the rest of the case?

Why he has got to make a point of saying the evidence was accusatory and inflammatory is beyond me. What does he think two opponents should say when they are in conflict over what to them is an important matter? In his upper class world of old boys clubs and whiskies, where men behave ever so gentlemanly, maybe opponents may behave like wimps, unable to raise any ire. In the real world, especially in business where people have built up businesses (a world which he no doubt knows nothing about) the fact is that it is a dog eat dog world. If he had had to put up with what I have had to put up with, maybe he would react to the accusations levelled at me and the fact that I had been on the end of a huge con designed to strip me of my business, my product and my life, in the same way.

However the crux of the matter is, that what was said and how (I refer to all the derogatory & irrelevant things) should have nothing at all to do with how he should deal with what was before him, and if he allowed any of that to influence his decisions. If it did then he was not fit to be hearing such cases.

Why he found it necessary to even mention my perjury trial or my copyright action is beyond me. I take exception to him saying that my copyright action 'petered out' as if my action was so weak and frivolous that it had nowhere to go. I gave a full explanation as to why it had stopped and surely he could see that I had been let down by my lawyer, as I pointed out. In anycase the copyright action had absolutely nothing to do with this registration hearing.

Similarly, when he says that those actions were not of assistance to him, except that they may shed light on my credibility or reliability. For he must mean it was my credibility or reliability, as both cases involved me. My question is if they could not assist him and they would be 'unsafe' to draw conclusions from, why even mention them? It all raises questions about exactly what was going on in his mind and just what he made of me? For here we have the possibility of the fact that because I was charged with forgery, I must have been guilty of it and you will see further on just how his mind has been affected by the fact I was charged. If you read between the lines, what he is really saying, is that those two cases show him that I am not to be believed and that I am a character who's integrity is suspect. It seems to have not even entered his mind that the action by RB against me over the alleged forgery may have been contrived and vicious.

11/ He now goes on to claiming that it is of a greater concern that doubt has been cast on the reliability of certain documents filed in evidence and are directly relevant to the case and could have a bearing on the outcome. He lists these as my document KC2, the Brightwheel Ltd document passing rights to me for the trademark, and he points out that RB said this was contrived so as to claim ownership. Then KC49/1 which was the forged Kunzli document which was confirmed by Kunzli as a forgery. Lastly RB7 the agency agreement which RB says I forged.

KC2 he deals with later on. With KC49/1 he agrees that the author said it must be a forgery, and the agency agreement was found not to be a forgery, by a Court. There will be more on this later.

12/ He complains that other documentary evidence from both sides are not properly headed for evidence, are photocopied when originals should have been put in, letters and other material that should have been properly subject to formal evidence by the authors, and the poor quality of the photocopies.

*Once again these comments show the state of mind of Reynolds and how he is very rigid in his thoughts on cases, even when the litigants are litigants in person. He obviously has no willingness to even begin to understand that we were not expert lawyers, so what does he expect? There must be some leeway in such cases and I know that decent HO's do give leeway. OK, neither of us headed each exhibit with a separate piece of paper, with headings saying what case they referred to etc. So what? Does that mean that they are all junk and should be ignored? If I could easily follow what they applied to, why couldn't he? Then, more importantly, comes yet another example of just how much of a grasp does this man have on the IPO's own laws and rules? For I have specifically read that documents can be photocopied and this is perfectly acceptable. So long as at the hearing the originals are present for inspection should they were needed. In my case I had all the originals concerned, yet he **never** even asked me if I had them. The fact that letters etc made out by witnesses to support my case, were not made in the 'formal' way so as to please such people as he, again he has to give leeway that we as mere amateurs do not know this (more on this later on). Lastly the question of poor quality photocopies. All my photocopies were of excellent quality and most of RB's were guilty of being poor. Why wasn't he specific about who was guilty of this?*

What I found about this paragraph to be so astonishing, is that he made absolutely no mention of the fact that RB's evidence content was largely irrelevant as was the vast amount of his documentary evidence. (Again I will comment on this aspect of hearing later on.)

13/ Now he does say that overall his overview of the evidence will not take into account much of what was said as it was peripheral. (I presume he really means irrelevant) he says that we both allege wrongdoings in a host of issues and have put forward motives for doing so. He says that he will stick to the real issues that affect the trademark issues, and his summary will stick to the relevant factual circumstances etc. *Well we will see about that in due course! For this is something he has to say to cover himself, but in reality he does take note of and is influenced by irrelevant content put into the arena by RB.*

14/ Here he says that a general problem with our evidence is that we seem to be retrospectively explaining and justifying our actions. That it is a long time since the actions happened and the date of filing the evidence. He says he doesn't want to be 'overly critical of private litigants' but it is clear that we did not pay sufficient regard to IP issues at the time and this has had consequences now. So it is not possible for him to reconcile the many inconsistencies in the evidence.

Yet again this paragraph, when you read in between the lines of what he is saying, it shows up what is in this man's mind. It is becoming quite evident to me that Reynolds is not living in my world and simply has no grasp of what being in business is really like. Like most civil servants he lives in a completely different world, away from the sharp realities of being in business in the UK these days. What is up with the man? Of course we are dealing with matters that took place 10 years previously and why is this I must ask? I will tell you ...Mr Reynolds, as he is obviously too far gone to be able to see it. **The IPO are completely to blame for the length of time it has taken!** *Firstly they took six years to hear my case versus Chrysler and* **they** *put this case on hold. They then allowed Chrysler to waste 4 more years before I was able to force them out at my cost. Then they take a further two years to get to this hearing. So much for yet another incompetent government department that is 'not fit for purpose'. Then one of their cringing minions blames us for us having to deal retrospectively with a matter that in any case should never have been allowed to even take off, let alone get this far (you will see why in due course).*

However no matter how far back the facts of this case go, I can remember them all like it was yesterday, for unlike Mr Reynolds this was **my life,** *my business, my baby, and I know every fact off by heart. Plus why should I not justify my actions, as I have a right to defend my actions, and in most cases I was forced to have to do this because RB kept bringing up crap about me that although I knew it did not have anything to do* with this case, I felt I had to defend. This is the fault of the IPO who do not bother to either weed out this irrelevant crap before it reaches the hearing or at least to make it very plain to the litigants what is allowed in evidence statements and what is not. Instead they idly stand by and allow absolutely anything.

I have already mentioned my thoughts on Reynolds mindset regarding litigants in person, which he now calls 'private litigants'. Yet again this phrase again shows just how his mind is working and how biased he is towards 'private litigants'. For who are private litigants? I say that all IP actions are brought by people or companies who are all private. No, what he really is talking about is his dislike of having to lower himself to having to deal with peasants from the street, as it were. He likes to only deal with lawyers whose only job in life is to deal with all the laws and rules of IP. This way his self important life is kept easy and he only has to deal with people who can stick to the point and not give him all this vexatious heavy work load (as seen by his remarks at the hearing re him being held up from getting home on time).

As for people who are in business, especially during the difficult setting up years when you are struggling to get your business off the ground, they are mainly underfunded because of bastard bankers, who like Mr Reynolds do not understand businesses and make it impossible for businesses to thrive. Trying to get sales and keep your head above water. Thinking about any IP rights you may have, simply has to take second place. The enormous cost just to even talk to an IP lawyer, rules out doing so. You constantly think you will deal with it when you have some spare money, so you do the best you can, as I did. I believe that it is the duty of all HO's to take this into effect and to put themselves into our shoes. Like in the case of my exhibit KC2 and the background surrounding all that.

As far as I am concerned the mark was brought into existence by me, as no company could do that. Companies are not people, so obviously are incapable of such matters. If I, who brought into existence this mark, want to keep ownership of that mark and not allow a limited company have it, for whatever reason, it is my right to do so. What law says I cannot do so?

15/ Reynolds says that the events that underpin this action took place between 1985/86 and to 18 May 1992 (that being RB's filing date for his application).

I am extremely annoyed with this man for saying this. The events in question **do not go back to 1986 at all.** For the simple reason that whatever I did with the mark between 1986 and January 1990 was covered by my opposition hearing against

Chrysler. *In that hearing I presented the same evidence as in this hearing. I only presented it in this hearing because RB saying ad nauseum that BRL owned the mark and I did not. Maybe I should have ignored that and taken the tack that the IPO had throughout this previous hearing agreeing that I owned the mark, and that is why I was awarded it and the Chrysler application was made was in Jan 1990. What Reynolds is doing is making me fight yet another battle covering the same period that was covered in the Chrysler case, and making me have to prove yet again that my rights are bona fide. Just how many times does one to have prove ones rights? So now I have to have Reynolds poking around a period of time that has already been determined.*

16/ In this paragraph he retells my story of how I started off in kitcars. *Why does he need to even retell this story as it does not have **any** relationship to what happened between myself and the Busbridges after BRL ceased to be?*

17/ Now he relates word for word what I put into my statement as to why I decided I must keep control of my IP. I put this into my statement so he could have on overview of the history up to my involvements with the Busbridges after 1989 and not for him to dissect, as it had already been dissected by HO Tuck in the Chrysler case in 1998.

18/19/20/21/ All these deal with my history up to the cessation of BRL and at that stage how I bought the assets I needed to continue from Zinlic and he makes reference to my exhibit which showed how much was realised for each of the assets and who bought them. He notes that this document was hard to follow and this was made harder by manual overwrites.

This document was not made for Mr Reynolds but was made for Zinlic, so the niceties of IP hearing officers like Reynolds was not even thought about and I do not see how it is hard to follow. If there is any problem, it is with Mr Reynolds not having been part of that business and being a bit of a dickhead. As for these so called 'overwrites' which he is referring to, these are the annotations I made by hand, next the each asset item on the list, to denote who those assets went to. I fail to see how hard that is to follow. He could have cleared up his cloudy mind by asking me at the hearing questions about this and anything else the dickhead couldn't understand!! Once again one has to say that whatever went on in BRL has nothing to do with this case, so why is he delving into the minutiae of this document and anything else to do with BRL?

22/ Late 1989 to April 1991. Here he goes over my starting up Classic Replicas and keeping on the Busbridges as agents, and by way of a written agreement. He notes that RB disputes this document and says it is forged.

*Now we are on the ground that Reynolds should be only looking at. Once again he annoys me by saying that the agreement is said to be a forgery. Firstly he ignores the fact that I have been through a long trial on that score, where evidence was heard that he is not privy to. So he should accept that and keep away from this, because all it is doing is pandering to the lies of RB. Secondly he completely ignores the fact that this alleged forgery is **signed by two people**, and all he is looking at is what **one of those two is alleging**. You will see the relevance of that little kernel in due course.*

23/ He magnanimously agrees that that it is not in dispute that there was a continuation of business after the demise of BRL.

24/ Now he lists several points I had made as to the business history onwards from 1989.

When he describes the incident when Dr Bechtolsheimer got RB to make a car I had no time to make, he describes the witness statement that Bechtolsheimer made for my 2000 trial by saying: 'to illustrate the somewhat conflicting messages it contains and the difficulty of placing reliance on documents containing overwritten material' This man Reynolds, is in my opinion the pits. This witness statement was accepted by the Dorchester County Court and yet it is not good enough for his Lordship. It is perfectly simple to understand and Bechtolsheimer changed one word by hand.

*Reynold seems to have a petty '**thing**' about anyone changing a typewritten word to another by hand. The man had sworn this statement as it was presented, including the one changed word. Does this oaf not realise that the Police make up witness statements every day of the week and words get changed by hand and these are just initialled by the witness! Later on in his decision he again trashes this statement which let us face it was a very important witness statement by an independent person who verifies that he visited me to buy a **Viper** car from me and **I told him that I could not make it as I was too busy and... for him to go to Cobretti as they were my "agents"**. Had he believed this statement **that would have been the end of RB's case. For it would have proved they were my agents with no rights to my Viper trademark. So by refusing to accept this piece of evidence he is able to go on and find for RB... it is absolutely outrageous!***

25/ He now reproduces my paragraph where I stated that up to June 1991 I had controlled the advertising of Cobretti. How it was at my behest that they headed their adverts, that the sales of Vipers were 'Under new management' *As it* happens I also contributed to their cost, but at this time of this hearing, I had no proof of that. However you will see later that in 2010 I got hold of the proof that I paid contributions for their advertising from none other than RB. Too late to influence Reynolds, had he been willing to even believe that evidence! But it shows that RB knew he had that the evidence, so it proves he was lying when he stated I did not have anything to do with their advertising. I guess that when he put it into evidence for another reason, he had forgotten the relevance of what it showed, in that it showed I had paid them for part of their advertising costs which was part of our agency agreement.

26/ Here we have Reynolds showing RB denying that this was so, in his statement. Of course in doing so he is indulging in more of his outright lies and in particular, by stating that not one of the orders they made to me mention Viper. Plus some waffle about what constitutes a Viper.

27/ Here he mentions my talking about the number sales of kits RB sold, to May 1991.

28/ Mid 1991 to 18 May 1992. He deals with my evidence which showed that prior to leaving the UK to build the car in Switzerland, I sent the Busbridges letters setting out how they could continue to order kits from me. Thus showing I am taking every step one could to protect my mark and its sales.

29/ Reynolds says that I am of the view that during the time I was abroad all kits that RB sold were my own kits and Reynolds says he is not clear from the response of RB whether this was a case of copying. He quotes RB's paragraph 23.

I am not surprised he couldn't understand a word as it is a prime example of RB waffle, which in total means nothing. However his saying he was not sure, tells me that again Reynolds shows his lack of grasp of the written evidence put before him, by me. I showed conclusively that what had happened as soon as my back was turned, was that the Busbridge's persuaded my subcontractors to supply them kits without letting me know. That continued until such time as they had set themselves up to be able to copy my chassis jigs and body mould. This lack of ability to grasp this important point shows just how vacuous he is. For such illegal activities just show the lack of integrity and honesty of the Busbridges and RB had openly in these witness statements for this hearing, admitted copying my product. Yet this obviously has no effect on Reynolds and on how he perceives RB. I find this astonishing that a man of IP law can see that the stealing of my IP has openly taken place, yet it has no effect on Reynolds and on his deliberations and summing up and his eventual decision making.

30/ Now he compounds what I have just said in the above comments, by saying that it now transpires that Busbridge did have Mick Frost make a chassis but to his own design. Then he says we indulge in a somewhat inconclusive debate as to who owns the copyright of this chassis and he cannot draw any conclusion.

*Yet again this shows the lack of grasp of all the facts of this case, by Reynolds. For anyone with half a brain who read my statement, could see what I was saying. Frost copied my chassis **jigs**. (For those like Hearing Officers) jigs are the instrument from which chassis are made **from**. Frost did not make a chassis for the Busbridges, what he did was copy my jigs from which the Busbridges could then make chassis for themselves and these chassis were **identical** to my chassis.*

When an HO believes the unsubstantiated lies put forward by someone accused of copying, it does become impossible to know who owned the copyright. However the evidence I put forward shows that long before Busbridge ever appeared on the kit car industry, I had been making these Viper chassis. This is apparently too hard for the vacuous Reynolds to grasp.

Where I have huge problems in understanding how the mind of Reynolds works, is the fact that here we have a hearing officer who deals in IP. *Yet he is unable to grasp facts that are staring him in the face and if there were things that he was not sure about, he had the ability to clear up doubts by asking me at the hearing to elucidate and clear up those doubts. He did not do so. In fact he never asked one question in the whole hearing, as far as I can remember! Yet in the above paragraphs it is clear there were issues he says he did not understand. I also find it incredible that someone as high up as an IPO hearing Officer does not know anything about copyright, seeing as the IPO deal with copyright. He ought to know that copyright is vested in the person who designs a product or even to someone who pays someone else to design it for him. So it is as clear as daylight that as I designed the chassis in 1986, it is I who owns the copyright and if Reynolds was too stupid to realise this then he should have checked copyright law out before making his decisions. After all he worked in the right place to find out.*

In any case on the issue of the chassis IP, this strictly has no bearing on this case, only that had he had the intelligence to grasp that this was yet another example of the dishonesty of Busbridge, it may have shown him just how unreliable this man's evidence was.

31/ Here he deals with the fact that in the UK between June 1991 to when I returned to the UK in September 1992 there were no sales by me. He mentions my ordering 2500 Viper brochures in early 92 and he says that it is not clear how they were distributed or how many sales they resulted in. He then says it 'appears' that I had moved to Germany by this time. Anything that happened after then he was not interested in.

*This is getting monotonous. Reynolds seems he cannot grasp anything at all. Firstly, I produced the invoice for Viper brochures to show that like the previous brochures in 1990, here was proof that **I must have been trying to sell Vipers**. I did this because RB kept saying I never tried to market Vipers between 1989 and 1994. Is Reynolds so thick and so ignorant of normal business practices, that he cannot see that ordering 5,000 colour brochures in total, means that whoever orders such a sales product and in such numbers, must be trying to sell whatever product is featured on them! The fact that my mark 'Viper' is prominently featured on them, should mean to anyone with more than half a brain that I must be trying to sell 'Vipers', contrary to the lies of RB! In fact I made a point of pointing out, that the Busbridges took many hundreds off me from the first batch, thus proving that I must have owned the mark whilst they were agents of mine. Otherwise why would they not get their own brochures printed and why was **I selling** them the brochures, as evidenced in my exhibits of their invoices, where I specifically charge them for **brochures!**

His comment that it is not clear how the brochures were distributed is farcical. The brochures taken by RB went out to customers who sent in for a Viper brochure. This was in those days before websites, and the accepted way potential customers got information on a kit car product. How and when I distributed my brochures after May 1992 is none of Reynolds business as this is outside the relevant date of this case. Nor is it any of his business how many sales were got by even the first issue of brochures some of which were taken by RB. The number of kit sales is irrelevant to this case. The kit car industry is a small one and a manufacturer may only sell 20 to 50 kits a year but could send out many thousands of brochures. If this vacuous man had any business experience he would know that success rates for brochure outputs can be around 1% to 2% or even less.

He makes a reference to my statement that when I came back to the UK in September 1992 I eventually set about rescuing my business. His comment is somewhat snide in that he states 'when he set about rescuing his business—as he puts it' Once more it is none of his business, as it is outside the relevant date and I only made mention of my activities outside that date because RB put heaps of evidence into the arena about matters after*

May 1992 and I felt obliged to counter the rubbish and lies because I was unsure about how the HO who heard the case would take that evidence of RB. As Reynolds had firmly nailed his thoughts to the mast as to what he wasn't going to take notice of of anything outside may 1992, why does he go on to mention happenings after the relevant cut off date?

His observation that after I had sent the letter threatening legal action (July 1992) things between RB and myself had deteriorated. Is this man even madder than I already think he is? The relationship had gone off the edge in early 1991 when it became clear that they were incapable of running a business and subsequently when I found out at Christmas 1991/92 that they had stolen my business off me, they were then totally out of my control. Yet another clear example of how this man is incapable of reading the facts out of all the evidence given him and how he couldn't be bothered to ask any questions about anything, at the hearing

32/ **Cross examination (between myself and RB).** Now we have Reynolds saying that this was conducted in a combative spirit Questions were asked in a calculating manner, we had well rehearsed positions and were reluctant to say anything that might not support those positions. He said that whilst this cross examination did clarify some underlying factual circumstances, it did not resolve key areas where the reliability of documents is in question. He waffles on again about the retrospective explanations and the fact that the events took place a long time ago.

*Quite what goes on in his mind, I cannot understand. He is from another planet. Of course we were going to be combative, and certainly I was. Is it a sin to be combative? Or is it deemed that we should all be gentlemen and behave like the upper class twits we have in this country who have no backbone? Should being combative stop one from being taken seriously and deny you **justice**? Similarly why shouldn't one have a calculating manner, or should we all so drippy and muddled that we come across as not organised? I am glad that he did get something clarified, for he himself made no attempt to clarify anything by asking questions whilst we were cross examining each other.*

33/ *The law in relation to proprietor issues.* In this paragraph and in 34 & 35, he waffles on about case law, but the nitty gritty of it boiled down to common law. The first to use a trademark is the owner, in common law.

So in my case I was without doubt the first to use the mark. End of story you would think.

36/ He says that a finding that I own the mark would mean that if Busbridge was given registration for an identical mark, that would give rise to deception.

Too damn right it would, as I had pointed out, and what about the simple fact that I had already been granted ownership when I won against Chrysler? It shows here that in his mind he was taking no notice of that and he was going to try that case all over again and make his own decisions on that and that it was in his mind that I did not own the trademark.

37/ Ownership of the mark prior to the formation of BRL. He goes through the making of the document KC2 and says I agreed under cross examination that it was 'neither fish nor foul' He says it makes no mention of a payment for it or licensing it or pays regard to stamp duties.

Once again we have some pretty vacuous remarks from his lordship. Firstly the mark is unregistered and it is my understanding that you cannot assign an unregistered mark. If that is so then it follows that maybe you cannot license it? I have never heard any mention anywhere about having to pay stamp duty if you assign a registered mark and I have assigned my mark since it became registered, without having to pay stamp duty. So what is he waffling about? Plus I have to repeat what I said above about him looking into a time which was outside the time span he should have only been looking out, namely Jan 1990 to May 1992.

38/ He says that the document was ill conceived and muddies the waters.

As I have said before, if I were rich I would have taken legal advice. I was not rich and so was under the apprehension that if the board of a company wanted to divest itself of something, then surely what business was it of others? Even to assign it, if that were allowed, then am I going to pay myself to get the assignment? It is ludicrous. I and my son were the company and all that was happening was that we were removing it from the company (not that I ever felt it belonged to the company anyway) so that if any intending investor would think it did belong to BL, then we could say 'Oh no it isn't' Plus as I have repeatedly stated, what business is it to Reynolds what happened before the application of Chrysler in Jan 1990? He also ignores the fact that this document had already been taken into account by Tuck, the hearing officer who heard my case against Chrysler and had presented no problem for saying I owned the mark.

39/ He, in a nutshell is now conceding, especially as RB admitted it, that he had had no dealings with me prior to 1988, and so could not know what understandings I had with BL, or that I owned the goodwill and the mark.

Hurrah at least he is giving me that one. **However** *for the second time, why is he bothering himself with any of the matters prior to Jan 1990, for as I have said, I have already proved I owned the mark during BL & BRL and in my opinion Reynolds should have been butting out and only dealing with a very short time frame Jan 1990 (the date Chrysler applied to register and which I won against) to May 1992 (when RB applied to register)!*

40/ *Ownership of goodwill arising from the BRL business (and to paragraph 48).* Reynolds firstly deals with the fact that RB admits that he could not speak confidentially about the dealings I had with BRL or anything else. Then he waffles on about case law to do with goodwill in BRL and whether I had just given permission for them to use it and would not take action against BRL for passing off. He says that he has not been pointed to a written license agreement or a verbal agreement, between myself and BRL re this.

He says he has to come to the conclusion that any licence from me to BRL was no more than a waiver of the right I had to take action against them for using this trademark. He then waffles on again about case law regards situations like this.

He concludes that it must be that the goodwill generated by BRL during its trading under the mark Viper, belongs to BRL.

This is the trouble you have when you have lawyers or such like talking about business matters which they obviously haven't a clue about, having never started, built up and run a business. The **reality** *is that BRL as a viable company was always very suspect. Quite soon after I tied up with the Yanks it became apparent that if it ever succeeded, it would be a miracle. So it is no use going on about whether I could sue them for passing off. Why the hell would I want to do that anyway? If it died a death which I very much suspected, it eventually it would,* **what good is the goodwill then?** *It can have all the goodwill in the world but if it is no longer a viable company, in the real world and not the hypothetical world of lawyers and the like, what use is all that goodwill if it had it? I owned the design rights and the trademark, the Americans knew that, one was in Italy and legally unable to step foot in the country and the other did not know his elbow from his backside, let alone anything to do with trademarks and copyrights. So when BRL ceased and I continued, what ever goodwill that existed would automatically stay with the mark, whoever was making the products.*

Also let us not forget that goodwill was created in other areas of business not to do with the Viper trademark, such as our fibreglass business and our steel fabricating business, the Lamborghini Countach kit which had its own goodwill. The kitcar building business we generated where we could and did build kit cars of other makes. All that goodwill went down the swanny, but all I was interested in was the continuation of one part of the business to do with what I had created and owned. Namely the Jaguar based Viper kit. I was not interested in the Granada based kit nor the Cortina based kit and each of those had their own goodwill. I end up with only one product that goodwill could be said to be attached to and even there, because the company closed in the way it did, what was that goodwill worth, or what did it add up to, I ask? So all this waffle about the goodwill of BRL is a red herring, because I would virtually have to start from scratch again, building up confidence in that one Jaguar Viper kit car in a new company. Also yet again, what did the events prior to Jan 1990 have to do with Reynolds?

49/ He now goes into the non story about the fact that in May 1989, BRL applied for the registration of the mark Viper, which eventually was dropped, abandoned or whatever you want to call it.

Once again out of the time he should be only dealing with and none of his business.

50/ In this paragraph he reproduces my account of why this happened.

51/ He now states that what happened to this application is unclear and he then goes onto saying he does not find my explanation 'of this episode wholly convincing' and that allowing the application to be put in, in the companies name was an 'ill conceived strategy' and is now being used by the arch liar Busbridge to say that BRL owned it.

His Lordship can say what piffle he wants, but he was not a part of the business of BRL, nor running it, nor was RB. So neither of them can speak about what intentions I or anyone else had. All they can do is speculate without any hard evidence to back up anything. **What did it matter if the application petered out or was abandoned or withdrawn?** *I think that what really mattered was, did it go as far as it could, to registration, and the clear answer to that is it did not!*

Saying as he did that he found my story unconvincing is tantamount to calling me a liar, and without clear evidence that I was lying, and I find it hard to understand what was so hard to understand in my explanation. I say again at the risk on endlessly repeating myself, what went on in BRL is of no concern to him as it had already been dealt with by Tuck.

*It all boiled down once again, to this man's complete lack of understanding of what goes on in real life, and what was going on in BRL and my mindset at that time. Because of his **ignorance** of what had happened to me all through the BRL episode in my life, not having been there himself, his ignorance of business matters, his ignorance of the real world, he is incapable of being able to understand what I was faced with. Of course if he had more than half a brain he would have asked me to elucidate at the hearing in a fuller manner, until it had sunk into his skull. Instead he calls me a liar in this decision document, knowing full well it is too late for me to do anything about it. Of course he then uses his warped understanding to go on and make assumptions about the case and eventually come to a conclusion, having been helped in part by these type of crass misunderstandings of the real situation. It makes my blood boil. But then you see this kind of crass behaviour by upper class twit Judges in the British judicial system, each day of the week. What was it Shakespeare said? He should have said 'Hang all the Judges as well while you're at it'*

Put yourself into my position. My life in those years was my business. I worked at it 7 days a week. I wished for it to reach great heights. I had the experience, the product but not enough capital to do it.

Thanks to time wasting tyre kicking Brits, I had to go with two Yanks instead and against my better judgement. These two turned out to be typical Yanks, all bullshit and big ideas, but liars and dreamers. I was stuck with them and the longer it went on the harder it was to break free. However by early 1989 with the runaway success of my Cortina Viper, at least I thought this should enable them to be able to obtain funding. They made all sorts of big promises that they could get the funding we needed. So put yourself in my position. Now I felt that if only they would get funding, and this was no overseas order we had, but home grown orders by the dozens. Surely they would now get funding? I felt some confidence and if I were right, then I would have my future secured, because the business would then be secured and would surge forwards. For it had not been secure for two years. If I was right then it made sense to now allow the trademark to be handed over to BRL. After all if there was success then the fact that BRL would now own the trademark, it would be no big deal for me on a personal level. This because my deal with the Yanks was, that if the company was successful, the scheme that we all entered into would also forge ahead and I would really benefit monetarily to such an extent that any considerations for me still owning the trademark, would pale into insignificance.

I fail to see what is so hard to understand about that. But as I have said, we are dealing here with a HO who obviously does not understand business or people in it. Shortly after I asked Gee & Co to apply for it became obvious to me that the Yanks were indulging in just more Yanky bullshit and I would not get the funding I needed to cope with the extra business. So I just stopped contact with Gee & Co. I knew that they would just allow the paperwork to fizzle out. When the company ceased as I felt it would if no funding came through, I still owned the trademark as it had not gone through to registration or even got to the first post.

What is so hard for Reynolds to understand about this and what makes it unconvincing? I say it is his stupidity and his lack of understanding of day to day business and the real world. It is not about his airy fairy world of stuffy legal nonsense. Plus he could have asked me to explain more fully to him at the hearing.

*One thing I cannot understand about his stupidity, is why is it that he could not see that at the cessation shortly after the application to register was made, if BRL (and here I mean the Yanks with their debenture over assets) felt that it owned the trademark. Why didn't the Yanks make me pay them for buying it off them? After all, one of them had been in manufacturing and venture capital all his working life. He knew the score on such matters. Mr Clever Clogs (Reynolds) doesn't apply his masterful intellect to this... Oh No! Of course RB leaps upon this fact that BRL applies for the trademark and he spins his web of lies and fairy stories, none based on fact with documentary evident or witness evidence to back what he says the facts are. Reynolds slavishly panders to his lies and made up tales. However over riding everything I have said above is the fact **yet again** that all the facts about what went on at BRL was covered by Tuck in the Chrysler case. Yet here I am being forced by this Reynolds to be tried **twice** as it were.*

52/ Reynolds now says that as with a number of actions that underpin this case, it is hard to give a rational explanation for what has taken place. Then he says that my 'suggesting' under cross examination that the trademark application was filed by a trademark attorney and that I did not know how he did that. He remarks that if the attorney had not been instructed properly 'that would not be altogether surprising'.

What the hell is it with this man? What is he actually saying or implying here' Is he suggesting I am lying again? I gave the job to apply for the registration to Patent Agents. What more does one do when doing that? You just tell them to apply for you and you leave it to them to do. They are the experts, do they need to know from me how to do it? What is this saying I 'suggested' this or that? I just damn well told him what had happened. It is just another example how Judges and HO's they think they are so smart they don't need to talk in plain English as that would not be British. So they talk in what I call 'waffle speak'. It is all innuendo and a posh way of saying something that appears to be nice and mean one thing, when all the time you actually mean something else, but it is not the done thing to actually say outright what you mean.

53/ He says that as I was aware that it was imperative for me to have ownership of the IP rights back at July 1986, why was it that in 1989 I am willing to allow BRL to have the trademark? He says that I said that I had failed to check in who's name the application was going ahead in.

Yet once again this man's stupidity just staggers me. I **never** said that I was not aware of in who's name the application had been applied for. I was never even asked if I knew at the hearing and if the HO was unclear about any of this why did he not ask questions until he became **quite clear?** His comment that he then makes, that my answers were unconvincing, makes my blood boil for yet again this stupid man is saying I am lying. What possible motive do I have for lying? It is on the record in who's name it was applied for and I gave the hearing the same explanation as to why I had decided to allow BRL to apply, as I have given above. What does matter, as I have said 'did it get registered in BRL's name' the answer is 'No it did not' So that means I still owned it at the end of BRL. Quite why any of this matters one jot to anything is as I have endlessly explained, when I had my hearing against Chrysler in 1998 long after the demise of BRL, I had had to go through the exact same explanations to that HO (Tuck) and what I said was accepted and I was given registration to the date in question at that hearing of Jan 1990. So why am I being giving the third degree over matters that have already been agreed by the IPO, here I am being tried again, as it were and everything I say is treated with suspicion.

54/ *The position after BRL's demise.* Here he says that after the demise, who did the goodwill belong to? He says this is critical.

What he doesn't say is what goodwill he refers to, for as I have previously pointed out BRL had goodwill in several areas. It is fact that after BRL I only carried on with ONE PRODUCT.

Namely the Jaguar based Viper. Who designed this and owned the copyright? I designed most of it and what I did not design was still owned by me as the person who helped me design the relevant Jaguar parts, was in my employ. In law I thus owned the copyright of that part of the chassis, too. I never sold assigned nor licensed BL or BRL to use it. There was a verbal agreement between BRL and myself, that BRL could use the design as long as I agreed. It is undisputed that BRL made those Jaguar kits, but how can they accrue any goodwill that could arise from that? BRL is not an individual and any success from the sales of that kit were down to me as I ran the company and it was my design and trademark that allowed any sales to take place.

As for the verbal agreement, Reynolds says he was 'never pointed to it' Just how do you point a person to a **verbal** agreement? Other than have one of the persons who you made the **verbal** agreement with, verify it. In this case had I known of the whereabouts of either of those persons, I would have done that. One of them is undoubtedly long deceased as he was in his late 60's in 1989 and not in good health, and the other is probably back somewhere in the States.

55/ He now says that if the agency agreement could be relied upon, it may have been a pivotal document in determining the matter. He goes on to saying RB says this is a forgery. (Which he would, wouldn't he?)

So what we have here, is this Reynolds bloke being unwilling to accept that the agreement document was real, just because RB says it wasn't. (The agreement and the signatures if it were a forgery, could just as easily been fabricated by RB himself in 4 easy steps.) He is unwilling to accept the verdict of a Court who found me not guilty of forging it and it appears too hard for him to realise that the second signatory of the document has never been asked if the document was indeed genuine. He is therefore prepared to accept the word of a person whom I have shown by my documentary evidence is not a person whose word can be relied on and indeed is an habitual liar. I say this is all because he does not want to find for me. So an inconvenient document like the agency agreement has somehow to be trashed. This he does that here.

56/ He says that in the cross examination, the question as to this alleged forgery was not taken 'further forward' He says that I stuck to my assertion that as far as I was concerned on this matter, I had been tried for this in a Court and found 'Not Guilty' He then incredibly says that even so, this is not enough 'to render the disputed document a credible and reliable one' Although I gave in my evidence pages from the transcript of my trial, those pages did not deal with what was said about this document and whether it was a forgery! So he did not know what was said in relation to that issue.

This HO seems to have a trenchant for retrying all the hearings and trials held before this case, when surely his job is to stick to this case and this case only. This case is my opposition to RB getting registration of my trademark and we should be sticking to facts about only that, not about matters that have already been determined. He seems to think that my saying that as far as I was concerned that I had been tried for this and that is that, is some how suspect. For his part he can legitimately say it is a fact, that the accusation of forgery can go on ad infinitum. Saying he did not have all the pages of the transcript and that what he had, did not deal with anything to do with the forgery is yet another example of how this man simply doesn't have a handle on this case or the evidence and facts as presented to him. Those transcript pages were put into evidence by me and they were selected pages which covered the cross examination of RB and dealt only with his assertion he had never been my agent. Yet here he is complaining that it did not deal with the alleged forgery. What planet is he on, where is his brain when he was going through the evidence? Why did he not ask me at the hearing about why the pages I put in only covered what they did? Why did he not ask me for all the pages of the trial or better still make an effort to get them, for the supplier of those pages was clearly to be seen on each page. Had he asked I would have forwarded them to him before he made his decision.

It was obviously too hard for him to see that by my showing that RB lied at the court case over whether he was an agent, then admitted he was, then surely that made it clear that in all probability the agency agreement must have been a true document.

57/ The transcript he talks about (which he does not clearly state which actual hearing he is talking about, as he has just been talking about a transcript of a completely different hearing and now he is waffling on about yet another) he then says I am asked five times if this document is a true document. He says I equivocated or said I could not answer the question. My final answer being that it was the document that I had sent RB to sign and what I got back.

His wording of this paragraph shows me that he is definitely biased against me. If he was a straight hearing officer only interested in getting to the truth, he would not have made these comments or the comments in the previous paragraph. He would have got the whole transcript and he would have gone into this in more detail with me at the hearing. He did neither. The transcript he is talking about is actually the one for the Chrsyler hearing, so easily available from his own IPO.

Much more importantly there is a fact that he completely ignores and this proves bias. This document was signed by **two people... RB and MB**. As I have said above, why did he not even query why it was that all the accusations levelled at me were by only one of the signatories? Why did he not say because only one signatory had given evidence he could not be drawn into making any decisions on this document.

Why was he in anycase going over a case that has nothing to do with this case. If he is referring to the Chrysler hearing, or the 2000 perjury trial, those are outside the remit of this hearing!

Now readers, you will see later on in this book, why this is so important and why I say that this man is nothing more than a lazy, biased numbskull. A doddering old fool that should have retired years ago. For he is disseminating so called justice which had a huge impact on my case and my life and pocket. It also raises questions in my mind as to, was the IPO in on this? Was he programmed by the IPO to come to the decisions he did? I think he was.

Let us face it, civil servants are well known for being lying devious people who do not like being proved wrong. Do not like having the truth shoved into their faces. They will do **anything** to trash members of the public who stand up to them. The evidence is there in droves, for anyone who wants to see it, where members of the public have been fucked around for years by duplicitous lying toads in the civil service and in local government areas, just so they did not have to give in and admit defeat. We who pay their wages are treated like shit and of course these bastards know they can and do get away with it, for it is extremely difficult to prove facts against these people. Evidence goes missing, lies are told that you cannot prove are lies, every dirty trick in the book is used.

Now you may think, why should I think that this is happening to me? Well that is easy, because before this case I had shaken the pot many times. Ever since 1992 I had been complaining, sometimes vociferously, about the IPO not doing what they should have done re this man Robert Busbridge and his application. I had complained to the Ombudsman and to their CEO. I bet my name was dirt in the IPO. Also I had accused them of **maladministration** and had threatened to sue them. What better way than to trash me now and knowing full well I could not afford to appeal before the High Court, thanks to their archaic 1938 rules they had not retrospectively got rid of. Maybe they felt I would give in and go away? It therefore would not surprise me to find out that this hearing officer was instructed to find ways to trash me by whatever means.

They were very much mistaken if they thought I would give up. I am like an elephant who never forgets. Fortunately for me I am a fighter, because I was brought up in an area were you had to fight to survive and or you got your head kicked in. I was an *officer in the MN who had to control rough blokes and then in the Forces, where again I was taught to fight, twice on active service. In all my business life it was a fight against others trying to stitch me up, because that is what business life is all about.*

58/ This is yet another biased summing up of what he believes about this agreement document. He turns himself into a Judge on whether it could be a forgery. He comments on what he says is an obvious positioning of the signatories which are the same as another document. Says he is deeply mistrustful of the agreement document and that it is curious that I did not rely on it by putting it into evidence myself and he obviously does not believe my response to this, by pointing out that I did so deliberately as I knew RB would put it into evidence, which he did.

I did not put it into my opposition evidence because I knew that RB was just waiting to make mischief with it if I did, as he had said if I did he would go to the Police so I determined that if he put it in I would then deal with it. I also determined that if I put enough documentary evidence that showed without any doubt that the Busbridges had been my agents, because events and my actions towards them would show that to be the case, then this document was not really needed. (Of course I did not know I would end up with an old biased and programmed fool like Reynolds.)

Had he asked me what I thought of the fact that the two documents had signatures that appeared to be the same, I could have told him how easy it was for RB to have done this. The agreement was signed in October 1989, the second document was made in 1991. I put in the agreement document to Chrysler and RB knew that I would before I did, when he was trying to fool Chrysler he owned the mark. He knew that when I found out they were trying to fool Chrysler, I would try to prove he did not own it. Of course I would as would anyone. He knew the best way for me to do that is show the agreement document. So what can he do to stitch me up?

That is dead easy for all he has to do is copy the signature part of the agreement document and transpose it onto the second document. 'Hey Presto' you have two documents that have the same signature and they come from the document he knows I have and will show. He has a potential forgery. At my trial when the jury could see that could happen and that RB came across like the liar he is, they acquitted me. RB had said that he had an 'original of the second document which proved that I had made a forgery. However at no time have I ever seen this 'original document. Even if he has, there are an easy 4 steps way he could do this and end up with a purported original second document.

I have to point out that Reynolds again, did not even bring up the point of the secondary signature and why was this person not in the frame? Of course if you are having to rely on an HO who is biased, programmed or just plain lazy or thick, then you stand no chance.

59/ So now he says that if the agreement cannot be relied on he will have to rely on other evidence to determine what the position was post September 1989. He says that RB's claim to ownership presents a confusing picture.

Well of course RB's evidence presented a confusing picture. I believe this is for two reasons. One is that he had no real evidence that was clear cut. That he deliberately presents so much cluttered irrelevant nonsense as I have said above, that anyone could become confused, as indeed did this HO. However as I have said it is his job to clear up confusion and this he did not do at the hearing, as he was only thinking as to getting home on time. He had months to read up on all the evidence and then ask questions until he was clear. He did not do that.

60/ Now he says that from what RB said in response to questions and his evidence, that RB is uncertain as to what date he feels he can legitimately claim ownership.

Let us face it, to anyone with half a brain it would be clear that RB is trying it on. If he cannot set out a clear cut chain of evidence to back up his claim, then is it up to any HO to make it up for him? Reynolds tone suggests that he is going to be sympathetic to this liar and find this chain for him. You can see he does.

61/ In this paragraph we have Reynolds listing some of the various stories that RB made up for various people as to how he can claim the trademark.

(a) He was owed money by BRL. *Absolute rubbish.*
(b) By Kunzli selling him rights. *Kunzli never owned any rights to sell.*
(c) By BRL abandoning the mark. *BRL never owned it to abandon.*
(d) Moral rights. *I do not believe IP Laws are based on moral rights.*

*Why did he not list **all of the excuses which I exposed**?*

62/ He says that these conflicting claims show RB had uncertainty in his mind as to the proper basis for his claim. Then he says that RB is a businessman not an IP lawyer so it is necessary for him to look 'under the surface of the claims'

Well once gain the wording of this whole paragraph shows just how deeply biased this man is towards RB. Remember, I too am not an IP lawyer, yet we did not see Reynolds showing sympathy for me in my not doing things strictly according to business law, IP law or partnership law. I am only shown his disapproval and his inference that what I say is unreliable etc. So now he his going to look deeper into these claims, yet he is obviously not willing or able to 'look deeper' into what I have said, not up to this point or further on in this summing up.

Also why is it that he just cannot see that by RB presenting all these conflicting claims as to how he can claim ownership of the trademark are nothing more than **lies!** Therefore why does this not warn him as to what RB is really all about? Because he wants to find for RB. It is the only explanation. This is exemplified by him saying " RB had uncertainty in his mind as to the proper basis for his claim" By saying this it is obvious that in Reynolds mind RB should **be found** a basis to claim my trademark and I will damn well do that for him. How biased and corrupt can you get?

63/ He says the claim that he was owed monies untenable, as no evidence or explanation. *Hurrah, he sees the light on that one!*

64/ He can place no reliability on the claim that Kunzli sold him the rights especially as Kunzli said it was a forgery. *Another Hurrah! Give that man a medal.*

65/ Now Reynolds shows more bias towards RB for he now says that "Mr Busbridges primary claim , it seems to me, is that he was taking up the reins of BRL's abandoned business".

Yet again this sentence shows extreme bias in favour of RB and it is so vacuous, that I just cannot believe that he could say this. Firstly he turns what RB actually said: 'a moral right' to take the trademark over, to now read, as just taking over the abandoned business. He is deciding on behalf of RB what his claim is, when the poor unfortunate creature cannot do it himself. Are HO's allowed to make up what the applicants claim is? I think not.

The more I see what this man has to say the more my blood boils. Firstly he is doing a good job as a defence lawyer for RB by treating him favourably, by making up a claim that he did not make. RB did not say that he was able to take it over (sentence(d)) RB said he 'adopted' it.

The statement that BRL abandoned the business is a clear piece of fiction thought up by Reynolds. To abandon anything means you just up and away. The Yanks did not do that at all. They closed it down and disposed of the assets. That is hardly abandoning anything! What's more I bought most of the assets off BRL so I could continue the Viper part of BRL's business and using my ownership of the Viper.

If Reynolds is going to use a case of abandonment then IP law states that a period of 5 years has to take place before anything can be claimed to have been abandoned. Of course Reynolds knows this but chooses to have a mental blackout about that law. What in fact was RB claiming he did, if this one of many excuses is to be latched onto, it is that he could just take over everything BRL owned. This is fairy tale country and he knows it. People cannot just take over things. What does Reynolds think he is dealing with here? A squatters rights or something like that? What IP law says a person or business can just **"take over or as he says, take up the reins of another business"**? One point here is very clear and that is despite my clear evidence that it was I that took over the reins of BRL's business, that is ignored.

66/ Reynolds says that the business conducted between myself and RB is the same as the business conducted between BRL and the Busbridges, but there is no formal agreement.

'Oh yes there is you vacuous dickhead' However you have just trashed that without even asking yourself 'Could it have been a true document, why don't I enquire as to what the second signatory says?' Let alone all the other points I made. What about all the incontrovertible evidence I gave of all the business I passed onto them to the tune of around £110,000's plus. My comments that would one give that amount of business to just anyone? Of course Reynolds has already shown what a biased prat he is, about anything to do with business. So all he wants is something in writing, but not the existing something in writing, like the agency agreement. Then let us not forget that Reynolds has intimated above that RB took over the reins of BRL's business, yet here he is saying RB carried on doing business with me getting the same service of kits and parts from me that he got from BRL. What is it to be Reynolds?

67/ Here Reynolds says that RB admits he never tried to acquire the trademark through BRL's receiver, so it is necessary to look at trade after September 1989.

I have no bother with that, but why didn't RB do this? It is ignored because Reynolds does want to find for RB.

68 to 72/ These paragraphs deal with what happened to my trading history after September 1989.

He logs how it was apparent that many customers of BRL were upset at losing their kit deposits, which were mostly for £500 each. Not a great amount to lose. A few customers lost more than that. It is stated that some irate customers threatened me and so I wanted to distance myself from that threat and so from BRL. Much is made of a letter I sent to all the kitcar magazines (3) explaining what had happening and my involvement with the company.

Then he makes much of the letter to Kunzli from me outlining the disposal of the assets of BRL. He calls it an unsatisfactory document because it had handwriting on it. He describes who got what in the disposals.

*Here we have again this vacuous man showing just how he does not have a handle on the true events. He surmises too much when he could once again asked questions about anything he had doubts about. He makes the wrong assumptions because of his lack of investigatory work. For instance he says that there 'may' have been some in the kit car trade who knew about the financial backing BRL had. How does he know this? If he does not know for an absolute fact, then he should not make unsubstantiated comments about things he knows nothing about. However this comment has absolutely no relation to this case, so why bring it up? Even if they did know, so what? Then he says that because after the demise of BRL, the press made comments. Yes they did make comments but only to the effect that BRL had closed down due to the backers exercising their debenture to do so and sell off the assets. How did they know this?... because I told them, but what has all that got to do with this case? Then he comments that the kit car buying public **and** the press are likely to have seen me as 'the front man' of BRL.*

What the hell is that supposed to mean? You usually see that kind of statement made in reports about shonky businesses who have men in the back room wanting to keep their involvement in a rip off business, and employing someone else to be their 'front man'. This is an entirely biased comment made I think to convey that somehow I am somewhat seedy individual in all this. Where did he get that impression from I ask. Well if you study all the drip, drip of lies and denigrating remarks make by RB about me, maybe you will get the picture.

*He goes on to saying that it is not surprising that there were disgruntled ex customers and 'trade creditors' who regarded me as 'deeply implicated' in BRL's demise. Once again this paints a picture of me that could be said to be unflattering, to say the least. He has obviously come to the conclusion that there were 'trade creditors'. Where does he get that information from? I have never even mentioned trade creditors and even RB never mentioned them. In FACT there weren't any as BRL did not owe **one penny** to any trade creditor. So another wrong statement by Reynolds which shows he hasn't a handle* on the facts of this case, or more to the point it is deeply biased.

Then he says I was 'at pains' to distance myself from BRL problems by saying I was not responsible for it's debts. Why the hell shouldn't I do that? It was a safe bet that many members of the public that lost deposits would not know company law in relation to directors and what they could be held responsible for. Like the fact that directors are not responsible for company's debts and that is why limited companies are in existence. So that is why I sent that letter to all the customers and to the kit car press. Who wouldn't want to lessen the possibility that people may come after you... ***physically!***

Only one customer threatened me and actually came to Christchurch after me. (He was owed more than £500.) This was a somewhat rough and yobby type person who lost around £2,000. Nor did the Busbridges suffer any real problems either, according to Martin Busbridge, who told me that in 2010. So much for all the lies of his brother, RB, on that score.

Reynolds goes on to state ' such a public pronouncement was necessary and is a clear recognition how he (me) considered how the public would perceive my continued association with the **Viper** business and name'. Once again I consider this statement to be yet another outrageous comment made by Reynolds, who makes it without any clear evidence that that was why I made the statement to the kit car press and to each customer. How dare he keep making **assumptions,** for that is only what it is when he hasn't a clue. I view it more as a continuing campaign by him to paint a certain picture about me and what had gone on in my brain over what to do, at the time when BRL was in the throes of closing down.

The fact is, that the furthest thing from my mind at that time was how the public would think about me in **the future**. When I sent that letter to all customers of BRL and the press, it was done merely out of good manners to let the customers know what had happened and that it would be a waste of time going after me. What they or others may think about me in the future wasn't even in my mind, because at that stage I had not formulated in my mind exactly what and how I was going to go forward. It would take some weeks to do that and what I decided to do was nothing like what Reynolds says were my reasons. Certainly it was not to distance myself from the Viper name or product as Reynolds intimates without a shred of evidence.

I eventually decided that trying to run a big business on the lines that I had tried with BL & BRL was never going to work, because too much capital was needed and too many high quality workers were needed and neither could be found. Plus a large *expensive factory is needed. I decided that what I should do is keep it small and manageable and that as the Busbridges wanted to carry on, this time as my own agents, then this was the best way to go forward. They had a reasonable workshop, they were in a better part of the UK for retail sales than I was, and they had already some staff. Enough to carry on with a retail set up.*

I could concentrate in a small workshop, building up whatever fully built cars I could get orders for and have my chassis and bodies made by outside contractors. So it is apparent to anyone with the requisite half a brain that what ex BRL customers thought about me was of no consequence at all. I knew that within 3 to 4 months it would have all blown over, in any case.

That is exactly what happened and why RB and his brother had virtually no problems, from any irate ex BRL customers. Also why I was able to help them out at a number of kit car shows without a spot of bother from anyone? So much for all the hypothesizing by his Lordship, he of the know-all brainbox.

*Now to all the rubbish he comes out about the letter to Kunzli in which it is described how the assets are distributed and for what amounts. His comments are an absolute disgrace, for this letter as I have already stated, was not made up to satisfy his Lordship. Had I known at the time that I was going to have to satisfy the likes of him I would have got a solicitor to do it **and paid for it myself!***

He has to take into account why this was made up, for whom and why notations were made by hand after it had been typed and printed. It belongs to the growing list of comments made by him, where he has forsaken the ability to get a clear factual picture by asking questions at the hearing or doing some investigations.

So I have to repeat the reasons why this letter was made up. One Yank (Max Suite) was living in Lugarno which is on the border of North Italy and Switzerland, unable to set foot in the UK. Kunzli my Swiss agent lived in Winterthur, not so far away. He asks Kunzli to act as a middle man between Zinlic and H&S Replikas also in Switzerland (near Berne), who had heard of the demise and knew assets would be up for sale (he had heard through Kunzli who I was in constant contact with). Max asked me to draw up a list of what assets could be sold so they could get some of their investment back. He also asked me to put a value on those assets. I did this and posted it to Kunzli. It was shown to H&S and they said what they wanted. I indicated what I would buy. I was then asked to ship off the parts to H&S and take what I needed. In order to keep track of what went where I wrote in biro on this list, against each item, who took it. I added the total of what I owed Zinlic and put that onto the list. I took a copy and posted that to Kunzli with my cheque, so he could know what he needed to know. Hence the letter was as it was.

So what gives this cretinous man the right to question it? Or make the equally questionable remarks as to why exhibits KC12 & 13 were separate as they were all part of the sale of assets. What damn difference does it make if the three documents were shown as three separate exhibits? This man makes my blood boil for he sees everything I have said and exhibited as suspect, yet he says little about the masses of exhibits that were irrelevant rubbish, and the incomprehensible and illiterate documents, put in by RB.

Reynolds further shows his lack of credibility and qualifications to be dealing with this action by showing up his technical ignorance, once again. For he describes the assets that I took as 'Cobra Cortina chassis jig' and that H&S took 'Granada and Jaguar chassis jigs for a Cobra.' I believe it is essential in such a case which involves a technical matter, that the person who hears it is intelligent enough to be able to grasp the technical aspects of it. Reynolds shows again and again he just cannot get a grip of what I manufactured and made and he constantly hashes it all up with statements and comments that completely misunderstand the true position and this is seen here. The chassis jigs were not for a COBRA! The Cobra is a car that was manufactured by AC Cars in Thames Ditton and it had a chassis that was completely different to mine. Similarly the body was of hand beaten aluminium. The **'Viper'** is a Cobra 'Replica', and having said that, the chassis is completely different to the real car and the body is not exactly the same and is of fibreglass. It seems that these facts are beyond Reynolds to comprehend, and in mixing up his facts, in law he is actually saying things that legally incorrect. You cannot have cases where a judge or HO make statements that are factually incorrect. It begs the question of 'does the man really understanding all the facts about this case' For if the cannot grasp certain parts of the case, how can we have 100% certainty that he grasps other parts?

On this subject, he now goes on to make yet another factual mistake when he says that I had a chassis jig made up so I could produce cars with a Jaguar based chassis. No Mr Reynolds, the jig did not make cars, it made a chassis which was part of the **Viper** kit. A body/chassis kit is sold, which could with other parts, then made into a fully built car. You will see soon how he also is completely at sea over the question of 'parts' and these mistakes he makes do cloud his judgement over what relationship I had with the Busbridges.

73/ Reynolds refers to what he says he thinks are relevant exhibits for the period end 1989 to mid 1992. These are listed with remarks in Annex B & C. I will deal with each with my comments.

So you see here that Reynolds does admit that the relevant period he should only be looking at, is this ex BRL date to May 1992. So why did he go over all the facts before this date of Sept 1989 and about hearings etc that are outside this time scale? Not to mention that the IPO hearing of Me V Chrysler had already found for me up to the date of Jan 1990, yet he will persist in going back to Sept 1989. It is nothing more than incompetence and or bias.

My exhibit documents:-
(as picked out of all the exhibits I put into evidence, by Reynolds)

KC 15:- This is a copy of a witness statement that Wheels Abroad made for my trial in 2000 by the lawyers representing me. It confirms that the owner Don Salvage gave me the order for the remaining 4 Viper V12's after the demise of BRL and that Cobretti were my agents. His Lordship trashes this as it was not headed for this case or any other case and is not an original document.

It is obvious why it is not an original as my lawyer has that and that it had been made for the 2000 trial. This is another example of Reynolds trashing an important document because he is biased and yet he allows other documents that are also not originals, especially those of RB. He never once asked at the hearing to see the originals I had with me. On this question of originals, he seems to have a thing about this, yet he as I have said he is not consistent. How one is supposed to have all the originals when in many cases an original just cannot be shown. For instance, I used copies of exhibits that RB put into evidence which themselves were copies, that I found to prove a point, so I copied them and put into my evidence. So how could I have the original? It is all ludicrous in this day and age. Another example of Reynolds inconsistency is the agreement document which he seems to accept OK yet this document that RB put in was a photocopy, yet he did not bat an eyelid about that. Reynolds obviously is ignorant about IPO rules which state copies are acceptable?

KC16:- A receipt/agreement from Frost confirming payment for the new Jag based Viper chassis jig. Reynolds makes snide comments that it is 'curious' and an open letter signed twice.

What he means by open letter I know not (it was a RECEIPT!!) and the fact it was signed twice is simply that the upper and first signature was made on a surface which Frost leant on that made his signature indistinct. I made him do it again. Why did he not ask me why it was signed twice? Shows to me that Reynolds is all too ready to jump on as much of my evidence as he can in order to criticise me and negate my evidence.

KC17/1:- This is my **order** for 2500 Viper brochures I made in June 1990. Reynolds criticises the fact that it is not an invoice, so how does he know if they were made and distributed? It also says I supplied the plates.

Now it seems too hard for Reynolds to get his head around why would I order 2500 Viper brochures if I did not need them. If I were not going to have them used, why would I order them? Having ordered them and given the printer the plates to make them, why would I not take them when printed. Also when you order a large number of brochures they could last you years, because they only are distributed when people send in for brochures and when you do kit car shows. I just cannot see why I should have to prove that these brochures were distributed. They were obviously ordered so that they could be used. Not to just sit there. Reynolds ignores the fact that in 1992 I ordered another 2500 and he had the invoice this time. Now why would I go and order another 2500 if the first 2500 had not been used? Too hard for his brain to work that out!

I included a sample brochure and as this brochure design had been still in use in 2000, the sample I had given him had been written on by me 'Ken Cook 551792. 2000' This seems to confuse him and he jumps on that to infer that the document is out of the date in question. He ignores the fact that the order document is dated June 1990 which is the date the brochure was printed. He is obviously too thick to see that it is my name and telephone number and the date when I was going to give it to someone and didn't, so used it as a sample of what the brochure looked like **and showed the brochure was advertising the 'Viper** had been still in use in 2000. He has ignored by written explanations on this exhibit and why I showed it

Yet another example of the bias of Reynolds. He jumps on everything he can, about my exhibits.

KC17/2:- This is a copy of the advert I used to advertise Universal Cobra Replica parts, using Cobretti to sell them.

I put this in evidence to show that I had set up at great cost so as to give not only myself extra turnover, but also the Busbridges. Thus giving weight to my contention that

they were, despite RB saying otherwise, my agents. For why would I do this with any old Tom Dick or Harry?

My explanation has obviously gone straight over Reynolds head and he makes this obvious when he says that he saw no trademark name of Viper, and this despite he himself stating that it says that it is for 427 parts of **any make** (and he emphasised the 'any make') To even a screaming dickhead it would have been obvious why no mention was made of 'Viper', because the advert was for **universal Cobra replica parts** and not specifically for Viper parts. Once again he completely misses the point of what I had said, or was it deliberate?

KC18:- He trashes a statement from one of my suppliers who says he had supplied me with specialised *Viper* parts since 1986. Dated 2004.

Not good enough for your **Lordship** because it is not done in proper evidential form. You will note soon that similar letters from RB do not get the same remarks from his **biased Lordship.**

KC 19:- A copy of an advert that I used to put into Classic Sportscar magazine for fully built Vipers. He trashes that because it doesn't actually say they are for 'Vipers'.

Yet another example of either his inability to understand the kitcar scene or the classic car scene especially in relation to Cobra Replicas and his unwillingness to ask questions, so that he can understand.

My replica of the Cobra was unlike any other replica (as I have already explained). It had much wider wheel arches. Anyone who saw a picture of my Cobra Replica would know it was a Viper and a Replica. Because of its distinct shape. So it is no more necessary for me to say it is a Viper than it is for Ford to show a picture of a Ford Ka and actually say in big letters '**just for you ignoramuses in the IPO, this is a Ford Ka**'! The advert was for Vipers, no matter what this ignoramus says and I got two orders for fully built Vipers from it. The people who ordered were sent my brochures which clearly stated the cars were Vipers. and showed the picture page as talked about above. (This in the days before the web.)

KC 20:- The witness statement by Bechtolsheimer again made for my lawyers for the forgery trial. He calls it 'deeply flawed'

Why is this? Why is it good enough for the trial at Dorchester County Court? Why did the CPS lawyer not bring up the same exception to it as his Lordship? It is yet another example of his extreme bias. This statement by Dr Bechtolsheimer actually shows *how someone saw the above advert his Lordship did not like as it didn't say Viper, and came to see me to order a car. He told me that he had been to see RB and why were the two cars the same? This statement backs up my assertion that this showed that RB was acting as an agent for me I passed the order onto them. Bechtolsheimer states that they were my agents and of course this does not fit in with the desire of Reynolds to trash all my evidence so he can find for RB!*

KC21:- No comments on this.

KC22:- A headed letter from me to Cobretti over 427 parts and he states that the letter heading does not mention Viper, but only 'For all your 427 Parts' (as opposed to Viper parts).

Once again showing his utter ignorance, as this letter headed paper was specifically for my 427 Universal Cobra Replica parts business, hence why no mention of Viper and shown to show the business between us **as supplier to his agent!**

KC 23:- This was an invoice sent by me to Cobretti for the cost of all the parts used in the Cortina based Viper they made for me.

Note he did not criticise that this did not even have Cobretti's name on it and could be for anything. All he can bleat about is that it did not mention 'Viper', yet elsewhere he admits when dealing with the invoicing between us that we both knew we were dealing in Viper kits and parts and felt it was not necessary to keep mentioning that everything was Viper, as this was basically all we dealt in anyway. So he conveniently forgets that and trashes this as an exhibit not of worth. Thus proving yet again his inconsistency and his bias, because this important document showed that I had given the work of building up this demo car to Cobretti and they were to use it for sales purposes. Another case of a document that was important for me, so it is trashed.

KC25:- He deals here with the exhibit that shows the one and only type of advert that RB had monthly in *Which Kit* magazine.

He makes no comment as to my comment that, as it says 'under new management' that was because I insisted that was what would be said and that it does not in any way imply that they are the 'new owners' Now I wonder why that is?

KC26/1-17:- These are copies of orders that Cobretti sent me over the relevant period, for Viper kits and Viper parts, and in some cases for universal parts.

What he states when he says that these orders were under the 'parts scheme' shows yet again what a bumbling oaf this man is. He just did not get the set up between me and Cobretti and as I have said this was important. The universal parts business was not set up until about mid 1990 and these orders cover a period from Jan 1990 to June 1991. Then he goes on again that the name Viper was only mentioned once. (in fact mentioned FIVE times out of around 12 orders which isn't a bad percentage.) So what? As I have explained above, re the number of times Viper was ever mentioned in much of our business dealings, so I will not repeat myself.

KC27/1-49:- These are copies of my invoices to Cobretti and we get the same remark about only one mentions the word Viper, yet in fact Viper is mentioned five times.

Now you may say 'What only five times over 18 months. Well for a start I would only call the body or chassis separately, or the body+chassis as a kit, by the name Viper. For parts only, even though some parts were specially designed for the Viper and would only fit the Viper, they were never called Viper this or that. They were just parts. Now how many kits did I supply Cobretti and RB over that 18 months? Well it only amounted to 14 body chassis kits and 2 bodies. Five times they are called by the name Viper! I think that is a good percentage.

What has to be remembered is that I had set up with the Busbridges, where instead of me paying the subcontractors for a body and chassis and then adding my profit and invoicing them, they could pick up a body and chassis directly off the subcontractor, pay them the wholesale price and I would bill them for what I termed a commission, but was in fact my profit. So all these invoices were made out for kit commission or chassis commission or body commission. That meant that it was unlikely for me to mention Viper and so bloody what, I ask? Had I known at the time what was going to happen and later on in life I would have to put up with some dickhead hearing officer making a big thing out of me not calling my kit by the name Viper each time. This to someone I trusted and who I knew, that he knew what the hell he was buying, I would have called even a screw I supplied... a 'Viper screw'!

KC28 & 29:- These deal with two letters from Cobretti to me over the payment to me with a rubber cheque.

Reynolds shows again he doesn't get it, as I was making the point in my statement that this was when things started to go down hill between myself and the Busbridges.

KC 32-35:- These are the letters I sent to the Busbridges where I outline how they could continue to order kits from me even though I am in Europe.

Reynolds here admits for once that even though he says mistakenly there is only one mention of Viper, he concedes that these letters were about the supply of Viper kits and parts. Hoorah! But he **still refused overall in his decision to admit they were my agents.**

Now I wonder why that was?

KC 37:- Yet another example of Reynolds vacuousness because this was a letter from Cobretti to a potential customer in Holland sent in Jan 1991 quoting for kits.

Yet Reynolds contrives to think that they are selling my body moulds. 'Is this man completely mad?' I asked myself when I saw this comment. One point here worth mentioning is that I gave Cobretti license to sell in the UK only and here they are showing a willingness to try for business abroad, unknown to me and this was MY territory. It shows what untrustworthy bastards they were even before they nicked my business, trade mark and IP.

KC 37/1:- A letter from Cobretti to a potential customer quoting for a kit and put into evidence by me because it showed that the letter heading says they are "Suppliers of Vipers".

To anyone other than Reynolds, this 'Suppliers of Vipers' would meant they were acting as agents for the manufacturer of Vipers (from **me**). He vacuously says that this does not show who owned the mark. What a tosser, I could cry with frustration over this man.

KC 38 & 39:- The documents which showed that when I knew the Busbridges had stolen my trademark and product, I took back my jigs.

He makes no comments here and I have to conclude that he views the criminal actions of the Busbridges as being quite OK. Anything they have done even if it is illegal is fine by him and beyond reproach!

KC 40:- My letter to the Busbridges complaining about their stealing my business etc.

Again no comment from Reynolds. Are you getting the picture now about this man?

KC 42:- The invoice of February 1992 where I had ordered the second batch of Viper brochures as I had run out of the first batch.

All Reynolds can say is he cannot see how they were used. In other words I am such *a twerp, that I go and order another 2,500 brochures just so as I can look at them. Shoot that man for Gods sake! In any case this date is outside his relevant date of May 1992, as said already.*

KC 51:- This is an article by Cobretti in which he lies about how he acquired the trademark.

No comment from Reynolds. This again is showing he sides with RB's actions.

KC 54:- My selection of copies of my adverts from 1986 to the current time of the hearing and which show the gap between Sept 1989 to mid 1991.

I did explain why there was this gap (due to the theft of my business) but it has obviously either gone over his head or more to the point he would rather ignore that and side with RB.

KC 57:- Another copy of an article about Cobretti showing yet another lie by RB as to how he came about the trademark.

Again no comment by Reynolds. I had hoped that evidence like this and a lot more which Reynolds has ignored would show any HO how Robert Busbridge lies throughout his evidence and how he has stolen my trademark and product and is therefore a man who's word cannot be trusted. I was wasting my time.

You may note that above are 28 different evidence documents put in as exhibits and in only 5 has Reynolds put any positive worth to them. I think this tells all don't you think? I also ask you to think about the fact I put in 84 documents and he has picked out only 28, so are we to take that all the rest are rubbish in his eyes and that all their worth has been trashed and ignored?

Robert Busbridges documentary evidence:-

RB 6 & 6a:- Magazine articles about the demise of BRL. No comment from Reynolds and I have to say what relevance are they?

RB 7,7a & 7b:- Is the waffle from RB about the agency document being a forgery. Of course Reynolds thinks the document is of no use as the agreement is a forgery in his warped and biased mind.

RB8:- This is merely the confirmation of the Wheels Abroad order to me at BRL and has no worth to RB's evidence, so why include it as it is really my evidence? Reynolds makes no comment.

RB9:- My letter to Kitcar International re the demise of BRL. Says he will comment in the main body of comment.

RB11:- The copy of the Bechtolsheimer order, which although he says is barely legible and partially reconstructed, he really does not make the kind of adverse comments he made on documents of mine he did not like. I wonder why again?

RB13:- Kunzlis alleged letter to RB selling him the rights to Viper. I have already commented on this and Reynolds does at least say he cannot give it any weight Hurrah! *However the fact that it is obvious it has been forged by RB does not faze Reynolds. Nor does he say that RB should be charged with forgery! I had even included a copy of Kunzli's affidavit that it was a forgery but of course Reynolds ignores that.*

RB14:- A copy of comments about RB's own bankruptcy and why this is included as it is outside the date and only tells us that RB is a useless businessman.

RB15:- No comments as same as RB6a.

RB21:- Copy of a request for a quote for a Viper kit from Kunzli. This is dated outside the relevant date and why it is shown beats means it has no relevance as had Reynolds read my evidence he would have seen that Kunzli and I by then had split.

RB23:- A copy of my Stat Dec for my registration application made in 1996 and well outside the relevant date. Why is it shown and picked out by RB?

RB30:- These are literally dozens of copies of Cobretti adverts and adverts for his copy of my Viper. All are post 1992 and are irrelevant to this case as outside the relevant date and if pre 1989 are irrelevant as he was my agent for BRL. Those between Sept 1989 & June 1992 are few. Reynolds sees little wrong with them and even though most are appallingly badly copied and unreadable and undated, Reynolds shows his bias towards RB by his silence about this.

These documents are 95% all adverts or other material were shown in various places, *post May 1992* and up to the 2000's and are under various trading names. The few documents that relate to pre 1992 are mostly just letters to potential customers and sent out during the time they were agents for me 1989-1991. The few articles included are BRL era and cannot count for anything.

There are no adverts relating to the Sept 1989-May 1992 era at all. Certainly as far as I am concerned the last date that any advert should be counted as within a relevant date, should be no later than June 1991 as that is when they stole my product and trademark.

What I cannot understand is Reynolds trashed all of my adverts which I put in only to show my involvement with the mark Viper from 1986 to 2002, by saying that I showed no adverts between 1989-1991 and they were all BRL era or after 1992. Yet here we hear not a peep out of him over these alleged samples of how Cobretti advertised and marketed this Viper trademark. Does he think that we are all blind and stupid? But then did he care because he knew that there was bugger all I could do about his deception and extreme bias to RB? It is nice to know that the IPO employ such people.

RB33:- A statement by a third party slagging me off. Once more an entirely irrelevant and out of the relevant dates, as it is made in 1997, and is hearsay by a person who knows nothing about me or the BRL business. Why is it in, even though Reynolds does say it doesn't say anything about the ownership of the trademark? He should be trashing or better still not even showing it. Bias again.

Out of the above documents which number 15 he picks out of about 40 exhibits and there are only ***two*** which Reynolds discounts. The rest he makes no anti statements and indeed, mostly he says nothing. If you compare the two sets of documents it becomes clear that in my case he has hardly a good word, pro what the document has said, yet in the case of RB's documents they are all OK. Doesn't this show bias towards RB?

Whilst it seems that I put in many more documents than RB, the opposite is true and RB put in exhibits that were made up of multiples of documents.

Continuing with comments on Reynolds summing up paragraphs.

74/ He now makes another one of his incomprehensible statements that make you wonder what planet he is on, for he says that exhibit RB30 purports to show the volume of trade RB made.

It again shows that he hasn't a clue about business. Apart from the fact that I commented on this above, about that exhibit, over 95% of that exhibit consisted of copies of adverts that were made outside the May 1992 cut off date. They were made in a variety of companies names and not in the name of RB or of Cobretti Engineering. None showed advertising made in the relevant period of Sept 1989 to May 1992. On top of this Reynolds is out of his depth regarding business and how it proves turnover (he calls this 'volumes of trade... very quaint!) If he had ever been in business he would know that you can advertise as much as you like, but that doesn't equate to how much turnover in sales you achieve. Quite what levels of advertising expenditure has to do with whether you own a mark, or whether you are generating heaps of goodwill through **sales**, *beats me.*

On my part I showed my turnover of **sales** *of kits and fully built cars during the relevant period of time as I had to show in my statement that is referred to. Those sales were either made by BL, BRL or Classic Replicas or were made by people under license to do so. Even those sales under license, are sales that are legitimate for me to claim that my mark was generating sales. Sales do not have to made by ME as I only have to show how many sales are made with my trade mark.*

75/ Now he carries on with more of his comments which also show his lack of business acumen and his lack of understanding of the Cobra Replica market. For he says that the fact that I sold 'generic' Cobra parts.

I have explained above on the paragraph that dealt with the exhibit showing all the orders and invoices generated, about this business of the difference between **real cobras** *and Replica Cobras and Vipers. It is only difficult for Mr Reynolds to understand as he seems to have a lack of ability to understand such matters. In that case he should not have been hearing this case, for he ends up out of his depth and I am the one that ends up suffering because of that.*

However he does at the end of this paragraph admit that what I was selling the Busbridges over this period were **Viper** *kits, bodies and chassis as these were the only* products that I was selling. However he bangs on again about the fact that not many referred to Viper. Again I have explained about that above. However you have to wonder once again how a HO can admit that I was indeed selling Viper kits to RB yet somehow I did not own the mark, Viper.

76/ Once again here he is banging on about the lack of the mention in the orders and invoices of the mark Viper.

*That has been explained in depth above. Also it is again apparent that some of the documents that **did state Viper** have been missed by him (deliberately?).*

*However he does again admit that it is not necessary for us to **have to mention the fact that each and every part, body or chassis is a Viper**. This as we both knew full well what commodity/product we were dealing with. This was not a case of me invoicing a member of the public and had that been the case each and every sales invoice would have clearly stated that what was being sold was a Viper body, chassis or kit, or part. This man is totally and utterly inconsistent. One minute berating the fact that adverts and invoices did not mention Viper, then saying that was OK as we both knew what we were dealing in. Why did his summing up and his decision use his perception that the mark was not used by me and that meant I had to have no rights in it because of this?*

77/ This paragraph once again drives me to despair over this man Reynolds and of course the duplicitous arch liar Robert Busbridge. Here Reynolds says that an argument developed between me and RB over what actually the trademark could be applied to. He reproduces an extract from one of RB's statements where RB is waffling on about how the name Viper can only applied to a fully built car. That the body, chassis and parts used cannot be called Viper, only the finished product.

Now here is a prime example where Busbridge has deliberately tried to create a story as fact, which he knows full well is disingenuous and a lie. He tries to have it that Ford makes a universal platform that can be made into a Ford or a Jaguar car. (Ford at that time owned both Jaguar and the UK Ford Motor Co.) So that platform would not be called by a trademark name.

What complete and utter tripe and a deliberate lie, that is as the analogy is completely and technically absurd. For Busbridge knows full well that he is trying to confuse the hearing officer that will hear the case. Hoping that he will be a dickhead that doesn't know the difference between a old style car chassis and a modern monocoque body. For in the kit car world 99.9% of all kit cars are made with a chassis that is particular to that model of kit and nothing else. This because a fibreglass body is not strong enough to give a car the strength it would need. So a steel frame or chassis is made and the body sits on that. That chassis will only suite the body that has been designed to sit on it. So my chassis was a Viper chassis that was totally different from any other Cobra Replica chassis. My body was different to any other body from any other Cobra Replica body and it would only fit my chassis. So by definition that too was a 'Viper' body and so on. The fully built car was obviously a Viper too.

Yet again we have a situation where Reynolds simply did not understand what the hell I or Busbridge were talking about. He could have asked questions at the hearing to educate himself and didn't. He could have researched on the subject and obviously didn't. So he ends up blundering around on a topic he knew nothing about, yet the outcome is that I suffer tremendously from this fact, as you will see.

78/ Now Reynolds makes more statements that show he simply isn't up to the job.

He says that he understands that the point RB was making above was something to do with the 'parts scheme' when what RB has said above has nothing to do with the parts scheme. (427 Universal Parts) and that it is the car not the parts that carry the trademark Viper. So he has been indoctrinated into believing a load of crap and lies. For he now goes on that Cobretti was advertising and selling the **cars!**

No, Cobretti was not advertising cars, they advertised Viper kits that could be built up into cars, and the necessary parts to enable that to happen. He fails to add that they were advertising them **as my agents.**

79/ Now after indulging in many paragraphs of inane waffle that has nothing to do with whether RB stole my trademark, he says that all the arguments as above are not of assistance to RB. It seemed to him that who was marketing the Viper goods is the crux and **hence who would be able to claim ownership of the resulting goodwill.**

This statement made me immediately groan for this absolute dickhead of a man was now saying that anyone who was an agent of a manufacturer could, because they were at the retail end of the supply chain, claim ownership of any trademark. Is the man completely and utterly mad? To give an analogy and one in the car trade:- Any main stream car manufacturer in the UK, who all have dealers (and this is absolutely the same as being an agent), run the risk of losing the rights to their trademarks that apply to all their models of cars that the dealers will be selling to he public. We all know that that is mad and simply not the case.

I have worked in the car dealership world and I know how dealerships work, and I certainly know that no dealer in the world would be able to say 'well I sell the Ford Focus. So therefore I can claim ownership of the trademark, Focus'!

I have already explained in detail why I kept Busbridge as an agent, so that I could concentrate on only the manufacturing of the kits. Now I have this raving lunatic Reynolds saying that by doing this Busbridge can just say 'Ta ever so I'll have your trademark rights, for I have been advertising and selling your kits for 18 months now, so piss off while I rip you off.

You will see how this now pans out.

80/ Here he merely is saying he has set out his overview of the main parts of the evidence and how the Viper was presented to the public. He says as far as he is concerned the business is a 'run off' of the BRL business and the continuation of the Wheels Abroad order proves this.

I simply do not agree with that view at all. The business was set up in a completely different way, many of the models of kit were not continued and the order given to BRL as mentioned was cancelled and reissued to ME at my new company and half of it was subcontracted out to RB by me.

81/ He restates my statement where I say that during the years 1990 to June 1991 the advertising was under my control and vetting.

82/ Here he deals with the example I gave where in Cobrettis advert it is said they were new managers of the retail of Vipers. He goes on to state that most of my documentary evidence is 'of little or no evidential value' and fails to refer to 'Viper' or are outside the relevant period etc.

In other words all of my evidence was irrelevant trash, but as he makes no mention of what RB put in as evidence, one has to take it that all or nearly of that was 'gold plated'! **Does this man not realise he is showing to the world that he is determined to find only for RB?**

Then he has yet another go at the Dr Bechtolsheimer witness statement which he said could have formed a link between me and RB and Viper, but then goes on to restate that it was also trash.

This is simply because Dr B overwrote one word in the last sentence as he wanted to correct it, and this according to Reynolds means that Dr B was only reporting 'what I told him to say' In other words according to this cretinous man Reynolds, I dictated that witness statement and told him a story to spin on my behalf. He is so stupid that he cannot see the fact that this statement is headed by the solicitors firm Coles Miller and was done for my 2000 forgery trial, seems to ring no bells in Reynolds empty head. For I had absolutely no contact over that statement with Dr B as it was Coles who rang him up and Coles who crafted the letter after consultation with Dr B.

Let us see what changes Dr B made to the statement. Coles had written 'Mr Cook said that if I were anxious to have the car built immediately he could arrange for Cobretti to build the car and that he would supply the necessary kit, which he did.' Dr B crossed out 'and that' and wrote under the following; 'I don't know if the kit was supplied by Mr Cook or if Cobretti had one in stock.

Also Coles after the above wrote 'To my knowledge and belief Cobretti Engineers were at this time working as agents for Mr Cook' He crossed out 'and belief' and wrote 'because Mr Cook had told me so'.

Now I ask anybody with average intelligence 'what does all that say to you?' First it was obviously Dr B's writing and he had just objected to the way some things had been said. The statement about him not knowing if Cobretti had one in stock or whether I had supplied one, is so irrelevant to this case as to not be worth commenting on. It certainly does not imply anything untoward or whether Cobretti was my agent or not. Then he merely says that he could only know that Cobretti were my agents because I had told them so. What is the big deal about that, I ask? I cannot believe that when he visited them to place the order that Cobretti did not agree they were my agents. Then we have the fact that I included in my exhibits the very orders RB gave me for all the parts to make this car. So Reynolds could see that the kit and parts were indeed ordered off me, thus making what Dr B had said, correct.

Another factor one has to take into account is that is the Bechtolsheimer statement could have shown a link between RB and myself, (as Reynolds says) what the hell did all the orders from RB to me and the invoices for same, provide, if not another link? Then there are also others links Reynolds cannot or will not see.

As far as I am concerned Reynolds was working to his own agenda (or more probably the IPO's agenda) because as Reynolds says this document is important, it shows that (a) I was advertising a magazine for Viper cars so much so that Dr B saw it and called out of the blue on me and (b) after asking me why both my advert and Cobrettis adverts were for a car that was obviously the same, that I had told him that Cobretti were my agents and sold my kits etc.

Other facts in my evidence show all this to be the true facts, such as the invoice from Cobretti to me for this very kit, and that after the car had been built as Dr B was dissatisfied with its quality, he came to me to have it sorted and not to RB. (in actual fact he drove it all the way to Germany for this and then when I had finished he had me sell it for him). Now why would he do all that if he did not recognise me as the manufacturer of that kit?

Why was Reynolds unable to come to the conclusion that here, the evidence was overwhelming as here was a case that a man sees my advert for the Viper, comes to me to have it built and as I am already building a car, I am willing to just pass over £25,000 worth of order to someone else who is not even an agent of mine? If Reynolds was not biased or a screaming vacuous dickhead, that is what he would have been deliberating on. However if he has been programmed to make sure this case goes against me, he would find some way of trashing this piece of evidence.

I pointed all that out in my evidence, but Reynolds chose to ignore my comments. So what is it to be? I know what I think, but you can take your pick of which explanation YOU go for. One point you should realise is that, as Reynolds had said when making snide comments on the fact that as far as he was concerned the most important document in this case of the agency agreement, was likely to be a forgery. He says to explain why he thinks that by using the fact that in civil law one does not have to prove things 100%, but cases can be decided on the balance of probabilities. In all probability he said, that document had to be forged. He ignores the fact that to win the forgery allegation the CPS had to prove things to the higher level than in a civil case and could not do so. So why is he allowed to, as it were, prosecute this case a 2nd time on a lower level of evidence AND with absolutely no evidence, just the words of the liar Busbridge?

Now with all my crucial exhibit documents like this Bechtolsheimer one and others, he refuses to apply the same evidence level to them. Anyone else would think that in all probability it was safe to accept them as true documents of worth using "the balance of probabilities" level of evidence. So it is another example of his bias and duplicity and double standards.

83/ Reynolds is again repeating that out of all my evidence of adverts, none show me advertising the Viper, during the 1898-1992 period.

Yet I had provided explanations as to why this was and they included that from mid 1991 to mid 1992 RB had stolen my business off me. In the above paragraph we have Dr B saying he saw one of my adverts and that is why he wanted me to build his car. Then there is the question as to whose car was I building when he called in Jan 1991? That was a car for a Belgian who also saw my advert and had me build a car. Had I known that I was going to have to suffer all the crap I had to suffer, thanks to the lies of Busbridge, I would have kept documentary evidence to show things clearly.

However because of this constant reference to my not advertising the mark, I went to great pains to explain that if you are a manufacturer and you decide not to involve yourself in retailing your product and take on a dealer or agent to do that and you give them the right to use your mark, then the advertising is down to them. Yet according to Reynolds this means you are stuffed, especially when you get tossers like him poking into your business and making up fairy tales about how you have stuffed yourself up. Sure I stuffed up myself for being a trusting fool with the ratbags at Cobretti.

84/ Here we have even more vacuous remarks by Reynolds for he goes on again about my adverts for 427 parts. According to him this is consistent with my wanting to distance myself from any association with BRL. Really it makes me so mad I could happily throttle this old buffoon. I have gone into great depths about what the 427 parts meant and it was not that they were Cobra parts, for Cobra parts means the **real Cobra** who's parts are not all the same as parts for **replicas!**

However it is what he says next which wants me sending round a van to his house full of men in white coats to cart him off. For apart from the nonsense he states about this being an example of me wanting to distance myself from BRL (it was nine months along the road from that and the public had forgotten all about BRL) **and 'there is no mention of Viper'** (in the advert).

To repeat for the umpteenth time the 427 parts were **not for Vipers** but for all other makes of Cobra Replicas... Have you got it Reynolds? Obviously not! But it is yet another nail in my coffin in this opposition case, as you will see.

85/ We have here yet another reference to the mass of poorly copied adverts from RB.

I have commented at length about these above. How over 95% of them are from post May 1992, only one from Sept 1989–May 1992. He says that many of these adverts have their date handwritten on them, the alleged date of publication that is. In my evidence, any handwriting on evidence he says is not allowed, but because he is biased, with RB's evidence it is allowed! He says that RB gives a list of the publications and the claimed dates and that is perfectly OK. We can believe what RB says as he in the eyes of Reynolds is gold plated. He overlooks the fact that this list does not cover every document in this bundle of evidence. His last statement beggars belief and I wonder if he is looking at the same bundle of adverts as I am. I repeat over 95% were for after May 1992 and **only one refers to Sept 1989 to May 1992**. A lot are simply letters he sent out, to potential customers, which not credible evidence of anything.

86/ He says at the hearing he asked me if there was evidence 'that the advertising was under my control and whether for instance there was an agreed schedule of advertising'

I had said our agreement on advertising was verbal and that I had insisted it be monthly and should show that they were 'Under new management'. Of course the execrable Busbridge denied all that and we will see who Reynolds believed.

Of course, once again had I known what would go on to happen to me over all this, I would have not trusted them and got absolutely **everything** in writing. (And they would then have been said by RB to have been forged.) However if we all possessed hindsight what a wonderful world it would be, especially when we end up have to deal with absolute tossers like Reynolds (who can go on and ruin your life).

It has to be pointed out here that many of the copies of adverts that RB said in handwriting on them, were from the relevant period, were in actual fact lies, as they were after May 1992. Had I known how Reynolds would conduct this case (hindsight again) I would have looked more seriously at all of them and would have raised objections. Yet I cannot help thinking that I have raised objections throughout this case only to be ignored every time by Reynolds.

87/ Here we have an example of what I have just said above for Reynolds quotes a Which Kit Guide Advert.

Now this advert is said to appear **summer 1990 and contains lies put out by RB as to how they are now manufacturers of Viper**. All the ways that I pointed out to Reynolds as to how RB had lied to various magazines, has been comprehensively ignored by Reynolds. On top of that there is something deeply suspicious about this advert. There is only one such advert in the whole bundle and it says that their address is in Bishopford Rd, Morden. Yet in the Summer of 1990 they were not at this address for it was a two car workshop and the business I had given them alone required a much bigger workshop. They were in their workshop at Westmead Business Centre at August 1990 as seen on many of the letters they supplied in this bundle of advertising evidence. Anyhow it is headed Cobretti Viper and I simply would not have allowed that as it was not a Cobretti Viper, that at that date they were advertising, but a Classic Replicas Viper and my verbal arrangement with them is that all adverts were to call it just a 'Viper'.

The wording in this example advert is nothing more than a pack of lies that was used by the Busbridges when they stole my product after June 1991. My continual pointing this out in my statements has been ignored by Reynolds throughout and he obviously chooses for reasons best known to him to side with what RB says. Although he must be able to see the truth of what happened and exactly what the Busbridges decided to do. Once again one has to question what went on with Reynolds.

88/ Now he says that he finds it 'scarcely credible that I would have accepted Cobretti's claim to have taken over the Brightwheel Cobra business

Well clever clogs Reynolds, did I know what they were saying behind my back? They did not do many adverts, only one a month in Which Kit and I was unaware that they had taken out adverts in this guide. Plus Reynolds is being disingenuous once again, for all the claims that Cobretti made such as this, were made post June 1991 after I went to Switzerland. I cannot be held to book for that, not by anyone who is independent and has an open mind, that is!

Reynolds now refers to other instances of similar claims and refers to one in Car Builder June 1991 (after I had departed) and all the others he refers to are post June 1992. Yet of course he does not stick to the same rules for RB as he does with me.

89/ Here he concludes from all our evidence that:

(a) After BRL I continued to make Viper parts and kits.

(b) I elected to distance myself from the BRL business (the deceased business, I presume) but then astonishingly claims that this means also from the Viper name.

(c) My advert for 427 parts made no mention of the Viper.

(d) All advertising was by and in the name of Cobretti making no mention of me or Classic Replicas. He is not persuaded I had any control over advertising in any way.

(e) That Cobretti openly claimed it had taken over the business of BRL.

(f) No evidence I took steps to correct the messages put out by Cobretti about how they had taken over the BRL business, if I felt that it was a misrepresentation.

Of course all of the above needs commenting on as all are ludicrous and totally mistaken assumptions.

(a) Well at least he admits that after BRL I continued to make Viper kits and parts

but what he does not say and this is important, is that **I continued to make fully built cars after BRL.** In fact I made three cars and passed four onto Cobretti. If these cars were not Vipers, then what were they, I ask his Lordship?

(b) How does he make this decision and for how long did that go on for. I say I did no such thing as the BRL business was defunct and therefore nothing to distance myself from. I did wish to make myself scarce for obvious reasons, but only for a couple of months, and then I was back in the open. The astonishing claim that by making myself scarce for such short period means I also that I was also distancing myself from my trademark, is so vacuous that it defies logical explanation as to how he comes to that assumption. He gives no reasons as to how he can come to this statement. I can; it suits his fairy story which he has to make up so as to be able to eventually take my trademark away from me. It is painfully obvious as you read all of this biased document, as to where he is heading, and as I have said, I believe that he has been programmed to do his dirtiest on behalf of the IPO. You may scoff at this claim, but you have to read the whole of this story, from beginning to end to see how the IPO have behaved towards me from day one, over and over again. There emerges a clear course of actions and non actions, which are not normal and the only assumption from all that is that they wanted me to lose.

(c) He still doesn't get the true picture about the 427 Parts Scheme and I cannot believe he is that thick that he cannot get it. The 427 parts adverts of course would not mention the trademark as they were advertising non Viper parts!

(d) Why should Cobretti's adverts mention me or Classic Replicas? In the trade, the mark Viper was synonymous with me and Cobretti only advertised with one magazine in the relevant period and it's owner was in regular contact with me and knew what I was doing with the Busbridges. In fact the advert that RB puts into evidence that Reynolds glows about, for a free Viper to be given away as a prize, was set up by me and the kit was to be donated by me. It is quite normal for manufacturers who take on agents and dealers, not to be mentioned themselves in adverts instigated by those agents. In the kitcar world of which Reynolds is entirely ignorant, it happens all the time that various kitcars are mentioned in the press by their model name (trademark) and the actual manufacturer is not mentioned, as in that small world everyone knows who makes each model of kit. So in the case of Cobra replicas you get the following models mentioned Dax, Pilgrim, SR, Hawk, CR, and so on. They are all made by manufacturers who have company names that are different to the trademark itself. So why is he making this cretinous remark? Because he has little real evidence that he can properly use to make a decision against me, so he has to make up stories to justify himself. He has to twist certain evidence to suit his decision making.

(e) Then he compounds his crass and cretinous remarks by saying he thinks I had no control over the advertising. He produces no clear evidence to back up such an assumption, so that means he takes RB's word for it. But hey! There was someone else involved in all this... his brother Martin. Has Reynolds ever mentioned him in this long and sorry document, not on your life. It is as if he never existed. Yet you will see eventually what he has to say about all these goings on between Sept 1989 and May 1992 and about the advertising and whether I had any input to the advertising which Reynolds says I did not. Later on in this story you will see that RB puts a document into evidence that clearly shows me paying my part for advertising. Unfortunately for me I did not keep every scrap of paper that dealt with these times. It appears RB did and recently in 2010 he put in documentary evidence into the last hearing, that helps me, as they were copies of other invoices I sent them, which I never had copies of, and included the invoice where it shows me contributing to advertising. Also an invoice that showed me charging them for brochures. Had Reynolds been truly unbiased and a top hearing officer he would not have come to such firm conclusions about a lot of things when there was no collaborating evidence from Martin or anyone else for that matter.

(f) Once more we have a statement by Reynolds that shows his appalling ignorance and inability to delve more deeply into the story, ask questions about stuff he could not have been sure of etc. He absolutely refuses to believe my explanation about why their adverts in this time to when I left for Switzerland stated that they were 'managing' the sales of Vipers, because that was **exactly** doing, **managing** them, for **me**! And why those adverts did not call this car a Cobretti Viper, as it then became called after my back was turned? Similarly he refuses to believe my explanation as to why the minute I left the country the adverts changed and all editorials contained stories about how Cobretti were now 'manufacturing' the Viper and how they justified themselves being able to do this. He obviously sees nothing wrong in them having stolen my designs, which then gave them the opportunity to be able to apply my trademark to their copies. For without a product the trademark is of no use! So how was I supposed to stop them from making these tales up in the press? I had not been able to stop them from carrying out a far more difficult process of theft which required a physical effort. This being the copying of my body and chassis. Where the telling of tales to magazines requires no effort at all.

First of all to be able to complain or take steps to put a stop to their subterfuge I had to know about it. How do I get to know about it in a foreign country? It is a fact that I did not get to see many of these articles and adverts until many months later when I was back in the UK. They were history by then. Plus Reynolds could see that when I did find out about the copying of my kit car and the use of my trademark, **I did complain straight away!** What good did it do? Nothing, is the answer and Reynolds could see from the documentary evidence that in reply to my letter to them from Germany, they merely replied cockily that 'they noted my comments and put them on file' So for Reynolds to make this remark beggars belief and again shows his bias for Busbridge. You cannot force someone to stop a course of action they want to take (and even though Reynolds refuses to acknowledge that the likely reason for their actions was greed, by hoping to get a lot of money off Chrysler for the mark and here he obviously thinks that too is OK) apart from going round and breaking their legs or worse. Or if you are rich like his Lordship you can engage one of his cronies, a mega expensive IP lawyer to take immediate High Court action to take out an injunction to stop their crooked games.

These comments and reasons given highlight his bias and slanted thinking.

Now Reynolds says he turns to what the law says… and that filled me up to the brim with overflowing confidence. This because my attitude to British Law and all those that are engaged in the top end of it, is far from complimentary. In fact I feel another book coming on!

90/ Reynolds says that it is well known that goodwill does not exist away from the business to which it is attached. That goodwill will not necessarily go to the manufacturer or supplier of goods and may go to the agent or dealer. He goes on to quote case law Medgen Inc V Passion for Life Products in 2001.

Then he gives an example of a case of which I will not state word for word, as it is too long. The gist of it is that a US manufacturer took on a UK distributor and this entity was claiming all the goodwill because they sold it in this country under their name and the public did not know of the manufacturer, and the advertising the distributor did made no reference to the US manufacturer. Had there been any problem with the product they would have gone to the distributor and not the US manufacturer.

Yet this example is light years away from any similarity to my case and I say it is disingenuous to put it forward as an example of how he can then go on to say that RB can steal my IP, using this as an excuse.

Now this is what I mean about British Law. This seems a typical example of how in Britain we have laws and Judges and Hearing officers who make what I think are wholly vacuous decisions as they did in finding for the UK distributor. If it was heard by an IPO hearing, I would not be surprised if Reynolds was the hearing officer. I will not go into why I think that decision was barmy as I have my own case to defend. In my case I was in this country AND I was manufacturing and selling the product too, and any problems with what I supplied RB with they would have come back to me for sure. It is not comparable. Also, for how many years in the other case, did the agent sell that product for? In my case RB only sold my product on my behalf before stealing it, **for a miserable 18 months!** Yet in Reynolds corrupt mind that enable this conman to be able to legally steal all my IP and my business! Do you agree this is lawful and right?

91/ In relation to applying it to my case as Reynolds now does, shows again just how Reynolds is willing to twist facts to enable him to say with conviction, his decision is that the above case can be applied to mine. Firstly he says that using the principles of the above case it suggests that Cobretti could claim the benefit of goodwill arising from the trade under the mark Viper after BRL's demise.

By that statement he is suggesting that the minute BRL stopped trading, that was what they could claim, just because they had been BRL's agents?

Now the above case did not as far as I could see involve a manufacturer that had ceased to trade. Then he completely ignores the fact that while BRL was trading, did it own the trademark? Yet he has said throughout the above chapters, that after BRL 'I was manufacturing and selling to Cobretti, VIPERS'. He therefore is admitting that I owned the mark and surely I must own it as I had already proved that I had a claim to it, and that is why I got registration in 1998. He is inconsistent. His assertions about goodwill are nonsense. I would like someone to tell me how anyone can just take over anything that does not belong to them. In any case the goodwill the Jag based Viper belonged to me and not BRL.

Then we have the fact that while BRL was trading, Cobretti was only an agent for a small part of the UK. When BRL ceased to trade, Cobretti were in no position to be able to trade in anything and take over the BRL business as Reynolds says they could do, as they had no expertise nor machinery, nor any money, to be able to manufacture and sell Vipers. I did and I owned the mark and the design rights to the chassis and was able to set up a manufacturing process. So without my cooperating with them they would have had no ability to trade in goods with the trademark Viper attached to them, or benefit from this **'goodwill'**.

Another fact unlike the above case is that, in that case the manufacturer was not in this country and I was. Not only that, I was also selling and advertising the Viper myself. I have already described how that was the case. That is a big difference between these two cases and which Reynolds ignores. Also in my case there was no packaging involved which played an important part in that case.

He says that Cobretti did all the marketing and sales of the products, and once again he is wrong as he ignores the fact that I was advertising the VIPER fully built, and what was being carried out by the Busbridges through Cobretti and was through an agreement with me, which Reynolds refuses to rely on, having trashed it. My adverts did not have to state my name (Cook) or Classic Replicas or even the trademark Viper for reasons I have already stated above. Anyone ringing me from that advert, as many did, resulting in two sales for fully built cars which were ordered from me, got through to me where I said who I was and all the quotes given were in writing and on Classic Replicas headed paper, plus they got Viper brochures. On top of that I was the one producing of colour brochures as part of the marketing process and that can be seen by previous evidence, which were used in this marketing Reynolds said RB was doing for the Viper mark.

He then mentions the trade and presumably he means suppliers of general auto parts as would be needed to complete a car, would understand that BRL had ceased and Cobretti had picked up the reins of the reins of the defunct business. Excuse me Reynolds, you are a raging ignoramus, for you know nothing about what went on in these specific instances, as you were not there. How dare you make up fairy tales to suite your biased mind!! You know nothing about how the business of making kits or fully built cars operates, yet you are somehow a World Authority and can make these statements.

First of all, all the trade people I dealt with at BRL knew full well that when it ceased I had carried on to make the product, as Classic Replicas. As I have said no trade company was owed money by BRL and I carried on using those same trade suppliers in order to **make my Viper cars** and obtain Viper specific parts and universal Cobra Replica parts and general automotive parts. Most of my trade suppliers did not do business with Cobretti as they had their own trade suppliers. So your fairy story made up to suit your twisted biased ideas, are totally false. How you can say that Cobretti picked up the 'reins' of the BRL business is beyond me, as they came crawling to me as Martin Busbridge has now testified, in 2010, but more about that later on.

Reynolds also says that informed kit car enthusiasts would also know that Cobretti had taken over BRL's business. Now Mr Reynolds how do you come to that conclusion, where is your evidence that that was the case? How about those who would have heard through the grapevine that I was still involved or those that saw and met me at kit car shows when I was helping Cobretti? How about those who rang Which Kit and spoke to the owner Peter Filby to ask if I were still involved? How about those with enquiring minds who on seeing the adverts would ask themselves as to how they were only managing the sale of Vipers, if they supposed to have taken over the 'reins' of the whole business? Fancy answering those questions, your Lordship? Like I said you are an ignoramus and unfortunately for me, people like you act like God in our useless judicial systems and get away with it after having ruined peoples lives and businesses.

Now Reynolds makes such an ill informed statement that he should be transported to Australia! He says that any customer that bought a product that they had a problem with, would go back to only Cobretti to get it fixed or sorted. Now how does he justify making such a sweeping statement as if it were fact.

The true fact is anything that I supplied to Cobretti would come back to me if there was any fault. There is no way that Cobretti would have done otherwise as they had no **expertise, experience or tools to do repairs to bodies or chassis etc**, and once again this is yet another fairy tale that Reynolds makes up to fit his hypothesis. Of course he did not know that Dr Bechtolsheimer did not in 1992, go back to RB to put right the car he built, **he came to me!** Had I known Reynolds was going to come up with this gem of a statement I would have made sure in my statements he was told about Dr B's actions.

Reynolds says that this position would have lasted from Sept 1989 right through to May 1992 and even while I was in Switzerland. Of course he once again ignores the reality and truth of what happened, For once my back was turned the public were no longer getting supplied with kits manufactured by me as the Busbridges had by now copied my product and stolen my UK business off me and the mark (with **Reynolds** approval it seems). They were only able to fund this copying because Martin borrwed money against his house...more on that later.

He says my letters to the Busbridges complaining about this stealing, does not shed light as to who owned the mark. Yet elsewhere in his document he stated that I was making the Viper and selling it to Cobretti and he for the umpteenth time ignores the fact that I had proved I owned the mark to his own bosses the IPO at the Chrysler hearing in 1998.

92/ He says here that he takes the view that at May1992 Cobretti Engineering was entitled to claim ownership of the mark Viper.
I think I have commented at length at what I think about this view.

93/ Now he says that he has ignored the argument I made that Busbridge only wanted the mark to sell it to Chrysler.
This even though I provided evidence of this. Reynolds prefers to say that I too tried to sell it to Chrysler and he therefore ignores my evidence which shows this to not be the case as it was they who approached me every time. That is a completely different scenario to the one that existed with RB.

94/ He says that the opposition fails under Section 17(1).

95/ Now he states Section 11 which deals with registering a trademark that would cause confusion etc.

96/ Basically he trashes this as well by saying it will not cause confusion.

97/ He says that under Section 11 my opposition fails as well.

98,99,100 & 101/ He states that my opposition under section 12 must also fail as Busbridge filed his registration before me.
He does not take into account the fact that Busbridge had no legal right to even apply, because of the fact he went bankrupt and that when the partnership failed he lost rights to all the assets (if indeed they owned the asset of the trade mark at all) as they were not sold to him by his partner and the application made in both their names was also illegal as Martin never gave his permission to make it. Thus Reynolds ignore partnership law. It should also be asked, can anyone just apply for any trade mark that may already belong to someone else but not registered but who has then gone on to prove ownership to a date well before the applicant can prove?

102/ **the assignments (alleged)** It is said that the application in the name of Cobretti Engineering (a partnership) had two changes of Ownership recorded since the application in May1992.

103/ It is said that on the 22nd Oct 1992 Autotrak Ltd was assigned the assets of Cobretti. This was not recorded by the IPO until 2002. It was said that the assignment was not perfected (made legal) until an Addendum was added at a later and at an unknown date.
Reynolds conveniently does another of his assuming exercises by saying it was probably done at the time of the filing. He also ignores the fact that RB did not have permission of Martin to assign the assets to Autotrak? Proving once again that in

Reynolds mind Martin is invisible and partnership laws don't exist.

104/ Another assignment was said to have been made on 18th March 2002 which now took it to Robert Busbridge.

105/ The IPO have recorded these and the application now stands in Robert Busbridges name only.

106/ Reynolds now says that I objected to the legality of these assignments by saying that in 1993 Cobretti Engineering went bankrupt and Busbridge cannot resurrect Cobretti so that all these assignments can be made legal. He says that I had expanded on my claim in my evidence in fuller detail.

107/ He says my claim gives rise to a number of issues. Is it open to me to be able to challenge the legality of these assignments in the grounds of an Opposition?

My answer to why I did so, is that Busbridge put in copies of these two alleged assignments into his evidence. They looked amateurishly done and when I saw them for the first time in 2003, my immediate reaction was why haven't I seen these before and why has it taken him 10 years to notify the IPO of the one allegedly done in 1992? My view was that as he knew my opposition was coming up soon, I would make much of the fact that he had become bankrupt in 1993 after his application of 1992. So how could he have been able to proceed with the application? If he could show that in fact the application as an asset had moved away and before his bankruptcy, to a limited company, now how convenient would that be. He ends up with it on paper, showing that he doesn't own it. So he now has to show before the hearing, the application asset is back with him. Not to mention that how can he still have HIS application remain ongoing when he is producing paperwork that is supposed to show he no longer owned it from 1992 through to 2002 as this Autotrak Ltd did and he had suffered a three year period through bankruptcy when he could not legally trade anyway!

As I say I was very suspicious of it all and the first assignment document was so amateurishly done with no payments having been made. It certainly had not been done by a lawyer. So I swotted up on assignments and under the TMA 1938 he had broken several of the laws by not putting in the notification within 6 months, was for no consideration and it appeared that the IPO should have made sure that it had been done legally.

So as he himself had brought it into the open, I felt I had to make these concerns known. This is what Reynolds now was addressing and he admits that there was the question as to whether the IPO had been right to record these two assignments.

108 to 116/ He here waffles on and on and I will not repeat what he has said as you can read elsewhere what he has said.. The main thing is that eventually he says that he thinks that the recording of those assignments were errors of procedure by the IPO (another example of IPO errors which have blighted me) and that the IPO should deal with that and the application, which if you remember had been changed into Roberts name only, should go back to being only in the original names of Cobretti Engineering (a partnership).

That for me was a minor victory, but how could a registration be given to a partnership that was no longer in force and had not been since 1992, and a company no longer in business. Even after all that, the IPO still went on to make several more errors that taxed me and I had to lay complaints. They still gave him a registration certificate in his name, thus giving him the ability to go round swaggering and boasting how he had beaten me, and waving this incorrect document. I had to get that changed.

That was now the end of a disastrous event for me and I just could not understand how all the mistakes that I felt had been made when it was obvious what had gone on with this criminally minded person, Robert Busbridge.

It was bad enough that the IPO had allowed Busbridge to be able to trade with my mark since 1992, by allowing him to keep this application in and to ignore all my protestations that it should have been made null and void due to the break-up of the partnership and his bankruptcy. Now it had just given him carte blanche to carry on.

I could not appeal as I have already said, as under the 1938 Act it had to be at the High Court and I could not afford a potential cost of £20,000 plus. So I had to give up and let that warped decision stand, to the delight of Robert Busbridge and his friends in Kit Car magazine (Mr Den Tanner) who had been backing him for years.

How the decision should really have read…

At this point I have to ask you, the reader, who I will take it are an independent person, what you think about this matter up to this point of the story. You have read the history of my involvement with the product and the trademark and what RB has said in evidence, what I have said in evidence and what this Reynolds bloke has said about the hearing.

I say that I think that any intelligent, thinking, fair minded and independent person would on having read all of the above, could only come to one conclusion. That is that the hearing before Hearing Officer Reynolds was a travesty and an injustice of the first order.

What Reynolds should have said is as follows;

"The evidence already on file at the IPO shows that Mr Cook had proved in 1998, when he opposed Chrysler, that he had the earliest use of this mark, going back to Jan 1986. That on showing to the IPO HO this evidence, he was granted registration. That Mr Busbridge could not show that he or his brother, trading as Cobretti Engineering, had used the mark in their own and legal right before June 1991. (This even though I say his use was illegal as how can theft be legal.)

That using the level of evidence as used in civil cases, which required only for there to be a "balance of probabilities" it had been shown that Mr Cook carried on the business of making Viper kits and parts after the demise of BRL. That he was able to do that as he had rights to the copyright of the product as he had designed them and rights to the trademark as shown in his case against Chrysler. That case covered a time period up to and including Jan 1990, which was *after* the demise of BRL.

That the balance of probabilities was that he had taken on Cobretti and the Busbridges as continuing agents for his new company in Oct 1989. This having been shown by the facts that firstly an agreement was entered into to give them an agency for Classic Replicas and secondly the supply of kits and parts to them from end of 1989 through to mid 1991. On top of that, the passing over to them of substantial orders to the value of over £100,000 over that period, would surely never have been made to a third party that had not been an agent of Classic Replicas. It was inconceivable that any sensible businessman would hand over to a non agent, such high value orders especially when he could have taken on locally sub contractors to build those cars. Thus accruing the high profit levels in them.

Furthermore the funding by Mr Cook of a demonstrator which Mr Busbridge was paid to construct in order to give Mr Cook and Cobretti the ability to market a new version of the Viper, would not have been done by a sensible businessman, if Cobretti had not been agents.

The advertising and marketing on the balance of probabilities was under the control of Mr Cook and that was shown by the fact that Cobretti's adverts said they were *"managing"* the sales of Vipers and not 'manufacturing' them. Also the fact that Mr Cook had paid for marketing tools as in the printing of brochures so that Cobretti could send brochures to their potential customers and use them at kitcar shows, showed that Mr Cook had paid for such marketing tools and why would he do that if he had no say in advertising and marketing.

The question of did he pay for a part of the advertising as he claimed and which RB denied was inconclusive as neither side was able to, at that time, show evidence as to what was the real case. That had Martin been part of the application and evidence process, we would have had his evidence which could have been at odds with Roberts evidence, not only about advertising and marketing but over much of the evidence.

The accusations that Mr Cook forged the agreement document had not been proved at a higher Court and using higher levels of proof, so that I am not going to interfere with that Courts decision, nor to try to try that case a second time. That the evidence from the second signatory, Martin Busbridge was absent. So to make a ruling on whether it was a forgery was doubly out of the question.

Mr Busbridges evidence throughout had shown many inconsistencies and and contained many statements against Mr Cook that amount to invective, which is not allowed in evidence as per CPR's on evidence. That it was apparent that deliberate lies had been indulged in by RB which Mr Cook had proved to be so, by documentary evidence, including a document said to have come from a Mr Kunzli which was said by Mr Kunzli in an affidavit, was a forgery. This should be investigated and pursued by the relevant body.

The evidence from Dr Bechtolsheimer on balance, showed that he had seen an advert by Mr Cook, despite it being said that Mr Cook never advertised the Viper, and that he had been directed by Mr Cook to Cobretti as they were his agents and could build it for Dr Bechtolsheimer as Mr Cook was too busy. This again on balance, showed RB was an agent of Mr Cook and Mr Cook did advertise his product which was known as a *Viper*. The picture shown in the advert could only have been a *Viper* due to its distinctive shape which was well known in the kitcar and even the mainstream car trade and the telephone number shown was that of Classic Replicas as shown on their letter headings in evidence.

Finally the claim that because Mr Busbridge applied before Mr Cook to register the mark Viper, he has the earlier right, has to fail as the IPO put his application on hold because they saw that the evidence supplied by Mr Cook showed an earlier right and it was right that he should exercise this right against Chrysler who applied before Busbridge and if successful he would have the registration and the Busbridge application would fail as it could not show an earlier usage or right to Mr Cooks claim.

So I have to find that Mr Busbridge has not proved any rights to the mark and his application has to fail."

Now that is the kind of decision Reynolds should have come to, based on all the evidence you have seen above, or at least along those lines.

What you have seen through the above story is a travesty and an injustice, that defies belief and unfortunately is the type one sees in British courts by damn awful judges who simply defy description and are in effect corrupt… what do you think?

What happened after Reynolds?

Throughout the rest of 2004 after the decision document of Reynolds which was issued in late July 2004, I had to contact the IPO many times to get them to carry out the decision by Reynolds that the Registration of the Mark had to be put into the name of the original applicants, namely "Cobretti Engineering (a partnership)." I heard nothing from the IPO as to who or when there was to be action taken to determine this issue about the alleged assignments, as Reynolds said had to take place.

Some time later in 2005 the IPO notified me that a hearing would be held sometime in August 2005, to consider the issues about the assignments. So it took these incompetents over a year to even get round to having a hearing. I was barred from attending this hearing or putting in evidence to it, which I found to be inexplicable and yet another weird way the IPO works and their ridiculous rules. The hearing would not have taken place had I not made the submissions at the Reynolds hearing about the alleged assignments. What would happen now was of direct interest to me as I was still the other registered owner of the mark Viper.

Chapter Fifteen
The Hearing Held by a Mr Landau into Irregularities in the Evidence in the Reynolds Hearing

I eventually got the decision document which was dated the 31st August 2005. (Landau got this together in record time as the hearing was only on the 24th August.) It is clear that Robert Busbridge was present and he supplied the hearing with five copies of letters mainly from his solicitors Taylor Willcox. (Now here I have to ask why is it that I was considered when it came to sending me this copy of the decision, yet I could not attend the hearing?)

This document is 25 pages long but the first 4 and a half pages only repeated what Reynolds had said in certain paragraphs of his document numbered 102-116, which dealt with these assignments. Landau now goes on to start making his comments on what happened after the opposition decision and my not appealing, meant that the decision of Reynolds had became final. He says in paragraph 3:

3/ On the 26th Nov 2004 the IPO got a letter from RB with a form TM16 which is a form to register a change of name of the proprietor. The form stated that the current proprietor was Autotrak Ltd and the new one was RB. It was signed by G.Busbridge (wife of RB) and an assignment document was attached. Another TM16 was included which said that the current proprietor was Cobretti Engineering and the new one was Autotrak Ltd. This had taken place on 22nd Oct 1992 and it was signed by RB in his position as partner. It too was accompanied by an assignment document saying all the stock and assets including Cobretti and Viper trademarks had been purchased by Autotrak Ltd from the former proprietors of Cobretti Engineering. *Signed by three people who Landau does not state who they are, but on examination I see that one is RB, the second is his wife and the witness is Colin Bruce a person RB was deeply involved with. Here the big point is that GD Busbridge is not the legal other partner of the Cobretti Engineering. As the document has no heading as to whether it comes from Cobretti Engineering or Autotrak Ltd I cannot see what legal worth it is. Certainly if assets from the partnership were being assigned to somewhere else, then surely both partners would have had to sign any documentation and at the date on this document of 22nd October 1992, Martin the other partner had been gone since June. (Although he could have signed if asked as RB knew where he was) So I say that this document is not legal in any way. What will*

Landau make of that?

The addendum which has obviously been added and at a later date, when they realised that to be a 'legal' document of assignment it had to be made for a consideration or money had to pass hands if it was going to be allowed as evidence.

Now these documents had been offered to the IPO in 2002, when they sent me copies and that started my complaints to the IPO that they were not bona-fide and my saying that, in my statement before Reynolds. Hence his edict that these had to be looked into. Yet here we have this cheeky git (RB) trying it on again in 2005 **After Reynolds had decreed that the application should remain in the partnership name and not in Robert Busbridges name, until it had been sorted by the IPO.**

It goes to show how slack the IPO are in that they did not appear to immediately tell RB to hold off until they had taken steps to look into the whole business of these assignments. It shows what a slippery, crooked man RB is and how he ran rings round the IPO. Also the company Autotrak Ltd had by then been struck off as I have already pointed out and this to the IPO. Does anything ever sink into their thick heads?

4/ Next we have RB quickly following the TM16's up, with a request on the 29th Nov 2004 to renew his registration and in his own name. This even though both he and I had been told that his registration was to be held in the partnership name only, this by Reynolds.

Landau now goes on to say that because of failings in the registry, leading to confusion and incorrect statements as to the status of the trademark and the TM16's that RB had submitted . They wrote to his Patent Agents Reddie and Gross to point this out and then they wrote to RB himself on the 4th Feb 2005. Landau shows copies of this and all the other letters that followed.

<u>This just shows how dysfunctional the IPO are.</u> They simply do not have a handle on what is going on with this case and they seem totally unable to keep pace with the goings on of RB and his masses of lies and crooked actions.

5/ It is apparent to me that the IPO had completely ignored the decision and edict of Reynolds that the IPO had to sort these alleged assignments and that is why there had been no action taken by the IPO since July 2004, even though I had been writing to them complaining that RB had a registration document in the incorrect name. You couldn't make these people up! (Littlejohn in The Mail should write a piece on this incompetent mob as he seems to think the same about civil servants as I do! None of them would last 5 minutes in business!)

In their letter to RB of the 4th Feb, they said that before they could consider his requests they needed to ask him some questions re the first alleged assignment. Do not forget, I had banged onto the IPO about this and given them a number of questions that needed to be asked and here we are now, many months later and they have just got round to it:

1: When was the assignment document dated 22.10.92 drawn up?
2: Is it an instrument of Transfer or a retrospective certificate that such a transfer occurred?
3: If the latter, was there an instrument of transfer?
4: Please state who each of the signatories are, and in what capacity they signed?
5: If Cobretti Engineering was partnership, have all the partners signed the document?

I can imagine the panic that would have put into RB, but he is such a pathological liar he would have quickly got together a load of lies to answer them.

6/ RB replied on the 22nd Feb 2005 his reply was:
1: 22/10/92
2: It was an instrument of transfer.
3: N/A
4: The signatories were RB partner of Cobretti and a director of Autotrak - G.Busbridge, director of Autotrak - C.Bruce Design Engineer of Cobretti/ Autotrak. *That sounds grand especially as he was no engineer at all or qualified designer, but I got from Martin that he was a know-all who had a big hand in a lot of RB's crooked goings on at this time.*
5: Martin Busbridge retired from the partnership on 29 June 1992. and he enclosed the letter that had already been in evidence at the opposition hearing where MB resigns.

7/ Now the IPO reply to that and ask:
1: The document shows the partnership Cobretti Engineering dissolved on that date. Was there a written partnership agreement? Is there a copy in existence? Or was it a partnership at will?

2: After the partnership ceased who owned the assets after it ceased and how did they acquire those assets?
3: Who are the former proprietors of Cobretti Engineering?

8/ Busbridges reply:
1: The document shows that MB resigned and the business carried on and the partnership was verbal.
2: As I was the continuing partner/proprietor of CE, I owned the title to the assets and continued in business with my wife.
3: The assignors of the transfer are R.Busbridge and G.Busbridge (wife).

9/ The IPO then wrote a longer letter which basically said that the partnership had been 'at will' and was dissolved on 29th June 1992 The trademark was an asset of that partnership when the application to register was made on 18th May and once it became registered it became a property right and was then deemed to have been that at all times. The partners are therefore entitled to assign that property to another, but that does not appear to have happened during the partnership.

According to the 'Saxon' case when the partnership was dissolved both partners were entitled to their share of its assets, but neither became automatically the legal proprietor of the assets.

So there appears to be a gap in the chain of title as no request to record a transfer of the ownership of the mark from the partnership to yourself. So it is not clear how you became the owner of the trademark which you claim you have assigned to Autotrak Ltd.

So we cannot record either assignment because (a) the partnership ceased to exist so no one could sign the TM16 and (b) the documentary evidence you supplied cannot suffice as an alternative as the signatures are legally ineffective. So the second assignment is ineffective.

So your request to renew the registration will also have to be rescinded because it was made by a person who was not the proprietor of the mark. You may request a hearing if you do not agree.

All this was manna from heaven for me and I thought 'get out of that you lying bastard'. *I felt that at long last the IPO had listened to all my complaints about these alleged assignments and the lies of RB. The fact that as the partnership was finished how* could the application have gone ahead. What totally pissed me off was that the vacuous Reynolds had ignored what I had said about the partnership finishing. Why did he not come to the same conclusions and ask the same questions at the hearing. I had laid out all the same basic questions as to the validity of what had gone on after the partnership ceased. Of course even now the IPO never asked if the claim for the Viper mark that RB made were bona-fide, because when he made the application he knew I owned it, and that has been ignored both by Reynolds and Landau and the IPO, even now. Now here I have to point out that for once the IPO got something right about the legalities of this application by RB. They did miss other legal points like the bankruptcy etc, but what is shocking that after this point and the Landau decision they seemed to go into a deliberate state of amnesia as in all the other hearings and actions post this, they never ever allowed these facts and statements they made on this to surface again. It was all conveniently forgotten and brushed under their carpet as was Landaus decision. It is from this point on that it is absolutely clear that the IPO embarked on a campaign to deny me any victory or justice and that by corrupt actions and decisions by them.

10/ As no response was forthcoming from RB to the IPO letter of 4th April 2005 they wrote again on 6 May and said if he made no response by 20th May they would rescind the renewal and the status of the trademark would expire. I guess that RB was shell shocked and at a loss, for he did not have a leg to stand on.

11/ RB replies on the 10th May that he is sorry but as he was not aware of the procedure of the IPO he overlooked things in the application. (A rubbish excuse which just shows he is just trying it on as usual.) He also astonishingly ignores all that had been told him and states he is enclosing yet another TM16 to 'correct the register' *I cannot believe this nasty piece of lying crap. How does he think he can get away with this bare faced cheek and disregard everything he has just been told? He also asks for a hearing.*

He applied for a recordal of the transfer of the trademark to Cobretti Engineering, Robert Busbridge T/A' He states this transfer took place on the 29th June 1992. *It is a breathtaking piece of lying, once again. He has already been told that by law, as he did not own 100% of the trademark he could not authorise assignment or anything else, yet here he is just ignoring all that as if it has never been said. So you can see just what I have had to put up with since 1991.*

12/ The IPO replied that they could not accept his signature as the company had ceased to exist as they had pointed out. If he did not agree he could have a hearing.

13/ He replies that he cannot see why his signature cannot be accepted because the IPO had done so since 1992 when he first applied for registration. *He either simply cannot or will not accept that as he did not get his brothers agreement to apply or had legally bought him out, he has no jurisdiction to act on behalf of the partnership. He just cannot admit that since 1992 he has lied at every turn as to his alleged ownership of the assets of Cobretti.*

He then proceeds to go into yet another one of his long waffles as to why he is right and of course accuses me of wrecking the partnership etc, etc. All irrelevant nonsense and lies. He does go on also, about the fact he gave his brother an indemnity for any actions against the company. (As if that had anything to do with this.) He again asks for a hearing.

14/ Landau states that the letters are included in the annex, but I must point out we have seen all these before in the opposition hearing. So I will not describe them.

15/ Landau lists a table of events since 26th November 2004 which is the start of all the letters to and from RB and the IPO. So as we have covered all them above I will not repeat them.

16/ The hearing was heard on the 24th August 2005 at which RB was present.

17/ Landau states that what Reynolds said about assignments was correct and he draws attention to the Act which states that the recording of an assignment which is not registered cannot take place (I have noted this elsewhere and above).

This lays it open once again to show the reader just how dysfunctional the IPO are as they accepted and recorded the assignments. Even though I objected to their lack of credibility. It shows what kind of government department I am dealing with and who with their uselessness since 1992, have put me through years of a never ending nightmare.

18/ Landau discusses various issues relating to law on assignments and includes some case law. I will not relate any of this as all that important is what is the end decision.

19/ Landau lists a number of inconsistencies in the various requests by RB and his agents Reddie to change various aspects of the application names. *Basically they are all lies and jiggery-pokery and I am surprised that Reddie got involved in all these lies? They must have been able to see the inconsistencies, or were they putting him up to all this. Advising him to lie etc. The main point in all this is what RB was trying to play, with his game of musical chairs with these applications to change this and that, is that none of them had the signature of Martin Busbridge included.*

Yet another example of how the IPO accepted forms and never ever questioned as to why, when they were dealing with a partnership, that only one partner was doing the signing. What utter incompetents! **and they have also already said in writing that RB could not act alone in a partnership without the acceptance of the other partner!**

20/ Now Landau says that the IPO have made yet another mistake! In that they asked RB if the partnership was 'at will'. He points out that in actual fact a partnership with no written agreement is a partnership by 'parole' he also points out that a partnership at will is where there is no fixed term agreed to in a partnership and this was the case here, (then it seems to me that it could have been both) Anyway Landau decides that it was a partnership at will and he says that in these, when a partner retires from that partnership, it will cause the general dissolution of the partnership. With this, it forces a full scale winding up of the partnership and they would need to dispose of the assets, including the application. *(Of course we all know this did not happen!)*

21/ Landau uses this paragraph to lay out the fact that normally the IPO does not 'look behind' requests to assign a trademark or application. *My remark on that pronouncement is, 'Why not?'*

Why is it that the IPO never looks further than the end of its nose? Any crook or conman can tell the IPO anything and they take it for granted that they are being told the truth! This has been an ongoing problem for me throughout this case and from day one.

When I told them that this conman was applying for something he had no legal right to and provided proof, they ignored me. They could only say, 'take your remarks to an opposition hearing' When I then pointed out that he was now a bankrupt, they unbelievably said in a letter I still have, that how could they know that he was actually a bankrupt? Obviously it was too difficult for them to pick up a phone and ring the Insolvency Service, or look it up online!! Similarly when I told them that the application had been made in the name of a partnership that no longer existed and a company that no longer existed, deafening silence from the IPO!

I ranted on for months and months that it was obvious that these alleged assignment were a con and were made out of time and the first one in 1992 was not a legally composed document, so was flawed. Of the fact that Martin had not agreed to the assignment, and the fact that it was signed only by Robert Busbridge, that the IPO should have realised their mistakes straight away.

It was many months after Reynolds made his decision and my constantly complaining about the fact that they were doing nothing to implement the request Reynolds made, that this question of the assignment be looked at, that they eventually acted. Even then it was only because they suddenly were bombarded with requests from RB to deal with TM16 requests that were obviously going against what Reynolds had decreed, that they held this hearing. I doubt if they would have even done that if RB had not asked for it.

So here we have Landau listing all the inconsistencies about the claims that had been made by RB over his supposed ownership of the application. He points out that there is no documentation to show that the assets were disposed of correctly after the partnership dissolved. That none of the TM16's were also signed by Martin. That the alleged assignment of assets to Autotrak, left out Martin, so had he agreed to the assignment? That there was no proof that any indemnification to Martin had ever been given. The whole act of dissolution had been done unsatisfactorily, with no documentation, and so on.

Now at this point I have to ask; "*Again why the hell didn't Reynolds ask these questions?*" About the assignments and whether the breakdown of the partnership had been done legally. For I had raised those questions in my written evidence. Instead of granting Robert Busbridge the registration, he should have looked into what Landau had looked into and come to the same conclusion back in June 2004. While he was at it, he should have looked into the fact that the agency agreement could have been genuine and that fact could have been verified if only he had asked that Martin be present and if he could not then, it was entirely unsafe for Reynolds to have said what he did, about it being very possibly, a forgery and by ME!

22/ Landau says now that RB needs to satisfy the IPO that following the break-up of the partnership, he took over the asset of the application legally. He says there was a time limit to do so, for if it had not been done by the time he became a bankrupt then the assets would go to the Receiver. *That is precisely what I had been banging on about, to the IPO since 1993/4. I was ignored on each and every time I brought this point up and even when I made it to the CEO of the IPO in 2002.* The bastards would just not give me an answer... Now I wonder why that was?

On top of that you will see that the reply I got from the Insolvency Service was as vacuous as anything I ever got from the IPO, for they said; 'the Patent Office have ruled that the registration of the assignment was not correctly dealt with, there is no evidence that the assignment did not occur' They beggar belief, for if the assignment was not done correctly for whatever reason, then the assignment could not be said to have been legal! They just wanted to wash their hands of my complaints to them, that they had not handled the bankruptcy of RB properly and that he had run rings round them as well and defrauded the creditors. Yet another dysfunctional government department and I will have more to say on that subject further on.

23/ Now Landau says that the request from RB made in 2002 to record that the assets held by Autotrak Ltd to himself as he stated that there had been no change in the ownership, when obviously there had and RB had constantly said in evidence that the partnership had broken up in 1992. Landau goes into great detail about how all the events from the time RB tried to move assets away from the partnership to Autotrak Ltd then back to himself were incorrect, as in all of them Martin Busbridge had no part in them and as he was the owner of 50% of the assets he had to give his signature to all that went on.

As we know he did not and RB had even said on many occasions that he did not even know where he was after the break-up. (which we now know to be lie) What it tells me is that RB went on a deliberate campaign to deceive the IPO as to how he was able to take over the assets of the partnership. On that subject there is another example of RB's deceiving the IPO because this application made in 2002 to record the alleged assignment to Autotrak Ltd and then to assign it to himself from Autotrak, was a complete fiction This company had stopped trading many years before. RB had even acknowledged this in his statements given at the 2004 hearing. Companies House had struck it off for persistent failings to post accounts and returns. Yet here he is saying to the IPO in 2002 that it is still an entity and he needs to move assets from it to himself. How crooked can you get and all this flies over the IPO's heads. They are just so dumb, that an ill educated bum like Robert Busbridge can run rings round them.

24/ Landau now says that TM16's are to report to the IPO the reality of proprietors of a trademark not to 'create one'. *I think he is being too soft on RB here, as he should have said 'not to lie about the reality' (or truth).*

He even points out the fact that RB was advised by his very own solicitor that he needed to formalise (make legal) the transfer of the assets of the partnership to Autotrak. *Again Landau is being soft on RB as it is as plain as your nose that RB was up to skulduggery here. For in saying that after being given that legal advice RB, did nothing. He doesn't seem able to ask why that was, so I will state why.*

RB knew that to do so, he would have to go to his brother (and he knew how to find him, contrary to what he claimed) and grovel to him to get him to sign over his half of the partnership. He knew that would never happen... so he ignored that advice and crookedly blundered on!

25/ So Landau has to say that the application has to stay in the original names:- Cobretti Engineering a partnership of R.Busbridge and M.Busbridge... **hurrah!**

26/ The request to renew the trademark was not made by the two partners, so that cannot be renewed... **hurrah! But you will see this does me not one scrap of good in the future as the IPO simply ignore all that Landau decreed.**

27/ In this paragraph Landau is merely stating how Busbridge bleats on about how hard done by he is and he had only carried on doing the business and how he was ignorant of all the laws and how the rest of the World viewed his running the business Blah, Blah, Blah!! Then he makes one of his usual lying statements to Landau by saying 'he had no doubt that if he had asked his brother to sign a formal assignment of the trademark, that he would have done so'. *'Oh yeah, pigs might fly too' and you will see later on, how the* **real truth about the relationship and what really happened in that den of inequity, that was Cobretti Engineering.**

NOW Landau completely blows it for me for I had begun to think that here was man that was an honest one, who was rooting out the truth regardless of what his bosses in the IPO may have told him to do. He lets himself down big time when he says; "in his answers to my questions he gave me the impression of being **'honest and straight forward'**... I believe he simply did not understand the implications and ramifications" etc. *It made me want to spew when I read that bit!*

You see what we have here is a prime example of how a good conman works. He goes into these hearings looking like an extremely inoffensive little chap. A hangdog expression and demeanour, butter would not melt in his mouth. A quiet, pleading voice that gives off an aura of 'Oh I am just a poor, ignorant little boy who would never lie or deceive, or do any wrong to anyone, it's everyone else who is at fault and they are all trying to do me in. Have pity on me your honour for I need to be able to make a living, and I never stole anything off anyone, they have stolen it off me' Blah, Blah, Blah, Ad nauseum. It makes me sick, every time I think of the little wretch.

Anyway enough of that before I burst a blood vessel, for Landau finishes off this disgusting paragraph by saying; "Consequently, I consider my hands are tied and that the only finding can be that there was no valid assignment from the partnership. The ownership is to stay in the name of a partnership that no longer exists and the effect of this is that the trademark cannot be renewed"

28/ Summarising, he says:-

1: The trademark could have been assigned at the dissolution of the partnership.
2: The trademark should be in the name of R.Busbridge and M.Busbridge T/As Cobretti Engineering.
3: The trademark cannot be renewed owing to the non existence of the partnership and the registration expired on 18.May 1999.

I was ecstatic as this represented a huge win and justification for everything that I had said all along, even if it did not address many things it should have. What would happen now? Indeed what would happen now, and what did happen was **nothing**, in real terms, as you will see as you read on.

However you should be noting this; All the events up to this point have shown conclusively that the IPO are either a supremely ignorant and incompetent organisation or they carried out a lot of what they heaped upon me... deliberately! What is it to be? At this point of this sickening saga is that it could be said that maybe they were just incompetent. However when you read forward from here and you see how they continue onwards with this kind of behaviour, so you then have to be asking serious questions as to, maybe they do have a hidden agenda? For instance someone in the IPO who can pull strings could be a Mason, and so could Busbridge be. It may sound far fetched but Masons have a reputation for this kind of thing. I have long said that it was almost as if

Busbridge had a relative high up in the IPO, pulling the strings for him. Being Masons is the same as having relatives helping you. Remember that Busbridge had working for him, and ex copper and we all know how many of them are Masons. This man definitely had a hand in advising RB what to do and how to get round the law etc. Was he able to use his influence if he was a Mason?

The facts are that had justice been done at the Reynolds hearing, that would have been the end of Busbridge and none of what has gone on since would have happened.

Chapter Sixteen
The Events After Landau, 2005–2008.

I found this period of time as frustrating and stressful as any that had preceded it. Considering I had been told that I had won, I certainly expected things to wind down quickly. However all people who have to deal with the IPO will find that it is an extremely slow and cumbersome body, that oozes incompetence and where things only happen in slow motion. I ended up facing several actions and the first one was when eventually on the 7th October 2005 the IPO informed me that Busbridge was appealing the decision of Landau.

I do not know about you, but I believe as in criminal law, you should not be able to appeal unless you can prove that the hearing officer erred in law or some other compelling reason. What on earth RB could say was not done properly and as per law, I do not know. Yet he was allowed to appeal as if it were a matter of course. I was told I could not take any part in that appeal, which again annoyed the hell out of me, as I would not be given any information as to what grounds he was going to appeal on.

The appeal would be heard before a QC (Hobbs) who was put forward by the Treasury Solicitors. I thought that at least that would mean it would be heard by someone not connected to the IPO. *God, how wrong I was there, as you will see in time.*

So I sat back and waited to be told when it would be heard. However it was to be a long wait and by the 12th December 05 I still had not heard anything, so emailed the Head of the Law section of the IPO, a Raoul Colombo (RC), asking what was going on. From now on you will get another look at what a lot of duplicitous ass****s the IPO really are. Here is the itinerary:-

17/12/05:- I write to RC that I see that RB is showing on his website a copy of a registration document which clearly says that he, Robert Busbridge is the registered owner of the trademark Viper. He boasts elsewhere on the site of this fact. Now I am sure your memory can still remember that a few pages back you saw that Landau had clearly said he wasn't and it had to remain in the Cobretti name. Once again we see how RB does not respect the law at all and he just does what he wants to do. The Hell with what the IPO says is the case here. If it doesn't fit in with his warped take on everything, he just does it his way and if he is brought short, he takes no notice.

I was then told that this was not a job for the IPO to sort and that I had to complain to the Trading Standards and they if you do not know are worse than the IPO as they will not act on anything. I had already tried to get that shower to act against RB over the misleading advertising he does in magazines and on his website. He claims cars he shows were made by him when they are pictures of cars made by me. He claims that he has been in business making the Viper since even before I had even started and long before I even met him. What a liar this wretch is. I replied giving RC an earful.

24/1/06:- After my complaining about the above, the IPO actually send RB a letter pointing out he is breaking the law by these untrue statements. He is forced to take them down, but he could have taken no notice had he known that the IPO had no jurisdiction over this kind of law breaking, even though it has to do with their laws (according to them).

14/2/06:- RC tells me that the Hobbs hearing will take place on the 22/3/06. Now I entered a period of extreme frustration and continuing lies and evasions from the IPO which all border on the CORRUPT!

Here is a list of what happened:

2/6/06:- Three months after the hearing and I have heard nothing. I ask RC what is going on.

14/12/06:- I get a letter from the IPO CEO as I had complained through my MP that the IPO were failing to notify me of a decision. He says that after the Hobbs hearing matters were suspended (a lie as RB had in fact dropped his appeal) after submissions, in order that the IPO could get RB to assemble further information. After a period of time RB asked for more time to do so.

Obvious that the IPO knew all along what the state of affairs was, yet they lied saying they did not know!

I eventually found out that the IPO, after RB had been given advice from Hobbs to try and get Martin to sign over his share of the assets, had asked him to try and find Martin and they actually sent Martin a letter asking if he wanted to sign over his share to allow RB to carry on and rectify the Register. I found all this absolutely amazing and mind blowing. The IPO had been telling me since April 06 that they did not know what was going on, yet here it is quite clear they did and not only that they were being complicit in giving RB time to find Martin, *and* were even doing his job for him by writing to Martin. They even gave him an extra three months to do this. I thought that even if he found him and I did not think he would even bother to try to ask him, that there was no way Martin would agree to this.

6/1/07:- Now *nine* months after the hearing and nothing. So I complain to RC again. I get the same answer that the IPO cannot question an Appointed Person as they are independent. So you see that they are still acting dumb and *lying!*

8/1/07:- RC tells me that Hobbs has said the case will be restored on 12/1/07. I am flummoxed as I thought it had been dealt with and a decision made back in March 06. Or maybe it was to do with what RB had found out, about Martin.

8/1/07:- I ask RC why another hearing?

11/1/07:- RC replies he cannot tell me as it is out of his hands, so he was still *lying!*

3/3/07:- I write once more to find out what is going on.

5/3/07:- Same answer as before from RC.

What is appalling about all this is that the IPO knew full well what had gone on with that Hobbs hearing, Whether RB had won, or it had been suspended so RB could contact his brother and he had been given TWO extra periods of time to do this yet he had done nothing in that time. For the IPO knew this because they ***actually had written*** to Martin. Yet they lied ad nauseum to me and even to my MP saying they hadn't a clue what was going on and using the excuse they couldn't question the Independent Appointed Person. What a bunch of lying bastards they are and even prepared to lie to a member of Parliament.

What can you do about this… absolutely nothing as they are a law unto themselves it seems.

Chapter Seventeen
My Complaint of Maladministration to the CEO of the IPO

I had, like anybody else would, become extremely fed up with the IPO messing me about and I knew they were up to no good and quite obviously lying to me. So despite having got nowhere before in 2002/3 when I complained to their CEO and the Parliamentary Ombudsman, I decided to have another go as their CEO was yet another new and useless, supposed top civil servant.

I fired off a letter to this man, a Mr Marchant on the 3rd April 2007. I will not detail the whole letter but I will list the most important points I made to him.

I said that I and my Patent Agent had warned the IPO back in 1993, that RB had no rights to apply for a trademark that belonged to me, as he was my agent and I supplied a copy of our agency agreement. Also that RB was now bankrupt, and the partnership had ceased. Yet the name that the application was in was in the partnership name. These had been ignored over many years. When the alleged assignments had been made in 2002 I had pointed out over and over again to the IPO that they were severely short of legality and should not have been recorded. Once again I was ignored.

That after the Landau hearing and Busbridge had appealed that decision, which had found all that I had been complaining about to the IPO for years, was entirely correct. I had then had to wait for over a year for the decision of that appeal hearing. Of course each time I had complained at the delays, I was lied to by the IPO. I had been told time and again by no less than the Head of Law a Raoul Colombo, that his hands were tied and he knew nothing. Yet while he was saying this the IPO had known that Busbridge had dropped his appeal and the IPO had given him time to find his brother.

I complained about other matters that I had had to endure because of the IPO's actions and I wanted compensation.

On the 23rd April I got a reply, not from Marchant but a Mr Webb, Head of trademarks and astonishingly he made comments on my complaining, that Busbridge had been able to appeal to an appointed person re the Landau hearing yet I had had to appeal to a High Court re his registration opposition hearing decision. He ignored everything else I had complained about and it was as if I had never written about those important criticisms.

Now this is a favourite trick of the IPO, for if you make a valid complaint that they have seriously failed to carry out proper procedures over a complaints or mistakes, they think that by ignoring you, you will just take that as an answer.

He ended by saying that RB had dropped the appeal, and this was the first I had officially heard of that fact. He failed to tell me that RB had been given time to find Martin or that he was now applying to rectify the register (this in Jan 2007 before Webbs letter). What a disgrace and typical of the disingenuous way the IPO works when put in a corner. As I say, RB had applied to do this on the 3rd January with a form TM26R accompanied by a statement stating his reasons to ask this.

Once again a statement full of perjury. He claims that his company Cobretti Engineering (the very same company he has previously said wasn't trading and which all his adverts after 1993 had not shown it as trading) had been run by himself since 1992. Martin had left in June 1992 and everyone knew him to now be the owner. (Forget about how he had never paid his brother for his share.) He says he not been in contact with his brother for some years and he says he had tried recently to contact him in Spain with no success and the last time he had seen him was in Spain in 2003 (another lie as you will soon see).

In return he was told in a letter dated 30th Jan 2007 that he should make a statement of truth about his brothers last known address and he should formally withdraw the appeal application he had made before. (This during the time the IPO are lying and saying they don't know what was going on!) Also that he agreed that the IPO should treat this application as a request to remove matter (from the register) that has ceased to have effect.

It appears he did give this statement of truth and his brothers last known address as on the 23rd April. The IPO then sent Martin a letter to the address given them and asking MB to agree to RB changing to register to read RB as being the owner of the mark. Of course he never replies because the address given is fictitious and one where Martin had never lived at. More on this point later on.

Now what you have to remember here is that Landau had clearly stated that the application was at an end for the reasons he gave. RB had appealed, but now had dropped that appeal, yet the IPO instead of now enacting the Landau decision, were now allowing RB to ask for the IPO to remove Martins name from the application... this is absolutely astonishing and despite my asking the IPO why they can allow this to happen, they refuse to answer me... incredible and corrupt!

Either the IPO are screamingly incompetent or they are being deliberate in what they were now allowing RB to do because they had felt that Landau had come out with a decision they did not like.

It is also worth knowing that on the 11th of *April* Colombo sent me an email about my complaining that RB was being allowed to appeal this business about the assignments to an A/P even though his application to register was under the 1938 Act, he clearly lies by saying that the appeal is still ongoing. More lies, because as I have said he had dropped the appeal in September 2006 and had already applied to rectify the register. Either he is being incompetent as I said above, or he is lying.

I sent Colombo a reply asking him why he had been saying every time I had asked him what was happening about the decision of Hobbs, he had said he did not know. Why was he lying? *I got no answer* and this is obviously because he knows he is at fault and of course he will not want to be truthful and admit that. This is the umpteenth time the IPO has refused to answer a direct question.

On the same day I sent that above letter, I sent a second asking why a previous letter on the 13th was not replied to and I asked why. I also go into many of the other complaints I had over the way they had been dealing with Busbridge of late and basically why was I having to put up with all the lies of the IPO and why they were bending over backwards for him. Why was he now being allowed to apply to rectify the register to drop his brother off the application etc, especially when Landau had clearly said that he could not do anything about the fact that the registration was null and void for various reasons?

While I was doing all this letter writing, I also fired off a letter to Mr Webb to whom my official complaint to the CEO had ended up with and who had completely ignored all I had complained about. I repeat my complaints and ask him to get on and deal with them.

On this very same day I sent that letter to Webb, which by the way I had got from him through Colombo (so you see, you make an official complaint to the

CEO, it gets passed down to a lower order—Webb) and now it is with an even lower order bloke, Colombo… that's what the IPO think of your complaint! It is like being in a restaurant and making a complaint about crap which you say you want putting through to the Chef, and you get a reply from a dishwasher! All that is said is that RB has put in his request to rectify and that the IPO has written to Martin at an address provided by RB in his statement.

On the 1st May I send another letter to Colombo, further to the other two of the 26th April and I complain that I am being asked to oppose RB's application to rectify, when what should be happening, is them enacting Landaus decision and not forcing me into more time and expense to oppose another bunch of lies from R.Busbridge.

I get a reply from Colombo on the 9th May. He ignores everything I have said about how the IPO and he has lied and how they are not enacting Landau's decision. He merely says he is sorry I am not satisfied with the way my original complaint of maladministration (fails to mention all the other letters I had sent him about his lying) and cheekily says if I want to do anything, I can oppose RB's application to rectify. Then he says 'I am unable to assist you any further'. In other words—bugger off and stop pestering me!

On the 10th May 2007 I get a reply from Webb which is just more disingenuous waffle. Basically he is saying that once the Landau decision was made, the case is closed and he cannot open it or even comment on the issues I raised! It is so against natural justice that I cannot believe it is true, in fact I think it is just another complete IPO *lie!* You may as well say that a Judge says a man is guilty of murder, the guy appeals, then when told by a QC how he can go off on a different tack to get out of his situation and to drop his appeal, which he does and follows the advice, then the original decision of the Judge that he must spend 25 years in jail, cannot be carried out! Also no one can comment or give answers to questions about IPO chicanery and their refusal to enact a decision made. Bollocks is what I say.

So I am forced to put in an appeal against RB's application to change to register, which I do mid June 2007.

On the 5th October Busbridge applies for an extension of time to deal with his application and gets it to the end of 2007 on the 28th December. The IPO bending over backwards for him, once again.

What you see in this chapter highlights the disgraceful way the IPO was treating me. First Hobbs gives RB free advice at the appeal he heard (more on that below). So RB drops his appeal and on this advice from Hobbs and then outlined to him in letters from the IPO, he goes through the motions of trying to find his brother Martin who is in Spain. The IPO are thus actively giving RB advice on how to go ahead and circumvent the decision of Landau.

Not only that but all my efforts to find out throughout 2006 and into 2007 what the decision of Hobbs was, I and my MP are lied to by the IPO through Raoul Colombo and their CEO, that they don't know what the decision is and cannot find out. When all the time they know full well as RB is in touch with them and they are writing to him giving him free help to go forward. My complaints to their CEO are brushed aside and demoted to lower orders who refuse to answer and deal with the complaints.

My insistence on knowing why the IPO are not enacting the decision of Landau is either ignored or when I am given an answer by RC, it is absolute lying rubbish.

RB commits perjury once more in the statements he made during this period about his trading with Cobretti Engineering and the IPO have on record that RB has previously admitted that he was trading with Autotrak Cobretti Ltd, yet they ignore this. <u>He also commits absolute perjury when he gives a fictitious address for Martin knowing full well what Martins address really was!</u>

Chapter Eighteen
Transcript of what Hobbs QC Said at the Appeal Hearing 2005

As I told you above I wasn't allowed to be present at this hearing and so I had no idea what Busbridge had said to Hobbs, nor what Hobbs had said. At first I was not bothered what had gone on as at the end of the day, RB had dropped that appeal. I thought that it was because he could see that there wasn't any way he could get round it legally. It was to me, a pretty water tight case against him. It wasn't until much later that you will see how I began to get doubts about this whole section of this sorry saga. I could leave telling you until much later but in order to keep things in chronological order I am putting it onto the stage now.

In 2009 I got off the IPO, a transcript of this appeal, and I only got it because I sent in a letter to a general office instead of to Colombo or someone high up. So I dealt with a clerk and was told that I could always have a transcript of what was said. I got it like a shot, and I have wondered ever since if that clerk made a mistake in giving it to me. If it was a mistake, then it was only one of dozens the IPO made, but one which went my way for once. For what I found in it explained a lot, one hell of a lot if you read between the lines. It is 46 pages long and the behaviour of Hobbs who heard it, explains why the IPO were allowing RB to go ahead and were not bothering to enact the Landau decision.

The first thing that got me wondering what was going on at this hearing, was when I read that at this hearing was non other than a person from the IPO called Mr Allan James. He is the Head Honcho of the Tribunal/Law Section. I had always thought Colombo was, as he had sent me many emails where it had said he was. (I subsequently asked that section why I was being told that Colombo was Head, when it later appeared that James was. I never got an answer, which is quite normal behaviour for the IPO. They it seems, like to keep you in the dark as to exactly who you are dealing with.)

The first 32 pages are pages full of what I think is all typical legal waffle. These two characters engage in this long conversation to do with law issues and case law to do with partnerships. I will not bore you with it all the nitty gritty of it as it does not really affect the story directly. What you have to do is read between the lines and if you do you will see it reads like two old chums sitting in some posh old boys club, chewing the fat over how they can justify getting RB out of his dilemma (the dilemma that the lying bastard should lose his ill gotten gains in the trademark stakes).

When you carefully pull to pieces the whole of this hearing, it gradually becomes clear what these two are up to. I now realise that all this discussion about case law is to impart to RB what they think the law says about his situation re him and Martin and how he can circumvent the problem that the decision of Landau presented him with (which was largely to do with partnership law). Hobbs actually has the arrogance and cheek to now ask RB if he understood all of what they had been waffling on about. This because he wanted to find out if their ruse had worked and that RB had realised that he was clandestinely being given advice, by them going over case law. (This discussing case law at the very beginning of an appeal hearing is most unusual, as case law would be gone over only in the decision document after the hearing to back up what the hearing officer decides in law.) Now that is what I call corruption and it is made clear that this was a deliberate act of corruption when you take into account how the IPO behaved towards me after the hearing.

Elsewhere I have detailed what the IPO did in this period, but I repeat this so you can see it in context with the above. Obviously even though I was not allowed to be present at the hearing, I wanted to know what the outcome was. Had he been successful or not? For the outcome was of great importance to me. If he had lost, then he loses the registration that Reynolds had corruptly given him and I would have my registration remaining secure. If he wins then who knows what.

So after a couple of months and not hearing anything, I naturally start asking what is going on. You can see elsewhere what the answers or rather non answers, were. The IPO were lying because they did not want me to know that RB had dropped the appeal and that they had given him a certain number of months to seek out his brother. Then RB messes things up for the IPO by wanting *more time*. That means the IPO have to keep lying to me and my MP, that they don't know what is happening because the hearing officer Hobbs QC does not need to tell them. Hogwash and lies as their very own Mr James had been present and knew full well what the outcome had been as did their tribunal section who had been writing a number of letters to RB.

This confirms that the IPO were up to their necks in lying, corruption and obfuscations to hide their involvements in this scam. More on the hearing:-

You should note that on the first page of this hearing transcript document, it says that this is a hearing about the matter of the trademark registration 151099 in Cobretti Engineering (a Partnership) and the operative word is *'partnership'*. Yet here we have a hearing about this partnership and only one person from that partnership is present... Robert Busbridge! ***This after the IPO in the form of Landau and their own tribunal section office, had told RB that he could not represent the partnership on his own!*** And here are these two sods sitting there for hours talking about how they can do that partner out of his rightful share of that partnership! What case law will allow them to do this? They make me sick, but not as sick as I become further on, for from page 32, Hobbs takes over and actually starts to bring RB into the proceedings, whereas up to now he had been out of it.

It is what Hobbs says next to RB that beggars belief, for he says 'I have looked at, as you know, the Registry record. You can get them off the internet, with all the case details, the case history—*the long sordid history'* Busbridge says, 'I have a couple of those, yes' (an inane remark, typical of RB).

Hobbs then says ' I have the history at the same time, relating to Daimler Chrysler on a mark which was 265 (part of the application reference number of their registration application which I opposed) and this looks like a ***complete and utter mess*** to me' RB replies 'It is' (can I kiss your arse while I am at it, your highness?').

So here we have this QC, who to me sounds like he is full of himself and feels he is in a secure environment where he can safely state what he likes. What is he actually saying? Well he's talking about my opposition against Chrysler and obviously also the Reynolds hearing which I was part of and firstly he is saying that in his opinion 'It has a long sordid history' He also thinks specifically that my case against Chrysler was an 'Utter mess' What does he exactly mean by this and the former statement and what has all that got to do with this hearing? He is expounding his personal thoughts about a hearing and about cases that have nothing to do with the appeal case he is supposed to be dealing with. He is saying things about me ***and I am not there in person to object*** and defend my reputation. I am not a criminal as I have no criminal convictions and the only time I have

EVER been charged with anything criminal was when that reptile before him, trumped up charges against me. Hobbs now started to question RB about Martin and the break-up. RB then went into his usual act of lying through his back teeth. He ended up by saying they had an argument of a personal nature, and he walked out. (Funny how in his statements in the opposition case, he blamed me entirely for that.)

Hobbs goes into detailed questions about my starting copyright litigation and he also touched on the forgery action. Quite why he brings these into the equation, as he was supposed to be dealing with RB's appeal over the assignments and these questions about me are totally irrelevant. I suppose it was to fill in time, maybe show he knew all about what an asshole I was and maybe get RB at ease by appearing to commiserate with him? It all smacks of corruption to me and is against all the Judges Rules on how a Judge is supposed to act.

Then he gets down to the point and starts asking if it would be possible for him to find his brother, kiss and make up and get him to agree to sign over his share of the business. Before he goes further on, he goes into RB's bankruptcy and asks a load of questions on that. I believe here Hobbs is trying to find out just where the Receiver stands on all this. Of course RB lies again and tells him that all is sweet with him and he's been given a clean bill of health by the Receiver. (We will never know the truth about all that as they are as incompetent as the IPO, as they have destroyed all the files on RB, so they say!)

He asks RB if he is professionally guided and is told that he cannot afford it. Now he asks if RB understood the 'technical' conversation he had had with Mr James. This Hobbs, I can see is a crafty bastard. What he is doing here is sounding out RB to see just what he understood about all the legal hints that were included in that long conversation. Hints that if RB wasn't an empty head, he could have got their real meaning and purpose. Of course RB answers that he really did not grasp it all and there he shows just how empty headed he is. So Hobbs has to try another tack.

Hobbs then says to RB 'Let me just recapitulate (doubt if RB would understand that word) with you now, the essence of the conversation that I was having with Mr James.' He tells RB that he is caught in a game of snakes and ladders as no sooner had he got registration than it was taken away (referring to Landau's decision which in any case has never been enacted). This comment makes my blood boil for it was clear to Hobbs that I was the rightful owner of the Mark and had it legally registered to me, and I was now on the slippery road of losing it to a conman. Yet Hobbs has no sympathy for me. Now I wonder why that is? Now here is where I get really mad, because he now says to RB *'I cannot advise you as I am the tribunal'!* What he should have said is that it is not legal for him to be advising him in any way shape or form. He further drubs it into RB by going on to say, *'So you must understand that I am not advising you as to what course of action you take'* it is clear to me that this is being said so Hobbs can turn round to anyone who queries it, and can say that here he is making it clear he cannot give advice. He goes on to say that RB should get legal advice. Yet what he has just said above *is nothing more than legal advice!*

Now the trouble is (for Hobbs) is that in his next breath, ***that is exactly what he goes on doing for some time more, to give… advice!*** On page 40, lines 15 to 25 and then onto page 41 line 1 to 8, you can see an unashamed exercise in Hobbs giving RB, clear and free legal advice. He tells RB that if he withdraws the appeal re the two assignments, it would remove a 'distraction'. (He is quite prepared to overlook the fact that RB had been with these 'distractions' trying to illegally play around with the trade mark ownership, by hiding it away from the Receiver.) It would then make the application as being in the original names it was made in IE The partnership. He then goes on to make the astonishing claim that the IPO would not stand in his way if he as a person, authorised to seek renewal of the mark (it had expired seven years after application date of 1992). What about partnership law which says that a partner cannot carry out actions unknown to the other partner. Especially as in this case this action, if done would deny the other partner of his share in the assets of the partnership! and the IPO had said he couldn't do this) He points out that even after this, it would remain 'untidy' as because Martin had left causing a dissolution, so his share of the business had to be sorted. In other words RB would have to buy him out. (So RB is now aware of the implications which Landau had already told him about.)

Quite frankly I think this man Hobbs is appalling. Here is an eminent QC in IP, who is breaking all the rules of his job as a hearing officer, where he is supposed to be unbiased and completely independent, above reproach etc, etc.

The whole hearing is an example of governmental jiggery pokery of the highest order. Firstly an appeal is supposed to be a legal process where the appellant applies to have a hearing decision looked at again. You would think that it would be necessary to have to come up with legal reasons for asking for an appeal. To show that due legal process had not been carried out, or that the HO had erred in law and so on. It should not be an exercise where you simply do not agree with the decision because it did not go your way. The latter seems to be the norm as far as the IPO are concerned.

In any appeal you would be expected to make a statement as to what grounds you are appealing on. Yet here there does not seem to have been any statement, for one is not mentioned anywhere within this transcript. As I was told by the IPO to butt out of this appeal, I of course did not get to see any of its documentation like statements by RB. Busbridge. He is not asked any questions by Hobbs re anything he may have said in a statement, nor are any facts that would have been given in a statement, alluded to by Hobbs. All that this hearing dealt with is a cosy old boys discussion on law and case law, a few vacuous irrelevant questions asked of Busbridge, and then a great spiel by Hobbs where he gives endless advice and points RB in the direction where he should go with 'his problem'

It is nothing more than an appalling act of an abuse of the legal process, carried out by a person who on the face of it is nothing more than the up market face of the IPO. For if you look at this man's working record, he is up to his neck in work *for the IPO!* He is practically a full time employee of the IPO. He acts as a hearing officer for them *and* an appeal officer. When acting as a hearing officer, he must get paid by the IPO, so he then becomes an employee of theirs! So how can he be said to be independent?

On top of all that, when you look at how the IPO have behaved throughout all my contacts and hearings with them, and now this, you cannot help wondering what has been going on. Their actions smack of a concerted effort on their behalf to make sure I never win anything, with a blip when the renegade Landau went and failed to do their bidding. (For he came out with the *truth*.) But since then they have concerted their efforts to nullify him as if he had never existed. You will see their future behaviour only strengthens this belief of mine in their skulduggery, and their reasons as I have said before, are that they do not wish to be shown up as being incompetent or admit they have messed up on many occasions. Always hoping I would give up in despair or die of old age or have another heart attack. I can imagine they have a shrine to RB at Newport HQ and where each day the bastards go to pray I will kick the bucket and then they stick pins in an effigy of me!

Hobbs further on, repeats his advice and tries to hide the fact that it is ***advice*** he his giving, by saying *'If in the hypothetical situation I am considering'* Who does he think he is kidding? What he is doing is giving advice and it has nothing to do with 'hypothetical', for what he is dealing with is fact and not hypothetical and all this bullshit is to try and hide the fact he is giving ***advice!*** He says the loose ends after dropping the appeal can be dealt with by RB asking for a rectification of the register to remove his brother and so end up with the mark in his name. Then he goes on to saying that RB should seek legal advice, but I am inclined to think that saying that is a smoke screen, as all RB has to do is apply to rectify and that is exactly what the twat does... thanks Hobbs you corrupt bastard. He doesn't need a lawyer or advice for that, and Hobbs knows that. As you will see, and he doesn't need to get Martins OK to do it. Martin is conveniently air brushed out of existence. He even goes into what the wording of a statement should say, if RB did get Martin to agree to handing over his interest in the partnership.

Of course what Hobbs does not know is that RB knows there is no way Martin would hand over the substantial interest he has in his share, and Martin knows RB has no money to pay him, even if RB would splash out. On page 44 line 6 he expounds how things could work from now on. He could adjourn the appeal and give a 3 month cooling off period and he would 'invite' the registrar (James) to consider if he will accept the position that they have cosily worked out between themselves at this so called appeal and would not object to RB asking for a renewal etc. RB then says that he has already applied for a renewal, but Hobbs replies that it was under sufferance rather than unconditionally accepted. I suspect that that is not true either since when does the IPO do things "under sufferance"?

He then asks James if any of that sounds impractical or difficult for him? James grovels, calling him 'SIR' and saying that the assignment was the only thing casting doubt as to the proprietorship and if the assignments were withdrawn the renewal request would stand. (A renewal request made by only one of the partnership and illegal in partnership law.) James here is suffering from yet another IPO bout of amnesia as he conveniently forgets what his own department had said on the legalities of RB's position as to his ownership, as outlined above when they wrote ,many letters to RB asking many questions and then telling him that he could not have ownership of the trademark! He asks RB if he understands and has any questions. The dickhead is too thick to see these two crooked bastards have just handed on a plate, to him, the answer as to how he can kick me in the balls and complete the stealing of my trademark from me. He says he is somewhat confused, but will speak to his Patent Agents, Reddie & Gross.

You could not make all this up, and it makes me as sick as a parrot that the IPO through James and Hobbs can have openly and illegally carried out what is no more than a corrupt action to pervert the course of Justice, by manipulating this alleged appeal hearing.

This hearing or rather meeting, was not a bona-fide appeal hearing as I have said above. It was not controlled as an appeal would be controlled to take the form it normally would and therefore discuss appeal matters. This is because it was never intended to be a pukka appeal hearing. The IPO have to get round the decision that Landau made as it interferes with getting me out of the way, so I cannot end up suing them for over a £million. For them I believe that Landau must have been a renegade person, for he came to a decision that they did not want. Maybe they had to put him in charge of that hearing, for I do not know how officers are picked for the various hearings, and maybe they knew they could not get him to play ball with the way he decided things.

As RB had actually asked to appeal, then they have to give him that right and I believe that here is where they see they can work things the way they want. This by using this 'private' hearing to manipulate things to their way. Hobbs no doubt will do anything for his cred with the IPO and James is one of the top managers who no doubt would be most affected if I were able to sue the IPO, for he is responsible for the section that has done me in. So the hearing is run by just these two people... how convenient for them, but in reality no mistake, for it is deliberately so. You have to ask why it is that for this hearing the IPO send one of their TOP managers. I think you will be able to see through that one!

Not to mention how they can get me while they are at it. Hobbs even says he will see to it that a transcript will be sent to RB, so he can have it all in writing to refresh his thick memory and then take the appropriate steps. I have never heard that said in any hearing I have been through or know of that the HO would say "No problems sonny, I will help you and send you a transcript, so don't worry your little head."

So ended this travesty of justice appeal hearing, or should I say the free legal advice session, where no appeal against what Landau decreed, was ever enacted. Well eventually, way off in the future after I had got this transcript in 2009, and having let it all sink in and had read deeply between the lines, I was so enraged that I reported the bastard Hobbs to the Treasury Solicitors. They prevaricated for two months, thus wasting my time, before saying they were not the people to deal with it and I had to go to the Office for Judicial Complaints. A comprehensive complaint I made to them was brushed under the carpet, and this enraged me even more. So then it had to go to Judicial Conduct Ombudsman. Because of my past experiences with all Ombudsmen I was not filled with confidence.

Chapter Nineteen
My Complaint to the Parliamentary Ombudsman about the IPO.

Because the IPO had treated my complaint to their CEO with such disdain, arrogance and ignorance, I felt it may be worth it to have another bash at going to the Parl/Oms. True I got nowhere the last time, but a lot of things had happened since, that warranted another more fuller complaint. So on the 20th May 2007 I slapped in a large statement of 6 pages with 41 documents to back up what I had said verbally. Many were letters that I sent to the IPO and their replies.

I will not go over each and everything I said as most of what I said is contained in all of the above facts of this saga to date. The salient points I made which I think showed rampant maladministration, was the IPO's ignoring evidence that RB was now a bankrupt and that the partnership was dissolved, and therefore the application should be voided. Plus the fact that I gave them evidence that we had an agency agreement and that made his application to have been made knowing full well someone else owned the mark and thus was not bona-fide. That all meant that the application was thus made against laws that existed concerning what should happen to this alleged asset, and was the application bona-fide as the partners were no longer partners? This should have meant the IPO's questioning if the remaining partner who made the application, was legally entitled to go ahead without legally owning 100% of the alleged asset (which as you can see they did-only for this to be forgotten and brushed under the carpet).

As the IPO sat on this from 1992 right through to 2004, this had meant I had been forced to allow this conman to trade with my trademark and produce a copy of my product, thus causing me great losses and a lot of stress which culminated in a heart attack. All this despite the fact that at the same time I had been fighting an opposition against Chrysler which in the end I won and proved my usage of the mark to a date long before RB even applied to register my mark.

The Parl/Oms is allowed to investigate such acts by a government department, which to use their own words 'Consider complaints about government departments, where there is evidence that they have not acted properly or fairly, or have provided poor service' I cannot think that any fair and intelligent minded person who knew the facts of my case would come to any other conclusion that my complaint fitted those requirements, to a tee. Plus I had also complained of very poor service with inordinately long reply times and many letter ignored, in which high proportions of what I had said or complained about, were ignored. Then the evidence that I and my MP had been lied to when we were pressing for an answer as to what was happening with the decision reply from the Hobbs hearing. This last point had absolutely clear evidence of lying and evasions when the IPO knew full well what had been happening.

What did they do? Eventually on the 7th August 2007, they come up with… Well guess what? Yet another typical civil service whitewash document. On their very first page they jump in by stating they will not investigate my complaint. This is a strange way of stating what they will or not do, as surely this quite long and detailed document means they have obviously investigated what I had said. Also some of the things they said, made it plainly apparent that they had been heavily in contact with the IPO. So what this means, is that a member of the Public makes a complaint against some governmental department and the first thing the Ombudsman does, is go running to that department blabbing out that someone is complaining about them. What then happens? Of course the department will then know what has been said against them, and all they then do is get all their forces together to deny and rubbish the complainant. I hate to think exactly what the IPO told the Ombudsman about me and what their version of events said, for you never get to see that.

The Ombudsman said that they can investigate the administrative actions of the IPO and she needs to see evidence of administrative fault, evidence that the fault cause a personal injustice to Mr Cook, and reasonable prospects of a worthwhile outcome. I don't know about you but the vacuousness of those statements gets right up my nose, especially when it was then said that those requirements had not been met. So the fact that on several counts, the IPO ignored its own rules re bankruptcy, bona fide applications, and applications made without the knowledge of a partner and the partner making the application had no legal authority to do so, all that does not count as administrative faults. Please, Mrs Ombudswoman, do me a favour will you?

They then go on to say that at all stages I had the ability to appeal whatever the IPO had done wrong, to a subsequent independent hearing or to a Court. These civil servants make me sick. Firstly I did just that, as I was forced to do so by the IPO failing to carry out actions according to its own rules, and that hearing was 11 YEARS later, during which time all the damage to my reputation, my business, my health and losses of profits, all were done. Far from being independent, these hearings are a sham as they are conducted by an IPO employee. All your evidence of wrong doings are totally ignored, because to find for you puts the IPO in a bad light. The one hearing that did go your way is brushed under the carpet and ignored like it never happened.

    I then complained about this Ombudswoman under their own internal complaints procedure and I tore apart everything she had said. Of course I knew I was pissing in the wind and I was right. A reply to that on the 21st November 2007, was yet another knock back. The complaint was dealt with in a 100% correct way etc, etc, blah, blah, blah. In other words you just cannot win against any governmental department. Democracy, don't make me laugh! The government is there to beat you down every time you complain. None of their employees can be seen to be anything other than gold plated. All are angels!

Chapter Twenty
The Rectification Application

As you could see above, I had left off after explaining what had been said at the Hobbs hearing, at the point where RB had now applied to have the register rectified. He had rapidly dropped his appeal as I had been informed by various managers at the IPO. Then he had wasted nine months by pretending he wanted to find his brother and then had applied to have the register rectified. I had been tartly informed when I had complained about not being told about the outcome of the Hobbs hearing, that I could oppose the application, but at a cost of £200. So I paid that and put in my first statement as to why he should not succeed. All the below statements describe the chain of events.

RB's Statement of Grounds, made 3rd Jan 2007

First of all I have to deal with the Statement of Grounds that he put in when making this application which went into the IPO on the 3rd January 2007. I think that he was getting legal advice on how to deal with this Rectification Application, plus wasting time as he did not need to be in a hurry.

He makes his claims by numbered sentences and I will comment on each sentence with my remarks in italic:-

1/ He confirms he is the same person who appeared before Hobbs QC. *I suppose just to let all those at the IPO know that they could liaise with the right person and carry out what Hobbs and James had worked out for RB.*

2/ He says he is asking for the registration to be rectified to show the proprietor as being himself and not Cobretti Engineering because that had been the position long before the trademark became registered. *He omits of course to say it was a partnership and that his brother had never given him carte blanche to register the trademark or run off with his half of the assets of the partnership. Also his registration dates back to May 1992 and prior to that date he cannot claim that the proprietor was only him as he was in partnership with Martin. See what a liar he is.*

3/ Now he says that first the registration has to be in the partnerships name (which straight away is at odds with his claim in para 2 when he claims he was the proprietor) as that was the case when it was first applied for. *As I say above, he doesn't say that his brother never even knew that it was being applied for.*

4/ He states his brother left the business and there is a document to the effect that the partnership was being dissolved and that Martin never had anything to do with the business after that. That everyone knew the business to be owned by him since then. *Forgets to tell us or the IPO that he never legally acquired Martins share of the business and therefore had no legal right to continue the business, or that Cobretti Engineering could not carry on trading after he went bankrupt in mid 1993. Or admits that the IPO had told him he had no specific rights to the trade mark after the break-up of the partnership.*

5/ He refers to a letter from his solicitors talking about the partnership dissolving and him giving Martin an indemnity. *No mention that no indemnity was ever legally drawn up and even if it had it was worth diddly shit, as he had no money. Also that in law Martin would still have been liable for debts.*

6/ He defended the company from then on against all the litigation started by me. *His enemy and why shouldn't he, I ask, as Martin had gone anyway and there was only him to deal with legal matters and he was on legal aid to do that.*

7/ He has continued to trade as Cobretti Engineering and has a website and advertises. *No mention that firstly he could not trade as Cobretti after the bankruptcy and then he advertised right up to 2002 under the banner of Autotrak Cobretti Ltd, until he woke up to the fact that he aught to resume using Cobrett Engineering as that was cleaner to do so, for his IPO cases. Also that in any case Autotrak Cobretti Ltd had been struck off in the late 90's.*

8/ He had withdrawn the assignments. *As advised by Mr Arrogance alias Mr Hobbs QC.*

9/ I have not been able to make contact with my brother for years despite attempts to do so. He had even tried to do so recently in Spain and the last time he saw him there was in 2003 and had not seen or heard of him since. *Lies again as he knew most times where his brother was and he had spoken since 2003 to him and had even visited him at his home on one occasion in 2004. Plus he attended his Fathers funeral and met Martin. Their Mother knew where he was, as she lived close by in Spain and had his phone numbers and address.*

10/ Here he slags off his brother by saying that he had tried to contact Martin since 2004 when he visited his Mother, but he had moved. He then goes on to intimating that Martin was in trouble with UK authorities and that was why he had changed his name and moved out of Europe! *What an ass**** this reptile is. He tries to make it appear he has done all he could to find him but Martin had disappeared into thin smoke, due to him being a less than honest person who had had to disappear. This is done so the IPO will think that there is absolutely no way Martin is traceable so they can all say that it will be perfectly in order to rip him off and out of his part of the partnership. As I said above he stayed at Martins house in 2004, so all he said was outright **perjury**.*

11/ Then he makes the statement that because of all that, it seems to him that the inclusion of Martins name on the register is an error which needs correction etc. *How very convenient and of course he has been schooled to say this by the lovely Mr Hobbs QC.*

My Statement of Grounds made June 2007.

I then made a statement in reply to all this nonsense and that was done sometime in June 2007. So this is what I said in my reply to his lies above, and I deal with his chapters of consequence, by their number.

2/ I point out that he could not have traded as Cobretti Engineering ever since the application in 1992 and reiterate the question of the bankruptcy. I point out that this statement is made under oath and that it constitutes perjury.

4/Audi A4I point out that him saying that other entities such as the tax authorities treating him as a sole trader, does not confer on him legality. I point out that Martin never assigned or sold his share of the partnership on its dissolution. So he never owned 100% of the partnership, up to the bankruptcy time and after that, the ownership of the application should have been owned by the Receiver. I say that the copy of the dissolution is not a legal document and could have been made at any time or even forged and more importantly, it does not assign or sell to RB, Martins half of the assets.

5/ The document from the solicitors showing they discuss a dissolution is worthless as it does not show a legal act of indemnity.

6/ That my entering into litigation against them is irrelevant in this case.

7/ I point out that this statement, again made under oath, is a lie and therefore perjury… *again,* I prove it by showing copies of adverts made by RB from 1993 (after his bankruptcy) to the present date none of which show the trading name of Cobretti Engineering, and I also include an up to date advert made in June 2007.

So more perjury is committed!

8/ I complain in this paragraph that the decision from Landau that the assignments were not legal and I question strongly why is it that the Landau decision has not been enacted after RB dropped the appeal, which was over these assignments. That should mean that the decision should now be enacted. I strongly ask why the IPO can now just act as if the Landau hearing never took place?

9/ to 12/ All these just confirm that Martin went away and has allegedly not been seen since. I repeat that he never assigned his share of the partnership to RB. I also castigate the IPO for allowing RB to ask for changes to what the real facts of the RB application were, when I am not afforded the same kind of convenience.

I then go on to make several observations to back up my assertion that this rectification should not proceed;

(A) That the IPO's letter to Martin in Spain to ask if he would sign over his assets to RB, is perverse because here they were siding with an ex bankrupt fact of which they had been warned by me, over and again, not to mention the non bona-fide acquisition of the Cobretti assets, only to be ignored.

(B) They had also ignored my telling the IPO that the application had been under the names of a partnership that had dissolved. That the application should have been discontinued. I complain that this was ignored by Reynolds. I ask why Reynolds could not have seen all the points that Landau did?

(C) I ask how the IPO can go over the wishes of the person (Martin) who may not want to lose his share of a business, just because it is said he cannot be located. *Had I known then when I made this statement what I know now, I would have said that far from being lost, RB knew exactly where Martin was.*

(D) How can the IPO hold a hearing when one of its officers (Landau) has said what he did and what the situation had to be (legally) after his decision. I state word for word what Landau said and say that the IPO has no legal right to allow the assets to be given to RB by way of a hearing.

(E) I say the rectification application should be discontinued.

RB'S statement in reply to my Statement of Grounds, made in Dec 2007.

I deal with his statement paragraphs in his order and my remarks are in italic;

2/ He says that my stating he has not traded under Cobretti Engineering is not true and he produces various copies of adverts where he says the trading name is shown as Cobretti. *Of course once again he is being disingenuous and really lying, because the adverts only state Cobretti. AND he only supplies selected adverts as there are others where he uses Autotrak Cobretti Ltd.* **This is simply not the same as the trading name he used in full before his bankruptcy and we all know that was 'Cobretti Engineering' and that was the name he used to apply for the trade mark!**

He used variations of all sorts from 1993, so much so that it was difficult for anyone to actually know who they were dealing with. I have already commented on this, and here he shows only the original name *after* 2002 and even then it was not consistent.

He then waffles on further about how he can call things what he wants etc. He finishes up by saying he can trade as a bankrupt. So the legal world will have to change all their books on law because he has decreed it.

This is yet another case of how RB comes out with out & out lies and statements that are just not correct and the IPO does nothing and says nothing. His application to register the trademark was made under the Cobretti Engineering banner and would have been registered under that. To prove ownership you have to also prove usage under the name you are applying under. So saying that he can trade under any name he likes is incorrect and not using the mark under the applied name, surely weakens his claims and case, especially as two of those names used were limited companies in which he **was not a director!**

Then the lie he waffles on about, re being able to trade as a bankrupt is so outrageous, the IPO should have commented on that, but deafening silence... of course.

4/ He says his receiver knew everything he had been doing and had no interest in the assets of the application. (Of course they did, as he never told them of the truth and they were kept in the dark about the Viper trademark application asset, until I told them. Then he lied through his back teeth and they being as incompetent as the IPO let him get away with it. It was too easy for them just to accept whatever he said. Regarding forgery, of course he has forged documents as I showed in my evidence at my trial in 2000 and at the Reynolds hearing.)

5/ He then tries to bamboozle our intelligence by claiming that because he carried on the business through thick and thin against my legal actions against him etc, that proves his 'commitment'.

What the hell his commitment has to do with anything? *Of course he continued with the business because right up to recent years he knew there was always the possibility that Chrysler would still buy the trademark, but only if he got rid of me,* **which is what they had told him to do!** *Of course they told me the same.* On this 'commitment' theme, what about **my** commitment in trying to protect MY mark against him which was ignored and even brushed aside by the IPO.

6/ Now he is lying buckets because he is accusing me of being responsible for the break-up of the partnership. *More perjury as he knows full well this is not true.* You will see that Martin will have told what the truth about this break-up was, further on in this story.

8/ He claims that the assignment from Cobretti Engineering of the assets to Autotrak Ltd in 1992 was legal. *Of course it was illegal as he did not own the assets 100% as I have shown, Martins share was never assigned or sold to him, so the assignment, if it ever took place was illegal and in any case it was not done in a legal format.*

9/10/11 He says Martin abandoned his rights when he walked away. Either he had this alleged legal indemnity or he abandoned his share, what is it to be RB? He also says that I abandoned the mark when I shut my business in 1989 and disappeared with deposits. *Well of course Martin never abandoned anything, and I did not shut the BRL business nor did I disappear, as I have shown many times above. It must be said that Busbridge has a fixation with the words 'abandoned' and 'disappear', and I expect he has had it drummed into him by Reddie & Gross to keep harping on about these points, as they will indoctrinate the IPO into believing them and that shows just what a legal company will do for its clients... deal in lies when they must have seen he was a liar.*

This document is yet another of RB's lying, fictious and mostly irrelevant pieces of nonsense. How the IPO will react to all this is to be seen.

My second statement made in Feb 2008.

My reply to his above statement & I reply to his paragraphs that need me to comment on.

2/ I reiterate the FACTS about his copies of adverts where he tries to justify his claim that he has used the trading name Cobretti Engineering consistently since 1992 to 2008. I again go over the real evidence that he is lying about.

I also state that there has been no evidence that his brother has agreed to having his name taken off the application records. I accuse him of committing perjury by making this statement about what trading name he has used. I point out that I have before made accusations of RB making perjurious statements and that the IPO seem to think that is OK, for they never take action.

4/ I remind the IPO that I was *found not guilty of forgery* and that RB making comments about it all the time in order to indoctrinate the IPO's mind against me, should be ignored. (Of course Reynolds did not ignore this at all, in fact it formed part of his decision to go against me.)

6/ I state that if Martin had taken no part in the business after the break-up, why didn't RB make sure he legalised that? I also castigate the IPO for not enacting the decision of Landau which dealt with this fact of omission. I also query why is it that the IPO refuse to answer my questions as to why they refuse to enact Landau's decision.

I reiterate my past comments re the alleged assignments and again point out that they were not legally done and as Landau said they cannot be taken as proof that RB gained ownership, for Martin never gave his agreement for this assignment.

I then reiterate that the Receiver was incompetent by not insisting on seeing a legally made up assignment. (One signed by Martin as well.)

I accuse RB of perjury again by pointing out that when he stated as he did, that he had not dropped his appeal and I mention various letters I had had from the IPO which stated clearly to me that he had dropped the appeal.

9/10/11/ I again claim that RB is committing perjury by stating that I had abandoned my trademark and had closed BRL, when he knows they are not the facts. I list the facts as they had happened after the cessation of BRL, just in case they have forgotten them and I accuse RB of muckraking to denigrate me so the

IPO have a low opinion of me. I say in any case all of his claims in these paragraphs are irrelevant to this case.

RB'S statement made 17th March 2008, in reply to the statement of mine.

This unusually for RB, is a short statement. Really it is just a statement full of irrelevant waffle and says nothing much of consequence or that is new, so is not worth repeating here.

However once again he commits perjury about whether the appeal before Hobbs has been dropped. This even though I quoted letters from the CEO of the IPO and the Ombudsman. So he insists that it is still alive. ***The man simply cannot stop lying!***

I reply to the above with a short statement dated 3rd April 2008.

I summarise the position we are in at this moment from a legal point of view. This regarding how he has not done things as per the law, with relation to the dissolution of his partnership, and that the decisions of Landau should have been implemented and that the IPO should enact that. I point out that RB has no right in law to rectify the record because of the way the law has not been enacted over the partnership break-up or the assignment or anything else.

It is worth noting that because I brought up the question of him perjuring himself, by claiming twice that the appeal is still ongoing, the IPO sent RB a letter on the 9th April telling him that there appears to be some confusion and that the appeal was dropped... *full stop*. No castigation about making perjurious statements and I say this is because as far as the IPO are concerned, Busbridge making perjurious statements is not a bothersome event that they would ever take action against.

Now we have reached the stage of a hearing date of April 2008 when this Rectification Application was eventually heard. I cannot say what the actual date was because as I was 'ex parte', yet again The ridiculous system the IPO have of keeping interested parties out of the loop even though I am allowed to oppose his application, and so I was not told when it would be heard. This even though I had a right to attend as a member of the public. You would think in a normal world, that I as the person who first started using the mark and who also has registration, I would have a great interest and right to know what was going on. The most astonishing fact about this farce and denial of my rights, was that I could put in all those statements and evidence against rectification but I cannot be part of the hearing.

So what went on and what was said I was unaware of, no matter what I thought and I waited to get the inevitable knock back decision. I had no faith by this time that anything was going to be seen in a positive light for my position. As far as I was concerned it was a travesty of justice that the hearing had even been necessary for had the Landau decision been enacted as this action would never had been necessary? It has been allowed by the IPO simply to enable them to eventually give Busbridge the mark by hook or by crook. It is the culmination of conniving by James and Hobbs as a way they can do this.

The hearing was to be heard by yet another hearing officer called Foley.

Chapter Twenty One.
Foley Rectification Decision

Well hearing decisions usually take no more than two months, this one took *seven months*, and after two, I was in constant contact with the law section of the IPO complaining as to the delays. Of course I got nowhere. You have to ask why this was? Was it deliberate, just to annoy me? Was it because they had to take their time in order to concoct the right story in order to find for RB? Was it incompetence? You never get to know. Eventually in mid November 2008 I got the decision and 'Hey Presto!' I was dead right, the decision went against me despite all the statements I put in. Once again the decision document can be seen on the IPO website. Below is a breakdown of what it said by paragraph number with my remarks in italic:-

4/ He starts by saying that this application is to change the recorded proprietor from M.Busbridge & R.Busbridge trading as Cobretti Engineering to R. Busbridge trading as Cobretti Engineering, on the following grounds as stated in RBs statement:-

(a) Martin had left the business in June 1992 and since then everyone had accepted that RB was the owner. He mentions the termination document.

(b) Two letters RB's solicitors confirming this and asking for an indemnity from him to MB against future debts. *Talking about giving an indemnity is not the same as actually giving on… something that seems RB cannot grasp!*

(c) RB carried all future liabilities including my litigation against him Martin walked out because he did not want to be involved in that. *Well he had to defend any litigation, didn't he, as Martin had gone. But he still had not given Martin a **legal** indemnity.*

(d) He was still continuing to trade as Cobretti Engineering. *I have shown many times that this claiming he carried on trading as C/E uninterrupted throughout the years is yet another lie.*

(e) He had asked for two assignments to be recorded but now has withdrawn them.

(f) He has not been able to contact his brother for years. He says his brother travelled to the Phillipines, New Zealand and Australia. Then he moved to Spain in 1996 and was in contact with their parents. He saw him in 2003 at the funeral of their father. He has not seen or heard from him since. *Now here he shows what a duplicitous liar he is. At this point in time he thinks he is safe to say whatever he wants. Lie through his back teeth. He has already seen that the IPO are not in the slightest bit interested in whether he lies. His brother is away in a foreign land and is probably unaware of what he is up to. We will see further on in this story if this state of affairs with Martin changes.*

(g) In 2004 he tried to contact him and had travelled to Spain to see his Mother and had gone to the last known address of Martin but he had moved. He then says that he thinks his brother had moved out of Europe because of difficulties with UK authorities. May even be using another name. *Here we see the example of how this wretch will slag off people **including** his own brother. His attempt to claim to the pliable IPO how his brother is so far away that there is no way he could be contacted and asked to confirm anything he says. Again you will see just how many lies he has made here about Martin, when you read Martins affidavit.*

(h) He thinks that keeping his name on the register is an error which needs correction as he left long before the mark was registered. *Well he would say that, wouldn't he!*

(i) Martin has had no involvement with the business since 1992. *He couldn't stand working with you, you lying duplicitous ratbag.*

5/ Foley says that these above submissions are accompanied by various extracts from magazines etc. Although they are not presented in the formal way that the IPO love, Foley says I asked what they were worth as real evidence. *Now again we will see how duplicitous the IPO and their staff are.* For he now goes on by stating that even though I question their validity as evidence, I did not question as to whether they were real (not forgeries). So he then says 'that in the circumstances of this case I consider it appropriate to accept them at face value and where appropriate, take them into account in my decision. *He completely fails to mention that I had also questioned how they prove his assertion that he traded as Cobretti Engineering at all times as they mostly show copies of adverts for trading company names that are not in that name. Remember that Reynolds would not accept various exhibits I had put into evidence by asserting they had not been presented properly or had some minor piffling thing wrong with them, in his estimation. Here you see the bias of the IPO at work , once again, because this h/officer will accept badly presented evidence.*

Badly copied as to be almost unreadable and no dates on the copies of magazine adverts and articles. (Well he would, as it will help the IPO find in favour of RB.)

6/ He says that much of what I say in my opposition goes to the substance of this case and to the truthfulness of the claims made by RB. (Well isn't that nice of him, but as we will see it mattered not a jot) He says he will take what he considers to be relevant in determining this case. *But he absolutely fails to say that he will fail to take much notice in real terms, of what I said. So he can come up with the end result that will favour RB and what the IPO seems to want.*

He also says that I comment on the outcomes of earlier proceedings (that would be the Reynolds hearing and Landau). Then the cheeky bastard says that he will not revisit those proceedings as they were a matter for appeal. *You will shortly see that throughout the rest of this document he does just that—revisiting previous hearings, but only when it suits him to do this so he can eventually find for RB. Now that is what I call biased and I could see that I was up against yet another biased, pre-programmed employee of the IPO. Even one of his fellow hearing officers Annand in the next hearing says he has revisited other hearings and should not have done so!*

He now listed what he said he believed were the grounds of my opposition:-

(a) That since 1993 RB had not traded as he claimed in the name of Cobretti Engineering.

(b) That just because RB claims to be the sole trader of Cobretti Engineering does not confer any legality. That after his bankruptcy he could not have traded with that trading name, and he could not have owned the business himself as the partnership was never properly and legally wound down. That after the bankruptcy the Receiver should have taken ownership of the assets of Cobretti Engineering.

(c) The termination letter was not a legally made up document, it was a photocopy that could have been made by anybody at any time. Nor does it deal with a legal assignment for money, of the assets of Cobretti Engineering.

(d) The letters from solicitors merely discuss a dissolution document and that is all.

(e) My copyright action had no relevance or bearing on this case.

(f) His copies of adverts did not show what he claimed re Cobretti Engineering and even his current website did not say he was called Cobretti Engineering.

(g) The assignments were found to be incorrect and were withdrawn by RB, and that the IPO should enact the Landau decision.

(h) Martin had never assigned his share of the partnership to RB and it could not be an oversight as RB claimed, as he was under legal advice at the time.

(i) That RB should never have been allowed to have his application proceed due to his bankruptcy.

(j) The application was under the name of a defunct business and should be discontinued.

(k) That the assets should not be handed over to RB just because MB cannot be found, as he may have other wishes.

(l) The trademark cannot be renewed as the partnership no longer existed, so expired in 1999.

(m) That the application should be discontinued on the grounds that it is not lawful and that Landaus decision should now be enacted as RB had withdrawn his appeal to the A/P.

Foley ignores all the above compilations, and those made throughout the three statements which I made for my opposition of this application, and the many accusations that RB committed acts of perjury. All those acts evidenced by statements he had made or documentary evidence. Plus why the IPO can allow and hold a hearing on a subject one of its hearing officers has said is at an end...

7/ Foley now mentions the two alleged assignments which RB had used to try to show he now, in his name, owned the trademark. He says that I challenged the legality of those alleged assignments at the Reynolds hearing. He goes on to say that Reynolds had said they were an error and that eventually they would need to be the subject of a post registration application for rectification. *This shows more incompetence as Landau did not hold a Rectification hearing but just a carry on hearing of Reynolds. By this Foley revisits other hearings. Now the crux about these assignments is that neither Reynolds nor Landau and now it would seem, Foley, have even bothered their heads about, is for the first alleged assignment to be legal RB would have had to get Martins permission in writing to allow it. For RB to simply assign away all the assets of C/E which were jointly owned, is not legal! So simpletons like Reynolds and Foley cannot gloss over the legalities and go on about these assignments as if they were perfectly legal. Also why are we still talking about them when RB has dropped them at the Hobbs hearing?*

8/ Now Foley shows that the IPO hearing officers are simply too slap dash and not fit for purpose, for he goes on to say that the assignments became the subject of an application for rectification by me (K.Cook). Then he goes on to state what Landau said in his decision.

Firstly I absolutely never applied for a Rectification at any time. (This shows straight away that Foley isn't with it and fills you with apprehension about his quality.) I will not repeat what he said as it has been said above in that relevant part of the story. However Foley had said he would not be revisiting past hearings, yet here he is doing just that, and he is heavily guilty of carrying on throughout this wretched document with him revisiting Reynolds, then Landau and then Hobbs and Hobbs was not a hearing in the sense that it was never finished due to RB dropping the grounds for it. Yet you will see that Foley relies on what the great 'His Lordship Mr Hobbs QC' said. (I have another two words for QC and they are not Queens Council!) Foley seems to me to be in awe of Hobbs the way he keeps referring to him and I feel that this shows just what an influence this man has on the IPO) I believe that once RB dropped this appeal it can no longer be called a hearing. So why can other IPO officers keep going back to what he said as if he was setting precedents. Surely all it amounted to was a discussion which went nowhere in legal terms?

9/ Bearing in mind what I have said about Hobbs above, here we go with the slavish repeating of his great announcements; Foley says that after Landau, RB appealed before Hobbs and he says that during the hearing there were 'discussions' and Hobbs said he thought that if RB dropped his assignments appeal, then the renewal (that Landau said could not be renewed) could be renewed. RB then wrote to drop the recordal of the assignments. *Now isn't that nice of His Majesty, King Hobbs? He can virtually say 'Fuck you Landau your nothing, I am the great authority here and you are nothing, and I say that the renewal can take place, so there!' But Landau said the mark could not be renewed because the application etc was not legally done and it had nothing to do with the assignments as claimed by Foley.*

10/ Foley states that Hobbs said that 'It would appear that at the time of the hearing, the understanding was that after withdrawing the assignments, the registration would revert to being in the name of Cobretti Engineering, a partnership.' The rest of what he also said is irrelevant. *Foley when he listed what Landau has said in paragraph 8, 'the trademark cannot be renewed' and he said in sentence 2, that 'the trademark should be in the name of R.Busbridge & M.Busbridge trading as Cobretti Engineering. So what is going on here with Foley misrepresenting* the facts? This because Hobbs never said any such thing.

11/ Foley now says that even if this were not the case the two events create the same effect. Then he waffles on with a lot of irrelevant nonsense and ends up stating that the registration is in any case in the names of R.& B Busbridge. So what was all that about Mr Foley? Page filling waffle, I say.

12/ He now says the bleeding obvious, that if the renewal did not happen there would be no registration to rectify. That is **exactly** what Landau said should happen and what I have been banging on about to no avail to the IPO, in effect why are we here at this point with this ruddy hearing? What is the point of the IPO, having Hearing Officers who make decisions when they are deliberately ignored as Landau was?

Foley then says that Hobbs after one of his cosy chats with James of the IPO, that although the IPO HAD renewed the registration, it was under sufferance rather than unconditionally. You cannot make up the stories these bastards make up, do they think the Public are all thick and they are the only ones with brains? The IPO had renewed it by making yet another error, another cock-up, another case of them not knowing what the hell they are doing. Landau had said what he had said, and even if he hadn't said that, why were the IPO allowing a renewal and in only one name when before it had been in the name of a partnership. Did they not say 'Hey hold on here, where is the paperwork that says we can do this, as you cannot just like that, change the details of who owns a mark,' What had happened was that straight after the registration was granted RB went trotting along to the IPO clutching his relevant form, this in November 2004, and renewed the registration in his very own name. This even though the IPO's own CEO Mr Marchant and Mr Webb Head of the trademark Registry, plus a Mr Kevan Badar, Head of the Law section had said in writing in 2004 after the Reynolds hearing, to me, that it had to stay in the partnership name until a hearing had been held to determine what the position was to be. RB was being his usual cheeky self, trying it on and the IPO were being their usual not fit for purpose, self.

I have the very form in front of me, as I write this, it is dated 29th November 2004. Also I have the certificate of registration made out to only RB signed by Marchant and dated 12th Nov 2004.

I had to complain most vociferously to the Law section about all these cock-ups before they corrected themselves. Now we have here this Foley bloke saying that it had been renewed 'under sufferance', what the hell is all that about? No one told me it had been renewed and I was under the apprehension that it was suspended until the outcome of due process. (if there is such a thing in the IPO's world... due legal process and all that!)

13/ Foley says that I had said that I thought that RB should never have been allowed to carry on with the application as he became a bankrupt and then the partnership collapsed.

14/ Now in this paragraph we have Foley going on about what happens if an applicant for registration suffers a bankruptcy. Some of what he says is crap and he shows he prepared to believe whatever lies RB tells him and not to look too closely into the equally incompetent Insolvency Service (IS) actions. Firstly Foley admits that as a bankrupt RB should have lost his assets to the Receiver. But strangely he only says that the trademark application 'Might be affected' as it would depend on what the circumstances under which the licence was granted.' What the hell is the man talking about? In the first case he damn well stole the mark off someone else (me) so how can he have a licence for it?

Then he goes on to say that there is nothing in trademarks legislation the even suggest that a bankrupt would stop his registration application in its tracks. *I have several letters from the IPO over several years where I asked this question and I got on each occasion the same answer and that was; if the IPO knew that an applicant was now bankrupt, the IPO would approach the Receiver to see what he wanted to do with it. IN this case even though I told the IPO many times they refused to act. Plus I found a rules document called 'Work Manual' Chapter 26 Law Section dated April 1984.*

I was sent this by the IPO in the early 90's. In the section headed 'Law section-Opposition to Registration... Transfer of Applicants Interest—Bankruptcy. 'Should an applicant for a trademark become bankrupt after formal opposition has been filed the proceedings may be continued in his name or the Receivers'. Then it goes on to say if the application is withdrawn etc etc. Now to be bloody minded, Foley or anyone could say that this says that the Receiver could either continue the application, as presumably he thought it was worth some money (the trademark) or withdraw it. Also they could say that this applies to an application where an opposition has been taken out. In this case the bankruptcy took place before it got to the stage where I had to oppose it. So what I say is; it shows that the IPO had rules on bankruptcy and I refuse to believe that the IPO does not have rules or laws which tackle bankruptcy issues with someone who has just put in an application to register. The IPO are just hiding from me its legislation. We will in due course see the truth. In the meantime I see no difference in the thinking that can be seen in this document that does cover bankruptcy issues. I see no difference between what it said and what would be probably said in this case. It is also worthwhile to know that I brought up this document several times from Reynolds onwards only to have it ignored by the IPO.

Now Foley deals with the fact that RB said that the IS had said they were not interested in the trademark asset. We are expected to believe RB when he tells us that he informed the IS of the trademark application.

Foley goes on to say that there was no formal evidence of that he did not. (So is he saying that we have to believe the liar RB?) However he says there are letters from the IS that say that the examiner was aware of the application. Then a letter saying they did not have an interest. Foley says one of those astonishing claims that HO's seem to like to make. *'Even without these letters it would be reasonable to infer that the examiner knew of this application: there is an onus on a bankrupt to declare such matters'.* The only saving grace for this idiot is when he says that 'If I have any concern.. It is that the examiner has not formally disclaimed the application as property falling within the scope of bankruptcy' Well, well, well!

Here we have a whole nest of vacuous 'assumptions and inferences' made by this Foley bloke. Let us be brutally honest here… the IS are as big a rabble of incompetent wankers as the IPO.

At the time of the bankruptcy in 1993, the country was just coming out of a bad recession. No doubt the Croydon branch of the IS was inundated with bankruptcies. Are we to believe that each and every small bankruptcy was dealt with by a microscopic examination? Well the IPO may well be that naïve, but I am not. I am willing to bet that RB never even got a visit from the IS in 1993. Foley does indeed show he is naïve when he says that the examiner would have known of the application. I ask, "why the hell should he know"? Do you really think that RB was going to tell him even if he did get a visit off the IS not long after he applied for bankruptcy?

This is a man that deliberately moved away all the assets Cobretti Engineering owned, when he knew that it was heading into financial meltdown. This is a man who went to Chrysler posing as the rightful owner of a trademark he'd pinched off the rightful owner, and who asked them for £500,000 for it. And he is going to tell the IS that there was a potentially valuable asset lurking about… do me a big favour… please! All this shows to me is that Foley and the IPO simply did not want to believe me and preferred to be taken in by RB. It seems to suit them more to do this, for some reason best known to them. Maybe RB has a relative working in the IPO at the top somewhere? Or maybe he is a Mason or Masons are mixed up in this, as RB had an ex copper working in his office at that time and he is still to this day mixed up with this bloke. How many coppers are Masons?

Another point is that it was not until I told the IS what RB was up to, in 1993/1994 that they even talked to him. This they did in early 1994. I have a letter to RB from them asking him to attend a second interview on the 10th March. They say that they want to ask him about the Viper trademark. (So one has to assume that in mid 1993, the time of the bankruptcy, they did not know about the trademark, otherwise why wait a year to ask him about it?) They then, in another letter ask him to also provide all the details of the assets sold to Autotrak Ltd and for how much, and where that money went. So he goes bankrupt in mid 1993 and it is not until my letter to them telling them he is trying to deceive them, that in March 1994 they start asking questions. Of course he fed them all his shit about Cobretti no longer owned any assets as they had been assigned to Autotrak Ltd in late 1992. God knows what lies he told them about how much he got for the assets? Probably told them it was for a nominal £1. It seems that the IS just took that in without lifting an eyebrow or asking delving and pertinent questions.

This seems to me to be the normal civil service way of doing things these days. They ask people what they have done or are doing and they believe every word they are told. This is seen all the time when illegal immigrants arrive here and tell humongous lies about where they came from and why, and without a scrap of evidence, they are believed by IPO style civil servants and are rubber stamped into the UK!

Or to take another example of civil service dickheads who believe everything told to them... take the gross examples we see where tens of thousands of Brits have conned the DWP into believing they are such human wrecks health wise, that they simply cannot work and they want loads of money so that they can idle away their lives. No questions are asked and they go on to enjoying a wonderful full life, courtesy of the tax payers. Similarly all the liars who con Blue Badges so they can park anywhere for free. I see these bastards parking at my gym right by the doors and they hop out full of life and run up the stairs and go off for their strenuous exercises on the running machines etc. The country is full of liars, it is the National pass-time... lying ones heads off. In fact it is these days it is the only thing Brits are still good at. Now at last the Conservatives are in at least they are saying they are going to sort this. But I will believe it when I see it, so it remains that every shyster is believed at face value, yet they are all liars like RB.

As Foley said, there are no letters from the IS shortly after these meetings RB had with them, to say that they were not interested in the trademark asset. We do not see any letters from the IS until into the 2000's AFTER they had told me that all their records were now destroyed and they could not say anything for sure. It was in November 2007 that RB sent a letter to the IS **asking them to provide him with a letter confirming they had no interest in the asset of the** trademark. So we have to take it, that back in 1994, not only did they not then confirm that they were not interested, they never even gave him the formal letter disclaiming interest, that Foley mentions above. The whole thing stinks, both from the way the IS have behaved throughout the whole bankruptcy from 1993 and on, but also how the IPO and their Mr Foley have behaved. The IS have potentially been so incompetent that had RB been successful in screwing Chrysler for £1/2M then the creditors of Cobretti would have missed out big time as RB would have not been seen for dust.

Do not forget that this is the man who has slagged me off for closing down BRL and diddling the creditors (neither of which happened as he said). BRL owed a piddling £40,000 made up of £20K to customers for their deposits and £20K to the HMRC, yet here he owed to his creditors an unknown amount which he has kept quiet about, plus whatever the assets of the trademark application and all the tools and tooling that he siphoned off to himself and to elsewhere. **Do not forget he was not a limited company either** so not personally protected.

15/ Here Foley says that there is nothing to stop a bankrupt who is self employed from starting to trade again albeit subject to certain restrictions. One of these is that there is a prohibition on them carrying on a business (directly or indirectly) in a different name from that in which they were made bankrupt, without revealing the name in which they were made bankrupt.

I do not believe a word of all that and I have to say I have never heard such nonsense. Maybe it may be considered OK if say a window cleaner carried on after bankruptcy, but then his business needed no valuable assets to carry on his business. In this case to carry on making kit cars requires much expensive tools and jigs and moulds etc. In RB going bankrupt and then carrying on with exactly the same assets and business, would mean that the bankruptcy laws were a farce. Even the carrying on in a business with a different trading name is not allowed, although you can be an employee. Now what did RB do? He had if you remember, started up Autotrak Ltd in 1992 and he was a director. All he did was to stop using Cobretti as the trading name, and he continued as Autotrak. It wasn't until I notified the DTI he was still a director six months later, as a bankrupt, that he was forced to resign. A complete and utter disregard for any British law, from this conman. Far from advertising the fact that he was a bankrupt from his days under Cobretti as Foley stupidly says he must do, that of course that was never done by RB Can you imagine RB saying to a bloke about to order a kit and having to pay say £1,000 deposit, "Well mate I am taking your deposit but I must tell you by law, that I am a bankrupt!

Foley carries on by saying ' It is reasonable to infer that, subject to any action that the receiver may take, RB could continue to trade under the name of Cobretti Engineering and use the name Viper. *Is this man completely mad, as what he has just said is completely against all the bankruptcy laws that I know about after 45 years in business. Maybe it is I that is the fool?*

16/ Continuing, Foley says that RB provided evidence to show that he continued to trade as Cobretti Engineering and using the name Viper. He says the papers filed show that RB, Cobretti and Viper had a continued connection in trade, but it is not formal evidence 'which I do not challenge the authenticity of' (meaning I did not challenge). Then he makes yet another astonishing statement to add to the many already uttered. That is, he says that all this information (even if it is not formal) is only useful in establishing a continued connection with the partnership.

This man is a raving lunatic, and the whole of this paragraph is madness. Of course I do not challenge the authenticity as the adverts were indeed made and what I pointed out was that all of them did not show that RB used the name Cobretti Engineering. He used at least 4 other trading names until about 2002/3. Just how can these adverts show any connection with the partnership that was defunct from mid 1992? What this and many of the previous paragraphs show is that this man Foley goes exceedingly soft on RB and all the wording of the statements he makes re RB are in a very sympathetic tones. **In other words he is rampantly biased. Everything RB does and says is treated sympathetically and all his lies and inconsistentcies are ignored and isn't this familiar** *to you, as Reynolds did exactly the same? In civil cases the people who do the judging, take things not as black and white, as in a criminal case, where things have to be absolutely proved. Foley shows he is prepared to infer this or that or say it is reasonable to infer or take as, etc etc, when he deals with RB, but in my case all my evidence is not dealt with in the same way. Any old excuse to leap in and rubbish what I say, and he is there dishing it out just as Reynolds did. It is all there in black and white on paper, if you read his decision document.*

17/ The core issue I make, he says, is that the assets of the partnership should not be handed to RB against the wishes of Martin simply because he cannot be located. He then goes on to state that the termination document is flawed for the reasons I stated. Hurrah, I eat all my above words… I think not!

*This was not the **core issue** as it is only one of many issues I raised. Again here he shows his biased nature towards RB. For he seems incapable of even considering where Martin is and that RB says he does not know where he is, could be the subject of lying by RB. There has been no absolute proof that would really stand up in a **real** Court of Law, that what RB says on this is 100% true, and we shall see later more on this. But here Foley is siding with RB yet again.*

18/ Here Foley deals with the letters from solicitors about the alleged indemnity, but again he has says that I do not challenge their validity, so he thinks it seems appropriate to take them into account.

*Again this thing he has about me not screaming from the roof tops that they are not valid. For in every such case when I have said that their evidential value is not there, I mean that they are also not valid as well. He will not see that I am a litigant in person and not a lawyer. It is OK when he deals with all the mush RB said in all his writings, but in my case he has to nit pick and criticise. The **fact** is those letters are worth 'Diddly Shit as they do not deal with any valid indemnity, all they do is **talk** about it.*

19/ Now he turns to his hero, 'His Majesty Hobbs of the QC'., when he was asking if RB could contact Martin to get him to transfer his share of the assets. He says that even though it would have been 'tidier', it didn't happen. Then he repeats what Hobbs said about a handover for a valuable indemnity being the same is if RB had handed over money for Martins share.

God these two must be relatives of RB they way they are unashamedly biased towards RB. Well I am not at all convinced that what Hobbs thinks about this is really the LAW as it stands. It sounds a lot of bollocks to me. First of all why wasn't there a valid and legal indemnity actually drawn up by their solicitor?? Would any such indemnity be worth a crock full of shit? The partnership collapsed because they ran out of money and Martin lost his house to the bank. RB admitted this. So what was RB worth in real terms and in reality? It is obvious to everyone except Hobbs and Foley that RB was worth **zero**, so any such indemnity wasn't worth a zack.

It is also obvious that this is why Martin never got an indemnity, and we will see all about this later on.

20/ The whole of this paragraph is absolutely full of crap and is so biased and slanted that I rage reading it. Bear in mind what I have said above. Let us face it, Foley here is faced with an unpalatable truth, ***there had been no legal indemnity given.*** So he has to think of ways around it. So he waffles on about the wording of the two letters from the solicitor and comes to the conclusion that as the wording changed from one to the other, that means that there was '***clear intent*** by Martin to leave the partnership and get his liabilities in order'. 'He was clearly ***prepared*** to relinquish his interest on the basis of a suitable indemnity'. So it would be *'reasonable'* to take the partnership as having passed into the ownership of RB.

Do you like the way he did that? It is like watching a magician with a sleight of hands. One minute it is all up in the air, next it all belongs to Robert. Hey Presto! Aren't I just so clever! It is so outrageous and how does he think he can get way with it or think I am going to take all that lying down? It is obvious that these IPO hearing officers are so used to getting their own way, that especially when they are faced with private litigants like me, they think they are on a winner. He put words and thoughts into Martins head, especially when he was not there to contradict the utterings of this biased IPO madman. Again you will see what Martin did think about all this... later on.

21/ He reiterates that RB was entitled to file for renewal, despite Landau saying otherwise. He again says it is '*clear*' Martin was prepared to relinquish his assets, this despite anyone actually asking him if that was right. Now he says it is '***also reasonable to infer that an indemnity was granted even though no legal document has ever been seen. So this puts the ownership into the hands of Robert Busbridge.***'

Again this all makes me so mad with the bias of it all and the chicanery used to put words in people's minds and mouths. It shows to me an absolute determination by the IPO to put this registration into the hands of RB, no matter what.

22/ He reiterates there is nothing in trademark legislation about bankruptcy, so that makes all that I complained about worthless. So he orders the registry to read that Viper is in Roberts name. Hey Ho and up yours, Cook.

Fait accompli by the crooks of the IPO and the lies of Robert Busbridge, super crook, and the 'Worlds Biggest Liar'. I bet he went out the night of the day he got this decision and got himself well pissed up. It certainly gave his ego another boost as again as you will see later.

I must point out here that after reading Foley's decision document I was so appalled at what I read about the Hobbs hearing and what seemed to have had gone on there, that I resolved to see if there was a transcript available to me. I approached the IPO as I have recounted previously, to see what I could get. I was sent a transcript and I wondered if the person who sent it realised just how what I found was a pointer as to just how rotten the whole IPO system is.

It goes without saying that I was not going to accept any of this decision of Foley and once I calmed down I set about appealing the disgraceful decision. I sent in a letter on the 1st December to say I would be appealing and I enclosed my first statement date 28th November 2008.

Chapter Twenty Two
Statement of Grounds for Appealing the Decision of Foley, Dated 24/11/08.

Although I knew that this statement should only deal with what was said in the Foley document, I decided to include a rant about my general dissatisfaction of the IPO from day one and going back to 1992. I knew that the appeal person would not take it into account but I thought that it would get to those within the IPO hierarchy and it just may concentrate their minds and show just how pissed off I was with the way they had treated all the cases etc that had now come to this point. So I will not comment on what I said as the content is contained within this book and on the prior pages to this.

I voiced my deep concerns at the length of time it had taken between all the hearings and I was of the opinion that this could be due to the fact that the IPO was just hoping I would 'kick the bucket' before it all came to an end. I also voiced the fact that I was trying to find a way to either sue them or get a Judicial Review. I wanted to rattle cages and whether I did is anybody's guess.

In hindsight I now believe that this is the reason that someone in the IPO had decided because of what I had said on a number of occasions that I was trying to get a Judicial Review or to sue them, they would make sure they would never allow me to win at any stage. To do so would be tantamount to admitting that somewhere they had cocked up and that would give me grounds to sue. So they keep making me lose and then to sue I would have to find grounds to do so and have a damn good lawyer present the case *in a high court*. That would cost big bucks which they knew I did not have. To force a JR, I was out of time and it too would cost more than they knew I could afford.

I set out the paragraphs of Foleys document in their order:-

4/ I deal with Foley quoting various statements of RB presumably as he thought that what RB said was relevant and truthful. Then I go into whether the original description on the original registration application was correct and I query exactly what Act RB is relying on to be able to apply for rectification.

I query why RB did not ask the IPO immediately after the dissolution of the partnership to change the name of the application. I again show that RB never bought out Martins share of the business. I ask why Foley seemed to accept the statement by RB that everyone knew him to be the only owner of Cobretti after 1992, when it had no legal relevance and how RB after his bankruptcy used other company names to trade under. I go on to say that much of what Foley said about RB and Cobretti was waffle.

I then go into RB's trading activities in depth, to show that RB is lying when he tries to say that his use of the trademark Viper was unbroken from 1992 through to 20004, when for various reasons it was not, and not least because of his bankruptcy in 1993 and enforced inability to trade for three years after that. I say that I believe that most of what Foley said was padding and just made out to try and show he was doing his job, but in actual fact did nothing about the legitimacy of what RB had done or was trying to do. Of course this also includes the alleged assignments which he dropped after the cosy legal advice from Hobbs.

I say that all the claims by RB about trying to contact his brother are irrelevant as he did not do that in any case.

5/ I then deal again with the adverts RB showed and I reiterate that they do not show RB traded as Cobretti after 1993 and nearly all are after 2000. I point out that when Foley said I did not question their validity, that this was rubbish as what did he think I was saying when I made those comments. I accuse Foley of being slap dash.

6/ I then tackle the fact that Foley said that in my evidence I had quoted previous hearings, but he wasn't going to do likewise. However he then went on and did just that. I ask in any case, why did he ignore what Landau had said., especially my points about what he had said should have been enacted after RB dropped his appeal.

I point out that Foley is slavishly following what Hobbs said in the appeal he heard. I then say that Foley is turned his hearing into his rehash of the Landau hearing with his own slant on it, and then he overturns what Landau had decreed and this in favour of RB.

I accuse Foley of cherry picking what I had said in my statements and ignoring much of the rest of what I had said, which was relevant. I pointed out that due to the fact that RB had said many irrelevant things in his statements, that forced me to reply to them in case some biased IPO officer took them to be valid.

7/ I say that Foley had brought up the question of the alleged assignments when in fact RB never brought them up in a big way. Only to say he had dropped the appeal and the question of those assignments. I said I thought it was just to make a case in order to for him to eventually say that RB can rectify the records.

8/ I then point out that Foley hasn't got a grip on the case when he says I applied for rectification (Landau hearing) when I did no such thing.

9-11/ In these paragraphs I point out that Foley is going on about the Hobbs hearing. I remonstrate that Foley had come to a conclusion that although Hobbs never made any decision as the case was dropped, Foley thought that what Hobbs really meant was that RB could drop the assignment issue and then the renewal of the mark could take place. That Foley was using everything that Hobbs had said and it was influencing his own thoughts. When you take into account that Foley had said he wasn't going to revisit other hearings, here he is doing that in a big way with what Hobbs said. He hasn't a thought or decision to make of his own. I complain at the number of times Foley says 'he thinks that this was meant' and that he is always putting thoughts and words into peoples mouths.

12/ Once again I complain that Foley is using what Hobbs had said, as a basis for what he will say. I point out that the Hobbs hearing was supposed to be an appeal hearing about what Landau had said about the assignments etc, yet it patently was not an appeal hearing but a cosy chat amongst all (except myself of course) about how RB could circumvent what Landau had said must happen and the corner he was thus in.

I also complain that having read what Foley repeated all the time about what Hobbs had said, and that the Hobbs hearing was nothing more than a free advice session, which is continued through Foley. I then showed by producing a document that Busbridge was so cocksure after hearing the advice of Hobbs, that he was going round in the press boasting about how he had won and the mark was now in his name. It was obvious to me that Foley did not want to entertain the fact that Landau had said that for various reasons the mark could not be renewed and that meant also that no rectification could take place. Yet Foley had said that it could take place.

13&14/ I now say that we should not even be at this place if the IPO had done their job properly back in the 90's when they were notified of the bankruptcy of RB. I did not think that this would have any effect on my appeal to the A/P hearing this case, but I threw it in, in any case and showed documents all from the

IPO to show them saying that had they known about the bankruptcy etc, they would have acted.

I then make the statement that Foley is being naïve when he believes that what RB states is true, when I have shown time and again he is a liar.

I go into the facts about the Insolvency Service and how the document that RB shows which formed a large part of what Foley thought about that section of my complaint, that had the IPO acted about the bankruptcy, I would not have had to fight an long battle against RB. I tried to show that the IS were completely incompetent and that letter shown by RB was made very late in the day (2007) and not at the time around the bankruptcy, and made when the IS even admitted they had no records left to really back up their thoughts on the matter. How the IS could not give me any comments when asked, yet when RB asks them to confirm they were not interested in the application asset, they can suddenly remember they were not interested.

I complain bitterly that for Foley to once again make statements like the examiner of the bankruptcy *'must have known'* about the asset, because *'the onus was on RB to tell him'* was astonishingly naïve of Foley. I said that it smacked of bias for RB, once again.

15/ In this paragraph I again say that Foley was being naïve and biased when he made statements that it was OK for RB to have continued in business even though he was a bankrupt. I try to show once more how RB is dishonest over the way he traded for the 10 years after his bankruptcy and this was an indication of the type of person he was, yet he is believed by all in the IPO.

16/ In this paragraph I once more complain about Foley's lack of business experience when he thinks that the trading pattern I showed Foley, did not gel with RB's claim that he had always traded under Cobretti Engineering. I give documents to show during the period that RB showed copies of adverts, my own advertising was much more intense and I produced copies of my own advertising.

17/ Once more I complain that Foley was willing to accept copies of advertising shown by RB as formal evidence, yet my evidence is not 'formal'. Similarly when I objected to certain evidence shown by RB by saying it was irrelevant, I was accused of saying it was not 'authentic'. That it seemed to me that Foley was once more being biased.

Then when Foley said that all the RB evidence of adverts, showed a connection in trade to the partnership, I queried how he could say that as there was **no partnership** after 1992!

I then explain in detail how in the Reynolds hearing he had castigated me for not advertising my mark, and I then explained all about my trading history with RB from 1989 to 1992, and how despite all that, *Reynolds found that this none advertising meant that I was not in control of my mark. Yet here we had a case handled by this hearing officer, who says it is quite OK for a trader not to actually trade and be still able to claim ownership of a mark. Thus showing inconsistencies between hearing officers and thus showing bias towards RB by the IPO through its hearing officer employees.*

17/ I said here that I actually agreed with what he said in this paragraph.

18/ I complained that Foley had said that I had not said that the two solicitors letters RB showed were invalid. I point out that it was because I thought them irrelevant. Yet Foley thought they were terribly relevant.

19 & 20/ Here I complain that Foley once more relies heavily on what Hobbs had to say about how the offer of an indemnity, somehow meant that RB could legitimately claim ownership of his brothers share of the Cobretti business. I point out that both were under the guidance of a solicitor at the time, yet nothing legally was done. Yet Foley leaps on what Hobbs had said, once again!

I complain that Foley makes the astonishing statement that 'it would be 'reasonable' to infer that the matter was concluded' (Meaning that a legal handover of Martins share to RB) I point out that RB had no intention to find his brother to get a handover, and even if he had, Martin would never had done this. I continue to complain that Foley is always putting thoughts and inferences into the arena, when facts would be more to the point.

21/ I disagree that by withdrawing the assignments from the arena, gave RB the right to renew the mark (which the IPO had on hold) I ask what law Foley is relying on ? Then I point out that Foley saying that this gives **'Richard Busbridge'** the right to have the business in his name, when there is no Richard. (This shows Foley is so slap dash that he cannot even get the names right.)

22/ In this paragraph I say that I have shown that the bankruptcy was badly dealt with by the IS and the IPO. Legal requirements were not carried out and it was not tested legally if a bankrupt could hold onto an asset that at the time was valued at £500,000. That the so called proof that the IS were not interested in the mark, was a letter written 11 years after the event and after the IS had admitted it had no records to check against. It was seriously flawed.

I then asked that the case be looked at by an *independent* Appointed Person, who was not a stooge. (Little did I know then what I now know about AP's. More on that later.)

It must be pointed out that as is normal, I had been given a date by which I had to put in the above statement. All the time I was making it out, I was also trying to get some sense out of the IS re just how they could 11 years after the date, categorically state that they had not been interested in the asset of the trademark application and this back in 1993/4. This when they told me over and again that they could not answer my questions about the chain of events after RB's bankruptcy, due to the fact they had destroyed all their records. The two factors did not add up. I decided to contact their manager of the Croydon branch of the IS, that had dealt with this matter.

I then entered a surreal world that you only get when you try to get some dysfunctional and duplicitous civil servant, to tell you the truth. It was something like it was out of the mad hatters tea party. Emails went back and forth with non answers and me then replying by castigating the writer for not answering the question etc. Of course each answer took ages and the time went on and on, and the deadline for me getting in my statement to the appeal, loomed up. So when it arrived I did not have my answer and I thought that if only I could get the bastards to admit their letters to RB were unwise and not really truthful, it would be worth keeping it up.

So I wrote to the Treasury Solicitors to ask if I could put in an additional statement which I thought was very important. You couldn't believe the song and dance I had to go through, and this annoyed me because RB had twice asked to be allowed to have additional evidence allowed, and was allowed.

Here I was being buggered around as if my asking this was a crime. I was eventually told to put it in to the appointed person, who by then I knew would be a Professor Annand. I found out that she worked for a firm of IP lawyers in London and at some Uni, in their law section. I thought that being a woman she may be more independent and not an IPO stooge. How naïve I was, but then I didn't know what I know now.

Second statement to appointed person, dated 18/2/09.

I drew up this second statement, and I will briefly set out its contents:-

Firstly I point out that it was necessary for this statement to be made due to the slowness of the IS replying to my various requests for information and clarification as to why their examiner Hawkins made up his letter to RB stating the IS was not interested in the asset of the application.

I said that because Foley had placed great reliance on this letter (probably 50% of his decision on it) this required an explanation from the IS.

1/ I charted out in this paragraph the whole history of the how the applicant RB went bankrupt and when this happened.

2/ I said that I first sent a letter to the IS late 1993 informing them that I thought the IS had not taken control of the asset of the trademark application at the time of the bankruptcy. I got nowhere with this as the IS ignored my letters.

Later on I had found that after my letter, they had interviewed him and I asked if they had asked about this question and if they had dealt with his assertion he had assigned this away from his bankrupt business? Had he given them proof he had done this? I pointed out that according to IPO laws this assignment was not legal. That the assignment document stated that RB was the proprietor and I maintain that the document was made after the date of the bankruptcy, so then he would be the former proprietor (and not even a lawful proprietor as he had not lawfully been given ownership of all the assets).

3/ I go over in detail about how the IPO had repeatedly ignored my request for them to drop the application due to this bankruptcy. Then they admit several times that had they known of it, they would have contacted the Receiver.

I say that Landau brought up the fact that when the partnership was dissolved as Robert did not buy out his brother, then he did not own the application, so could not assign it or carry on with the application. Despite this, Foley had used the bankruptcy as one of his main reasons for allowing rectification!

4/ I say that now, because of that, I have to look at this bankruptcy in greater depth and I then go into the whole bankruptcy business. I carry on to discuss the whole story of what RB did after his bankruptcy re the asset and what he is supposed to have said to the IS. How RB relies on an assignment which is shonky to say the least and is it legal? Why was it that the IS seemed to believe what RB told them about what the asset was worth and his lack of conviction as to their worth, even though the assignment had taken place recently, to the IS asking him their questions.

How, in any case, as RB did not legally own the asset completely, how could he legally assign it? The IS even though the business was a partnership, seemingly they completely ignored that fact and to question RB as to how he could therefore assign away an asset he did not fully own?

5-10/ I query how in 1993 could the IS rely on what RB said, as to him actually owning the mark asset?

In these paragraphs I detail all the letters and emails between me and the IS and the machinations of the IPO over the bankruptcy and the assignments. All of the subject matter I used is already gone over in this book so far. So to detail it all again will not be necessary as you will shortly see.

Robert Busbridges statement in reply to my first statement.

This was exceedingly short for him and basically he just denied everything I had said about the facts surrounding his bankruptcy and his talks etc with the IS.

It is his last sentence that is of interest, though. Here he tells the A/P that to show what type of person I am and what he has had to deal with for 16 years, they should read my blog on the IPO!

In turn this shows what a devious shit he is, for what I may say on a blog about the way the IPO have treated me over this case, is totally irrelevant to the pending case in question. He does it to try and influence the mind of the hearing office... of course, and even admits it is irrelevant, but he has a duty to inform the A/P of some of the things I say. Talk about a humongous hypocrite, as here we have a conman and pathological liar who has stolen the IP of another person, then complains when that person will not allow him to get away with it. Of course one wonders what Annand (and of course the big wigs in the IPO) will make of that… we will see later on just how my blog did influence the shits of the IPO and it raises the question of how it is obvious they set out to stitch me up because of it and what I said in it!

I make up a skeleton argument for Annand comprising of 16 paragraphs were I condense my main points for the appeal.

Chapter Twenty Three
The Appeal Hearing Before an Appointed Person, Prof Annand

The appeal was heard in London on the 16th April 2009. Straight away it became apparent that Annand was going to conduct this hearing in a completely different way to how the Hobbs appeal was conducted. Straight away she said that she would only take note of ***relevant*** points in the main statement of mine. She would strictly deal, only with the law related to the facts of this appeal.

She said she was going to first deal with whether she would allow this additional evidence I had requested, be added. It quickly became apparent she wasn't going to allow that because she said three main conditions had to be met in order to allow new evidence. Firstly I had to show that I could not have got it together along with the rest of the evidence. It must have an important influence on the case, and it must be credible.

My first thoughts were, that it fulfilled all of those, and I thought she would allow it. Only to be quickly shot down as she said that it was argument, already in the case, on the registry file and not fresh. She then admits that my copies of emails between me and the IS was fresh? Then she says my reason for late production was I had not realised that importance was being attached to a letter sent by the IS to RB saying they were not interested in the asset.

She says that my emails were to verify why, that late in the day a statement was made about facts that could not be verified, as all the files had been destroyed.

She says she will not allow the evidence as it will have no effect on the outcome. Even though they concerned what Foley had said about the bankruptcy, and thus ignoring the fact that, as I have said, that Foley relied on this business about the IS allegedly not wanting the trademark asset, and that allowed him to come to the conclusion, wrongly as I said, to allow RB to have possession of this asset. Had he not been allowed to have it, how could he have then continued to get it registered? Obviously this was too much for Annand to handle in her biased brain. She is no more than yet another IPO stooge!

Whatever the outcome of this appeal the register will still state that the trademark will remain in either the name of both brothers or in RB's name only.

So once again, my pointing out that Foley had used this letter as one of his main reasons for saying that RB could claim ownership seems to either go over her head, or she was instructed to brush aside even relevant claims and points. I believe this was VERY relevant and it is another way my evidence is just kicked aside. It also has a core connection with the fact that RB had no legal right to even still have that asset under his total control as he had not bought out his brothers part of the Cobretti business. She especially annoyed me when she went on to state that these proceedings were to remove Martin from the register, yet as I have just said the bankruptcy and the letter from the IS show that RB was still using an asset he did not completely own. So how can the IPO through Foley or her, just decide that Martins rights are to be taken away from him... just like that?

I was asked if I had any questions and I said I did not as all I had to say had already been said in my statements. Busbridge who was present did not ask any questions either. So within half an hour or so it was done and dusted.

Now my point is here that the Hobbs hearing never took this course at all. Busbridge was not even spoken to right from the beginning. Nor was he ever given the chance to ask any questions of James (he was representing the IPO). It was right from the start, a long discourse between Hobbs and James. Then a lecture from Hobbs to RB on how he should do this or that. Whereas this appeal was strictly to do with the grounds of the appeal. Did I, as the appellant wish to add to what I had already stated or have any questions of her. (Note here there was no member of the IPO present for me to question if I wished, as there was at the Hobbs appeal.) Busbridge was given the same rights, which he declined, so as neither of us wished to say anymore, the hearing was over and the A/P could make up her decision. At the Hobbs appeal there may have been a statement put in by RB and if there was, it was not alluded to by Hobbs. So I think I was very right to be suspicious of the Hobbs appeal hearing and of the actions of Hobbs.

I had hoped that the decision would only take the normal two months maximum I had been told by the IPO was the norm, and not the 7 month and 13 month times taken with the last two decision documents to get to me. I got the decision three quarter way through May, so it had taken just over a month. However it was no joyous event as it went against me... yet again. But I really had not thought it would go for me, as the more I looked at all the evidence of the previous goings on, I was convinced I would never be allowed to prove my case, by the IPO making sure of that.

As I am not an IP lawyer I cannot be certain that Annand was strictly neutral and had only dealt with what evidence she had before her, and it was just a case that me not being a lawyer, meaning I had not presented a case with enough hard new evidence to sway her or in the proper legal way they all like to see. That said I still had this feeling that it was all a put up job by the IPO as usual. I certainly did not feel justice was served.

For me, I felt when putting together my statement for this appeal, I was a bit war weary. I had in the past used all the points and legal arguments I could think of and every time it was all ignored or pooh pooed. I could not think of any more to say other than what I did say. So I will leave it up to others more knowledgeable to come to conclusions on that one.

Chapter Twenty Four
Transcript of the Annand Hearing
(Obtained by Me in Oct 2010)

I went to some lengths to get this so I could compare how Annand had conducted this appeal hearing compared with how Hobbs had conducted his sham of a hearing. I will deal with those aspects separately under my comments about this Hobbs bloke.

However it is interesting to refresh my memory as to what I said and what Annand said and what she covered, rather than using my memory as in the previous chapter. Straight off it is clear that she spends an inordinate amount of time and energy going over my asking for 'additional evidence' to be allowed out of time. I will not go into what she said or what I said as none of it is relevant to what I want to show here. Although I will point out that in the end it boiled down to her saying that whatever Foley had said about the Insolvency of RB he thought it relevant to his decision, which of course made me apply myself to replying to his nonsense and this turns out to be a waste of time for me. When I said that Foley had dealt with it, so if it was not relevant why did he do that? Her reply was "I do not have to agree with Foley".

Where I take issue with Annand is why didn't she just tell me straight off about this instead of waffling on for 24 of the 40 pages of this transcript, when it was all irrelevant?

This shows yet again that Hearing Officers are making mistakes all the time and I will show you further on a list of mistakes specifically made at each of the relevant hearings. All this hardly gives anyone confidence in the IPO and their hearing officers, which I will again comment on further forward.

She now went into the reasons for my appeal and at the point where she deals with RB lying about MB's Spanish address by swearing in an affidavit that the last known address of MB, it should be noted that she did not say anything more about this. However at this point in time Martin had not reappeared so I did not know that this statement was a sham and perjury.

Now she makes comments about the TMA section under which Foley covered his hearing and decision. It being TMA 64 (1) and she says he was mistaken and it should have been 64 (5). She says that had the appeal have to be heard under that section or 64 (2, 3or 4) the appeal would have had to take a different direction. She she is proceeding under a completely different section of the act and quite how she is able to just change things like that, I do not know. Surely if Foley made a decision under a wrong part of an act then his decision must be trashed on a technicality?

So we have here yet another mistake by this Foley bloke and there is more to come.

Foley had said in his decision that there had been an "error made in the Registry" I had differed to that and in my evidence had said so. She agrees with me and said it was neither an error nor an omission. *So another Foley mistake.*

Now she goes into asking me if I had any points to make. I point out that Foley made mistakes in saying RB could acquire Martins assets merely by giving an implied indemnity without the OK from MB, thus giving him the right to a Rectification and into his own name. She makes no comment.

RB is then given a chance to comment on that and here he gives the game away regarding this Hobbs bloke and his corrupt hearing. For he says "My appeal with Hobbs, his comment was that in the case of a partnership breaking up, you can also obtain a handover (of assets) where my brother had nothing to do with the business"This makes it obvious he was given ADVICE from Hobbs. RB goes on to say that therefore he took over MB's assets legally etc etc.

He goes on to perjure himself again over MB's Spanish address by saying "my brother lives in Spain somewhere" when he knows full where he lives having visited him and stayed there and also knew his telephone numbers. He repeats this a second time further on.

Then he again shows how corrupt the Hobbs hearing was by saying "as I said, Mr Hobbs reasoning for a handover and not a cash or financial benefit" for this is again admitting Hobbs gave him advice.

At this point Annand shows how complicit she is with the IPO and Hobbs for she jumps to Hobbs defence as she has now realised RB is admitting advice. She says "I should make it clear, actually, that Mr Hobbs was quoting from a textbook. He was not actually making this up," in other words "Whoops he wasn't helping you but quoting from a case history text." Bollocks you complicit woman.

I then go into a long spiel about the Hobbs appeal and him giving ***advice!*** Annand ignores all that I said about Hobbs and other things RB has said so far in this hearing and she says she must bring me back to this hearing which deals with changing the Registry to take off MB's name. ***It seems to me that whatever I said about how the evidence given by RB is tainted and wrong or irrelevant, matters not.*** Yet RB can talk his head off about Hobbs and that is OK.

Now we get to the crux of how this transcript shows that this hearing was conducted along proper guidelines and only dealt with the Foley hearing and his decision and the evidence and points I had put in and whatever RB had said in evidence. Whereas Hobbs had not dealt with ***one point of evidence nor even RB's statement of grounds***, which is what an appeal hearing is supposed to deal with. Also he had referred to other hearings.

Annand states; " I must say I have no powers to say anything about Mr Reynolds decision or your fight with Chrysler" " What Mr Hobbs said is nothing to do with me" "They were different proceedings. So it is not up to me to say anything about advice" (from Hobbs) "It is not my jurisdiction".

I ask Annand why was it then that Foley had revisited Reynolds and Hobbs and saying it was strange. She says "Yes I agree with you Mr Cook, it is strange and Mr Foley actually says in his decision as you correctly point out that the present proceedings have nothing to do with the past proceedings" I say, "So why comment on them?" She replies, "I agree".

From this it is clear that once again Foley has made mistakes, yet as always they are ignored by the IPO. It also shows that Hobbs visited previous hearings when he should not have done so. Thus tainting his hearing which in any case is as corrupt as hell throughout.

Now Annand nails it for me by saying something that makes it clear that I have had to suffer hearings that were not conducted along the proper lines as per various laws and rules which I will deal with later on. She says;" I know Mr Cook, and I regret that both parties really have put to perhaps unnecessary angst when the boundaries of what is happening has not been really truly appreciated".

To read this in normal English, what she is saying is that the hearings prior to hers have not followed the guidelines and rules that a hearing should follow. A damming indictment I think, which vindicates what I have said many times before, to be ignored. However even though she commiserates it makes no real difference to me as the IPO will not be reading her decision and noting that, let alone make amends. So it changes nothing for me!

One thing that annoyed me with what she said there, was by commiserating with RB as well as me, when this criminal, lying, bastard is the one who was **absolutely responsible for all the hearings I had to put up with and their incompetencies!** Can't she see that from the reams of evidence that show he stole my IP and therefore is a crook, so needs no commiserating with.

Then she makes a statement in which she is entirely wrong by saying something that revisits a previous decision which she has so far said cannot be done as per the rules. For she says " Can I just say that Mr Landau's decision evaporated because Mr Landau decision was concerned with assignments that were withdrawn." This is not the whole truth and had she read all his decision she will have seen that there were a number of legal reasons for his decision that were quite apart from any alleged assignments. In any case why is she commenting on a previous hearing when she has constantly said this is not within the boundaries or not under her jurisdiction? Especially as her next comment which I point out and that is "What Mr Landau said or did not say is not within my jurisdiction! These legal people blow me away. Don't they realise how incompetent and inconsistent they appear to others outside their little cloistered and incestuous world?

The next to last statement she makes which I comment on, shows to me that she had in fact made her mind up what her decision was before she heard any verbals from me or RB. She says, " I will give the decision in writing. It should not be too long getting to you" It in fact took only a week and that folks is the fastest decision that has been made in all the hearings I have had to put up with. I wonder why?

The last statement reiterates her wrongful sentiments and could be said that she really only commiserates with the blue eyed boy of the IPO, one RB, the Biggest Liar in the World. "really I feel for both of you in that you have had to do a lot of proceedings" (poor grammar for a professor) Once again who has been responsible for all that… Why, Mr Liarman himself.

Chapter Twenty Five
The Annand Decision Document
Dated 12th November 2009

Paragraphs 1 to 5 dealt with what the TMA 1994 said about applying for rectification, so I am not going to comment on that, apart from the fact that a lot of it is written in the usual legalistic gobbledegook, which only lawyers can make up. I think this gives lawyers the ability to put various interpretations on how they see it. It justifies their existence if you like. In this case I had to take it that RB had an apparent right to ask for rectification (only according to the IPO) and what it boiled down to, was did he really have the right when you looked at the way he had gained registration? Was that legally done, according to all the laws and rules? I obviously felt he did not gain it legally, but by deception, perjury, forgery, perverting the course of justice and so on. I knew that the IPO and probably this lawyer, were not in the slightest bit interested in any of that, as they view everything they do as 100% right.

In paragraphs 6, 7 they deal with his application and what he said in his statement as grounds to be able to apply. As I have already commented on all that in detail, I am not going to repeat it all.

8/ This deals with a letter the IPO sent RB where the writer details that the way he sees it, is that the application should be one that removes matter that has ceased to have effect. That is if RB agrees to this.

They propose to proceed as follows. 'The evidence you have provided will be regarded as sufficient to present a prima facie case that has ceased to have effect'. The registrar will write to Martin and if no objection is received within 3 months, Martins name will be removed.

I think that letter says it all about the way the IPO were treating this case. I find it astonishing that the IPO are telling RB how they will do things, and he doesn't even have to think about it as they have done that for him. You can see the influence here of Hobbs and what he had agreed with James of the IPO at his appeal hearing. I ask is this strictly legal and kosher?

9/ Of course RB replies that that is all OK and he provides the last known address of Martin, in Spain.

You will soon see what transpires about this act by RB and I can say now that it was yet one more act of outrageous **perjury!**

10/ This simply says that the IPO sent a letter to Martin. No response from him came back. *You will see in the future why this was.*

11/ Here we are told that the registrar wrote to me to notify me of the above in paras 8,9 & 10 and that I could oppose this.

12/ In this paragraph Annand nails her colours to the mast by making comments as to how she cannot understand why the IPO did this as I was not party to the most recent process (presumably she means the Foley hearing). That the hearing of my opposition to RB's registration was decided and I did not appeal.

What has it got to do with Annand what the IPO decided to do in letting me know what was going on. I find this comment by Annand perverse. She makes a big deal about me not appealing the Reynolds decision and ignores the fact that as it was before a High Court and I could not afford that and had said so. I have noticed that various people in the IPO use this fact to beat me with, as if this not appealing had meant that either I had no case or that I agreed to the decision. It makes me a suspect person, in effect. What about the fact that in the Foley hearing I had been allowed to be part of it (but was denied to be a part of the actual hearing) and I put in written evidence as to why I opposed it. So why shouldn't I be sent this letter?

Either way it showed to me that this woman was behaving like someone who had an agenda.(Yet again!)

13/ Annand now says I had the right to oppose the application.

14/ Here she says that she takes it that this case would go forward under Section 64(5) and rule 45. *Re my application to put in late evidence.*

15/ She just states that I made the application to do this and that I also had asked that the CEO of the IS be made to attend as a witness to clear up questions over their handling of RB's bankruptcy. She also says that at the hearing I then agreed this was not necessary.

16/ Here she is setting out what conditions must be met to allow this evidence.

17–21/ It is set out how, at the hearing we discussed these criteria and the evidence I was trying to have admitted. How she came to her conclusions that it could not be admitted as she thought it would have no effect to the outcome of this case for the various reasons she stated.

22/ Annand stated that Foley granted the application to remove Martins name so that RB would then be shown as proprietor. She goes on to saying I argued that there was no evidence that Martin had given up his interest in the business or the mark. She also says I complained that Foley had strayed into the other proceedings of the IS, the renewal of the mark, and my opposition to RB's application to register the mark and that I was justified to do so.

Well double hurrahs, but whilst it did nothing for me in this case, it does show that IPO hearing officers do not conduct hearings in 100% correct ways. But that in this particular hearing Annand will also go into matters she should keep out of, as well.

23/ Here she sets out what Foley had said in his paragraphs 17/18/19/20/& 21. So I am not repeating all those as they can be found above under my comments on those paragraphs.

24/ Annand says that I complained that Foley was repeating what Hobbs had said throughout his hearing (which never came to any conclusion or decision). *She then goes on to do exactly the same thing by repeating what this Hobbs bloke had said and she takes up paragraphs 25/26/&27, doing that. I think she has a damn cheek doing this because as Foley had said he was not going to refer to previous hearings and then did just that, she is doing the same. She is probably another devotee of this bloke Hobbs.*

Lastly in her last line of para 27 she says that as Hobbs was merely summarising law, she sees nothing wrong with Foley referring to Hobbs.

Well I disagree as this woman Annand has a brain of her own, why doesn't she quote case law etc off her own back, without visiting cases that have nothing to do with my appeal and dealing with the grounds I put forward for my appeal. She could quote her own views on whatever case law she thought applicable. Plus I do not know if it is legally correct to quote what was said in another case that has nothing to do with this one, especially as she has said I was justified to complain about HO's continually referring to other cases. Plus the Hobbs hearing was never a true full blown hearing as RB dropped it.

She uses the excuse to revisit previous cases, which she had at the hearing said was not allowed in appeals, that I had asked her to read Landau and Hobbs so as to acquaint herself with why I had complained about actions that RB had taken and so as she could understand the previous history. Now she uses this to excuse herself from the fact that she now goes into quoting Hobbs over and over.

28/ My other criticism is said to be the lack of evidence of an express indemnity having been entered into. However she says an indemnity can be implied on the part of a continuing or surviving partner and she quotes Lindley and Banks on Partnership, and the cases mentioned therein.

We have only her word for that and later on my own lawyer (in my Invalidity defence in 2010) begs to differ over this, as you will see. Also following events will show how crass her comments are. But this is lawyers for you as they, like her and Foley and Hobbs are too quick to jump to conclusions and to infer this or that happened, without any effort to check if what they say isn't a load of uninformed crap made just to win a case. They see it as black and white and in a way that suites what ends they wish to achieve in their case.

29/ Here she deals with Section 64(5) of the 1994 TMA. She says under this section the registrar is required to take into consideration what the circumstances were at the time when the application to rectify was made and whether to remove matters which have ceased to have effect. Then she states that it was undisputed that Martin had taken no active part in the business since 1992. That the letters shown from solicitors, Willcocks, that the partnership had been dissolved **and indemnity arrangements in favour of Mr Martin Busbridge discussed**. Martin had gone abroad in 1992 and had not returned. *(We will see how inaccurate that is in the future.)* That RB had continued the business and had assumed all liabilities, so the registrar had followed the correct rules and had served notice to Martin. That RB had supplied the last address of Martin in Spain under a statement of truth. So as Martin did not reply she believes that what the registrar did in removing Martin from the register was lawful and now it showed that RB was the proprietor. She goes on in paragraph 30 to say the appeal is therefore dismissed.

It is the above two paragraphs that show me just how dysfunctional, biased and incompetent the IPO is and through its employees like Reynolds, Hobbs, Foley and now Annand. Forget about Hobbs and Annand being independent because that is bollocks. They gain most of their work and wages from the IPO (or at least a substantial part of their wages) and only a naïve fool would believe they are independent. It is pronouncements like the above that make me **'raging mad'** *(the name of my blog). So let's dissect what she has said:-*

(a) Her statement that it is undisputed that Martin had taken no part in the business. How does she know this and who is making this decision that it is undisputed.

How does she know what went on in that business? **The fact is that she like all those before her had only Roberts word for those assumptions.** *Is his word to be believed? Why has she and the others not taken note of all the acts of perjury he had committed that I had shown and complained about? If she had she may have preferred to ask questions of RB to get at the real truth.*

(b) The fact that an indemnity was discussed does not mean it was ever legally made out. In fact Foley states categorically that no document of indemnity has ever been forthcoming. The fact is that no indemnity was ever made. The excuse they make that it can be said that an indemnity was given even though it wasn't, defies belief. Is it actually legal as they say it is? I doubt that Martin would agree to this. It would be exactly the same to say that Martin talked with Robert about him handing over his share of the business, but never actually doing it, so after a period of time Robert could legally say, "Well we talked about it, so that gives me the right to just take it" I think that we would all say that was a load of trash and an attack on his legal rights. The case law they quoted was trash and was for a completely different set of circumstances. I don't think it is legal to just quote any old case law in order to legitimise what you want to do. More to the point what does Martin have to say about all these pronouncements about this taking away of his property and rights??? You will see soon enough about what he has to say.

(c) It is said that RB continued the business, yet despite my banging on ad nauseam that he could not carry on the business as from 1993-1996 he was a bankrupt, so how does a bankrupt carry on a business? You see this very fact is continually ignored by all in the IPO!

(d) RB is supposed to assumed liabilities. Tell this ignorant old fool how a bankrupt could do that? How does a person who is so lacking in money that his partnership with his brother breaks up because they have no more money and then in short order he goes bankrupt, afford to assume all liabilities? And liabilities for what I ask? How does she know he assumed all liabilities I ask? Is she going on the perjured word of a liar like Robert? She shows her ignorance of the law on partnerships, for Martin even though the partnership was over, was **still liable for the partnerships liabilities because the dissolution was not done legally.** *So what has she to say about that? You will hear more on this later on in the last hearing of this bloody saga.*

(e) Then there is the statement saying Martin had left the UK in 1992 and had never returned. Where does she get this from? Once more it is the perjured word of RB that supplies this and as **no evidence is ever offered that this is what did happen how**

can it be taken as the truth? *Again you will later on see more on this.*

(f) How can the IPO and Annand be sure that this address given up by the liar RB, can be taken as factual? When I read the letter from the IPO to me saying that this was the address they had written to, I remember thinking it was all bollocks as **I knew that Robert would never want his brother to be actually contacted.** *It was obviously not in RB's interest to actually contact Martin as he knew Martin would never give up his share in Cobretti. It seems I have more brains than the IPO, for it was obvious to me that a man who has lost his £60,000+ share in his business with his brother, and who had lost his house, lost his marriage over it all, would ever give away whatever collateral he had in the business just like that. Don't forget when he left that business there were still assets left in it, apart from any possible value in a potential ownership of a trademark that may not legally belong to the business, which maybe could be sold to Chrsyler. No, Annand is a fool and as big a naïve fool as the rest of them. So I never believed that this alleged address was a genuine one, nor that RB would ever go to Spain to confront his brother. This address business is yet another act of perjury by RB and you will see the evidence for that later on.*

I say that the act of using all of the above excuses to give RB this registration and this rectification to enable him to keep it and in his name, is a deliberate act by the IPO to illegally strip me of my trademark. This stage in proceedings would be just a step towards achieving the end that the IPO wanted to achieve.

Chapter Twenty Six
What is My Position Now?

When you look carefully into the content of the Annand document you will have to come to the same conclusion as I did in that it is mostly padding. Page after page of repeating what Busbridge said, what Foley said, what Hobbs said and what I said. Plus throwing in paragraphs repeating what the TMA says. I think it is more guilty for what it doesn't say. For instance how RB is able to take over his brothers half of the business and lie through his back teeth, and Annand makes not a peep about that. Not a thought for me as a victim of this conman, nor of Martin who ends up stripped of his investment into the Cobretti business, without a thought for his rights. A document meant to show that the IPO were doing their job and therefore that demanded a document full of many pages, so they needed to be made up any old crap, to show this.

You see to these oafs in the IPO all this is at arms length to them. It is just another messy job to them. They don't give a stuff that what they are discussing and messing about with is peoples lives and businesses. They just want to get it done and get it all out of the way. The fact that all what they have done is by sheer incompetence, and corruption matters not one jot. They know no one can touch them and they can carry on with their cosy overpaid lives, patting themselves on the back for being great people doing a great job and being a great service to all the peasants in the UK who have to put their trust in them.

On the question of open perjury and blatant forgery, it isn't even considered. I think the IPO and most of its employees are morally bankrupt and a sop to thieves, crooks, conmen and perjurers. They blindly follow their stupid laws which are outdated, belonging more to the 19th century than the 21st. So I was pretty upset after reading it, I can tell you, as it showed me once again that the IPO were not interested in justice.

Of course now this seemingly never ending string of actions and hearings were obviously over and this lying bastard Robert Busbridge now stood, no doubt gloatingly, with the Viper trademark firmly in his grasp. He had been able to pull the wool over, during the past nine years, firstly the Police (but then they are so thick that would have been dead easy to do) then progressively over the IPO, who I have no doubt, were sick of me having complaining bitterly since 1992/3 over their incompetence. They chose to believe every lie he ever told them, even though they must have known he was lying, for many times I provided documentary evidence of this. I have said before that some in the IPO, in my opinion must hold grudges against me for the shit I stirred up. Maybe some of them suffered in their jobs because of it, who knows? What I do know having been an avid reader of news all my life, is that I would not be the first person that the might of the State, through state employees, knows no bounds of decency or for revenge. I have read of dozens of cases, of people who's lives were ruined by avaricious civil servants who did not want to give in and admit defeat or that they were wrong. Who will hate you for standing up to them. That is why I believe what I do.

You only have to read through all of the above information on this case, see how each hearing was conducted and how the HO's came to their conclusions, to be able to see that something is going on here.

I racked my brains as to what I could do about all this. With no money to pursue the IPO for maladministration, how could I get justice? After 2002 when I had my heart attack and had to retire, I lost any ability to carry on earning whatever I could get out of my depleted business. I had to sell it for buttons, so that was more loss. In this wonderful country of ours, legal aid is a long forgotten luxury. For now only immigrants, criminals and crooks get that. Justice is only for the rich!

One thing that still bugged me was that RB had applied to make my own registration, invalid. I ask you to try and imagine how you would feel after being notified that this lying, cheating, conman bastard, who had pinched your business and was making a good living off your back and your efforts, was now cheekily trying to have your own registration made invalid. Not content with doing what he did, he now wants to complete his crooked actions by twisting the knife he had already plunged into your back, to finish you off. If I lived in say Russia, this piece of excrement could be flushed down the toilet and out of your life. However, I am a law abiding person and I would have to rely on trying to get justice out of our crap British, so called Justice system, even though it may see me into my grave.

I was first informed that he was trying to do this, around the end of 2003. Of course he had to wait to do this until I had achieved my own registration and that happened in mid 2002 when I finally got rid of Chrysler. That in itself gave me the shits as he too had put in an opposition to Chrysler. Then he sat back and let me go through the expense and hassle of seeing off Chrylser. (Due to the fact that the IPO had not followed its rules and let him oppose Chrysler first, when he had in fact applied to do this before me!) That done now he jumps back in to try and get me out of the way.

However he had also applied to register the mark as you will well know, having got this far through the story. His application to oppose had been put on hold as had his application to register.

Now Chrsyler was out of the way, thanks to my efforts and costs, he is allowed to put in this application to make my mark invalid!! This once again raises questions about what the hell the IPO are up to. First of all his opposition application to Chrysler was put in before mine, yet they put that on hold and allow mine to go forward. He may have even asked for this to happen, I may never get to know.

Then you also have the fact that my application for registration was also put in *after* his application. Mine in 1996 and his in 1992, yet the IPO lets mine go through before his. Why was this I ask? There are some real pertinent and serious questions to ask here. What the hell are the IPO up to here? As if there were not already enough serious questions to ask the IPO.

Anyway I got this notification in November of 2003 and his application for Invalidation had initially been knocked back for the want of certain information that was lacking. I complained that as I was preparing a case to oppose his application to register, as this case would determine whether he really had registration, because if I was successful and he did not get registration, then this application was a waste of everyone's time. Funnily enough they agreed and it was eventually put on hold.

At this point I should point out a fact that would be a real important point for anyone going into registering a trademark. I think that all readers will agree that I should have got my trademark registered as soon as I started to use it. However, now I can tell you that at whatever stage you do this, for Gods sake get a competent Patent Agent or IP lawyer. (if you can afford one) Double check on their competence. In my case I ended up with one who although he won my case against Chrysler, he did make one monumental cock-up that has resulted in me having to put up with all the crooked goings on by Busbridge. That is to say that he should in January 1992, have applied for registration. This was when I first saw him and then paid him to apply for my registration. He never did it until 1996, and he erroneously thought that by winning against Chrysler would mean my showing use back to a time long before RB applied. Of course he was dead wrong (or maybe *he was right?*) but as I am not a lawyer I cannot find out the answer to this) and had my registration application gone in before RB, then RB would have been blown into oblivion years ago. In fact he would never have stood a chance and I could have got him for 'passing off' back in 1991/2, when I could have got legal aid.

When I got notification of RB's application for Invalidity, I also got a set of notes from the IPO which dealt with Statements of Case and Counter Statements. It said that in the past the IPO had not scrutinised these but now they were doing so in order that poorly drafted and elliptically worded documents which could cause confusion and waste time etc, etc, would be required to be amended. Also these documents had to contain the grounds on which they were going to rely on in the hearing.

They even reproduced what my dear old friend, no less than the Mr Hobbs QC, he of highest order of Big Heads, who knows all there is to know about all things to do with IP, had to say on the matter. (This is more proof of his standing and lack of independence in this whole area.) They quoted what his illustrious self had had to say in a case called Demon Ale (2000) when he was again an Appointed Person.

I tell you this because I wonder if they should have applied this sensible approach to *all* the *statements* made in the run up to hearings. Certainly if they should do it, they did not do it in the cases of Robert Busbridge, for all his statement were badly drafted and contained such a lot of irrelevant nonsense that could not be used in the actual hearing. In the case of RB's statement of grounds to apply for the Invalidity, the IPO did indeed pull him up for several reasons. In three or more paragraphs he was asked to clarify matters and identify matters. I have made notations that what was asked was generally ignored and not done, yet it appears that the IPO never made an issue of that. Why I ask? Anyway I was too late to object myself to RB's statement of grounds for the opposition hearing in 2004, as they were already in.

In the case of the Foley hearing in 2007 I must admit I forgot about these notes, as they had been filed away and I had forgotten about them. Never the less I doubt that whatever I may have said, would have had any effect on matters. It does show though that anyone who like me runs these kinds of cases themselves, they do not do themselves justice and you can lose a case, when if you had professional help, it could turn the case your way. Of course in my case I simply did not have the money. So it appears I was doomed. However you should note that in the case of Busbridge he never once had a lawyer appear for him and most of his statements were drafted by him with little legal help, yet he was able to win over the IPO, hands down. It raises the question as to how was he able to do this, yet I was totally unable to make any impression on the minds at the IPO, even though I took on lawyers on a number of times to advise on how to frame my statements and as to the laws that should apply etc. In the Invalidity case a lawyer handled it completely, yet on every occasion I lost out. As far as I am concerned it only once again shows that the IPO must have determined that for reasons known only to them, they had determined that I was to be stopped at all costs.

How can one ever find out why this was so obviously the case. If I were rich you can bet I would be able to find out as money talks!

Chapter Twenty Seven
The Application for Invalidity Against My Registration

The Statement of Grounds by Robert Busbridge for the invalidity case. Eventually submitted 14th December 2003.

This case got off to a very complicated start because of the IPO making RB redo his original statement of grounds due to the above stated reasons. The eventual application statement read as follows;

Para 1/ Here RB is stating Section 47(2)(b) and 5(4)(a) due to an earlier right in respect of my registration on the grounds it was contrary to Sect 5 (4) (a) of the 94 TMA.

Just how he can claim an earlier right when I started in 1986 and he was only able to copy my product and therefore use my mark on that copy from late 1991/early 92? Well you will eventually see that the IPO in the cases re RB, did not take into effect when I first used the mark... **only** *when you actually put in your application to register it.* **This seems utter madness to me.** *Yet in the case of me versus Chrysler, they did grant me registration based on my earlier use even though I had no registration at that stage. Surely your rights go right back to when you first used the mark in every case you may get involved in and not when you got round to applying for registration and here you have to ask what about ones common law rights applying to Busbridge as they had been applied in the Chrysler case?*

2/ My mark should not have been registered because its use could be said to be passing off 'The use of the mark by the applicant and his predecessors in title commenced as early as 1987 and has continued since that date up to the present time'.

Another clear case of wanton perjury. Firstly since it was not until September 1987 that he even met me and not until Feb 1988 that he gained with his brother, the agency for BRL. Secondly he cannot as I have shown many times, claim continual use of the mark in his own legal right to the present date (of 2003) because his bankruptcy of 1993 made a three year break. Not only that but the bare faced cheek in accusing me of passing off. He pinches my product and trademark and then accuses me of passing off his product!

3/ The extent and manner of use as above has been set forth in detail in relation to opposition 90677 by the present proprietor to the applicants trademark 1501909.

He has included the whole of the Reynolds decision document (and by doing so he repeats all the perjury that was to be found in that document, for a second time).

4/ RB says my registration is contrary to TMA Sect 5(1) and/or 5(2) **and** 6(2). So my registration is invalid. *Now if he is right here then the IPO have given me registration and broken their own rules in doing so!*

5/ That my registration is identical to his application and the goods are identical.

Another example of his utter cheek, as it is being claimed I am the one guilty of passing off, not the other way round. It is also when you think about it an admission that he has copied my product, but then he has brazenly admitted to this in the past and sees nothing wrong with that as do the IPO!

6/ He asks that my registration is made invalid.

It is obvious by the wording that this document was made up for RB by his patent agent as it is too short and to the point, for him to have compiled it. He has paid an agent to do this for him. The first time he has done this.

After this statement of grounds along with his application was put in, I replied with a Counter Statement.

My counter statement dated 26th January 2004.

(I took legal advice from Lawdit LLB as to how I should make this up, with regard to IP Law.) The paragraphs are numbered as per RB's Statement.

2/ I deny my registration was contrary to Sect 5 (4)(a) and the applicant has to prove it should fail on an earlier right.

3/ The applicant is required to prove the facts and it is denied that my trademark amounts to passing off. I am the owner of substantial goodwill and have used the mark continuously since 1986.

4/ I deny that RB has title to the mark since 1987 as it was only in 1988 that

RB started as an agent.

5/ That I was a director of Brightwheel Ltd and was assigned all IP by BL and that I remained the owner of the goodwill.

6/ In 1987 BRL was formed and at that time I did not assign to it any IP, including the mark.

7/ Whilst as agent for BRL, Cobretti was allowed to use the trademark Viper and it was not assigned to him.

8/ In 1989 I resigned as Director of BRL and set up Classic Replicas and continued with the mark Viper. I took on Cobretti as agents for the UK and they could continue to use the mark as per our agency agreement.

9/ RB advertised the product and the mark and in 1990, continued to use it, advertising that the retailing of the product was under 'new management'. Then in 1991 new wording was used in the advertising contrary to the agreement and it was clear they had copied the product and had taken over use of the mark. It was made clear to the applicant that this was not acceptable.

10/ RB continued to use the mark without my consent and he was informed that he was 'passing off' and should desist.

11/ The applicant applied to register the mark and I had filed opposition.

12/ I am unable to admit or deny the details set out in paragraph 3 (of RB's statement of grounds) as the applicant is required to set out the facts on which he relies in his application of invalidity.

13/ I deny that and set out in paragraph 4 with reasons as set out above in paras 2-10. and I deny that the mark was registered contrary to Sect 5(1)(2), Sect 47 (2)(a) or sect 6(2) of 94 TMA and application should be refused.

I further point at that at the time of this statement I had asked the IPO to stay his application until my opposition to his registration had been heard.

So for a period of time there was this suspension of the proceedings in this invalidity application. Even after RB won his registration application, because I could not afford to appeal that decision, he could not proceed as there remained the Landau hearing to be heard, then his appeal against that, followed by his application to rectify and my appeal against that. So this invalidity action was simmering away until late 2009, until all other matters had been cleared out of the way.

Nevertheless he did put in another statement in late 2004. The IPO objected to something in it and he had to do an amended statement. This was put into the IPO in March 2005. From Jan 2004 to 2009 there was regular contact between myself and the IPO over various issues to do with this application.

As I have already stated above in the relative chapter, that after RB's registration the IPO failed to carry out its own hearing officers decision that the certificate should be in the partnership name and yet they issued it in RB's name. So several letters went back and forth about that. I complained to a Kevan Bader, that he has not replied to my questions to him re RB's bankruptcy and why the registration application was allowed to go ahead when the IPO have in letters agreed that the application should have gone to the Receiver. It does not appear that I got any reply to these questions from Bader. Par for the IPO course.

Statement from R Busbridge, dated 20th March 2005.

My comments are in italic after each paragraph.

2/ He says he is now the registered owner having won his application proceedings and he shows as evidence the decision of that hearing.

*This is more evidence of his duplicity as he was not the registered owner because Reynolds had clearly said the registration has to remain in the partnership name. Quite why he includes a document that both I and the IPO already have, is beyond me. However in one way it strengthens my **perjury** claims because it means he has repeated the bulk of his perjury, a **second** time, even though he knows I have complained about perjury in those documents. It shows he views that he is **invincible** and that the IPO are in his clutches.*

3/ He says he has used the mark since 1987.

Yet again he perjures himself as he knows full well that he was not allowed to use the mark in 1987 and even from 1988 it was under licence, and that he used it as an agent of BRL then for myself trading as Classic Replicas.

4/ He goes into a big spiel about the history of both his actions and mine and ends up asking why my application to register the mark was allowed to proceed ahead of his, which was made before mine.

Note here that he does not complain that the IPO let me oppose Chrysler ahead of his own opposition application. Oh no, he was quite content to sit back and let me do that as he had absolutely no grounds to win an opposition against Chrysler. His question about why I was allowed to get registration ahead of him is one I want answered too. Of course the IPO will not answer that either to him, nor to me.

5/ He merely confirms that his invalidity has been suspended until after matters of his registration are finally decided.. He produces a copy of the letter from the IPO telling him this.

6/ He says my registration should not have been given due to him applying for registration before I did. He also says that Reynolds had said as much.

Nowhere does Reynolds touch on this subject in his decision making. More lies.

7/ If my registration is allowed it will cause confusion etc etc. *The cheek of RB defies description. He nicks my designs and mark then accuses me of causing confusion!*

8/ He again goes on again about his application being made before mine.

9/ As there are now two marks on the register for the same name this is contrary to trademark Rules.

He doesn't say which rules say this and in fact there CAN be two marks for the same name. However I am against this myself and his should be the one to go, as mine was won on prior and legal use. His being stolen and illegal.

On the 3rd July 2009 I decide to blitz the IPO and in particular Mr Colombo as he is the Head of Law Section, or was, as to why the Landau decision has never been enacted. I also threw in a question about perjury and what should happen if I say it has been committed and show evidence that it has. I think you will see from the emails and the replies I got, up to the last email sent of the 8th July, that they will show just what the IPO are up to.

Up to now all the hearings right up to my appeal before Annand, had been heard and decisions handed down. These questions as far as I was concerned were at the heart of matter, as had Landau been enacted I would never had had to put up with all the crap I had, since 2004. RB would have rightly lost the registration. So I sent an email on the 3rd July 2009 on this. He gave me a cock and bull explanation which was that as the appeal to Landau's decision was dropped, and an application to rectify was made , the matter was left to be dealt with once proceedings were finally concluded.

Now excuse me Colombo, you may think I am thick, but that means that whatever Landau decreed should happen, has now to be quietly forgotten about, because RB then applied for a rectification. The fact that he applied for something else should have nothing to do with it. According to Landau he now owned nothing, so how can he just apply to apply for a rectification of nothing?

Then on the perjury question he merely says that if I thought there had been any irregularity on any document then I could take legal advice. What a reptile, as he is saying that if you think the IPO have not followed the correct steps, even if it is to do with perjury which is a criminal offence, you cannot complain to us, get legal advice! I had also asked if it is the IPO that take action or the Police? He ignored that question. *Fast forward to 2009 when I go to the Police about this perjury as it is plain the IPO will do nothing and when the Police contact the IPO what are they told? "Leave it to us as we are best placed to deal with it". Talk about liars and duplicity, you could not make up these twerps in the IPO. Then later on towards the end of this story when the Dorset Police and Met approach the IPO to ask about the perjury, they are clearly told a pack of lies that ranges from no perjury was committed, to it is a civil matter that Mr Cook has to take up himself by going to a solicitor!*

I lambasted him on that answer, saying he had access to the Landau wording of the decision, and he should read it, for it was unequivocal. 'The trademark could have been assigned at the time of the partnership dissolution and it was not done'. Also that the trademark could not be renewed as the partnership was no longer. In other words RB did not own the application as he did not buy it off his brother.

I made the strong point that in law, if someone does not like a decision handed down and they appeal, then if they drop that appeal then the original decision has to stand and in this case it was ignored, so why was that?

I point out that he did not answer what the IPO do re perjury and I also pointed out that one case of perjury I could prove beyond doubt, was the fact that RB lied to the Reynolds hearing when he denied being my agent, and this was provable by the transcript of my trial in 2000 where RB admitted he was my agent and bought Viper kits off me.

His reply said it all, *again*. He says that Landau refused the assignments, so the application stayed in the partnership name. There was no change of name. An appeal was lodged about this decision and then dropped. He says he cannot understand why I am asking why the decision was not enacted when it seems to him that it was.

I hope you can see that he is deliberately being dumb on this as if he does not understand what I am getting at. Also the assignment part was only a small part of the decision of Landau and he has ignored the rest of what he said had to happen. Typical IPO duplicity, do not answer anything that may incriminate us. Just ignore it.

Re the perjury, he said that if I believed that someone had provided false or misleading evidence then it could be brought to the attention of the hearing officer who would decide what to do at the hearing. (*Of course this ignores the fact that there may not be anymore hearings… then what?* And what about perjury that has been committed in past hearings?) Is Colombo saying that once a hearing is finalised, any questions re perjury are dead? If he is, that is a nonsense as perjury is a criminal offence and IPO laws cannot alter that. I believe that the IPO have a duty to deal with perjury no matter how old it is, once it is brought to their attention. If I can be charged for alleged perjury allegedly committed two years prior, as I was in 1999, then so can RB. What I also wanted to know is why the IPO had ignored it in *every* hearing, when I brought up allegations of perjury in my evidence and in most cases gave documentary evidence of it, nothing was done and the hearing officer did not even discuss it. This behaviour re perjury is an absolute disgrace and the IPO know it and this is why Colombo was being very evasive. On top of all that, is the fact that Colombo had already said I should deal with perjury myself through a solicitor. He is as bad as RB for lying and forgetting his past lies.

On the question of Colombo's last answer re why Landau was not enacted, I fired off yet another email on the 7th in which I again asked why RB was allowed to carry on after Landaus decision said he could not, and I ask not to be subjected to a spin answer. I also again ask why Landaus decision was not carried out.

On the perjury I pointed out that some of the perjury was still ongoing and to do with the current Invalidity case as RB had put in documents that contained gross numbers of perjurious statements. I ask who actually takes action re perjury (meaning is it the Police or the IPO?).

In his email answer of the 8th he says that he has read Landaus decision and he says the decision was not enacted until the outcome of the appeal (as if I did not know that already). He then tells me again what I already know that during that appeal it was discussed that if the assignments were withdrawn then RB could apply to rectify the register. God this man annoys me as they all do, for I have complained until I am blue in the face, about why should RB dropping the appeal allow him to now go on to rectify, and that meant having it show RB as owner, when Landau said that the register could only be in both names as RB had never legally taken over his brothers half of the partnership. The assignment were never legal in any case. It is just a case of Colombo grasping at straws to try and explain away a situation he knows is flawed, wrong and illegal, by whatever lies and obfuscation he can think of, just to fob me off.

He then went on to say again that the cosy agreement between Hobbs and the registrar James agreed that if the appeal was withdrawn RB could renew the registration (which as far as I was concerned he did not legally own) and that it would stand because the renewal request would be made by the proprietor on the register.

I hope you can see how duplicitous the IPO are here, how they squirm and invent excuses which they think you are so stupid you cannot understand the complexity of. This last statement is so vacuous it defies belief. Landau said that the register had to be in both names so how can RB be on the register? How can he be the proprietor when both he and his brother legally are the proprietors? After he allegedly could dupe the IPO into accepting against all odds, that he is the proprietor, he can then apply to rectify the register to read he is the proprietor, which he already supposedly is on paper.

It is then stated that the rectification was allowed and I appealed that and lost. So Landaus decision was no longer relevant. So because of all that jiggery pokery, Hey Presto! Robert Busbridge now becomes the registered owner of the mark. He did not even have to try very hard to get there as the IPO had mapped it all out for him and smoothed the way for him.

Of course this email, a supposed explanation as to how the decision of Landau was circumvented, is nothing more than a scam and disgraceful further episode in the long history of lies and evasions and shonky actions by the IPO.

On the question of perjury he gets out of answering any of my questions by saying I should write to the case examiner on the Invalidity case and outline setting out my case, which I did.

I emailed him right back and in great detail, went over the whole facts about what he had said above, and how it was all bollocks. I also state that I believe the IPO have not allowed natural justice to take place and by their actions have interfered with the proper process.

His terse reply within 5 minutes, was that he had nothing more to say on the matter and I think that said it all. "I do not want to know about perjury or Landau"!

I was not prepared to let them off the hook and I sent Colombo another email saying that I wanted to make an official complaint about my not getting the answers I need. His reply told me to send my complaint to the Head of the Tribunal the very same Mr James, whom I think is heavily involved in this cover up. Anyway I duly sent him an email on the 15th July asking how I can make this 'official complaint'.

He replies saying I need to set out what the question I was asking Colombo that he refused to answer.

At the same time I was corresponding with James, I was also in contact with the case clerk a fellow called Gittings. I had sent him a letter outlining the perjury that had been committed by RB in his statements for this Invalidity. In his letter of reply dated 16th July he said that it was open for me to submit any further evidence which could show RB committing perjury. Then eventually we would both be given the opportunity of a hearing and at that hearing this evidence of perjury would be taken into account (they call it a conflict of evidence, which is typical of the IPO. Play it down and let's not call it *perjury*, but a 'conflict of evidence'). Then of course his wording is the usual mush, that does not make it plain whether the hearing he is talking about is an fresh hearing to hear only about perjury claims or was he saying that the forthcoming Invalidity hearing would be where the perjury would be dealt with?

If there was sufficient evidence of perjury or a conspiracy to pervert the course of justice and if there is sufficient evidence then they would refer it to the authorities to investigate such criminal offences. (The Police or the CPS?)

Re a letter to James re Colombo, I have no copy of any email of anything I sent to James, so I may have decided to take another tack and complain directly to their CEO because I made out a long letter of complaint dated 20th July to their CEO, a Mr Marchant which I knew would take ages to be replied to, and as the reply was not sent until mid September, which taking into account the severity of my complaint, is another disgrace. On the 30th August I added a second statement to Marchant which *included an affidavit statement from no less than Martin Busbridge.* He came out of the blue and contacted me by phone and I will cover that in detail shortly and I will go over what I had said to this CEO. The point is that after sitting on my original complaint letter sent a month previously, now there were really serious events for this man to get to grips with.

I got a reply letter from Gittings dated the 18th August, re my email to him of the 17th August in which I had dealt with his last letter of the 17th July, in which he outlined how my accusations of perjury would be dealt with. I tell him that I now have a witness statement to add to all the accusations of perjury and I have sent it to their CEO, but I want them to start acting about this perjury now! His reply says that this perjury will be dealt with by the hearing officer at the Invalidity hearing. They do not propose to deal with it ahead of that. Nice of them, let it wait ad infinitum, we have all the time in the World and perjury is not something we care much about! I am also told that RB has until 28th August to reply to my last statement for the Invalidity case dated the 17th July. I am also told that if I have further evidence to put in then I have to ask to do this as there have to be good reasons for them to allow this!! Can you believe that?

I reply complaining about the fact I am telling them about perjury that was committed way back in 2003 and 2004 and why don't they start acting now? I complain that when faced with evidence of perjury, the IPO seemed not to be concerned. Then I complain that as a right, I can reply to RB's statement that he will put in reply to my last, without asking for permission.

His reply is pure IPO evasiveness as he says he has nothing to add to what he has already said. *So you see that complaining to even their top man or any of his minions gets you absolutely nowhere, as they just aren't interested in dealing with RB's criminal actions.*

My statement of evidence for the invalidity case brought by R Busbridge in 2003.

In reply to the applicants amended statement of the 20th March 2005. Made on 15/7/09.

2/ I deny RB has a claim to the mark from 1987 as he was not even an agent for myself at that date.

That he continued as my agent until 1991, when he copied my product and stole my trademark.

His evidence RBINV01 a copy of a registration certificate is not valid as at the date of it, the registered owner was Cobretti Engineering and not RB.

3/ Another false claim by RB stating 1987 as being when he could lay claim to the mark. See para 2.

Whilst he did initially oppose application 1410265, he did not carry it through as I opposed it to it's end in 2002 when I was awarded registration. This showed my use back to 1986 and to an application dated Jan 1990 which was before the applicants application date of 1992.

I posed two questions: Why had RB not gone through with his opposition to Chrysler? Why did he not oppose my application of 1996?

I believe that my registration followed the correct procedures, contrary to what he claims.

5/ I made no comment on his exhibit RB INV03.

6/ I disagreed with his claims in this paragraph. I also said that the Reynolds decision could not be tested by an appeal because of the onerous fact that I could not get legal aid, which made it impossible for me to appeal and I asked if my registration was not lawful as claimed by RB, why was it that the IPO registered my application for the mark?

7/ Contrary to my causing confusion by my registration, RB had caused it by copying my product using my trade mark and getting registration of that.

8/ The fact his application was back to 1992 is immaterial as I had gained registration based on an earlier right, back to 1986.

9/ RB's application should have been voided due to his bankruptcy, the partnership had broken up and he had not taken legal ownership of the asset of the application over his brother. The IPO had been warned of these three reasons for voiding, yet ignored them.

10/ If RB can have previous decisions be part of this application then I reserve the right to insist that the Landau decision be enacted. I accuse the IPO of an unlawful decision to ignore Landau's decision.

11/ Exhibit RBINV 02 which is a copy of the Reynolds hearing decision document, so it is a different hearing and irrelevant to this hearing.

12/ I repeat my assertions of my counter statement.

13/ My use of the trademark is well documented in the kit car industry from 1986 to present (of the date of that statement) and I had built up considerable goodwill. I show evidence of this. My actions since 1986 show my considerable involvement and show that no one would do as I have done to protect a mark and at considerable expense to me, if they did not legally own it.

14/ The facts do not show that I abandoned the mark and I list (a) to (j) the history of my involvement and the passing off carried out by RB. I show many documents in evidence to back up what I say.

15/ I say that far from abandoning my mark in 1989 as claimed, I did carry on using it and I exhibit documents to back this.

16/ I state that RB was purchasing Vipers from me up to mid 1991. I show copies of invoices and orders from him to show this.

17/ In Exhibit 34 I show that I was dealing in Vipers post 1989 by having 5,000 brochures made up and printed all which bear the trademark Viper on them.

18/ I go through the reasons why during the period 1991-1992 I was in Europe and advertising the Viper there and any break in business in the UK was brought on by the fact that RB stole my business off me in my absence. As soon as I knew what was happening I took all steps to safeguard my rights.

19/ On my return to the UK I took steps to continue using the mark through a licensee from early 1993 and up to end 1995 when I again manufactured my product in my own right having bought out the licensee.

20/ I then show transcript pages of my trial for perjury in 2000 where RB clearly says he was an agent for me and bought Viper kits off me 1989-1991. I point out that in his statement of January 2005 in the Invalidity proceedings that he had sold Viper products from 1987 to 2005, this was to try and show a longer involvement than was the case and with the lies made in my forgery trial, show acts of perjury. He had used the same claims under oath in his Invalidity statements and I invited the IPO to take action against him for perjury.

21/ I say that I believe that at no time have I ever abandoned my mark and I did my best at considerable expense to protect it and the fact that between Sept 1989 to mid 1991 RB was advertising my mark was because I allowed him under contract to do so as my agent. A fact he had agreed to, under oath, at my trial. Also that I was not guilty of passing off *his* rights as he had none.

22/ I point out that at no time since mid 1991 has RB ever contacted me to demand I stop using the mark Viper. On the other hand conversely I did immediately demand he should stop using my mark Viper, as required by law.

23/ I accused RB of not complying with IPO law in Invalidity cases where he should contact me with a view to settling. On the other hand I had contacted him and offered to sell him my rights and was ignored. *Here is yet another case of the IPO ignoring their own rules because they did nothing about this breaking of their own rules.*

The first official letter of complaint to the IPO CEO, dated 20/7/09.

I followed the above statement, by a letter of complaint to the IPO CEO and the contents are set out as follows:

I set out the fact that I opposed RB's registration application and lost and because of stupid IPO laws which under the 1938 Act meant I had to appeal at great cost ONLY to the High Court. I could not afford to appeal. I complain that people like me are therefore being denied justice. I then set out that Landau did find for me in a hearing that was held in relation to issues mentioned in the Reynolds hearing, that I was not allowed to participate in, again, because of stupid IPO laws. I say that the registration certificate was issued to RB in the wrong name and was not corrected until I complained, thus showing the slack way the IPO work.

I then complained that the Landau decision was never enacted and my complaints about that have either been ignored or I am given spurious and obviously incorrect reasons as to why it was not enacted.

Then RB appeals this and once again I am kept out of it due to more stupid IPO laws. I complain about the behaviour of Hobbs and James in the way they gave legal advice instead of actually carrying on a proper appeal case. That the whole process of that supposed hearing was a con and an abuse of the legal process and denied me justice. I then point out that the IPO kept the decision of that appeal from me, for such a long time and lied repeatedly as to why there was a hold-up. I was then told that RB had applied for a rectification before I even had known what had gone on at the appeal. That the whole process had been a disgrace and looked like the IPO were being biased.

I then complained that leading up to the Annand hearing I had complained to Colombo about the fact the Landau decision had not been carried out and was told that Annand would deal with that, yet she did not do so. I also had included with this letter copies of relevant emails between me and Colombo and I said I thought that the replies I got were mostly devious and evasive.

I summarised my complaints as:

1/ Lies from IPO waiting for Hobbs decision.

2/ That RB was allowed to renew before a decision had been made that he owned the mark and could do so.

3/ That RB was allowed to renew in his name only, before he was given the right to do that.

4/ The evasions and lies as to why Landau decision was not enacted as soon as RB's appeal was heard and he dropped the appeal.

5/ My questions as to what was Colombo's position within the IPO were ignored.

6/ My complaints about the perjury of RB were ignored at hearings, when I was told they would be dealt with.

7/ I ask him to answer my query to Colombo of the 20/3/09.

8/ I wanted to know why I was not told that the Hobbs hearing had been suspended and that RB was given time to hunt out his brother?

9/ Why was I and my MP lied to when we tried to get answers as to what was going on with the Hobbs appeal?

I give an example of what the lack of enacting Landaus decision was equal to in other legal cases, as an example of how wrong this was.

I say that RB has lied wholesale to the IPO and it has been complicit and had thus allowed RB to get away with stealing my business and IP including the trademark, from me. I complain that the IPO seem not to be interested in Justice being seen to be done.

I accuse the IPO of having a stupid and incompetent system with laws written in gobbledegook and not in clearly understood English. That the general public cannot afford access to the laws when acting for themselves, therefore do not get justice from the IPO. I accused his staff of being slow and the case has gone on for 17 years whilst he and his employees sit on high wages etc, paid for by us.

I finally ask him to explain why the Landau decision was not carried out… So these are all serious allegations and complaints and we will see how he answers, in due course.

Busbridge reply my witness statement of July 15th. Dated on 26th august 2009.

1/ RB indulges in more of his perjury as he says that my asserting that he was not an agent in 1987 as he claimed was untrue. He shows an exhibit which is a magazine advert of mine in which I state he is my agent.

Yet there is no evidence that the cover date is December 1987 other than his own handwritten date. It is an advert from sometime in 1988 and certainly not from Dec 1987. This is easily proven by the fact that you have to put in an advert **two months** before the cover date for the advert. So if you take that it **was** Dec 87, that would take my putting in this advert for publication, back to September 1987. This was before I even met Robert Busbridge and his brother, which was right at the end of September. December magazines appear one month **before** the cover date IE early November minus two months = early September. RB had to build a car before I saw it and agreed to make them agents. Furthermore RB states in other statements that he never became agent until Feb 1988. More perjury!

He fails to answer my assertion about the fact that his registration certificate exhibit is false as it shows him personally, as the proprietor.

He perjures himself again by stating that Reynolds had stated that the goodwill of the mark had been vested in BRL under a debenture of Atlantic Capital. **Nowhere** in his decision does he say this. He says he is inclined to think that the goodwill was in BRL and he makes no mention of the debenture in relation to the goodwill. In any case that is only a view and not tested in law and my lawyer begged to differ on this contentious issue, as do I. Also RB had no insight as to the goings on in B/L or BRL as he admitted.

2/ In this paragraph RB indulges in a mess of claims, none of which appear to answer what I had said in my paragraph of my statement that he is replying to and this is what he is supposed to be doing, not introducing new statements. He waffles on about the course of events to do with each application and oppositions etc which I never touched on at all. Then he continues waffling about the declaration I made in support of my application to register.

3/ Now he is telling us all about what the hearing officer said at my opposition hearing to Chryslers application. *This is irrelevant to this case and he was not a party to it, in any case.*

4/ He then says much of what I have to say has been heard in the Reynolds hearing and he does not intend to visit that, *yet he includes* **that Reynolds decision document** *in his evidence, so this evidence being included shows how his mind works.*

5/ Now he goes against what he has just said about the Reynolds hearing, by making reference to it again, by saying that Reynolds said that there was no evidence that BRL had disposed of any goodwill in the trademark, and then he makes comments about the fact that BRL had applied to register the mark and then discontinued it. *So what I have to say to this is; it has nothing to do with this case and it certainly never gave RB the right to steal my mark or even take over a mark, even if it did belong to BRL.*

6/ Here we have RB dictating what the history of my involvement was with BRL, *yet in a previous hearing he had admitted that he had no authoritative knowledge of what went on in BRL. Yet he can state that when BRL closed the trademark was owned by BRL and when the winding up was done (by whom?), the mark was abandoned and he was able to take it over and apply to register it. More fiction and lies as you will know by previous chapters on this era.*

7/ Here he is at it again yelling his fairy tale story about the break up of BRL. *This has been extensively covered already, so I am not repeating history except to say it is all made up to suit his view of affairs and to fit in with his stealing my IP property.*

8/ This paragraph is his slant on the decision of Landau and is pure fiction. *Again this has already been covered in depth before.*

9/ Now he tries to give an explanation to my charge of perjury and in doing so perjures himself again.

He says he has never knowingly perjured himself at any time. He then goes into an incomprehensible rant on my whether I or BRL owned the trademark asset. *On perjury, he has made so many perjurious statements that are all provable that this amounts to yet another act of perjury. The rest is all irrelevant to this case.*

10/ Re my claim that he never asked me to desist using the mark, he now says that his solicitor sent my agent a letter in July 1992 (after I had told him I would sue him). *On checking my records ,here I have to admit for once he is **right**. God bless him, I could kiss him!* So he did, but one has to say that it was a hollow threat as since then no litigation or legal acts were taken by him to stop me using my mark, nor did he give any evidence as to how he had legitimate claim to it, which as you know I have.

11/ Here he shows in evidence a copy of a rubbish, so called open letter that appeared in a kit car magazine. *It is totally irrelevant to these proceedings and full of libellous lies about me. It apparently was printed whilst I was in Germany, but in what magazine, we are not told. So how can that have relevance as it is not evidence that is credible as it is from an undated and unknown source and is hearsay. Rules of evidence should have dictated that he remove this document but we now know that the IPO is not interested in following those Rules*

12/ Here RB is saying that he has no legal reason why he should settle with me as I am not the legal owner of the mark, even if I do have registration (by default). *This is a typical example, along with this whole document, of what you have to deal with when you get mixed up with a conman of the likes of Robert Busbridge. The lies and twisting of facts just defies explanation and they come so thick and fast that I am sure that employees of the IPO could well be swayed by some of them. You end up in a cesspit of iniquity.*

All the exhibits were documents that have already been seen a number of times in other hearings.

Chapter Twenty Eight
The Sudden Appearance of Martin Busbridge

At this point I should tell you about the astonishing turnaround this whole story took, which I have actually already mentioned in passing above. That was the appearance of Martin Busbridge. I got a phone call one afternoon from him and I nearly fell off my chair, for I had always thought we had seen the last of him. Anyway he had returned from Spain due to the recession there and his wife had been searching the net for info on Cobretti. She had eventually trawled up my blogs on the IPO and a blog I had set up specifically designed to tell the Public what a liar Robert Busbridge is. I wanted to really get up his nose and I knew this blog would quickly be seen by people searching for his business site.

He told me that he wanted to help me for various reasons as he could see that I had been severely disadvantaged by Roberts lies over the years. We agreed to meet and I duly drove up to Kent where he was living. Over two days we had long talks going over the whole story of the days when he and Robert stole my business. He readily admitted his part in what had happened and was able to confirm the evidence and facts that I had relied on in the various hearings, also to fill me in on some very interesting facts which really surprised me. These being:-

1/ He confirmed that I had contacted them quickly after BRL ceased.

2/ That we had agreed that Cobretti could continue as my agents and I was able to continue to supply Viper kits.

3/ That this was quickly followed up with a written agreement.

4/ *That he had not known that Robert had applied to register the mark.*

5/ *That he had not even known about RB asking Chrysler if they wanted to buy the trademark Viper.*

6/ He admitted that they both had deliberately set out to cut me out and copy my kit so that they could make more profit.

7/ That his bust up had been over the fact that RB had been running the business and had lost much money which had been guaranteed by his home as collateral whereas RB lost nothing. Also the bust up was compounded by RB telling his wife he was playing around with another woman which he said he hadn't.

8/ That he had never been given any indemnity and that his solicitor had advised him not to accept one. He said in any case he knew that RB had no money, so any indemnity was not worth a light.

9/ He had never assigned or agreed to hand over his half of the business to RB and he believed he still was owed for this by RB, as he had left a considerable amount of assets in the business.

10/ *That Robert had never contacted him just before the Rectification hearing and that the address he gave for Martin was not his address nor had ever been and that in any case RB knew his real address as he had stayed there on one occasion in 2004.*

I tell you this to show you that a person who will do that to his own flesh and blood, will have no compunction to do much the same to someone like me, as he had done and also for money.

He said he would help me in any way he could. I suggested for a start he could make up an affidavit for me, putting the real facts behind what his brother did up to the time he left the partnership. As I was now dealing with the IPO's CEO over an official complaint about the way they were handling an application by RB to make my registration invalid, it would be sent to him. He agreed and an affidavit was drawn up and sworn in front of his solicitor. I had no input or hand in that affidavit, So I now list what it said:

Affidavit by Martin Busbridge for the IPO CEO, re Robert Busbridge perjury. Dated 26th August 2009.

I set out the relevant paragraphs for consideration by their numbers:

3/ MB says his brother has lied in all the statements he has made to every hearing, from Reynolds on and on a prolific scale. Also lied verbally, at hearings. He thinks that the lies had clearly clouded the judgement of Reynolds as can be seen in his decision and the way he came to decisions that were clearly arrived at, through the lies of RB that he believed. (I had given him some documents re hearings, other he got from the IPO or their website.)

4/ In the 2003 statement for Reynolds, MB says that it included dozens of lies about their involvement re the agency and the selling of Viper kits and making cars. He says there are too many lies to quantify but he would be willing to expand on all at any hearing or by statements.

5/ He accuses Reynolds of not having a grasp on the realities of business and the history of their involvement. He has believed everything RB said and disbelieved everything Mr Cook said, even when evidence was given by Cook to back up what he had said.

6/ He wants to set the record straight as he believes an injustice has been allowed by the IPO which has affected both himself and Mr Cook. That the IPO have not practised due diligence when dealing with all the applications of RB. Even though Mr Cook had brought to the attention of the IPO the lies of RB, they had washed their hands of those false claims and had always said the hearing would deal with them, when they did not. In any case those hearings were held years ahead of 1992 and that allowed RB to trade for years using a trademark which he was not entitled to use and to do that in his name (Martins) without his knowledge.

7/ He acknowledges that on BRL ceasing business, I had contacted them and they had been anxious to continue getting Viper kits off me. We had quickly agreed to an agency, verbally then in writing. *He confirmed the advertising was under my directions.*

8/ He acknowledged that the trademark belonged to me and had it belonged to Zinlic then they would surely have sold it on when they closed as they did with other assets. They would have had to agree to Mr Cook carrying on using it (with Classic Replicas).

9/ He explains how I did not want to be more than a manufacturer, with Cobretti being the retail agents.

10/ He confirms his brother began to express his desire to cut me out of things by copying my product when possible. They started to do this when I went to Switzerland and firstly by copying my Cortina based chassis. They got my chassis maker to supply them on the quiet with the Jaguar version, similarly with my body maker. (Both subcontractors using my jigs and moulds) They pretended when I phoned them that they were still acting as agents. Eventually they were able to make their own copies of my two Viper chassis and my Viper body. They changed the wording of their adverts to show they were now manufacturing a Viper kit and not as managers. He makes the point that I could not do anything about the wording of adverts nor articles, as I was abroad and unaware of what they were doing. (remember this was a plank of Reynolds decision that I had not taken steps to stop them) He admits that he had a hand in all this and wished he had not. He says that when I became aware of their deception and threatened legal actions, because his brother was running the company and wasting the money that he had put his house on the line to enable them to borrow via a bank loan, it all became too much for him. It led to a break-up of the partnership and he lost his house and marriage.

11/ Looking back at the records *he can see that his brother had deceived him by applying to register the mark without his knowledge or agreement. He had also tried to get money from Chrysler for the mark, which they did not own and unknown to Martin. (This also proves that RB intended if he got money from Chrysler, to keep that from Martin)*

He finds it strange that even though the IPO were told of RB's bankruptcy and the break-up of the partnership in which the registration application had been made in, they ignored that and carried on dealing with the application as if nothing had happened. The indemnity was never given to him as it was not worth anything to him, as RB had no money to back it up. Had he known that RB was trying to get £500,000 from Chrysler for the mark, he would definitely not agreed to any indemnity as that would mean he would get no money out of any deal.

12/ He is not impressed to read of the IPO's attitude toward his rights in the business and they talked rubbish about it all in the Hobbs, Foley and Annand hearings.

13/ He queries every decision reason that Reynolds made:

Re advertising, implying I had abandoned the mark because I had not advertised the mark, plus any problems with quality he would have sent to Cook, saying the adverts for 427 parts did not show they were Viper parts when they were not Viper parts, if Cook had complained about what we were doing we would have taken no notice and would have carried on, Reynolds showed bias against Cook, and the hearing was not held fairly as the IPO must have known to appeal, it was beyond the pocket of most people.

15/ He agrees with the decision of Landau and all the reasons for that decision, especially that RB had not legally dealt with the assets which he owned 50% of. Therefore his brother could not apply to register the mark, nor continue with the business using his assets which he had not paid for.

16/ He takes umbrage at the legal advice Hobbs gave RB especially on how he could get away with taking over his part of the partnership and the advice about how he could do so by supposedly giving me an indemnity. Then Hobbs believing RB had tried to find him, but did not know where I was, when he knew all along.

17/ With the Foley rectification hearing he says that the address that RB gave for his supposed Spanish address was a fabrication as he knew what his real address was and it was perjury, which should be the subject of criminal proceedings. That RB had no intentions of ever contacting him as he knew that he would never agree to signing over his share of the assets of Cobretti.

He goes onto saying that he believes that he and his brother never had any rights to the trademark and that he also believes that that his brother has been solely responsible for the systematic theft of it from Mr Cook. Foley's decision is flawed and should be declared null and void.

18/ The Annand hearing should also be declared null and void as it is based on the flawed Foley decision.

19/ As for the Invalidity hearing to be held, it is full of copies of perjured evidence from other hearings. He will attend and give evidence to these lies.

20/ He asks the IPO to take these accusations seriously and to take steps to remedy their refusal to listen to the truth and the Landau decision should be carried out and legal steps taken against RB for perjury.

It was signed and sworn in front of his solicitor and included in my second letter of complaint to the CEO of the IPO.

Chapter Twenty Nine
My Second Letter to the CEO of the IPO, Mr Marchant. Dated 30/8/09

I go over the ways the IPO have never listened to the accusations made by me that RB had lied and lied. I point out the fact that time and again I was told they would be dealt with at a hearing yet they never were. I also point out what the ramifications of the decisions against me by the IPO by believing the lies, on my health and business. I complain about the never ending incompetence of the IPO over the 17 years since 1992.

I told him that I had now been approached by a recent return to the UK, Mr Martin Busbridge who has made out an affidavit confirming the misdeeds and perjury of his brother Robert Busbridge.. I go on to list them all in a list numbered 1-11. I will not copy that list here as it contains all that appears above in the breakdown of his statement. I tell him that a copy of MB's statement is included.

I tell him that the IPO should instigate criminal proceedings against RB for the perjury, and I complain that even though perjury can now be seen to have been committed in all previous hearings, to the IPO recently and to Mr Gittings, the IPO have refused to act, saying it will all be dealt with at the forthcoming Invalidity hearing. I accuse the IPO of refusing to answer my questions as to why the IPO made certain decisions that were flawed because they did not follow their own rules. That the IPO have refused to answer my questions as to why I was not sent copies of evidence put in by RB at the Annand hearing. *(Yet another glaring avoidance of basic rules.)*

I ask that a meeting be held where both Martin Busbridge and myself can make our complaints to the IPO over their handling of events.

After sending off this letter to Marchant I send an email to Gittings on the 1st September 2009, asking that the Invalidity hearing be cancelled due to the fact that registration of the mark by RB was gained by fraud and perjury and this means that the Invalidity application made to cancel my own registration would not have been able to be made had the original registration application not have gone ahead as it did.

Needless to say I got no reply, so another example of how the IPO refuse to

answer sticky questions and requests.

On the 7th September I sent an email to Colombo telling him that I had just been to the Bournemouth CID to tell them of the perjury of RB. I tell him that he knows that I have already complained about this perjury to Gittings and that I now have been contacted by Martin Busbridge who confirms all these acts of perjury. I repeat once again that he has never answered properly the questions why Landau was never carried out. I tell him that in my letter to his CEO I have asked for the Invalidity action to be cancelled and the registration.

I ask him specifically how a hearing supposedly to be held to determine Invalidity can deal with acts of perjury going back to 2004 at the Reynolds hearing? Are the IPO going to hold a separate hearing to deal with perjury? I ask if it is guaranteed that the perjury will be heard and can I have Martin attend as a witness?

I get an answer of two paragraphs on the 16th September. He says: *'The issues of alleged acts of perjury by RB have been raised before the Tribunal as part of the application for Invalidity and forms part of the evidence you wish the hearing officer to consider.'*

This was utter and complete bollocks as nowhere in my written evidence so far, for this hearing had I specifically dealt with ALL the acts of perjury, nor had it ALL been contained in the statement made by Martin!

He goes on to say that should I wish to include Martins evidence (which as you can see came after I had put in my last evidence) to support my allegation of perjury, I will then be required to apply for this additional material to be admitted. (Oh yeah and they then refuse it as they did at the Annand hearing.) I wasn't having this and replied same day saying that Gittings had said I could just put it in without having to beg the IPO to be allowed. I castigate him for making erroneous statement about what I have already put into evidence and ask what the hell is going on here? I also point out that his own CEO has already said unequivocally that the hearing **will deal** with the perjury issue.

I now tell him that because of his behaviour and dis-ingenuousness and my inability to get straight answers as to where I stand on this business of the perjury, I am taking on a solicitor to handle matters.

His answer to this on the 17th is an about face to what he had said before. Now he says that if ALL perjury evidence is relevant to the Invalidity it will be allowed even if it was committed at previous hearings. ***This statement may come back to haunt the IPO if they do not deal with all the perjury of previous hearings!*** However if they do not have relevance to that hearing they will not take account of them. This is at variance with what they told my local Police. For I know they will say much of the perjury was not of relevance and that will mean ***nothing more than the IPO are not interested when you show them that acts of perjury have been committed at their hearings. They will invent excuses not to act.***

I decide to now wait and see what they do about perjury at the hearing and what comes up in their decision. If they miss out on the many acts of perjury I will be back off to the Police with a big dossier and will be insisting on action. I may even get my new lawyer involved so the Police see we mean business. I am told that if Martin has to give evidence he has to do this ***not in person*** but by a witness statement affidavit or Statutory Declaration and to be added to all the other evidence of mine and RB. If RB does not challenge it, it will be taken as true. (Remember this statement and see if it matches up with what actually happened at that hearing and in the eventual decision document!)

As you can see above I had told Colombo that I had taken on a solicitor and this was a decision that I felt I had to take, for the IPO ***were lying to me about all sorts of things I had put to them. They were refusing to answer many questions, or being disingenuous in their replies, giving differing answers which made no sense.*** In other words they were either being their usual incompetent selves, or they were deliberately trying to confuse me in order to mess up my chances of getting justice over this Invalidity case, that was coming up. I felt that if I did not get someone who cut through all this crap from the IPO, then I would lose this case and that would be the end of this whole case with Robert Busbridge since 1992.

I was able to borrow enough money from a good friend to do this and so I went ahead and looked for a local firm with an IP section. Funnily enough the company I came up with was the very same company I had sought legal advice as to my position when it became evident that that the Yanks were going to shut down BRL. I met up with a Mr Daniel Wallens and gave him all my extensive files after a meeting where I laid out in brief, what I was up against. I left it to him to read through all the large bundle of files in a large box.

Reply from CEO of IPO.

On about the 20th September I received the long awaited reply from the CEO of the IPO, to my last letters to him. It was what I had expected, nothing more than a complete and utter whitewash. They truly are a disgrace this mob.

I had sent two long letters listing a host of complaints of a serious nature about the way the IPO had mishandled all the cases from 2004 including mishandling everything from 1992 onwards to the first hearing in 2004. How they had lied to me and my MP and how everything had taken years to proceed. Many times refusing to reply to questions and of course the continual gross perjurious acts of Robert Busbridge. Not forgetting the affidavit of Martin to back up my complaints of perjury.

He ignored all of what I had said in my first letter which I sent prior to my list of specific complaints. To my complaint saying I had been lied to whilst waiting for the Hobbs decision, he said:

'There were no lies' But he admitted that Colombo had been incorrect to tell me in March 2007 that the matter was with the Appointed Person still. Just brushes it all off, just like that! *Completely ignores the odious fact that back in September 2007 his own department knew that Busbridge had dropped the appeal and they gave him time to find his brother Martin. That I had a letter showing that to be the case. No, if this was not a case of lying! Then what was it? Just another case of sheer incompetence, compounded but the fact that at every request by me from September 2006 to March 2007, I had been given the same answers...* **we cannot give you an answer.** *No apology given, which in any case would not suffice for me even if given.*

To my complaint that RB was allowed to renew his registration after it had run out in 1999, and even though Landau had said it could not be renewed and the appeal against that had not been heard. His excuse for this was that if it had been taken off the register, then anyone looking to see if it were registered would think it were free. *He competently forgets* **I had it registered so that would not have been the case!** *It would have come up as registered to me! It should have just been suspended until after the appeal. You cannot make this bloke up, what an incompetent or more to the truth, another liar!*

To my complaint that in renewing it they allowed him to do it in his name when Landau had said it had to be only in the name of the partnership, he then lies again or is himself bloody well incompetent, for he says that it was not recorded as being in RB's name only, until July 2009 after winning at Annands hearing. *Yet RB even put into evidence for the Rectification a copy of a certificate **signed by no less than Marchant himself and dated November 2004.** and in RB's name only.*

*The man is a complete and utter incompetent fool and here I was trying to get the useless civil servant dickhead to get me some justice! You would have to complain about him as well if only there were someone to do this that had any teeth **and were independent!** I gave up on this one.*

To my complaint that evasions and refusals to answer why the Landau decision was not carried out when RB dropped his appeal? He says that this was explained to me by Colombo in an email to me. *I have dealt with this vacuous explanation above. However I did not expect the head of the IPO to be fobbing this answer off onto one of his minions, about whom I am complaining about anyway.*

To my complaint that I could get no answer from James and Colombo as to what their positions were and what department they worked in and was I complaining to the right department? He says he is satisfied that they both correctly told me of their roles. *This is simply yet another lie as they never did any such thing. If they had why would I complain they had not? They never once answered my questions or to whether I was dealing with the right department. He has merely taken their assurances and he is saying they are right and truthful and I am not.*

To my complaint about all the perjury of RB from 2004 to date, to which I had provided evidence and which had been ignored. I am simply told that it will be dealt with at the Invalidity Hearing. He says that I had complained in a letter about the perjury of the hearing in 2004 (Reynolds) and the offending document is part of the Invalidity hearing. So it will be dealt with at that hearing.

Here he is being duplicitous again as I had complained about ALL THE PERJURY at all the hearings from 2004, only to be ignored both by hearing officers and the IPO in general. He ignored that I had just been told by Colombo that at the Invalidity Hearing they would only deal with perjury accusations that they deemed to be relevant to that case. So all the other cases of perjury would not get dealt with!

My complaint that I was not told about the Hobbs hearing being suspended or that RB dropped his appeal or was given extra time to hunt for Martin. His explanation for this is the old IPO kernel, "It was nothing to do with you so bug out" Again the IPO left hand not knowing what the right hand was doing.

The CEO admitted to my MP that I had an interest to know what was going on, and that I would be kept informed. That consistently, Colombo was telling me he could not find out as it was out of his hands but he would do everything to find out and let me know. These were either lies or hollow promises for it was not until well after March 2007 that I ever got to know, and belatedly so.

To my second attempt to get an answer on why I and my MP were lied to over what was going on when the IPO knew full well what was going on?

He again denies we were lied to yet I have shown above we were.

So all my efforts to get my complaints about maladministration to the very top man were once again a complete waste of time.

Now to my second letter with the Martin affidavit. He excuses himself from replying to anything I said in that letter as he says all that I said is subject to the forthcoming Invalidity Hearing and the Rectification application by Martin (sub judice).

Once again he is being selective and duplicitous as a lot of what I said in that second letter did not have to do with either of these matters but to perjury and general matters in others areas and times. Complaining as to the performance and antics of the IPO throughout. Similarly he ignores completely Martins affidavit which also dealt with non Invalidity matters. Such as why did Reynolds in 2004 allow the registration in the face of the lies of RB which were complained about at the time, only to be ignored.

This is all that the general public get whenever they complain to a government department. They are masters at twisting things so they do not answer your complaints. They grasp at matters that are not central and ignore the kernel of the complaints. They all make me sick and the IPO are just another rabble arm of the government, and who are the same devious rabble as all the other departments of government.

We are now at the point where Martin has applied to the IPO, to have his complaint about how RB was able to get the register changed to read himself as owner of the mark. He had written to the registry and they had obviously told him that he could apply to have it rectified (once more).

The application form TM26R was dated 15th August 2009 and accompanied by a letter/statement.

Chapter Thirty
The Statements of Martin Busbridge for the Rectification/Invalidity Application

Martin Busbridge complains that he was unaware that RB had applied to register the mark and he was also not aware of any of the other proceedings. That his brother had tried to convince the IPO that he had been unable to contact him at any time over an important subject as to him signing over his rights to assets of their partnership business, and thus allowing RB to become to sole owner.

He wants to point out that RB is not an honest person. The truth of the dissolving of the partnership is that they decided that they could not carry on the business due to money problems. He was about to lose his house as they were suffering a cash flow problem and the bank wished to foreclose on his house. They decided to terminate the partnership, but not for him to give up his rights to the assets including the mark Viper. His solicitor advised against him accepting an indemnity. Also he was not happy with the way his brother ran the business.

However RB had other plans and they did not include closing the business. With him out of the way he was able to carry on discussing with Chrylser about the mark of which he knew little having been kept out of those discussions. Had he known that RB may have been able to get money off Chrysler he would definitely have never have walked away, as by doing so he had dropped his rights to any future monies from Chrysler.

"RB states I left the country for good in 1992 and went to New Zealand and Australia for good". In fact I only went for a 5 month trip from October 1993 to February 1994. I was not contactable, yet on my return to London I was in contact with him to tell him of his trip." Martin says.

He accuses RB of twisting the real facts of what happened in these times to suit his story for the IPO.

He says RB has committed perjury at all the hearings right up to the last one, before Annand. He now made several specific points:

1/ He did play no active part in Cobretti after he left, but as far as he was concerned it had closed down and his brother went on to form Autotrak, a limited company. He had no idea of any legal entitlement to the mark (as he did not know it had been applied for).

2/ No legal indemnity was given him by Robert.

3/ He restates that he did not leave the country in 1993, permanently, only for a 5 month trip. It was in 1998 that he went to Spain and RB knew this as he had regular contact with their parents in Spain. He also knew I was living in the UK in Devon during 1996-1998. I had contact with RB in 2003 at their Fathers funeral in Spain and again in 2004 and at no time was any discussion held about the trademark or signing it over.

4/ So all RB's statements that he tried to contact him are untrue. As were his assertions he had trouble with the UK authorities and he had changed his name. Despite what he claims, RB did know my address as he stayed with me at my address in Spain in 2004 and writing to me at the same address. Also he had my phone numbers and my younger brother also had those, plus my email addresses.

RB did not WANT to contact him as he knew he would not sign over any rights to assets of Cobretti. He went on to say he found it hard to believe how the IPO could be so easily convinced and he could understand how Mr Cook had carried on trying to get the IPO to listen to what he was saying. He felt the decisions made by the IPO were wrong.

He says that the crucial point as he sees it, is whether or not he signed over his part of the assets of Cobretti to RB and as a result of the letter from the IPO to Spain which of course he never received. The statement of Jan 2007 by RB to the IPO re the Spanish address is perjurious.

Now my solicitor was in charge so I never made another statement myself but he now was working with Martin and two more statements of facts were drawn up to add to the Rectification process started by MB.

Second witness statement by Martin Busbridge for rectification.

Recounted in brief by relevant numbered paragraphs:-

1/ He makes this statement in connection to Rectification and Invalidity.

3/ He makes this to clarify his first statement.

4/ He has read all the relevant hearing decisions and evidence of all the previous cases.

5/ He supplies a bundle of documents in support.

6/ He went into business with his brother in late 1987 trading as a partnership called Cobretti Engineering. It terminated in June 1992.

7/ It was apparent to him that RB has in previous proceedings provided incorrect factual information as to the operation, trading, and dissolution of the partnership.

8/ Now he describes the agency they had with BRL where they would get kits for Viper cars for resale. How they arrived to that agency and the history of himself and RB's experience in the trade.

9/ During this BRL agency they dealt only with Mr Cook and the sale and advertising was dealt with by Mr Cook. When BRL ceased it was verbally agreed that they would continue as agent for Mr Cook in the same way as with BRL. They could not make kits themselves as they did not have the expertise, or consent of Mr Cook to do so.

10/ This oral agreement was quickly followed by a written agreement and signed by himself and RB.

Copy of agreement supplied as an exhibit.

11/ Mr Cook directed how the adverts should read (Exhibit 2) reading *'under new management'* and that meant the sale, advertising and sales of Viper parts and kits was being carried out by Mr Cook through the partnership as his agents. The use of the mark was strictly as agents in advertising or selling Viper kits and parts. At all times with BRL and then directly with Cook/Classic Replicas, also as agents. All goodwill in both cases was to go to BRL or Mr Cook.

12/ Mr Cook made it clear to the partnership that he wished to only be a manufacturer of Viper kits and parts on a smaller scale as to when with BRL. With the retail of same to be left to the partnership.

He did not distance himself from the agency nor to had given up the relationship, as he assisted the agency at kit car shows and by assisting the partnership with the completion of a Cortina Viper as a demo car.

13/ RB and myself discussed later on that we should not continue to purchase Viper kits from Mr Cook.

RB proposed to copy them, then manufacture and sell unlawful copies of the Viper in breach of the agreement. I agree that I agreed to this and used my house to obtain a bank loan to pay for the tooling, machinery, equipment to commence trading unlawfully, as proposed by RB. We first copied the Cortina Viper and got

Mr Cooks chassis maker to make us copied chassis jigs (exhibit 3 & 4). We also did the same with the body maker until we found a London company to copy the body. Then when Mr Cook went to Switzerland we were able to proceed with the RB copying proposal. We led Mr Cook to believe we were still acting as his agents so we could have the time needed to finish off our copying preparations. We altered our advertising to read '*under new ownership*' (exhibit 5) and the partnership prepared several untrue magazine articles (exhibits 6-8) representing Mr Cooks business as the partnerships and appropriating his goodwill, also contrary to the agreement. All untrue adverts and articles started after June 1991 when Mr Cook was unable to properly monitor the partnership activities. (as he was abroad)

14/ Towards the end of 1991 Mr Cook realised what was going on and started to send us threatening legal letters. (exhibits 9-11)

15/ In March 1992 my bank was threatening to enforce its interest over my house and neither my wife nor RB was supporting me. This culminated with the splitting up and falling out with RB and the termination (exhibit 12) and my losing my house to the bank and marriage.

16/ I can see that RB was working behind my back and unknown and without my agreement, he put in an application to register the mark Viper in the name of the partnership. I was also unaware of the later application to rectify the application. This was all in breach of his fiduciary duties to me as a partner. So he did not have the necessary powers to do this and it was in breach of our agency agreement.

17/ After the partnership finished RB unlawfully continued with the application to register the mark and I do not agree to the application having been made and it should have been withdrawn as it was not properly authorised.

18/ I see that from all the documents of the previous proceedings that RB says he offered me an indemnity in return for my agreement to transfer the partnership property to him. No agreement was ever reached and I knew he had no means and it was worthless. I took legal advice over this. I believe that Landaus decision in regards to this situation was correct. I note that the IPO have not sent me this Landau decision document. (*They did not want him to see it the duplicitous bastards!*)

19/ He says he regrets the partnership deception and wish to put it right and RB has embarked on a path of deliberately and incorrectly misrepresenting the position in previous hearings. (*Nice way of saying RB was lying and committing perjury.)*

20/ He also attempted to represent that the partnership was properly dissolved. Also that an address in Spain was my last known address. It is a complete fabrication and he knew what my address was, and he had several phone numbers for me.

21/ He had visited me at my address on one occasion. He did not want to contact me because he knew I would not agree to any transfer of rights and based on a meaningless indemnity. So I never received the latter sent me by the IPO (exhibit 13).

22/ As a result of the above matters if the registrar will not invalidate the registration as it was made in bad faith, then he should rectify the application or the registrar. If the registrar will not accept the untruths of RB, he should rectify the mark to show it in the partnership names and then invalidate it as being made without my permission and made in bad faith.

What are the odds the IPO will ignore all of this damning document? Also that they will do nothing about the perjury committed?

(I wrote this before the outcome of the hearing, so I was dead right.)

The third Martin Busbridge statement.

A third statement document was made by Martin soon after his second. Again I will report it in brief form.

Most of the second half concerns the way RB had treated him over their Mother who was also residing in Spain. As these comments do not have anything to directly do with this story I will not reproduce them. I do not know why he put them in.

I will once again comment on the paragraphs that are relevant by their numbers:-

4/ He says that RB has committed perjury to gain credibility with the IPO.

5/ He denies that he and RB had a falling out as described by RB, that even though offered an indemnity he refused it on legal advice as RB had no money to back it up. That RB collaborated with a Colin Bruce to engineer a bankruptcy. That RB had talked to Chrysler over selling the mark to them That the application to register in his name (a partnership) without his knowledge was done by RB. That far from fleeing the country straight after the split he only took a year later a 5 month holiday abroad. He states that RB says that he never took part in the partnership from 1992 to now, when there was no partnership to take part in.

6/ After the split he thinks that RB thought he would have a clear run to obtain much money from Chrysler. He does not dispute my rights to the mark Viper. He agrees that there was a verbal then written agency agreement with me and there was no forgery, and that by my supplying them with kits I was in fact helping them.

7/ The copying of my products was a true fact which he took part in. Why did they get my own chassis sub contractor to quietly copy the jigs whilst I was away abroad if as RB states they legally copied it.

8/ He also confirms that the Cortina chassis design of mine was also copied, this time by a person called Sangster Jones. He confirms that the business was run mainly by his brother, whilst he kept in the background.

9/ He confirms that RB was not a person to be trusted.

11/ The Landau decision should have been implemented.

14/ All the lies that RB told the IPO regarding his whereabouts when he knew all along where he was. Plus all the lies RB told about him changing his name and being on the run from UK authorities where made to the IPO to show that he could not get him to sign over his half of the partnership assets.

15-18/ He makes comments about the fact that RB knew full well where he was in Spain.

Of course RB replies to the above three statements, one is made out to his Invalidity action and one to Martins Rectification, but I am not going to waste a whole load of time on repeating what he said as what he did say was even more garbled than he usually is. I reckon he was going through a brainstorm because he just ranted on and on with a load of irrelevant garbage. He threw in everything except the kitchen sink as documentary evidence. The whole of his reply to Invalidity was about an inch and a half thick, when I got in through the post and it even included the whole of my long blog on the IPO. Then every page of my other blog on his wretched business (Cobretti Engineering) and what kind of conman he is, plus copies of everything he could think of and most of which he has used before.

On Martins action, his reply was a rant about how Martin and I were conducting a vendetta against him and he included paragraph after paragraph about family circumstances surrounding their Mother, which were totally and utterly irrelevant. He sounded unhinged, which I hope he is and in fact the sooner the men in white coats take him away and lock him up, the better. Or better still men in dark blue uniforms taking him for a spell in clink. However in this shit country of ours I very much doubt this will happen as the authorities seem less and less inclined to deal with criminals and put them away than ever, especially as we have that Ken Clarke in charge of the so called Ministry of Justice and he likes criminals, apparently. The way things are going, in the near future most will not even go to jail even if they are charged with offences. So what fat chance is there of RB ever getting charged with perjury etc?

However one good thing that came out of this mountain of garbage was that he for some reason included copies of invoices I had sent him and a few notes from me, back in the early 90's. As I have said before I never kept every scrap of paper to do with my dealings with the Busbridges. He proves what a liar he is, once again. He proves conclusively that liars, even good liars, trip themselves up eventually. For they tell so many lies that they forget what they have lied about previously. So with the two copies he supplies, one shows that I invoiced him in August 1990 for 1500 brochures. Cast your minds back to where I tell of the fact that I had 5,000 of these Viper colour brochure pages done so that he and I could use them to show our potential customers a selection of finished Vipers and on the front there is printed '*Viper*'. He told Reynolds that in no way had I had anything to do with their advertising and marketing, and he never used any of my brochures. Yet here we have the proof that I was **selling** him brochures for **my Vipers!** So that he could use them to sell **my Vipers!**

The second document was a note to Martin telling him that he could offset an invoice against certain costs that I owed him for. I say on the note that he can deduct off what he owes me the cost of my share of their advertising and I quote which adverts I am referring to and the magazines they appeared in. Again if you remember I had said that I shared their advertising costs, which RB had denied was the case.

Also if you refer back to Reynolds decision, the vacuous man uses as one of his main planks as to why I should lose my mark Viper, was because he said I had no control over their advertising. Of course at that hearing I could not fall back on evidence to the contrary, or Martin, and I did not have these two pieces of evidence. But they are yet more proof of the perjury of RB!

We are now at a stage where the evidence given by Martin Busbridge confirms all the lies that were committed by Robert Busbridge, in all the hearings, that I constantly complained about, and were true.

I feel that this vindicates all my complaints that I made about perjury and evasions of truth done by RB over the years. It remains to be seen just what the IPO will do, if anything, having now had three statements given by MB to these Invalidity/Rectification hearings. Will they once again ignore them? I feel that they would be extremely stupid to do that as by now even they must be able to see that I am not going to give up and let them get off. I feel that these truths now show just how sick all the decisions made by the various hearings that went against me, and especially the Reynolds hearing. Not to mention that awful arrogant Hobbs bum and his flouting of the rules behaviour at RB's appeal hearing in 2005.

Chapter Thirty One
The Invalidity/Rectification Hearing Held in London on the 28th January 2010

Just prior to this hearing Daniel my solicitor came out with a Skeleton Argument document which lays out to the hearing officer how he intends to make our points to the HO. Thank God Busbridge was not allowed to flood us with more truck loads of his garbage outpourings.

This is a long detailed document of 19 pages of 50 paragraphs. Once again I will break them down to the most relevant paragraphs and points.

4/ KC opposes the Invalidity action as RB has no earlier right. RB's trademark was applied for in bad faith and he has no authority to bring the invalidity application.

5/ He outlines the Busbridges connection to BRL as agents selling Viper kits and parts.

6/ In 1989 BRL ceased and then the partnership rolled into a relationship with KC the same as the BRL relationship.

7/ This relationship was as an agent for Viper kits and parts as supplied by KC and it was KC using the Viper mark. The manufacture of the Viper kits and marks by KC was consented by the partnership in accepting those kits and parts.

8/ This relationship deteriorated about 1991 and broke down in 1992 and the partnership broke down in 1992.

9/ Following this RB continued with the application in the partnership name to register the mark this was filed in May 1992 and the IPO had changed the register to read that RB was the proprietor.

10/ My application to register the mark was granted in 2002.

11/ KC's position is that the partnership had been permitted to use the Viper mark only as agents and that MB did not know or consent to the application by RB to register the mark. Also KC used the mark since 1986 and before RB commenced use of it.

12/ Therefore it is inappropriate for the Registrar to exercise its discretion to declare the mark 2070139 (KC) invalid on the basis of an earlier mark, because RB cannot be taken to be the proprietor of an alleged earlier mark 1501909. It is also inappropriate to do so on an earlier right as no such right existed which predates KC's rights to the mark. Considering the new evidence provided by MB which has not before been considered by the IPO, so this has to be considered freshly by the IPO.

13/The IPO should also exercise its discretion to dismiss the Invalidity application and the basis of RB's bad faith in seeking to rely on certain facts and matters which have been verified by a statement of truth, in which RB cannot have had an honest belief of the truth of such facts, having regard to this new MB evidence *(in other words he lied and committed perjury)*.

14/ KC further feels that the Registrar is required to implement the decision of Landau (2005) also having regard to this new evidence of MB. By implementing this, the invalidity should be dismissed.

15/ MB has been allowed to participate in the Invalidity application and he thinks that the application should be dismissed as not having been made with his authority and he seeks to have the trademark of RB rectified to include him as a proprietor and he does not oppose the Registrar making that invalid on the basis of RB's bad faith in applying for and to use the mark.

17/ It is stated that KC can rely on any evidence from the Reynolds hearing where RB wrongly asserts the opposite opinion. It should be noted that the registration of KC as proprietor of the mark 2070139 is prima facie evidence of the validity of that registration and RB has to prove the substance of his allegations.

18/ There is a complex history of previous proceedings and decisions which are included in evidence.

19/ RB relies on: Alleged earlier rights to the mark, based on Sect 47(2)(a) & (2)(b).

20/ 47(2)(a) RB says he is the owner of an earlier trademark as 2070139 was applied for after 1501909.

21/ KC says that 1501909 is no such earlier trademark and failed because of the foregoing reasons.

22/ Landau decided that RB's trademark could have been assigned by the partners after the partnership ceased, to Autotrak Ltd and subsequently to RB. However the partnership had not properly assigned the trademark or at all and there was no agreement between RB & MB to assign it.

23/ Landaus decision was appealed but withdrawn and RB applied to remove

MB as a proprietor. Foley agreed to this and the appeal before Annand failed.

24/ It was therefore determined that despite there being no agreement between RB & MB regards the assets on dissolution of partnership, it appears that the assets passed to RB as there was no evidence from MB and that an implied indemnity had been entered into.

25/ It appeared that the assets of the partnership had passed to RB as MB did not object to the application therefore the ownership of the trademark appeared to cease to have effect. However now new evidence from MB who had not provided evidence for Foley or Annand it can be said that no indemnity was given and it cannot be now said that MB did not object to the application. MB was unaware of the application for the trademark. There can be no implied indemnity in relation to assets of which a partner is unaware.

26/ Therefore regarding the above it now appears that the ownership of the assets of the partnership passed to RB is no longer correct. This is because MB was unaware of the application for the trademark which he objects to. Therefore Landau's decision remains valid. The registrar does not have any basis to declare the mark invalid because no earlier right can be relied on by RB.

27/ 47(2)(b) RB seeks to say he is the proprietor of an earlier right and is therefore entitled to prevent KC using the mark under passing off law.

28/ RB's allegation on passing off is fundamentally flawed and embarrassing for its want of 'Particularity' because:

28.1/ KC coined the use of the mark to describe body and chassis kits and specialised parts known as Viper. Manufactured and supplied by KC through BRL and then Classic Replicas. He has used the mark since 1986 and supplied the partnership first through BRL and then by CR until mid 1991. The kits would be marketed, advertised and sold by the partnership and following the partnership ceasing, RB sought to manufacture the same kits and parts as supplied by KC and using the mark Viper. It is erroneous to suggest that KC's use of the Viper mark is a misrepresentation for the purposes of RB establishing passing off, because KC's use of the mark represents KC is manufacturing and supplying the Viper parts and kits, not as manufactured by the partnership or RB. KC agreed with BRL that BRL would be permitted to use the mark but goodwill in the mark would accrue to KC. There is no evidence to dispute KC's use of the mark from 1986 or to dispute the arrangements between BRL and KC over the mark.

28.2/ KC has used the mark in relation to Viper parts and kits since 1986, before RB commenced using the mark either as an agent of BRL/KC or otherwise. Therefore there is no misrepresentation by KC that his use of the mark Viper relates to RB's use of the same.

28.3/ There is absolutely no evidence provided by RB that KC's use of the Viper mark has caused or is likely to cause confusion. KC has used that mark for such a significant and substantial period of time such that had confusion really existed, RB would have been in the position to provide evidence that some or all his customers had manifested an impression that KC's use of the Viper mark was connected with RB's use of the same.

28.4/ The act requires: There to be in existence as at an earlier date of the determination of the application for invalidity an 'earlier right'.

An 'earlier right' as at the date of registration of the trademark the subject of an application for invalidity, may be relied on to prevent use of the trademark.

28.5/ Even if RB could demonstrate that he had passing off cause of action against KC'S use of the mark on May 10 2002, (which is denied) that cause of action may not now be relied on in an application for a declaration of invalidity due to an earlier right, being no longer actionable due to passing of time pursuant to section 2 of the Limitation Act 1980. Considering that RB would be barred by statute from commencing a passing off action it would be inequitable for the registrar to exercise its discretion to declare trademark 2070139 invalid.

28.6/ In entering a trading relationship with BRL and KC it is inarguable that RB as a partner of the partnership was aware of KC's use of the mark. To enable the partnership to receive Viper kits and parts RB as a partner would have been required to consent to KC's use of the mark etc.

29/ Having regard to the above matters there is no 'earlier right' that may be relied on by RB. There is absolutely no evidence that RB has actionable passing off cause of action. The registrar does not have any basis on which to exercise its discretion to declare the trademark 2070139 invalid because there is no earlier right that may be relied on by RB.

30/ The partnership was at will where no fixed term was agreed therefore it could be dissolved by mutual agreement, which is what happened on June 29th 1992.

31/ This does not inevitably mean a winding up but usually this happens and usually the assets, debts are distributed to the partners. This partnership was terminated and dissolved.

32/ After dissolution each partner continues to have authority to bind the firm so far as necessary to wind up affairs. No steps were taken by MB or RB by agreement as regards their respective entitlements in relation to the assets of the partnership to deal with such assets in a winding up of the partnership.

33/ Goodwill and rights of a partnership in a trade name are owned by the partners, not in the individual partners and any goodwill of the partnership is an asset of the partnership and not belonging to an individual partner. Accordingly any rights of the trademark Viper or its application, were assets of the partnership.

34/ Any partnership, on dissolution is likely to have debts. If the business is to be continued, remaining partners may discharge those in the normal course of business. Any partner who has his share bought out, can be entitled to an indemnity against future debts or pre-dissolution debts.

37/ Considering the above points and that RB seeks to rely in his application for invalidity on him obtaining rights in the trademark 1501909 from the partnership, it is clearly inappropriate for the Registrar to exercise its discretion in circumstances where RB is not in a position to assert such rights.

38/ It is inappropriate for the Registrar to exercise its discretion to declare the trademark 2070139 invalid considering RB applied for the trademark 1510909 in breach of the agreement between KC and the partnership.

39/ It is inappropriate for the Registrar to exercise its discretion to declare the trademark 2070139 invalid considering that RB applied for the trademark 1501909 in circumstances where the partnership was passing off in relation to the mark Viper.

40/ MB disputed that the partnership was entitled to apply for the trademark. To give effect to section 24(8) of the Partnership Act, the Registrar is required to consider that a decision has not been taken by the partnership to make and continue with the application for the trademark 1510909. It is inappropriate for the Registrar to exercise its discretion to declare trademark 2070139 invalid on the basis of a trademark applied for without the necessary authority within the partnership.

41/ Consultation must take place between partners before a decision affecting the partnership is made, to ensure that the decision proposing partner is not imposing their decision on the other partner. In this case no such consultation took place and according the application should not have taken place. The Registrar is required to consider that a valid decision has not taken place and therefore it is inappropriate for the Registrar to exercise its discretion to declare trademark 2070139 invalid as the trademark was applied for without the necessary authority within the partnership.

42/ In partnerships there is a fiduciary duty to each other so each should disclose to each other all relevant information in his possession to his partner. The Registrar is required to consider that RB has breached his duties to MB in applying for the mark without disclosing this matter to MB. Accordingly it is inappropriate for the Registrar to exercise its discretion to declare trademark 2070139 invalid on the basis of a trademark applied for in breach of RB's fiduciary duties under common law and the Partnership Act. It is crucial that there is no evidence that MB was given notice by RB of the application for trademark 1510909 or the application for invalidity.

43/ RB applies for invalidity based on his alleged rights acquired in the trademark 1510909. For reasons as above in 30-37 any rights to proceed with invalidity for trademark 2070139 based on trademark 1510909 are vested in the partnership. It is appropriate to allow RB to continue with an application for invalidity based on the rights of the partnership without the necessary authority of the partnership, which has not been obtained for the reasons given 38-42 above and could not be obtained in any event, considering the partnership has been dissolved.

44/ It is inappropriate for the Registrar to declare the trademark 20702139 invalid because RB has provided the Registrar with evidence, verified by statements of truth, in which KC requests the Registrar to determine that RB cannot be considered to have an honest belief of its truth as follows, and in each following instance the Registrar is requested to make a finding as regards whether each such alleged instance amounts to dishonesty by RB (it is important to note that the Registrar has confirmed in an email from Mr.R.Colombo for the Registrar, to KC dated 17th September 2009 that the following matters will be dealt with in the application for invalidity):

44.1/ RB sought to provide conflicting information to the Registrar, verified by statements of truth, as regards the alleged assignments of the trademarks, as described in the decision of Landau, which he then sought to withdraw. It is alleged that RB cannot be considered to have honestly believed in such assignment if he sought to withdraw them, and such alleged assignments are so conflicting with each other that there cannot be said to be an honest belief of RB in each alleged assignment.

44.2/ RB asserted as verified by statements of truth, that the partnership no longer retained an interest in partnership property as a result of an implied indemnity and as a result of MB allegedly not responding to the application for rectification by RB. However it is alleged that RB cannot be said to have honest belief in such an implied indemnity or a genuine failure of MB to respond to the rectification application considering that an indemnity cannot be implied (see 22-26 above) and considering that genuine attempts to contact MB were not made by RB in relation to the rectification application.

44.3/ RB cannot be said to have an honest belief in his application for invalidity based an section 47(2)(b) because it is alleged that such an application ignores the facts that RB is aware as specified in paragraphs 27-29 above.

44.4/ RB has sought to prosecute the application for invalidity regardless of the incidents of alleged bad faith specified in 38-43 above. Despite knowing of such incidents of bad faith, it is alleged that RB has sought to verify by statements of truth that such matters do not exist, despite it being the position that he must have known that such matters do exist. In particular, but without limitation it is alleged that RB admitted on oath that the partnership was an agent of BRL and KC, a position which he now seeks to deny, and it is further alleged that RB has sought to wrongly mislead the Registrar as regards the address of MB.

45/ Considering the above matters, the Registrar is required to consider each of the above specified circumstances and determine whether RB should be permitted to proceed with the application in circumstances where KC alleges that there are clear incidents of dishonesty by RB.

46/ Section 48 of the Act says that where the proprietor of an earlier mark or other earlier right has acquiesced for a continuous period of five years in the use of a registered trademark in the UK, being aware of that use, there shall cease to be any entitlement on the basis of that earlier mark or other right. Considering that it is indisputable that KC has used the Viper mark (which is registered) as currently registered by both RB and KC) since 1986 and the Invalidity was not filed until 2003 (and the use by KC was not objected to by RB until at the earliest in 1992) It is inappropriate for the Registrar to exercise its discretion to invalidate the Viper mark 2070139 when it has been used by KC for such a significant and substantial period and such use has been acquiesced by RB for more than five years.

47/ It is of course important to note that 2070139 was registered before 1501909. It is likely that the registration 2070139 was allowed to proceed to registration based on the honest concurrent use terms of the Act, and where such use was for a significant and substantial period of time before registration and continues to exist, it would be perverse for the Registrar to exercise its discretion to declare trademark 2070139 invalid where it has already determined that KC has honestly used it.

50/ The application for Invalidity must fail because it is inappropriate for the Registrar to exercise its discretion to declare 2070139 invalid because:

50.1 The decision of Landau must now be implemented considering that evidence of MB that was previously unavailable at the Foley and Annand hearings, now indicates that such decisions can no longer be correct, accordingly there is no earlier trademark that may be relied on by RB.

50.2 Even taking RB's position at its highest, which is a position which is negated in any event in the evidence, there is no earlier right to the mark that may be relied on by RB, considering the use made of the mark by KC, to allow RB to establish passing off.

50.3 Considering the further circumstances of the application for the trademark 1501909 and the background thereto, and the dealings of RB, together with the benefit of the evidence from MB, this is an application in which the Registrar must not exercise its discretion as any such exercise would clearly be unsafe and prejudicial to the genuine and long standing rights of KC in the Viper Mark.

This is particularly so considering that at no point can it be said that KC has acted improperly or dishonestly throughout as regards the Viper Mark. The same cannot be said for RB.

I cannot think of a more damming document and list of criminal acts by someone in such an area as IP, as this is. Try and get out of that Busbridge! His day at this stage is near, and that is what I thought when I read it. Of course now it had to be used in action at the hearing itself. I was fooling myself *again. Thinking that our system of Justice would now have to act properly! I was being an fool yet again as you will see...There is no real Justice in this country unless you are RICH!*

The hearing itself:

Robert Busbridge was only given the skeleton argument at the hearing so had no time to even read it. He looked decidedly sick and more scrawny than he has before. I sincerely hoped it was getting to him as evidenced by his rambling last statement and reams of copied trash.

The hearing was held at the IPO London Office and was a video link job with their Head Office in Newport. The hearing officer was a large bloke with a deep booming voice. No doubt the IPO got their biggest bouncer/bother boyo in from the Welsh hills, in on the act, to intimidate us.

He first of all asked RB if he wanted to say anything and to be honest he just waffled on as he usually does, coming out with a load of waffle. So much so I cannot remember much of the little he did say, except that the HO seemed to me to be exceedingly soft with him.

He was sounding like he was giving him a lot of leeway, for he asked RB about this accusation we had made about him giving the IPO a deliberately wrong Spanish address for Martin. For the HO more or less told him after hearing RB's lies as to how he had not lied about that, as it seemed possible he had made a mistake which seemed perfectly possible to do. *This was an absolutely outrageous and brazen act of bias coming from Salthouse by excusing a clear act of perjury. He ignored every scrap of evidence given by MB as to how it was perjury and both MB and myself straight away knew we were going to lose, as the IPO had obviously decided that they would trash anything we said.*

Unfortunately I thought Martin was a bit weak on the way he gave evidence on that point, as if he was unprepared to be asked about it. Had he come across as more strong and sure with his statements about how it was a lie, I think that the HO would not have been able to give RB leeway on that point of, did he know his brothers address or not? It will be interesting to see what the IPO actually say on this one matter and I am convinced they will invent excuses to put down accusations of lying. This even though it is plainly obvious he is lying, as Martin was in contact by phone with his younger brother and his Mother both had his phone numbers/email addresses. On top of that RB and his wife had stayed at Martins flat in 2004 and his wife had written to there. All that was evidenced in Martins evidence statements. It does not auger well for all the other lies RB has made and we have accused him of as the HO never even mentioned those, especially my complaint about the perjury concerning whether Cobretti were or were not agents of mine.

After RB & MB had spoken, but only to confirm points already made in their statements, and that did not take long, it was time for Daniel to have his say about how he saw the evidence against RB. He read out the contents of his skeleton argument, with a few interruptions from the HO and a skirmish about whether goodwill can accrue to a person within a company. Otherwise his speech went well, I thought. However I have learnt by experience that with the IPO it doesn't seem to matter what you say at a hearing, what good and true legal points you put forward, the IPO have a habit of just ignoring what doesn't suit them, which is 99% of what you say or give in documentary evidence.

For instance in past hearings I have made the very same legal points such as:

(a) The fact that the application was not bona fide.
(b) The application was made by a partnership that no longer was in existence.
(c) The application being made by only one partner and this should have triggered the IPO to ask if the other partner had agreed to this action as required by partnership law.
(d) The assignment to Autotrak Ltd was not done with the obvious agreement of the other partner.
(e) The mark obviously belonged to me because the IPO had come to that conclusion in granting me registration in my opposition to the application to register the same mark, by none other than a multi national car manufacturer… **Chrysler.**
(f) That in 1993 RB became bankrupt yet the IPO did not think to ask his receiver what he wanted to do with this potentially valuable asset. (Do

not forget that RB had asked Chrysler for £500,000 for the mark and had ***turned*** down £250,000 offer, which was much more than the £66,000 they offered me. Or two of their Viper cars.)

There were other similar charges I had made which were the same as what Daniel had put forward, only to be ignored time and again.

The hearing did not last more than an hour and a quarter or so and that was it. My lawyer made no direct accusations of perjury having been committed, preferring to call perjury by every other word other than ***perjury!*** This is a trait I find most annoying with British lawyers, they are all wimps who will not ***fight*** for their clients and prefer to use low key methods and words for what I think is a phobia of upsetting a Judge, or in this case a hearing officer. Of course the IPO made absolutely no mention of the perjury I had complained about and had been promised would be dealt with at the hearing. They asked not one question of RB or me, or MB, who had also complained of the perjury of his brother, other than that one feeble attempt about the lie about Martins Spanish address. ***Cast your mind back to what Raoul Colombo, Gittings and Marchant the CEO had promised me they would do with ALL the relevant perjury I had constantly complained about. As RB had put in his main Reynolds statements into this Invalidity hearing that meant that all the 160+ lies in that were now part of this hearing. So despite all the promises made to me by various managers at the IPO, that the perjury that I complained bitterly about, was once more ALL being ignored.***

After this totally useless hearing, we all (apart from RB) had a coffee, once we got outside. Martin agreed that the HO seemed to show a soft handling of RB and seemed to be obviously biased to him.

Of course this is always par for the course with the IPO. So I was not surprised. However I did think that just maybe they would now have to listen to the litany of reasons why this application should never have been made let alone the registration RB got on the back of perjury and bad faith etc.

Chapter Thirty Two
The Decision of the Invalidity Hearing

It was now a waiting game and taking into consideration the IPO's history of breaking their own guidelines on how long various actions should take, (hearing decisions 4-6 weeks) we could be in for a long wait.

Indeed it did turn out to be a long wait, but this as I have said, I fully expected this. By the end of March I got my lawyer to email them asking what was going on. He was told that the hearing officer had just started dealing with it and he was expected to come to his decision sometime in April. What I wanted to know is why he did absolutely sod all for two months after having heard all the facts etc at the hearing? Also it is inconceivable that he had not already read *all* the evidence *before* the *hearing*! Maybe there was a reason for this, like lots of activity at the IPO to work out their strategy? (No doubt with the help of the Hobbs character.) Yet true to form we trundled into May and by about the 12th May I sent an email myself, to the IPO and was told they had sent my lawyer a copy of the decision on the 6th. They however sent me by email, another copy.

A 26 page document which took some trawling through it and to discounting all the padding these hearing officers always fill these documents up with. I suppose they feel that the more crap they throw in, the more it looks like they have done good and thorough job of summing up. *The end result was as I totally expected it to be... an utter and complete whitewash of my case and all the legal arguments my lawyer put forward. It was as if I had never had a lawyer put in solid & valid legal arguments, with all the points of law and plenty of documentary evidence... all totally ignored!* I may as well have saved a lot of money and done it myself as in the past. For I would have got the same warped decision. All the points raised about how RB had made the application in bad faith, knowing I owned the mark and he had signed a legal agency agreement which banned him from claiming the mark. How he had never even got the permission of his brother to make that application made in both names. How RB had taken over the partnership assets again without a legal right to do so, and of course that included the possible asset of the application for the mark. Plus a host of other valid legal reasons why the IPO should not allow him to invalidate my registration. *These were all completely ignored... yet again the IPO show they are simply not in the business of dealing in the truth or dispensing justice. They are an utter disgrace!*

Some months later when I had calmed down over this horrendous document and re-looked at it in depth, the first thing that leapt off the pages was how Salthouse completely ignored everything I, Martin and Daniel my solicitor had said as I have said above.

Pages 3-5 deal with Martins *three statements* which all contained many pages of comments and evidence, mainly to do with the period of time between 1989 and 1992 when they broke up and does not comment on all my tribulations with his brother after he left. I do not have these to hand as they were not part of my own case but it is obvious that when you see that all Salthouse could say was contained in just two pages and what he did divulge was heavily hand picked and sarcastically commented on. One such comment is about the agency agreement which I do know about and it is thus; "but I note that the signatures of Mr Busbridge appears to be considerably different to that shown on the agreement between Cobretti and Mr Cook." He is referring to a copy of the agreement between Martin and Robert to terminate their partnership.

What this wretched man is doing here is inferring as seems to be his style as he hasn't the guts to be straight out with it, that either the signature of RB, on their agreement is forged or his signature on my agency agreement is forged. Quite why RB's signature should be forged on either documents is beyond me as in the case of the document of termination this was put into evidence by RB in any case. In the case of the agency agreement, RB was always saying that *both* signatures were forged by me. So this is a case of Salthouse just throwing in words to make one feel that either I or Martin were up to no good, but he of course does not say why he feels any of this. No evidence is forthcoming other than sly intimations.

Now to my evidence and bear in mind that I had first put in a Counter Statement to RB's Statement of Grounds, where I put in what amounted to my own Statement of Grounds. Also bear in mind that as this document is supposed to an important document in any hearing, as it sets out your legal defence or case. I went to a well known IP Lawyers and the composition of that document was made by them. It consisted of two pages and 14 paragraphs of legal points. Salthouse not only completely ignored this document, he didn't even mention it at all, let alone discuss the merits of what I was saying.

Then my Statement of Evidence which was some 11 pages long and contained 23 paragraphs of firstly answering the many claims and lies made by RB, but secondly putting forward my own defence and legal points. Salthouse once again ignores everything and the only mention of anything I had said was condensed to *one paragraph* where he snidely says "Mr Cook claims to be the owner of the mark Viper" as if this was an outrageous lie by me, when the certificate of registration given me by the IPO confirms what I had claimed.

Broken down this is all he admits to my saying:-
1: Me pointing out that RB had only begun to use the mark after he was given an agency by me in 1988.
2: That I formed a new company Classic Replicas in 1989 and retook RB & MB on as agents.
3: That in 1991 I had found that they had copied my jigs and moulds. (Incorrect as I had stated 1992)
4: That I asked my Patent Agent to file for application of the mark in 1992.
5: I claimed that the Registration certificate first shown by RB was either a forgery or a legally incorrect. (Salthouse then lies by saying that my Exhibits 3&4 prove that statement incorrect.)
6: That I was selective when I described how I had won registration after defeating Chrysler.
7: I had pointed out that RB was bankrupted in 1993 and that because of this he could not take part in the business until his bankruptcy was played out in 1996.

Now here is the rub, for Salthouse now says "Much of the rest of his statement does not deal with specific facts but consist of invective against the Registry and Robert Busbridge. He also asks various questions in his statement; "neither the invective nor the questions can be regarded as evidence".

This is an horrendous and blatant lie by Salthouse as *all of my statements one & two, contained only facts about the history of my involvement and showing that all that RB had put into evidence was incorrect and mostly lies. There was no invective at all and you can check that on my blog.*

To quote Collins Dictionary *invective*: "vehement accusation or denunciation especially of a bitterly abusive or sarcastic kind" *vehement*, "marked by intensity of feeling or conviction"

I defy any *independent* and fair minded person to find ONE example of me being vehement on the whole of both documents either towards RB or the IPO. You will have read my brief breakdown as to what was contained in each paragraph of both of those statements in Chapter 24 and you can see for yourself It is yet another outrageous lie by this stooge of the IPO who only wished to trash me and my history and evidence, *so for some reason he could deprive me of my mark!*

Then their apparent wish that only Busbridge should have it will be completed. *But why is this the case, you have to keep asking yourself?*

This is what he says that I find offensive or is an outright distortion or lie with regards to my Exhibits. I will only list those Exhibits that contain these gross claims, and I will only state his statement as the description of what is in the Exhibit can be seen in Chapter 24. My reply will be in italic print;

KC 1 "At first sight it appears that it is signed by the three men, but I refer to my earlier comments at paragraph 15 above" *I have told you above what this refers to, which is about the veracity of the signature of RB. Thus intimating it could be a forgery, without actually saying so.*

KC 2. "These articles do not have visible dates" *Salthouse being disingenuous here because these articles were put into evidence by no less than RB himself and I was merely repeating them to back up my claim that he had copied my kitcar and trademark. Salthouse makes no such similar claims about any of RB's evidence, so it is yet another instance of how the IPO are willing to rubbish my exhibits and apply broken rules to them, but not apply those same rules to RB's evidence. Showing double standards and bias again.*

KC 10 "A magazine article , with a hand written date of May 1986... by the end May another manufacturer had joined the Cobra ranks" *This is another snide intimation that this article I put in as evidence of my earliest public use as shown in the article which clearly states that I had at the end of May 1986 joined the ranks of the Cobra manufacturers in the UK. You see the IPO and HO's like Salthouse like to rubbish* you if you do not provide absolute proof of a magazine cover date. Yet as I say it is clear what the date is without showing the front cover which I no longer had anyway. Once again RB put in masses of such copies of his magazine articles and adverts and almost none of them could be accurately dated... did the IPO ever complain about that? No of course not.

 KC 12. "An advert by Cobretti offering Viper cars and stating they are under new management . Attached to the advert is a front cover of a magazine the title of which has been blacked out. It is dated February 1991" *Another blatant lie by Salthouse as the exhibit can only have come from 1990.*

 Then of course and most importantly, there were all the allegations of perjury that I had constantly brought up over the years. Culminating with my recently made assertions that the IPO had to act on the perjurious statements RB had made in his witness statements to the IPO in 2002 & 2003, that he had never been my agent. That this lie had been shown to be a lie when he was cross examined in my 2000 trial by my barrister. I had given the IPO the transcripts of that cross examination, showing that RB had eventually conceded he had been my agent. Despite initially ignoring me once again, they eventually told me that they would deal with this and other acts of perjury at this hearing. *So what had they to say about the accusations by me and my lawyer that perjury had been committed many times? The answer is staggeringly, bugger all!* The only mention of perjury was made in a light-hearted and flippant way and that was about the fact that RB had also lied to the IPO about Martins Spanish address. If you remember he had been told by the despicable Hobbs QC at that hearing, to make it up with Martin and get him to sign over his share of the assets of the partnership. This led to the IPO asking him what Martins address in Spain was, so they could send him a letter The address he had given was completely fictitious and he full well knew it was as he knew his correct address, having visited MB only a year earlier to having given this fictitious address, and under the claim it was a truthful statement.

 What did the unctuous IPO have to say about this? They fobbed it of as nothing to get a sweat about, by saying that it would be easy for him to make a mistake and then they make a truly astonishing claim; *"in any case there was no legal requirement for him to even answer any question as to whether he knew where MB was in Spain."* So if that was the case why did they go out of their way to first of all suggest to him via Hobbs and then their own Tribunal section to give it, so they could write to MB? For asking him they did and to remind you, that at the appeal hearing before Hobbs and one of the IPO's top men in their tribunal section, a Mr James, RB was told quite clearly that if he could find Martin and get him to sign over his half of the partnership assets, then all his problems would be over! Then after that the IPO asked RB to send in a statement as to the Spanish address of Martin, he did so. Now they change their spots completely and have the cheek to say that where Martin was, was really of no importance and RB did not even have to tell them his address in any case. *What an absolute lying shower!*

Their excuse making on his behalf over this clear case of perjury is quite sickening, as far as I am concerned. It just shows that they were prepared to brush aside all my accusations and those of my lawyer, of perjury. They had cynically told me that the perjury would be addressed by this hearing officer, yet the only 'acting on' on the subject, done by the hearing officer, was about the Spanish address business. He did not even make a mention of other complaints of perjury I had made, and he never asked any questions of me or Martin about all the other accusations I had made of perjury being committed. Which their *CEO had promised me would be dealt with.*

Chapter Thirty Three
My Thoughts on Where I Am.

This shows me that once again the IPO had their own agenda, and that was; *'not to deal in any way with perjury'* For to do so would mean that they would have to report RB to the CPS or some other agency and that would not do if they wanted RB to win, so I would fail. For if I won it would be tantamount to the IPO admitting they had made many mistakes in the past and that would give me all I needed to take legal action against them which they knew was in my mind to do. (They knew this beginning from 2002 and even though I lacked the money to do this and I doubted that I would ever find a lawyer with sufficient balls and experience to take on the IPO, they still must have thought I would.) There are also other reasons which I will show you shortly, as to why they just had to ignore any evidence I put forward about anything that could help me to win. I believe that one of the reasons they took so long to finalise their decision was that they needed to confer with others who had better legal in-sights and experience in IP matters, than their own hearing officer. I bet any money there would have been a getting together of heads, within the legal department of the IPO. I would also bet any money that Hobbs would have also been involved at some point as he is, as I have already said, seen to be heavily involved with the IPO to the point that he could be said to be one of their employees. He has also obviously researched this subject of the trademark Viper and all the cases involving it, back to the Chrysler hearing which dealt with my opposition to their application to register. One has to ask why he did that and why he obviously had strong views on what he had read?

Why did this Hobbs fellow have to read up on my opposition application to Chrysler and to RB and the subsequent hearings? It had absolutely nothing to do with the appeal RB was making and what it does is show me that he had deliberately acquainted himself with the history of the Viper mark and my own history with that. That shows to me that things were going on here that need explaining, by the IPO. Why was Hobbs who is intimately associated with the IPO, taking an in depth interest in me and what I had been doing in the past, concerning this mark?

The decision of course went against me, regarding RB's Invalidity application against my registration and regarding Martins application to force a Rectification of the Registry to put back the registration of RB into both their names. I cannot say I was surprised, although I had harboured thoughts that as a lawyer had presented my case this time, they would not be so blatant as to ignore his case, as they had ignored all my past cases and evidence supplied. However it is now evident that the IPO are so arrogant and full of themselves, that they obviously think they are above the law and can act in whatever way they choose. Ignore evidence of perjury, bad faith, breaking of many laws to do with partnerships and so on. They no doubt were working on the base that I would not be able to afford a High Court appeal, or at least *hoping* I would not be able to afford one.

So what was I to do now? I was hopping mad at the injustice of it all and the sheer cheek and corruption of the IPO. However the real point is that in this wonderful country of ours it is that only the rich can afford *justice!* I would only be able to afford an appeal if my solicitors would do it on a no win no fee basis, and they knew *that* before they even represented me for this last hearing. It is my opinion that Daniel Wallen, the lawyer who handled the case proved to be too young and too inexperienced in IP to be able to handle this case. So he was cocksure he had formulated the defence in a strong way and that the evidence was so strong, that we had to win. This even though I had warned him several times about the IPO's past history and that I did not think we would win.

Because of this I feel that he should have been pre-warned to the extent that he should have made damn sure he had a watertight defence and case, that the IPO could not ignore. He should have taken advice from a more experienced and learned barrister and I even gave him carte blanche to do this, but he thought he was so clever that this was not necessary. He told me that he used a very learned barrister and wanted this person to appear at the hearing. I refused that as that would have cost me a bomb and for what? In fact Daniel had boasted several times to me when I complained that he was leaving things right up to the last minute in preparing our case, that he was a great solicitor who knew what he was doing, etc, etc,

So the upshot is that at the inquest on this damned decision document, was that all Daniel could say is that the IPO had ignored all the factual and legal points we (he & me) made. Well I had told him over and over that that is what they had done since day one. He even had all the evidence of this in the papers I gave him of all the cases and hearings from 2004 onwards. He also of course pointed out the obvious fact that the IPO had also ignored what Martin had said about how he had not even known that RB had applied to register the mark in both their names. That he had not given up his share of the assets of the partnership, and so on. That the IPO had relied on an implied indemnity to Martin that RB said he had given, so that gave RB the right to take over the assets and they included the application to register the mark.

Now here we have to remind ourselves of; *who said that this implied indemnity (even though the IPO agreed it had never been legally made) was good enough to allow the IPO to say that it was good enough. None other than His Majesty, Hobbs QC! As far as I am concerned the IPO through this Hobbs bastard, just made up law as they went along, to suit how they wanted this case to turn out.*

So the attack on my mark was upheld and I lost it. The grounds for this was simply that RB had applied before I did! Forget that the application was made in bad faith and perjurious statements by the hundreds, plus let us not forget... FORGERY. Forget that one of their own hearing officers in 2005 had said that the application had to be taken off RB as it had not been legally acquired by RB. Forget all the instances of perjury I had proved to them, which they lied and said they would deal with, and didn't. The thing that really gets me is the way the arrogant IPO did not even discuss all the evidence put before it by way of my statements and MB's statements, nor the many points of law made. Their decision document did not deal with or discuss *any* of that. How do they get away with it?

Of course Daniel said he thought I had been 'shabbily treated' and the way the decision had been arrived at, warranted appealing against it. I was told that if I wanted to later on sue the IPO for all their incompetence etc, it was important that I at least appealed and won and that would give me a 'springboard' with which I could then use to sue them. What he was saying was that because I had the opportunity to appeal this decision, no future Judge or court would look favourably on any attempt by me to sue the IPO. I simply do not agree with this at all and I think that I should be able to go straight into suing the IPO for incompetence for *all their previous decisions right back to 1992. I should be able to include this latest biased fiasco as well. It should be noted by any Court that being poor had meant I could not appeal the previous hearings that went against me.*

Why have to go through an expensive appeal, and then have to go through yet another legal process to get justice against the IPO? The law in this country is an ass and the only people who benefit are the greedy lawyers and hopeless Judges. The legal and justice system is a gigantic con act, in my opinion and I think most sensible ordinary Brits would agree with me on that, es[ecia;l;y those like me whjo have no money.

I hope you can see the madness of our stupid legal system here. For it takes no account of the fact that whilst one can represent yourself at any of the IPO hearings, which are just tribunals, appealing at the High Court is another matter which requires expert legal people to handle. Whilst it is possible to represent yourself I would have to undergo the long process of putting together of all the papers required and how do I know how to do that to their satisfaction? Plus I am sick of doing all this kind of work. I could of course appeal to an Appointed Person and that would be handled much the same as an IPO hearing (with bias for the IPO). However you will have seen that the AP's are in the grip of the IPO and are not independent. So even Daniel agreed that in this case I had to appeal to the High Court in order to get the whole case *away* from the biased and corrupt IPO and their stooges and even then I would have to hope I did not get a biased Judge who thought he would have to side with those in "his club".

One last point about the result of this yet another crazy/biased decision of the IPO, is that what it in effect it has meant, is that I have been forced ever since 2002 to fight an endless battle against not only Robert Busbridge but against the IPO. At considerable cost in time and money and all for nothing. The reason given for giving the decision to take away my registration was because it was under the rules of the TMA 1994. So why was I given registration in the first place only for them to take it back again and put me through all those legal battles over 8 years? The final bullet was delivered by these bastards in the IPO when I asked them to refund me the costs of my renewal of my Mark in 2006, which cost £200. For in effect they had asked me to pay this if I wanted to renew the registration which lasts for 10 years. As my registration started in 1996, in 2006 it needed to be renewed for another 10 years. However according to their decision document I should never have been given it in the first place. See what I mean? Each hearing required me to have to pay fees which probably amounted to at least a £1,000 and all those were also for nothing.

What was their response… well in as many words… bugger off! What a bunch of bastard and ********* they all are. I think all their attitudes and actions have all been expressly designed to stick the knife in and twist it as many times as they could. No wonder some people go off the rails as a result of how they are treated by the ruling classes and the Establishment and then go on to commit mass murder in order to get back at society. The two recent shootings by Moat and the taxi driver bloke in Cumbria were both as a result of hatred for society due to their perceived beliefs as to how they were treated.

Chapter Thirty Four
My Lawyer, Did He Do a Good Job?

So Daniel advised appealing and I brought up the question of how do I do that as I cannot afford it. I reminded him of what I had said much earlier at the beginning and that was, it would have to be done on a no win, no fee basis. He now told me that in order to do that he would have to get a second opinion as to whether we had a strong case. He quoted a figure of between £500-£1000. Bear in mind that not long before, he had been telling me I had a good case. This shows you how solicitors work, you always have a good case and if they do a bum job for you, they are on a *win win situation*. They never lose out, only you do… you sucker! I had paid this man £6,000 which I had had to borrow that as I was skint, (which he knew from day one) and thanks to the IPO and the crook Robert Busbridge, and because he had not formulated a case that the IPO could not ignore, thus losing it for me, when I had a very good case.

He wanted to ask his very good friend, this barrister chappy he always used, for a second opinion. No doubt by lining his pocket, he earns Brownie points, and this is the way these guys work at your expense. Now all this was done at the very last minute as we had to get into the IPO the fact that we were going to appeal. You only get about three weeks of time in which to make up your mind as to whether you will appeal. This is far too short a period to have to make up your mind and get legal advice. It is an outrage in my opinion and I had to put up with the same shit when I was deliberating as to whether to appeal against RB winning in 2004, his application to register the mark (even though I already had it registered).

Daniel had buggered off on three weeks honeymoon and had only arrived back on the 22nd May and his company had been sitting on the decision since about the 9th May. I had had to waste all this time waiting for him to get back. Then he had to read and digest it and give me his opinions etc. Now he wanted to get a second opinion and that had to be done before the 3rd June. The weekend before the 3rd was a bank holiday. I had only hours to make up my mind to have a second opinion which as I told DW that as I could not afford an appeal and it would have to be done on a no win no fee basis, meant he said that a second opinion was vital for his boss to agree for a NWNF basis. I had to make up my mind in hours and it was just another let down by this lawyer by again leaving things to the last minute. I cannot tell you how I felt. Although I had no money I agreed thinking it would be only £500, but I had no idea exactly how much I was going to have to pay or how.

The nitty-gritty was, that this barrister thought that whilst I had a good case, a Judge could think that the IPO were right in their decision on the application to make my registration invalid. This by rigidly sticking to the trademarks Act which at the relevant section says that an application made before mine has precedence over mine, no matter what. (Is this the exact, truthful interpretation?) So it was an end to going onwards and I have to drop everything.

Another case of lawyers winning which ever way. In my book, if there is a strong possibility that one could lose, the lawyers should clearly say that, and get you to sign that you understand that but still wish to go forward and pay to take the chance That did not happen at the beginning of him defending this case.

So I was simply not willing to try and raise the quoted £10K to £20K to appeal, when it may be all a waste of time and money. For who is to say that Daniel or any barrister will do a job that will definitely win for they are all unknown quantities as is witnessed by this lawyers futile efforts and maybe rubbish quality, yet he still gets paid. I think that now it should have been a case of YOU the lawyer put YOUR money where your mouth is and do it an a NWNF basis if your saying I have a good case for an appeal, as he was.

However what gets me is the fact that Daniel did not get a second opinion *before* defending the Invalidity case. Of course he was getting paid so didn't give a shit if he did a bum job. For had he got a second opinion from this very same barrister bloke, he would have got the very same advice and that was that the IPO could ignore *everything* we brought up about how the application of RB should never have even been allowed to stand for numerous reasons, which I have stated above many times. That the IPO could just rely on the Act re who had precedence, RB or me. If he was an honest lawyer he would then warn me that to precede with a defence would cost me £6K and I would undoubtedly lose. That of course would have made me abandon this defence, for let us face it, I did not care now if I kept the trademark, for what use was it to me now? I was not trading, I could not license it out for money, Chrysler were no longer interested in the Mark (I think). What I wanted was justice and only justice against the IPO and Busbridge for his lies and forgery.

Justice against the abominations of the IPO for 18 years, costing me my business, my health and my retirement money. Plus of course justice against that arch liar and conman, R.Busbridge, for also causing all my problems since 1991.

Of course Daniel will say that if I did not defend my own registration it would hamper getting justice against the IPO. Well is he right and on his record so far I am inclined to believe nothing more of what he say? To my mind why should it matter, for the IPO have still committed the acts they have since 1992, that have seriously affected my business and life and of course my IP rights.

So as I was never going to waste more time and money appealing to an Appointed Person (an IPO drone) as I would never get anywhere with that non independent person and I certainly wasn't going to be able to appeal to the High Court, that was it… ***end of the road to ruin.***

Some time later after I had written the above I was trawling through the Laws and Rules relating to IP and came across Rules that dealt with the fact that if a person who was claiming they owned a trademark did not act to stop another person using it, then they were in effect acquiescing to that person's use. This is exactly what RB did not do. (as brought up by my lawyer and what did Salthouse do about his very own law… ignore it?) Apart from one letter sent to my Patent Agent back in 1992 saying I was using it when they owned it, since then, over some 18 years and RB never once wrote again or constantly threatened legal action or took legal action. Unlike myself who wrote many times and started legal action.

Yet Daniel, my lawyer even though he picked up on that one he never made a big fuss about that, I think it would have been hard to believe the hearing officer could have ignored that very legal argument. It shows that Daniel did a sloppy job and all the evidence he put in an quoting of laws and case law, was for nothing.

Chapter Thirty Five
Justice British Style

Let us get this right; the IPO have allowed a crook to take over my UK business, copy my designs, steal my trademark and all with their blessing, you could say. They have twisted the law, lied, been totally incompetent, shown extreme bias towards this crook, been disingenuous, utterly corrupted, yet all this is deemed by them to be quite kosher. All above board and within the law. Of course those of us who are cynics about those in power, will point out that the law is twisted about, by lawyers and Judges, to get a desired result, every day of the week. With my own story this is seen when one IPO Hearing Officer, Landau, saw the law in a way that would take away the RB application and registration, yet the IPO refused to carry out his decision and never gave a reason for doing this. They then went on to have their subsequent hearing officers proclaim opinions that were the opposite of the Landau decision.

The IPO even gave reasons as to why RB could not legally keep the registration of the mark in a letter to him, yet they then go on to conveniently forget that they have said this and they then invent an excuse to actually allow him to do this. (Hobbs had his finger in that) However I do not believe they are right at all with this piece of lying rubbish, and I would like to get an opinion from somewhere on that, if only I could afford it. So where are the lawyers out there that have a heart instead of a money pouch where their heart is? (It is actually partnership law and nothing to do with the IPO.)

I have always thought that the law is an ass and if the British think that British law is the epitome of what is right and just, they are simply living in cloud cuckoo land. Time and again we see the law interpreted by lawyers and Judges in different ways. I am sure if you took ten Judges and gave them the task of interpreting a particular law, you would get wildly differing verdicts and views. This means that at these IPO hearings you get different hearing officers seeing the facts in different ways. All this is ignoring the fact that I firmly believe the hearing officers, Reynolds (2004), Foley (2009) Annand (2009) and Hobbs (2006) and finally Salthouse (2010) were programmed to manipulate the law to enable decisions to be made that favoured what the IPO wanted to see. Decisions that would let the IPO off the hook by denying me the ability to say that the IPO had acted incompetently or in a biased way, which would then enable me to go on to sue them for negligence, and corruption etc. (If only I had the money.)

I am positive that if a ***totally independent expert IP lawyer***, was to sift through all the history of my story from day one back in 1992, they would back up what I am saying. For we would be able to have everything the IPO have done during that time, put under a microscope and to see if they acted properly and within the law. I am positive they have not acted within the law on a very high number of times and I even have proof of that, but I am not an expert on IP law and procedures, or other areas of British law. So my word and thoughts mean diddly squat. The problem for poor peasants like me as opposed to rich people, is that; "how can I afford to have the whole history looked at independently"? So justice is denied to people in my position.

The country is full of people in my position. Oppressed in some way by the ruling oafs of this country. Only today in the Sunday Telegraph I read about how families are being oppressed by civil servants who are taking their children off them and giving them away to others, because they think they are right in assuming they are not fit to be parents for some crazy reason. I have no problem with yobby dysfunctional parents who couldn't bring a dog up right let alone children, being deprived of their poor children but how many times do they not step in when they should? So we get the Baby Peter situations over and over, but most of these are not yobs. In fact I think that these oafish social workers are scared of the yobs so don't do anything, but with ordinary non yob parents they know they will not fight back because they cannot afford it or haven't the fight in them. So these poor unfortunate people are trapped in a nightmare situation just like I am, as they have to fight civil servants who can do as they please and you cannot win if you do not have the money to be able to take on the countries elite lawyers to fight the bastards off. The Social Services people remind me of the IPO… same mentality and crooked behaviour!

In the last few days we have also seen another example of how the ***establishment*** had decided someone was guilty of murder which it was obvious they had not committed. This seen in the case of the school teacher Sion Jenkins accused of murdering his foster daughter, on decidedly almost non existent and dodgy evidence and then denying him compensation for ruining his life and suffering 6 years in jail, and when found not guilty on appeal. Yet another case where the establishment dig in because they do not want to be seen to be at fault in any way. They cannot admit they cocked anything up.

This means that in my case we have a situation were in my opinion the law and justice has been brought into disrepute by the actions of the IPO and especially by Hobbs QC. However the IPO and the likes of Hobbs and the various hearing officers, don't give a toss. For they think that they are secure from Public scrutiny because they can tie you up in knots for years using their skill at manipulating the system, and they know I am skint and cannot afford to bring any legal challenges. The object of this book is to try to bring this story into the open.

As my efforts to get justice through the IPO are now at an end, what else can I do? Well you may remember that back in August 2009, I went to the Bournemouth Police and reported RB's perjury. Then I was told by them it was best for me to rely on the IPO to deal with it and as we can see they manifestly and cynically failed to do that. As the Police had told me I could return to them if the IPO did not act, this was would I should now do. So what I did is compile a complete list of all the acts of perjury committed by RB, with the truth of the facts in relation to each statement made and what hard evidence I had to prove that the statement was a lie. I cross referenced all the lies to the actual document that they appeared in and referenced the hearing they were for. I also counted up the number of times key lies were made. These key lies covered points that RB had obviously been legally advised to keep banging on about, in order to indoctrinate the IPO into believing certain things that would enable him to win his attempts to legalise the theft of my IP. By showing that these key lies were made in large repeated numbers, this would show that an attempt was being made to influence by lies. I think this would fall under the charge of perverting the course of Justice? I sent the whole list which included some 200 lies, plus a covering letter, to the Inspector in charge of CID.

Would they act or would they like so many of our wonderful Police in this country, and just think up excuses not to act. How close was one civil service department (the IPO) to another (the Police)? So far, as I write this, things do not look good. For some weeks and a call from a Detective Constable ringing me up to say he has the file (and that took 10 days for him to do that). A further week goes by and I hear nothing, so I send him a letter by hand, asking him not to sit on this and that I had lost 10 months already, due to them not really wishing to act back in 2009 and passing the buck to the IPO. So far I still have heard nothing as to what they intend to do and when. I have not even had an official confirmation, in writing that they have my report and complaint. I am not impressed and it remains to be seen what and how this will proceed.

Of course should it proceed to him being charged and eventually found guilty of perjury and hopefully also perverting the course of justice, that would give me all I need to proceed to see if I can sort out the IPO, somehow. This for Justice, not only for me but for anyone else like me, so that maybe the IPO would learn a lesson. However I am deeply cynical of all British arms of the government and our so called justice system. Even if I could win such an action against the IPO and they were castigated or whatever, would they change? I doubt it. Have all those dysfunctional social services people who have been severely castigated in recent years, changed. The answer is absolutely not! We still get horror stories by the month. We are no better than a banana Republic.

On this whole point of whether the Police will act, I had a word with my landlord who is an ex Met CID Inspector. The upshot of his advice did nothing to give me any hope that the police will act on my complaint, for these days it is all down to *money* and justice and the law can all go to hell. Peasants like me do not matter in the scheme of things, only for the rich and powerful and our rulers, they do not have to put up with what we the peasants have to put up with. So the ruling powers who control justice etc, don't give a crap about us, especially when we are complaining about how *they* have treated us.

Chapter Thirty Six
My Efforts to Try and Get Other Government Departments to Act and Dispense Some Justice

These are the other government departments I approached:-

1: The Insolvency Service
2: Companies House
3: The DTI who are responsible for Companies House
4: Local Trading Standards at Sutton, Bournemouth and Dorchester
5: Local Government Ombudsman
6: HRMC Over Busbridges Tax Affairs
7: My MP at Christchurch, a Mr Chris Chope
8: Sutton Council Planning Department
9: The Bournemouth Police
10: Treasury Solicitor
11: Office for Judicial Complaints.
12: Judicial Appointments and Conduct Ombudsman
13: Office of Fair Trading
14: Parliamentary Ombudsman
15: Justice Ministry & Kenneth Clarke
16: Information Commissioners Office
17: The Independent Police Complaints Commission
18: The Attorney Generals Office
19: The Metropolitan Police
20: The Justice Commissioner.

You may wonder why I approached all of the above. That is easy, as all crooks will act crooked in more than one way, and so it was with the reptile known as RB. So here are the results of my efforts:-

1: The Insolvency Service (IS)

Once I knew RB had gone bankrupt in 1993, I knew he would not notify the IS of any of the truth about his business. This was borne out by the fact that there was absolutely no break in his business after he did go bankrupt. Also many of those departments you complain to are like the IPO and will not act on complaints, so you are then forced to complain to other useless bodies about the useless body who will not act on your complaint. In the end you run out of bodies to complain to. As is the usual way in this crap country of ours that is full of petty crooks getting away Scot free with all sorts of scams on the Public, and because of useless civil servants and that includes the Police, who let them get away with it. People who go bankrupt often do it deliberately with the aim of keeping going under another trading name.

This is exactly what RB did. He had created a limited company some months before he went bankrupt and he would have us believe that he moved all the assets of Cobretti Engineering into this limited company called Autotrak Ltd. However as you will have seen above he did not do this legally in any way. His wife ran Autotrak Ltd, as they always do in these cases.

I just knew that RB would never tell the IS the truth about the trademark if he told them about it at all. As he was trying to sell it for a Kings ransom to Chrysler, so the last people he would tell were the IS. I contacted them and told them to be aware of the true facts. I never got to find out if they took any notice of my letter and in those early days (around 94) I wasn't yet aware that ALL government departments were totally useless. Had I known then what I know now, I would have kept onto them. It was only in the later years of this sorry story, that I got onto them in a big way. If you remember I had been onto the IPO for years about the fact that they never stopped the application of RB to register the mark when it belonged to the Receiver.

Later on when I tried to get information out of the IS about events at the time of his bankruptcy, they eventually told me that they could not answer my questions because they did not keep files on bankruptcies for longer than 10 years. So they had been destroyed. Earlier to the 10 years time cut off I had got some replies to various questions and they told me that they had interviewed him and found nothing untoward. In his witness statements he had said that they had interviewed him several times and he had told them all about the assignment and that he had also told them about the trademark. He said they had found his explanations to be credible and they did nothing. However I think he is lying and because the IS say they no longer have files, which I think is typical of the civil service, they cannot tell me one way or the other if I am right. I am not prepared to believe RB's word on this.

I will not recount every word that passed between me and the IS, and they were numerous, as this story is long enough as it is. However in 2009 I had a big blitz at their CEO at the Croydon branch, over their uselessness and why they would not answer simple questions that I felt they could have answered. The stonewalling and evasiveness I got was typical of civil servants who have got something to hide. I got absolutely nowhere at all and this shows you yet again at how useless *all our government departments are… every man jack of them*. He knew he could answer my questions but to do so would be admitting that his department had failed the creditors of Busbridge as well as myself.

2: Companies House.

I contacted these people to check on RB's company details. I got print-outs on Autotrak Ltd and Autotrak Cobretti Ltd, just to see what I could dig up as he had hidden behind these companies. He had used them (both run by his wife) to hide facts from creditors and to confuse me and anyone else under just what company he operated his shonky business under. I had pointed out to the IPO in my evidence that far from operating as Cobretti Engineering from 1991 right through into the 2000's, he had switched from one company to another with rapidity.

Of course what I found was par for the Robert Busbridge course. None of these companies had ever put in accounts (it was around 2002 that I was making the enquiries) let alone had ever made a return.

I was staggered as this is supposed to be strictly not allowed by the DTI. How had they allowed this state of affairs to go on for nearly ten years?

I wrote to them pointing this out to them and asking why they were allowing it to happen and pointing out what kind of person they were dealing with. I got no satisfactory explanations, only that they were going to strike off both companies. No mention of fines or anything like that and of course all these vacuous civil service tossers, keep these things quiet under the excuse that they cannot discuss personal information to you. No saying 'thank you very much, we will hit this guy hard'! So yet another useless bunch of tossers, letting crooked UK businessmen rip off the State and their customers.

3: The DTI

I complained to the DTI who are responsible for Companies House and got nowhere, again. In fact they were even more uncooperative than Companies House. But can anyone expect any government department to be honest, especially when you are obviously complaining about their incompetency.

4: Trading Standards

Up to about 2000, the only avenue that RB used to advertise was in the kit car magazine called 'Kitcar' and from time to time he got writ-ups done on the product. These were written by the magazines various so called journalists, who were no more than an odd assortment of amateurs. They got most of their information on the product off 'Chief Liar' himself and of course he was anxious to let it be seen that this copy of my product had been legitimately acquired. So you can imagine the lies that appeared throughout all these articles on Cobretti and the Viper copy.

Starting from mid 1991 at the time I left for Switzerland they had no fully built cars that they owned as a demonstrator, which they could let these writers drive in to do their write-ups. So they had to rely on cars that either their customers had built from my kits prior to 1991, or they were cars built again from my kits, and built by RB and his brother for some customer who couldn't build it himself. In fact one of the best articles they had done in 1991, featured a red Viper V12 I had built in 1990 for the London company Wheels Abroad that I have spoken about above, and whilst delivering it I dropped off into Sutton with it and MB had a photographer friend take a number of shots of it with a model, in a Sutton park. The photos were said by RB to be wanted for future media advertising.

Of course when this write-up appeared in mid 1991 extolling this car and showing many nice photos of it, RB the 'Worlds Biggest Liar' failed to make it plain that the car had been built by me and was from one of my genuine original kits. This is known as 'Passing off' or better still as 'Conning the Public', for it was described as a Cobretti Viper! It still features today in 2010 on his website! Thus continuing to con the public.

A second article was done which featured the Dr Bechtolsheimer Viper and again it was represented as a Cobretti Viper. He has also used a shot of the interior of that car as one of his monthly adverts in Kitcar magazine. A third article appeared which showed three Vipers, two built by customers and one built by RB/MB. All were built from my kits but were represented as Cobretti Vipers. All feature on his website!

This kind of thing happened again and again but I was unable to get Kitcar magazine's owner, one Den Tanner to correct any of the misleading claims etc. For he hated me because I had got a better product and had trashed his own third rate Cobra Replica, the Sumo. Had I been rich of course I could have sorted him out too, but then I could have sorted liar himself out years before as well. When around 2000, RB started up a website, matters changed, for as I have said above he reproduced the very same three articles showing my Vipers but claiming they were Cobretti Vipers. So now I could go to the Trading Standards tossers (for that is what they turned out to be) this in 2004, to complain that RB was misleading the Public and giving all the reasons and evidence.

Give you one guess what the response of Bournemouth Trading Standards was! After wasting God knows how many months going through the motions, they declined to act by saying that this was a civil matter between two traders. This despite the fact I had told them I was reporting this as a member of the Public, but one who had inside knowledge as I was now retired and since Jan 2002. Of course no matter what I told them, they had no intentions of taking action even though they had a Statutory duty to do so. They just did not want to spend any money and when I complained at their refusal and pointing out to them that what excuses they had given were all incorrect and they had a duty to act, they merely said that 'It is not in the Bournemouth rate payers interest that we spend money on such a case' The hell with what the law said they had to do.

So RB went on misleading the public from 2004 to 2009 when I decided I had enough spare time on my hands to have another go. This time I complained to Dorset County Council who had now taken over from the Bournemouth Council. I also sent in the same complaint to Sutton Council who covered Morden where RB was operating from.

To cut a long story down, Dorchester (office of T/Std's for Bournemouth) said that as the trader resided under Suttons control it should be them that dealt with it. Sutton Council told me that as I had not actually been a customer of RB I could not make a complaint. They intimated that I had had a commercial relationship with RB, so I should take my own civil action, as it was not an appropriate use of Council resources to pursue a complaint on behalf of one trader against another! The same old usual lying evasive crap as before. They then went on to inventing the incredible excuse that all people who wish to buy a kit car 'would have specialist knowledge and would make their own detailed research before making a purchase'.

Here you see just how duplicitous Councils will be when you expect them to carry out their statutory duties. They just invent as many lies as they can think of. They knew I was no longer a trader as I had told them many times that I retired at the end of 2001. The crap about what a potential buyer of a kitcar knows is just too stupid to comment on. However they nail their colours to the mast in their last comments when they admit they do not have enough money to investigate.

So from this kernel of knowledge, all the British Public must now be aware that all Trading Standards departments around our land, view actually doing their job of protecting us from rogue lying traders as not worth investigating as they do not have any money!

Another tranch of useless British laws, we the public do not get enacted for our protection, by another bunch of useless civil servants.

5: The Local Government Ombudsman.

I was so incensed by this abrogation of their duty that I reported both these Councils to the above Ombudsman. Even though one of my MP's from a few years back had told me that to complain to any Ombudsman was a waste of time as they were all useless, I still tried to have a go. I may as well have not bothered… **again!**

I reported all the facts to this mob and after the customary wasting of many months when they went through the motions of trying to show they were actually doing something, their reply was a depressing tale of the same old excuses to do nothing. What it boiled down to was, they would do nothing as I had not been a buyer of a kit from RB so had not suffered an injustice. That I was motivated by purely bad feeling between me and Busbridge. (Now where did they get that information from I wonder?) It simply amazes me how all these civil servants believe RB all the time. Of course he gives them all the lies and excuses and that is all they need as they then have the excuses to not do anything with a set of their own excuses after having believed him. I do not deny that I dislike RB for the criminal acts he has perpetrated since 1991, but that is not a crime and in law does not detract from my ability to make genuine and reasonable complaints as to his misleading the Public. In fact it is only because I have the insider information as to the truth of his claims on his website, that enables me to bring the transgressions to light.

To say that I have not suffered an injustice by the misleading adverts and copies of write-ups on his website, is a gross distortion of the facts. Of course I have suffered an injustice as would anyone who was having his product, designed and made my his own hands (when he was in business) being portrayed on a website as having been designed and manufactured by someone else. The trouble with pen pushers like this vacuous headed man in the LGO who wrote this letter, having never owned a business in his life let alone having designed something, only to see someone else claim they had designed and made it and was advertising this fact on a website for all and sundry to see. They cannot see how that can serve up a heavy dose of injustice.

How would Rolls have felt if just after he designed the first Rolls someone had copied it and called the copy a Rolls, for that is exactly the same thing? Not that I designed car as good as a Rolls.

I then went onto a different tack and looked closely at the law on misleading advertising and I could see that the recent new act brought in, in 2008 that deals with unfair and misleading business practices, was over-seen by The Office of Fair Trading. A fancy named government department which I guessed would be as useless as all other government departments. All the Trading Standards tossers around the country in various town halls, are under their wing. I decided not to go in head first, but to act as if I were trying to get further information on what would be the case if someone who had not actually bought a product off a trader, but could see that the trader was indulging in obvious misleading information in their websites etc. I wrote in asking this question and asked if one could still make a complaint. I also asked if I had to reside in the traders area in order to get a complaint dealt with by my local trading standards or the traders local Trading Standards office?

The eventual answer they told me was what I basically knew was the case. You did not have to be a buyer of the product and you did not have to live in the traders area to complain to his local standards people.

All I needed, so I went back to them and told them about how Dorchester and Sutton Trading Standard's were trying it on with me. Go back to the Councils and complain which I did pointing out their lies and what the OFT had said. They both stuck to their original excuses and refused to do anything. You can't make up these people.

6: HMRC (Inland revenue)

I wrote to this mob on a couple of occasions to report to them that Busbridge was probably swindling them out of income tax/companies tax. I sent them a copy of an article from Auto Express in which he boasted about how many cars and kits he had sold from 1992. I intimated that he would probably have never declared this income or would have downgraded the figures. I also gave them other information which I thought they ought to know. Whether they acted on any of this who knows as they never let you know, which I always have thought hardly gives people the incentive to give such info to them. In fact if they had any brains they would pay informants a percentage of what they claw back and that would give anyone the incentive to dob (Australian slang for telling on someone) in all the tax evaders in the UK, of which there are millions at it, costing the State billions a year.

7: My local Member of Parliament

This bloke, an ex barrister called Christopher Chope. In 2005 I was waiting for months for the IPO to give me an answer as to what the outcome had been of the appeal RB made to an Appointed Person (Hobbs QC) over the decision of Landau that effectively took away his registration he had gained through perjury, in 2004. I was obviously being given the run round and something fishy was going on. So who better to get to give the IPO a kicking?

Chope being a barrister should have been able to give me invaluable help, had he only been prepared to do his job thoroughly. So all I ended up getting off him was a service of sorts where he passed on my letters to the IPO. I could have done that myself and in fact I had and had got nowhere, hence why I was expecting him to get answers.

He should have personally talked to the head of the IPO through the Minister responsible, and pointed out that I was being denied answers. All I got was a lot of duplicitous waffle and lies via letters sent to him which he passed onto me. I got very pissed off with his laid back attitude and let it go, for I eventually got my answers as you can see from the above story. However it showed me that we the British Public cannot even get our politicians to act properly for us, so what use are they? Now of course since then we have all been able to see just what use they are, the lying, robbing, useless bastards and hence why in my whole life I have never voted and never will.

In 2009 I had another go at him to try and get some help and information from him over whether I could be able to force a Judicial Review over the actions of the IPO. He was as unhelpful this time as before, with his offish attitude. So much so that I had words with him in his surgery and after wrote to him asking him to be more helpful. I got absolutely no reply from him.

Previous to this last election that saw the Conservatives get in, he now had no excuse not to help as he was part of a governing party and could no longer use the excuse that as they were in opposition they could not force Labour trash to act. Before the election he was never in the media, yet now he is there trying to make a name for himself as a rebel, but probably still too idle to help his constituents in a meaningful way. In fact as self confessed rebel himself you would think he would have some sympathy for me and my rebelling, but no, all he is interested in is himself. I may go back to him and see where I get, but it will be a last resort, and I feel that says it all about MP's when you feel they just are not worth bothering about when you need help.

This is democracy at work! If you think your are living in a democracy, your are living in cloud cuckoo land.

8: Sutton Planning Department

It came to me in 2009 in a blinding flash, that this robbing, conniving, criminal conman, bastard Robert Busbridge who has been boasting for years as to how he had been trading at the same address for twenty nine years, which in itself was a lie as he had not started to trade from his home address (which was what he was referring to) until around early 1994 after he went bankrupt. Either he is terribly bad at arithmetic or he is prone to exaggerating. I am inclined to believe in the latter.

Anyway, I realised that it is against planning law to conduct a business from your home such as garage services and the building of kitcars, which is what he was doing. His Council Tax would also be much different, had the Sutton Council known and allowed what he was up to. So I wrote to them and blew the whistle once more. What did they do? Bugger all once more, because they told me that if a person successfully keeps it quiet from a Council for so many years then they cannot act against them and stop the activity. Typical of this mad country we live in... you couldn't make it up.

So once again my efforts to get this lying twister of a crook to suffer some sort of action against him, comes to nowt, thanks to our useless civil servants, and British slackness and mad laws. The only pleasure I could gain from this effort is that just maybe he will now have to pay more Council Tax because he is using his home for business uses and business rates are higher than private council tax.

9: Bournemouth Police

As I have recounted above, they were the Force that charged me with 2 counts of Forgery, 2 counts of using a forged instrument and 1 count of Perjury and perverting the course of justice. They called on me on the 21st January 1999 and arrested me after RB had complained to the Met Police and it appears it was passed onto Bournemouth Police. They apparently visited him in November 1998 in Sutton to take a statement from him and in no time later I am arrested and charged. No slackness there by the Bournemouth Police on Busbridges behalf. Within two months of taking his complaint and statement I am arrested and charged not much later.

Now what kind of urgency are the same Police Force showing with my much bigger complaint about a whole bunch of perjury, in fact all 192 cases of it, plus forgery, and perverting the course of Justice?

When I first complained in August 2009, I am really in the end, fobbed off. Second time around there is deafening silence and no apparent action whatsoever. Not even a letter in answer to my first letter of the 19th May 2010, when I sent in the long list of all the perjury and forgery committed, not even a crime number.

I only got a crime number after I had rung the person who has had the case passed onto him, and he gives me no idea what or how the case will be handled. Nor what time scale I am looking at. So I am none the wiser if I will get anywhere. I will update the position at the end of this book as the last entry as it were.

10: Treasury Solicitors

This bunch are responsible for allocating a barrister to handle appeals before an Appointed Person. Supposed to be independent, but as you can see in the story above, these A/P's are far from independent.

When I finally twigged on to what Hobbs had been up to, I sent in a strong and comprehensive complaint over his behaviour, thinking that this department would obviously be in charge of these barristers.

The complaint took the usual months of delays and eventually I got a letter back saying that Hobbs had denied any wrong doing, (well he would wouldn't he, to use a famous phrase). Then what annoyed me was when they told me that in any case they could not deal with such complaints as they were the wrong people to do so and I should complain to the Office of Judicial Complaints. Isn't it amazing how every Government department has another government department shadowing it where people have to make their complaints to about department number one. But what really annoyed me about this particular shower, is that for months they went through the motions of handling my complaint, when all the time they were in no position to handle it. During that time they gave my complaint to the very person I was complaining about, so he could know all about it and have time to think up excuses. ***Yet another example of a duplicitous governmental department.***

11: Office of Judicial Complaints

All these departments stagger me and it just shows how in this country, because nothing works that has anything to do with the government, they have to have all these quangos or whatever to handle all the complaints that members of the Public are going to make.

My complaint about Hobbs went off to this shower on the 5/9/09 and as usual the months roll onwards, necessitating me to complain about this. I end up dealing with a woman with an African sounding name or could even be Asian, who knows. All I know is that she was obviously out of her depth. She doesn't seem to understand what I am complaining about, for when she sends her first reply, which was dated two months later, she says that they cannot find my original letter, so she asks me to send it in again, yet she then goes on in the next sentence to dismiss my complaint!

She says that my complaint seems to be about the outcome of a judicial decision and they do not cover those as I can appeal such things. I ask you, this kind of thing only gives me yet more material to be able to say that all government departments and those who work in them are bloody incompetent. She also says that all complaints have to be made within 12 months of the event.

I mean it is just a farce, as I was not someone who had taken part in any judicial hearing or court case but as someone who had heard that in a judicial hearing, the Judge hearing it had misbehaved by slagging me off in a very personal way, giving advice and being biased towards someone who I was in conflict with. The transcript been deliberately kept from me for a number of years and it was only when I managed to get hold of it, that I could see what had taken place and what had been said about me.

I of course replied and sent a copy of the missing letter and put her straight as to the facts and asked her to redo her reply. What I got back after several emails apologising for delays, in December, just before Christmas, so a delay of many weeks, was again a complete farce. All she did was send me another copy of her letter that she sent on the 10/11/09 and to which I complained to her about, asking for her to look at my reasoning and redo her answer. More emails to her from me brought no joy as she obviously would not change her answer or reply to my asking her why she would not see how her points did not apply. Nor would she give me the name of her CEO or tell me what qualifications she had to be dealing with such a complaint. She had obviously been told not to deal with it.

Is this the forces of the judiciary banding together to protect one of their own, at play here? I was told if I did not like what I read, to complain to yet another quango, the Judicial Appointments and Conduct Ombudsman. Not willing to back down or be beaten I did just that.

12/ JACO

I fired off a comprehensive letter outlining the whole complaint and background at the end of January 2010. The letter I got back saying that they had received it did not fill me with confidence as to these peoples intelligence, as they said 'The Ombudsman cannot comment on any aspect of your original court case' Are these people rampant dickheads of totally no intelligence, for this is the same crap I got off the last lot of disingenuous dickheads, the OJC lot. Either they are just plain stupid and unable to understand plain English, or they are deliberately pretending that I was involved with a court case when I was not even there, so they can eventually say it has nothing to do with them as they cannot interfere with court decisions (just as the last lot tried on) We will have to see, but the way it has gone since then is looking like I may not get a decision until next year or the next century, maybe?

These delays are due to the way they handle complaints... very bureaucratic and long winded with too many involved. First a case worker looks into it and she took about four months before she got onto it. That report goes to the Ombudsman and he does another report and sends that to the Lord Chancellor and he took weeks to do that. A reply is expected around the 20th of July, so we will see. But as you can see I started this complaint about this rogue Judge in September 2009 and we are nearly into August 2010!

Of course I am willing to bet all my non existent riches that it will be the usual whitewash. It will be riddled with faults because they have deliberately not understood what I have said. I call this constant state of affairs you always get with all civil servants as 'Selective Amnesia' or better still 'Selective word Blindness'

13/ Office of Fair Trading

Probably this department should be called the 'Office of Unfair Trading & Crap Treatment of the Public'.

I had first contacted them by email on the 30/11/09 asking them to clarify what the consumer protection regulations were. I got no answer so sent a 2nd email and still no answer so I phoned their so called Customer Service. I told the bloke who answered that I was phoning as I could get no replies to emails and that I did not think I should be paying for a phone call, so would he phone me back. He refused and tried to drag me into a long phone conversation wanting to know what the complaint was about. I would not get into this so asked him if he intended to phone me back, where-upon he put the phone down on me. I think this tells you all you need to know about this organisation and all other government departments who treat the Public like *shit!* I wrote to their CEO on the 12th Jan 2010 with a strong complaint.

I received a reply a week later, not from the CEO but from some clerk who said they will reply in full within 30 days. This now means that I will have been waiting a total of three months and still no answer to my original questions in Nov 2009. Anyway the eventual reply told me all I needed to know and that was that the excuses given me by Sutton and Dorchester were incorrect or better still, out and out lies.

They tell me that I could ring Consumer Direct about RB, but I have spoken to this mob and they are totally useless. Mainly manned by a bunch of youngsters that know nothing and this complaint about RB is too complicated to spend hours on a phone, only to get absolutely nowhere.

So I write back saying all this and complaining that Trading Standards at Town halls are a waste of space as they never want to investigate anything. That I have been through their own complaints procedures to get nowhere. I tell them that as the OFT have a duty to investigate such complaints even though they delegate these to Councils, if those Councils refuse to act then the OFT should act instead. I then ask what the OFT intend to do about this?

After this letter to which I got no reply, which again says it all about all these waste of spaces, I sent in two more letters to Dorchester and Sutton telling them about the information I have had from the OFT which shows that they were lying when they used the excuses they did to not act. I asked them once again to act. Of course after months of yet more time wasting I get two replies again refusing to act for the same reasons already given. Their cheek and arrogance knows no bounds, these utter bastards.

It was June 2010 and I had to write back to the OFT again, this time to tell them what had happened and demanding they act. Of course I only got the usual letter back which just told me that it will take the useless bastards another 30 days or more to reply. The upshot of all that was still no action against the robber and crook Robert Busbridge who merrily continued to mislead the Public, wholesale and it was now 8 months since I started this fruitless and frustrating exercise to get the very bodies that are set up to *protect the British public from crooks and shysters.*

There a vast bodies all over Britain, useless governmental departments, who the politicians boast are there to do all this valuable protective work on our behalf. All paid for at vast expense by the tax payers of Britain and all producing *nothing!* Are you happy about that, maybe like most apathetic Brits you don't give a monkies? That folks is why they get away with it, as there are not enough folk like me who will complain and complain and never give in.

I eventually got a reply from the OFT and it was exactly what I had expected, namely yet another duplicitous whitewash and that has taken them only nine months to get to this point! Briefly they tell me that they are separate from the TSS's of Dorchester, Sutton and Bournemouth, so I cannot castigate them. The letter went on to say that they could not intervene in disputes with traders which is not the case here as I am not in dispute directly with this trader (RB), over this matter, as I know it would be a waste of my time to ask him to remove the misleading website content. For if he will not do this for a TSS he certainly will not do it for me. The OFT then indulge in more duplicity by telling me to complain back to the TSS's concerned, which had they read my complaint properly they would have seen I have already *twice* done that! So nine months down the line the Office of Fair Trading act in such a way as to make the name of that department of useless civil servants, a huge bad joke. They are nothing more than a toothless, useless entity not fit for purpose, full of overpaid non job time wasters. Of course I am told if I am not satisfied I can complain to yet another useless mob of civil servants in yet another not fit for purpose mob called the 'General Counsel's

Office of the OFT". You couldn't make this lot up! I doubt if I will bother as I intend to send this book direct to whatever Minister is responsible for these useless shower.

One last remark on the OFT. What you have to understand is that we have laws governing crooked traders and misleading advertising and the OFT are supposed to be involved with all that, yet here you can see that in actual fact, they cannot or will not act in cases like the case I outlined to them, which is a blatant example of misleading advertising. So what really is their function, I ask?

Chapter Thirty Seven
Complete List of All the Failings of the IPO 1992-2010
(An expert could no doubt come up with more than this list)

1: They allowed the Opposition 35699 made by RB to Chryslers application to register the mark, to be stayed and instead allowed my later opposition application 35801 to proceed. As mine was made later, why did they do this? I say this is a deliberate act. *I cannot see how they could be right in law when you take into account how they gave the excuse they did to take away my registration in 2010... see paragraph 13.*

2: The IPO refused to take action on being notified that RB's application to register the mark was made in bad faith even after seeing evidence by way of the legal agency agreement, that he was in fact my agent. Thus allowing a crook to steal my IP.

3: The IPO refuse to take action on being notified that RB was now a bankrupt even though they admit they should have contacted the Receiver.

4: The IPO refuse to take action on being notified that the application made by RB to register a trademark in a partnership name, was now no longer applicable as the partnership had ceased. No effort to contact MB to confirm this or to find out if MB authorised the application.

5: The IPO did not take reasonable steps to check that the application made in a partnership name had been made legally.

6: The IPO allowed my later applied registration application to proceed ahead of RB's earlier application. Why was this?

7: The Opposition hearing I undertook against RB was so obviously biased, it was criminal and corrupt. The decisions made were so perverse that they were an affront to moral and actual justice. The fact that I had to appeal to a High Court denied me my rights to appeal an unjust decision as the extremely high cost to do so, denied me that right. They knew this and that gave them the excuse to behave whatever way they wanted to make me lose.

8: The IPO made procedural mistakes in allowing the recordal of alleged assignments of the application asset and this meant my having to fight this. No apologies ever given, yet they admitted the mistake.

9: My complaints to their CEO of the refusal of the IPO to deal with the issues of bankruptcy, partnership issues, perjury, forgery and bad faith, were all ignored completely. This is a complete abrogation of his responsibilities to deal with serious complaints.

10: The IPO made a mistake in allowing RB to put in further evidence after I had put in my statement in reply to the statement to which he wished to add further exhibits and comments. The IPO have time limits on you putting in statements and yet they in this case completely negated them. This was not only showing bias but meant I had to redo a new statement and re-post, thus causing me extra time spent and money for extra photocopying and postage. They refused to apologise or award me the extra costs. This extra evidence was not even relevant. When I tried to get in extra evidence in the Rectification hearing, I was refused. Bias once more!

11: At the hearing before Reynolds, he expressed a dislike of self litigants and this is against IPO rules as I am entitled to be a self litigant without having to put up with harassment. Also in this hearing Reynolds refused to allow me to make a further verbal statement in reply to something RB had said. Again this is against my rights. Reynolds also closed the hearing early so he could get home. What kind of hearing was this meant to be? It certainly was not fair to me.

12: The IPO lied to me and my MP over the extra long time it was taking for the decision of Hobbs to come out. Yet they knew full well what the reasons were. In fact they even had a hand in the delays. This must be one of their worst transgressions. Yet no admission or apology, only more lies and even from their CEO.

13: Allowing RB's application to register the mark they had just awarded to me, to be reinstated. I had had to prove my usage back to 1986 long before RB could legally say he was also using the same mark, which was in 1991/2, as the IPO knew full well.

In fact this only added to the list of incorrect actions of the IPO over when applications should be heard. This had started as per my points in paragraphs 1 & 6. I say that RB should have opposed Chrysler first as he applied to oppose first. Had he won, I would then oppose him getting registration on the facts that I had used the mark since 1986. However there was no way he could win as his application went in after Chryslers (theirs in Jan 1990). So Chrysler would have won and I would then, with RB out of the way, have opposed their registration on the grounds of my first use. I would then win as I did first time round. The actions of the IPO have meant that I fought Chrysler at great time and expense for nothing, because the IPO then allowed RB to reinstate his application.

Then they made a shocking and perverse decision that he should win the registration even though I had also got it. They knew full well I could not afford to appeal. Then they allow all the further hearings and at the end they cap it all, by a perverse decision at the Invalidity hearing which means RB has total control of the mark and I lose my registration. They base this on the fact that RB applied to register before me, yet with the Chrysler hearing they did not apply the same logic. To cap off their biased and corrupt actions, they say that I have to lose my registration because *'they awarded it to me in violation of their laws in which an earlier application gives an earlier right'* (Is that the real case or are they lying again?)

This perverse thinking does not match their thinking when they decided who would go ahead and oppose Chrysler, which also gives rise to an accusation of double standards. Of course they will try and negate this by saying that RB stayed his earlier opposition to Chrysler, yet when I asked for the history of this application they did not tell me this is what had in fact happened and were very vague, but I was told that it was still 'live'. Of course I have this in writing so it cannot be denied. I have tried to search on the IPO website for info on this opposition number and guess what, no records of it… mysteriously disappeared!

This means that not only did the Chrysler case cost me 10 years of my life wasted, but at a cost of around £8,000. The cost in time for all the rest of the hearings was another 10 years plus at least another £10,000 in costs. All for nothing because it was all waste of time and money. To top it all when my first 10 years of registration came up in 1996, I had to pay a £200 fee to renew it and again this was for nothing as the IPO have now taken that registration away. They refuse to repay me that £200. I say none of this can be right in law or anything else. Had I taken on legal representation instead of representing myself for all the subsequent hearings after the Reynolds hearing, I would have spent tens of thousands of Pounds. Would I have won the first one (Reynolds) had I a lawyer representing me? If I had won that none of the others would have taken place. (However we can now see that even taking on a lawyer doesn't guaranty you will win. For it can be seen that Reynolds must have been under 'Orders' to make sure that Busbridge won. Would he have acted differently had he faced a lawyer and not me? Well if you take the Salthouse hearing in 2010, you have to say that the IPO are no respecter of any lawyer or the law.

14: The IPO ignores my rights to the mark under Common Law, which states that the first person to use the trademark has the rights to it even if it is not registered. This is proved by the Chrysler case I won as at that stage I had not got it registered. This action meant that my use from 1986 went right up to the date in question in this case and that was Jan 1990, when Chrysler applied. By giving Busbridge registration over mine they ignored this and Reynolds in his decision ignored it. He also ignores the law which states that you cannot be said to have abandoned a mark until 5 years is up. Reynolds said I had abandoned the mark by not advertising it and this was for a period of only 1 year 6 months, and that was only because I was forced into that position by RB stealing the mark off me whilst I was temporarily abroad. So once again law is ignored.

15: The IPO continually ignored my persistent complaints that perjury had been committed and on a grand scale. I started to complain during the submitting of documents for my Opposition to RB's Application to Register the trademark in 2003 and it continued right up to 2009 in preparation for the Invalidity action of RB. In 2009 I complained for about the third time to the CEO of the IPO and he did nothing. I then complained strongly to Raoul Colombo in the Tribunal Section and gave him documentary evidence of the perjury RB had committed by continually saying he was never my agent. I provided copies of the transcript of my forgery trial in 2000 where RB admitted being my agent. He eventually told me that it would be dealt with by the hearing officer of the forthcoming hearing. It was ignored, so a deliberate false promise.

Mr Colombo also refused to answer my questions as to who was responsible for dealing with accusations of perjury, the IPO or the Police. He had the cheek to say that if I felt perjury had been committed I should get a solicitor and pursue that myself. (You will see at the end of this book how the Met Police and Dorset Police used this as an excuse to also fob me off after they had spoken to the IPO thus making it plain that the IPO was constructively obstructing my pursuit of Justice as legally this is incorrect.)

I and MB also complained about the blatant perjury RB committed when he gave a fictitious address for MB in Spain, when he knew full well what RB's address was as he had stayed there only a year previously in 2004, to when he made the statement in 2005. The only mention of perjury made at that hearing was some flippant remarks about how RB could have made a mistake. All other perjury complaints of mine were once more ignored. I believe all these actions by the IPO are highly likely to be illegal.

16: The IPO allow litigants in person to be able to put into evidence stuff that is completely irrelevant, and some of it highly invective and personal against the opponent. In a proper Court be it County or High, this is not allowed so why is it allowed here? I believe that all the reams and reams of irrelevant nonsense put in by RB should not have been allowed and in notes produced by the IPO they actually say that now they are scrutinising evidence statements and will ask applicants to change statements in order to cut this out and to keep to relevant points. So in the cases I have had to put up with, this has not happened at all. I believe it has been deliberately done, as I have drawn attention many times to irrelevant mush put into documents by RB, only to be ignored.

It has the detrimental effect on people like me who have to consider what is being said and many times it is personal remarks about your own integrity, obviously said to denigrate you, and to whether you should ignore it (and maybe to your detriment) or waste a lot of time replying to it and trying to defend yourself.

Another point is the sheer volume of perjury and irrelevant nonsense, must have an effect on hearing officers and this is totally out of order and counter productive to having an unbiased and fair hearing.

17: The IPO have ignored partnership laws and lied through their back teeth by trying to say that case law backs their arguments, so that it can be taken as a fact that RB could lay claim to the assets of the partnership by merely talking to his brother about giving an indemnity, but which never happened. Also they have ignored the partnership laws that say RB could not do things without the authority of the other partner, which is exactly what RB did, more than once. They then totally ignore the protestations of MB (and my lawyer) about all this, as if his rights matter not one jot.

18: *They refused to enact the decision of Landau.* Then when I complain about this and ask by what authority and law can they do this, they refuse to answer and when I force them to answer I get a bunch of lies.

19: They have invariably never acted within the prescribed times they have laid down themselves to do various things. Like never replying to emails and letters within time. Never giving decisions of hearings within time, except with the Landau decision. They have made errors of judgement, have never followed due diligence, have refused to answer direct questions made in order to query their actions. Even their CEO and managers have refused to answer questions, (not about law, but about their actions) and have lied many times. Have ignored basic laws of the land such as bankruptcy laws and partnership laws, as well as their own laws and rules. Have shown blatant bias in favour of my opponent RB and at hearings have ignored most of my evidence statements and documentary evidence that backed up my claims and evidence.

20: They have interfered in my pursuit of justice when using the Police, by trying to get the Police not to act. Then in July 2010 actually telling the Police that perjury was not committed as none of the statements were under oath. This is such a lie it is breathtaking that they have even tried it on. The Perjury Act clearly states that what RB did was perjury.

21: They lied to me when they said they would investigate the perjury at the Invalidity hearing, when they did no such thing. Perjury was never mentioned at the hearing by the hearing officer, (except for one action) no questions asked of him about it and no mention of it in his decision report. (The only question he did ask RB was, was it possible he got things "mixed up" when he gave that fictitious address? The hearing officer became blind and deaf to the perjury complained about.

22: I was told by the IPO before the hearing, if RB did not respond to all the complaints I made of perjury it would be taken as an admission. What another joke of a promise as that never happened as with all the other promises. RB never responded at all to mine and Martins accusations of perjury and he was never questioned about them except in a very biased and soft way about whether he knew Martins Spanish address. Of course his answer was yet more lies and this was accepted by the HO.

23: Failure at the Invalidity hearing to take any notice if my very important legal point that RB could not make my registration or use the mark, because

FROM 1992 onwards he acquiesced my using the mark by never telling me to desist or to take any legal action to make me stop. In IP Law this means he cannot proceed with Invalidity actions as for 18 years he did nothing to stop my use.

In other words the whole operation of the IPO in my case has been utterly disgraceful and has brought any reputation the IPO may have, into disrepute. The whole of my case should be looked into by a truly independent person or body, so what has happened to me may not happen to others. I feel that is it imperative that those who create intellectual property should be protected, for this creation is absolutely important to the well being of the business sector of the UK economy. It creates jobs and wealth for the country. At it's height my business employed 25 people and exported 70% of its turnover. That is until one Robert Busbridge came along!

The IPO is supposed to be there to do this but my case shows that it is not protecting the IP of people and in fact is doing the opposite and is actively protecting crooks to steal IP.

The way the IPO operates and some of it's laws need to change in a big way. No one should have to undergo nineteen years of litigation etc, in order to simply try and protect their IP, only to lose it because of the corruption and incompetence of the IPO.

In my case my life has been ruined. My business was ruined when I could have got it back up to the similar heights of before the recession of 1991/2. In the last fifteen working years of my life I could have been consolidating my business and saving for my retirement. Instead 60-70% of my business was stolen off me. The stress gave me a heart attack and this meant early retirement with a ruined business worth nothing, and very little saved, much wasted on trying to get justice. Now I am only a drain on state coffers and this at a time when the country cannot afford it. So state incompetence has meant it now has to waste money on keeping me when I could have been self sufficient. It is utter madness!

In contrast what has one Robert Busbridge done with his stolen business? He has worked from home only, certainly has not employed 25 people or got to a million turnover or over, nor created new designs and exported 95% of his fully built car turnover. He has been a one man business amounting to nothing. The only thing he has done is give the IPO (and me) plenty of work and to continually lie to his customers about his history and the history of his forgeries.

Chapter Thirty Eight
My Continuing Efforts to Get Somewhere

Whilst trawling through the mountains of paperwork so I could compile a dossier for the Bournemouth Police on the perjury/forgery Robert Busbridge had committed, I was forced to practically inspect all the pages of letters of all my documents I have stored. This meant I came up with some letters that set me thinking.

Firstly I found two letters from my Patent Agents, Kings. The first dated 31/7/96 says *'I do not think this Cobretti application (made in 1992 for registration) is really of great relevance, bearing in mind your prior use' (back to 1986).*

Then in a second letter dated 17/2/97 he says *'Your application (my application to register Viper) has proceeded because the Registry were satisfied that the evidence which has been lodged establishes use which predates the Chrysler application (made in Jan 1990). You have also achieved registration over the 'Cobretti' application. (made in 1992).*

Now this raises the very big question of, 'was he right?' certainly it was always my understanding that this was the case and why I was very upset at the IPO allowing RB to have his application allowed to proceed, the minute my opposition to Chrysler had finished. You have to ask if the IPO did say to Kings that they were satisfied I had established earlier use to Chrysler *(did they put this in writing to him)* and Busbridge and if they did and I have no reasons to believe that King would lie to me, then why did they behave afterwards in 2002 quite differently? For I brought up this argument with them a many times only to be ignored.

On this question of did the IPO actually say in writing to Kings how they viewed my application to register the mark Viper when Chrsyler had an application in and so did Busbridge, I went through all my files re Kings and on reading what he says is this; When I applied the IPO told Kings I would have to prove earlier rights and this is what I and Kings did. We supplied them with copies of advertising and articles and a Statutory declaration on what had been my turnover in kits and cars and what I spent on advertising. This I did from 1986 to 1995 which was the time when we were asking to register.

After looking at this they came back to Kings and said *they were satisfied of my earlier use and that is why they allowed my registration application to proceed.*

This is incredibly important to this whole case! Why? Because at this point in time they were saying that they recognised that I had earlier rights to Chrysler AND Busbridge. I believe this is why they put the application to Register by RB 'On Hold' and yet you can see that later actions by the IPO totally changed and those changes started post 2000 and steadily built up and carried on until the end when Salthouse implied very strongly that the IPO wanted shut of this Viper case once and for all!

Why would they start to behave this way post 2000? First of all prior to 2000 I was fairly quiet as far as me having anything to do with the IPO. I had a Patent Agent doing all that so did not need to be contacting them, but after 2000 I could no longer afford to keep him working for me in order to deal with Chrysler and them saying they wanted to appeal the decision. Once my trial for forgery was won and it became clear that the IPO were siding with RB and I started to have to deal direct with the IPO myself, I became extremely frustrated with the way they were treating me for I now knew that after Chrsyler backed down and I got the registration in 2002, that they were behaving as if RB had as much right to the Mark as I did and that made no sense to me. After all they as I have said, looked at the evidence in 1995 and agreed I had the earliest use and that had been backed up by my winning against Chrysler and getting registration. So why the change?

I have two theories, one is that they got pissed off with me complaining about how they were doing things and the unfairness of it. Threatening that I wanted to sue or get a Judicial Review and that set off some of the Rottweilers of the hierarchy of the IPO who decided to teach me a lesson and make sure that I lost the mark eventually, by doing all the actions they did, which you can see in this story. Ending in their taking away a trademark, they had earlier back in 1995 said I had a right to apply ahead of RB. It could be that the hearing that heard my opposition to Chrysler registering the Viper mark was deemed by someone in the IPO as having been a travesty and that Tuck, the hearing officer did a bum job, but one that could not be overturned. So the IPO set out to make amends for this by allowing RB to carry on with his application even though as Kings said, the IPO had said they were satisfied I had the *earlier* rights. Or that Chrysler put pressure on the IPO after the decision went my way, complaining that Tuck did a bum job in law. And that set the IPO to doing what they did.

Secondly, and this will be controversial, that the Masons are involved in this. Do not laugh at this as they have immense behind the scenes power. It is a well known fact that the wonderful Police we have are riddled with Masons. Who was working with Robert Busridge from 1990? None other than a recently retired on bad health, *Copper*. A Mr McCracken that I have mentioned before, a ex copper who I would not trust as far as I could have thrown the overweight tosser. If he was a Mason that could explain a lot, for I bet there are many in the IPO who are also Masons and it would fit in to what has gone on ever since. Remember I have said more than once, 'It was as if Busbridge had a relative working at the IPO".

Whatever the truth is, what I need to know is *what is the law on this question of who had the earliest rights... did I have precedence in rights over both Chrysler and the Busbridges? Again I need to find a lawyer who will elucidate on this. You will see how that panned out a few pages ahead.*

Another point to ponder is that it is clear that in my case, my application to Register the Mark had my supporting evidence scrutinised, yet I have to ask why wasn't the evidence of RB scrutinised? Because had it been done, they would have seen that nowhere could RB prove with evidence, that he had used the mark back to 1986 or earlier, as I had, as it was impossible for him to do so. He wasn't even involved with Cobra replicas until early 1988, as *my agent. (IPO evidence Rules state that when statements like this are made they should be backed up by evidence to support the claim.)*

Of course I cannot afford to seek full legal advice on this, as I have said already. I am hoping some kindly member of the IP law community who has some morals about these things, and to whom I will have sent this book to, will look kindly on my predicament and contact me to help me, get justice. Prove to me that there are some lawyers out there who are not totally money orientated.

I did also find a *third* letter which I wished I had realised would be of great significance had I picked up on it back in 2003/4 when I was fighting the Reynolds hearing. This was a letter I had sent to the Busbridges on the 13th May 1991. The Busbridges were short of money and wanted me to give them credit I was setting things up for my soon to be trip to Switzerland and was refusing that request (it would have been made for me to give them credit when I was abroad. I said to them "Let's face it if you can't or won't pay a small bill of £86 for the brochures why should I think that you will pay a bill for £500?" The significance of this remark is here I am talking about me having supplied them with brochures which they used to sell 'Vipers' I have covered the brochures in depth already and you may remember that Reynolds used the fact (as he saw it) that I had no part to play in Cobretti advertising or marketing. I have talked about a copy of a letter RB inadvertently put into evidence at the 2010 Invalidity hearing which was also an invoice for brochures. Thus it is now **very** clear that I was supplying them with brochures that I had paid to have created and printed and which clearly were to enable Vipers to be advertised in marketing. Why would I do that if the Busbridges were not agents for me and **my Viper?**

What is also important is that this document was used in my 2000 trial as evidence of this very fact and enabled me to win that case!

Long awaited reply from the Judiciary Ombudsman (Jaco) about the judiciary complaint

As you will have seen above I have been trying to get this Hobbs **** reprimanded in some way, since last November. At last they have replied with their decision and **yet once again it is another civil service whitewash!**

Put briefly they say that as it was what they call case management this is one area that their rules mean they cannot do anything. Once more we have a civil servant telling porkies so as to protect their own.

Their own rules, and I have them in writing, state; *"the OJC must dismiss a complaint if it falls into the category of a judicial case management and raises no question of misconduct".* They obviously do not understand plain English as this means that if misconduct has taken place they can investigate it! Well of course if you take it that their handling this appeal was a case management, then I made the complaints that covered bias in favour of RB, slanderous remarks about me, bad mouthing my case against Chrysler, which had nothing to do with this appeal. So that comes under a question of misconduct.

For the rules that cover judges handling IPO appeals as an Appointed Person, are; *"The Public must be entitled to expect all judicial office holders to maintain at all times proper standards of courtesy and consideration. The Lord chancellor and the Lord Chief Justice do not regard behaviour which could cause offence as consistent with the standards expected of those who hold judicial office. A substantiated complaint of conduct of this kind is in their view, capable of being regarded as misbehaviour".*

It also says *"The governing principle is that no person should sit in a judicial capacity in any circumstances, which would lead an objective onlooker with knowledge of all the material facts to reasonably to suspect that the person might be biased".*

Furthermore it says; *"Should not sit on a case if they have a personal, professional interest in that case".*

Finally it states; *" The Public deserves and expects the highest standards of conduct from those who hold judicial office".*

I say that my complaints about the behaviour of Hobbs fell into all those Rules and the OJC and their case worker who compiled the 13 page review was full of civil service wafflespeak, obfuscation and deliberately pushing aside my complaints with vacuous remarks, to exonerate Hobbs.

Then to cap it off a person identifying himself a Sir John Brigstocke whoever the hell he is, as he couldn't bring himself to identify in what capacity he was acting, in a nutshell, thought that although they took 9 months to finalise my original complaint started in Nov 2009 and this letter to me was late July 2010, he could dismiss all my complaints. Even though he agreed that the OJC had not handled my complaint as well as it should have... in effect... tough luck... no redress... whatever that would mean anyway. He had sent a draft of everything to the Lord Chancellor who as is usual just rubber stamped it and said "good job boys, carry on as usual chaps and bugger these annoying complaining peasants".

In other words if you still do not get it, all the pious words of the Judges Rules as outlined above mean **nothing and it is all smoke and mirrors which are ignored again and again by the Establishment and the Judiciary.**

Chapter Thirty Nine
Trying to Get the Police to Act

Bournemouth Police: update after initial approach in August 2009.

My landlord is an ex Met Police CID Inspector so I bent his ear as I have already recounted. I told him briefly about the problems I was having getting my local fuzz to act on this case and I told him how they had acted like greased lightening when RB reported me for alleged forgery and perjury, yet now they were being slow. He advised that I should get together my evidence documents and all the copies of the statements that the perjury had taken place in and I should ring the investigating officer to ask for a meeting so I could give him all this. At that meeting I should point out that I was the victim here and that it was unfair that the person that made me a victim namely RB should get quick results against me, but when I make serious and substantiated complaints about him, they are not acting.

A meeting was arranged and I noted that the constable who had also taken my complaints about RB last year was also handling this again, and he had another policeman who I was not introduced to, with him. No doubt to act as a witness etc etc. You know how they work, if they felt like it they could break my arm, then say I had attacked him and Hey Presto it is all backed up by *their* witness. Next time I go with my own witness. (You will see later on that this is exactly what these two duplicitous lying bastards did with a whole diatribe of lies as to how this meeting panned out. The document that you can see their lies on can be seen on my blog by the time this is printed.)

I said my piece and the transformation of this guy was amazing. He had always been polite and quiet and now his attitude was extremely aggressive. His face became as dark as a thunder cloud and his eyes became like two laser rays that tried to fry my brain. He went into a spiel about how he had spoken with the IPO, which he did say in a telephone conversation we had had two weeks previously, he would do. Then he said that they had advised him that no perjury had been committed!

No Sir, because the IPO hearings were not a Court where one took an oath for any statements made, so as no oath had been done, any lie could not be deemed to be perjury. What utter garbage and he must think I am a total idiot to swallow that. I immediately countered that by saying " Why then was I charged with perjury for what I had offered to the Chrysler hearing in writing and verbally and not on oath?" That caught him off guard completely and he stuttered a bit and then tried to blind me with science about how he could not possibly comment on something he was not involved in and that as by now due to the time gone by, there would be no files left as they would have been destroyed. Actually he first tried to insinuate that I was not telling the truth about this because in my evidence to date I had never said I had also been charged with forgery and perjury.

This revelation about perjury seemed to annoy him even more, for I had gone on protesting that I had the evidence of what had happened at my trial as I still had all the charge sheets etc. He shot out of his chair and stood up and said loudly to me that if I kept interrupting him and talking over his head and insulting him, he was closing the meeting. Quite astonishing and I decided to just play it cool, I showed him I was not flustered or bothered and I continued by talking to the other guy.

I said that I did not believe what the IPO had said and that I would check up on that, and I pointed out that some of the evidence was in the form of Stat Decs, which were on oath. I said I could not believe it either, because that meant that anyone could lie and lie, as RB had, for any IPO hearing and get away with it. He agreed and he must have thought I was that stupid I was taken in by that. Then his mate started asking me what I thought I was going to get out of all this, did I think I was going to get recompense? I knew exactly what he was intimating here and I also knew where it emanated from… ***the IPO!***

Yet another astonishing thing he said, aggressively, was that he had read my blog. He said it in such a way as to say "I now know what an ***hole you are and how you think about us civil servants" This would explain in part his aggressiveness and ***of course it was the IPO who told him about the blog and RB who told <u>them</u>.*** I told him coolly that he aught to now know why I was so passionate about getting justice and that all I had said, was what I felt and I had a right to free speech and if anyone did not like it they could take me to court as I would welcome that. That seemed to shut him up on that one, but it shows you all you need to further know about the way the IPO are working on this. Do not forget that recently Raoul

Colombo had sent me an email in which he said that even though they were not taking action on the perjury *"we will cooperate fully with the police!"* I knew when he said that what he meant and I was right again. Tellingly Colombo never ever at any stage told me that there was no perjury. No doubt Hobbs had advised them to use this ploy.

I had asked this Constable Scott Brimicombe bloke, on the phone, when he told me he was going to speak with the IPO, to take what they said with a pinch of salt as they would try to slag me off and I also asked him to be independently minded about what they would say to him. He had said he would do that. Yet it was obvious that he and his mate had been brainwashed. So the IPO had said to them that all I was after was getting money out of the IPO. (Plus no doubt denigrating me as well.)

I had to put them right and I told them that now I had no chance to get anything out of the IPO as I did not have the money to go to court and no legal firm was interested to take on such a case for free in the hopes they would win. That I would be dead long before I could get a resolution out of court proceedings against the IPO as they had the long pockets of the taxpayer to fund them. They could appeal if I won and it would go on forever as that is the way civil servants work. I had found that much out over the past 5 to 6 years of trying to find someone to take it on. It was out of time to get a Judicial Review, so that too was out. I told them both that it was now just a wish to get *justice* against a chiselling crook, who had got away with it for 18 years and ruined my life and business. Whether they believed or cared a jot what I said, I do not know but whatever they think it is going to be negative. (And so it was as you will see later on when my complaint about their handling and behaviour of this case and meeting, is finalised and we get to see their report.)

I then kept on about how perjury had been committed as per my own arrest and it had to be investigated. They said that they would continue to look into things especially with regards to the State Decs RB had made and I said I was going to investigate what they were saying about "no perjury committed".

It finished there and I got out feeling mad as hell, but not showing it.

Now in the days after that, I have looked at the Perjury Act of 1911 again, and what the Police and the IPO have said is **absolute garbage. it is quite clear that** *perjury is committed if you knowingly lie to a tribunal and what is more it does not have to be statements on an oath, either! I was quite right, what is more I have sent an email to the lawyer who represented me over seeing off Chrysler to get it in writing, from the horses mouth.*

I got my reply from the lawyer that I got on well with and we had a long chat about it. He confirmed what I have said above and that of course it was perjury and perjury can be committed in statements to IPO hearings that are always signed off as you having told the truth. Then there are the cases of the Stat Decs and the lies in the witness statement to the Bournemouth Police in 1999 which were admitted to evidence for the Court case and let us not also forget the lies said verbally during that Court case were on oath.

So in went a letter to the constable who came up with the garbage, with a Copy of the Perjury Act and the relevant parts highlighted. After two weeks not a peep and no acknowledgement he even received it. So as I am not going to pussy foot around with these bums, I sent a letter of complaint to the Inspector in charge of that CID, about the conduct from day one, of his department and this constables histrionics at that meeting. Where will it go, nowhere I bet so it will mean a trip up to the top man and maybe then to the IPCC. (This is exactly what happened as I have already said and you can see on my blog the whole letter which is full of lies and excuses which is all I expected and wasn't let down by our wonderful useless Police.)

A week later I did get a letter from this Inspector, who said that as the perjury took place in London they would have to get the Met to transfer the investigation to Bournemouth and that is what they were doing. He said that my complaint is being investigated, but that means what? And what I cannot understand is that in the charge I suffered back in 1999, the alleged offence also took place in London yet it was Bournemouth that investigated it and sent constables to London to interview Busbridge. On top of that, a lot of the perjury in this case was carried out by RB in Bournemouth when questioned by the Bournemouth Police and when he was at Dorchester Crown Court.

After a month I had to send a chasing letter and after that I got an answer from a different Inspector with the unfortunate name of Dixey. He is the champion Dorset Police whistler, who said that they would not be dealing with this case. His reasons were:-

1: *"The cases of perjury were carried out mostly in the Met area."*
2: *"Those carried out in Dorset and concerned the eventual County Court hearing in 2000 would have had the Judge at that hearing state that he wanted the person charged."*

Then he said that the Met had declined to deal with the case as *"in their opinion this was an ongoing civil case and nothing to do with them!"*

As I said above I expected these kinds of devious excuses to be made. I mean the Police are so thick they are incapable of hiding what they really think and that they have no intentions to do anything. Especially after having been brainwashed by the IPO.

In the case of:
1: One has to ask if this is the criteria that Dorset Police rigidly use, then why did Dorset Police charge me for ONE alleged act of perjury which also took place in London? You could also ask if I were to report a case of murder or robbery with violence that took place just over the border in say New Milton, would I also be told "Nothing to do wiv us Guv as that is not on our patch- know what I mean like"... ***holes!
2: When I put this to the hard man DC Brimicombe (who likes trying to intimidate 70 year old geezers like me) he had no answer!

My last contact with this wonderful and helpful copper Brimicombe, was on the phone when I asked him who he had had contact with at the Met and what department it had been? Now prior to this I had put in a request under the Freedom of Information Act to force him to divulge what contacts he had had with the IPO. I wanted copies of letters or emails between them. I also wanted to know what records they had on me on their computer as I suspected what they had was not nice towards me. I thought that it was highly likely that he would have accessed their records to see if there was any dirt on me personally. Obviously he got to know that I had done that.

So when I asked him, "Who did you talk to in the Met?" his answer was, "Get it under the freedom act you have started" and he point blank refused to tell me...

typical bastard copper!

Regarding the Met, well these dopey but sly coppers do try it on all the time, but I suspect they usually get away with it most of the time. This because too many Brits are scared of them or too thick to know their rights, the law, or maybe they are just too apathetic to fight the bastards.

So now I had to make the inevitable complaint to the Chief Constable, because folks I *never* give up, but I can assure you it will go nowhere. Why should I think it will go anywhere? Well you can now see with all the above history, of all the times and all the bodies I have complained to… they have all, to a man refused to deal with my complaints. They prefer to spend their time thinking of excuses and going through the long and tortuous motions as why they cannot or will not do anything even when you have legitimate complaints. Why is this? Well it's damned obvious… all government departments are under orders from someone, to prevaricate, lie, make excuses, in fact do anything or say anything, for they cannot admit to mistakes. I guess you have a few hundreds years of inbuilt mind-sets with these inbreds.

Some would say that this is because in these days they just have to save tax payers money. Yes if we are dealing with *today*, but my efforts to get justice go back 19 years and they were at it going that far back and even around the early 2000's when we were coining it in, in a boom and they were still at it. So it is just this mind-set that bastard civil servants have. I would sack the lot of them and start all over again with someone in control of the ******ers like a Sgt Major who would stand no nonsense, if you get my meaning?

I did complain to the Chief Constable about the behaviour of DC Brimicombe as I have said and I was interviewed by a civilian (but ex copper) bloke about what I was complaining about (even though it was all laid out in my letter). So went through it all again and off he went and no doubt bugger all will ever come of it. After all when the cops can murder people and get away Scot free, what chance have I got that this Brimicombe will get his arse well and truly kicked.

My dissatisfaction with the Dorset Police rumbled on over the Freedom of Info Act request I had put in. The eventual answer I got was no more than three pieces of paper that told me nothing, being only phone records of me ringing in to try to get hold of Brimicombe. So I sent another email reminding this bloke called

Shaun Walbridge what I had asked for. I got no reply and then I came across the two emails from the IPO & the Met Police bloke Walters that I explain about in the next section.

So I rang him up and told him I wanted any emails/faxes or letters between Brimicombe and the IPO as what he had discussed was not an investigation but that he had been seeking advice and had ended up talking about me on a personal basis. That I said, gave me the right to know what that was, as per the Act. He tried it on again by saying that he couldn't possibly tell me anything to do with any investigation. So I said he was making up excuses not to answer. He put the phone down on me.

So what we now have is me sending him another email demanding my rights as per the Act and if he doesn't co-operate, he will be part of my complaint to the IPCC. For this is where I guess Dorset Police will end up having to respond to for their actions. No doubt they will protect their cosy friends, the Police, like all so called Ombudsmen.

My application to the MET Police to register a request that there be an investigation into acts of perjury and forgery.

So it goes on and on and I now had to contact the Met as to why they are trying it on. I am also sure they would give me the usual run round and knock back, as they don't want to spend any money if its not a murder or a racial issue that they know will mean the media will be watching all their moves. I started by sending in an email on their online website asking who has knocked me back and what section they work in?

Guess what, I get a slow answer by probably a civilian, who makes excuses that he does not know what department Dorset Police got in contact with as there are so many. He tells me to go back to Dorset Police and ask them! This even though I had made the point of telling him that they had refused to tell me. I suggested he ring them as they would be more likely to tell him than me.

To cut a long story short several emails later to and fro and I have got nowhere, so I tell him that no answers from him and I take it to a higher level. Still no answer, so I fill in an online complains form and still no action. Next stop was the

Head of the Met, a Sir Paul Stephenson and a complaint goes into him about his poxy coppers pissing me around. Now they acknowledged receipt and say it has been passed onto their Standards people. If there is no action it is up to the next level and to the IPCC who are as non independent as you can get, and I am told they are toothless as well. Reading their pamphlet it certainly makes you wonder why they are in existence. I hope to reveal all before I decide to print this book off as I cannot go on for another year or so.

When I finally got Brimicombe to send me back my dossier on all the perjury and copies of all the evidence, I just put on my sideboard. A couple of weeks later I decide to start organising it all again just in case I have to show it all to the Met and low and behold I find that Brimicombe, the idiot, has left copies of two emails, one sent to him by this Sgt Walters of the Met, the bloke he wouldn't tell me about, and the other an email from Hayward of the IPO and he is brainwashing Brimicombe that only a court can order a perjury investigation. Doesn't say which Court though and that gives Brimicombe the opening to try it on with me and say it is the court that heard the case. That of course is rubbish as perjury could be committed at the hearing and the judge would not be in the know that it was perjury, until he was told by the defence or opponent, that it had been and after the event and some time later. So what happens if he can't be arsed, which is exactly what all these Hearing Officers of the IPO have done since day one?

What these emails showed me is that there had been emails and phone calls between Brimicombe and the IPO and the Met, as a fax is mentioned by the Met and a telephone conversation by the IPO.

So what went on there and what was said especially on a personal level about me?

When I finally got the records on me from my application under the Freedom of Information Act, all I got was two pieces of paper which were records of me phoning Brimicombe twice in 2009. Nothing about what records they have on me personally on their national computer, nor anything on what I asked for re copies of any letters or emails that went between Brimicombe and the IPO & Met, of which of course I now have these two copies, I can see there are more.

The Police make the excuse that as they were investigating, anything that relates to that in the way of records, I am not privy to. Being a duplicitous mob they of course do not accept that actually the truth is that they were not investigating my complaint at all, as they had told me quite clearly that would not investigate. They were merely obtaining advice from the IPO and in the course of that they had clearly involved themselves in discussing me on a personal level. This was seen when Brimicombe interviewed me and his attitude after having spoken with the IPO was decidedly anti me. He admitted that he had read my blog and he could only have got the information I had one, from the IPO.

I am therefore sure that any contact Brimicombe had with Sgt Walters would also have discussed me on a personal level. It is inconceivable that they did not. This email from Walters to Brimicombe shows that he had received a fax from Brimicombe and obviously from what he goes onto saying he had also been sent my file or dossier I had made up on the lies of Busbridge. I will repeat word for word what he said in that email as I think it will show you what I am dealing with here and I would hope you will be able to see that:

"I am e-mailing you regarding the fax received from you on the 6th July 2010 regarding allegations made by Kenneth Cook against Robert Busbridge—I did find the 47 page letter by Mr Cook a little difficult to follow.

The allegations largely surround submissions made to the Intellectual Property Office by Mr Busbridge concerning his business relationship with Mr Cook over the past 18 years. There is also an allegation that Mr Busbridge gave false evidence which led to being charged by Dorset Police with perjury in 1999—Mr Cook claims he is able to prove Mr Busbridge lied in his evidence.

It appears from Mr Cook's letter dated the 9th June 2009 to Inspector Travers of Dorset Police that the IPO have attempted what they refer to as an "Alternative Dispute Resolution"; possibly some sort of mediation to resolve this dispute. It is clear that this has failed, as there are a huge number of details around the history of events given by Mr Busbridge that Mr Cook disputes—and Mr Cook is now attempting to make criminal allegations against Mr Busbridge. The normal course of events in these circumstances would be for Mr Cook to pursue this dispute through the High Court—and for the Court to make a decision on the ownership of the IP concerned and award damages where appropriate.

If any party was to give evidence to the High Court that was found to be untrue then obviously this may well give rise to a criminal investigation. I will take further advice on this matter, however my view at present is that submissions made by Mr Busbridge to the IPO, giving his account of events and recalling his dealings with Mr Cook, do not amount to an act of perjury or attempting to pervert the course of Justice—they are simply facts that Mr Cook disputes . At present we will not be recording this matter as an allegation of crime.

It is obviously a decision for Dorset Police, but it may be appropriate for you to re-examine the circumstances of the charges of perjury and subsequent trial that Mr Cook states he endured after Mr Busbridge gave false evidence against him in 1999."

For those who have read all of this book up to this point and have understood the story and sequences of it, I am sure all will be able to see just what kind of person this Sgt Walters is. He is typical of Police today in that he obviously hasn't got a brain at all. Or more importantly he was indulging in what the Police are famous for. That is deliberately twisting the facts so as to make them appear to be something entirely different and innocuous. Here we have a Sgt in what is a branch of what would normally be called CID, but in the Met World of today some idiot has decided to call the Metropolitan Crime Management Unit, no doubt because it sounds better! He shows clearly that he does not know what he is talking about and is obviously incapable of understanding any of my dossier I sent Brimicombe through his boss, Inspector Travers, or the letter I sent with it.

Quite frankly if this is the calibre of the CID at the Met all I can say is that I am not surprised how easy it is for all the crooks and criminals that get away with all manner of crimes in the capital, as the PC Plods of the Met are just not fit for purpose and are too thick to understand anything. However I am really more inclined to think he is just another devious copper bent on not doing anything and lying through his back teeth in order to get the Met off investigating something he feels he can get away with not investigating.

I will disseminate all of what he says to show you how this man is "Not fit For Purpose".

1/ 1st paragraph:- "I did find the 47 page letter a little difficult to follow" It was not a 47 page letter, but a letter to Travers with an accompanying dossier showing all the perjury committed, in what documents and what the truth of each lie was, plus evidence to back up that they were lies. What this oaf should have done is interviewed me and I could have gone over everything in detail and at the end of that he *would have understood everything.* No that was too difficult for him, but in any case he is only looking for excuses not to act as this is what happens time and again these days when people report crimes. The only way the Police stretch themselves is in the inventiveness of their excuses not to act. Even then, what they say adds up to lying and twisting the truth.

2/ 2nd paragraph; This shows how this man just does not understand what this is all about even though he has 47 pages of evidence which show that. He says that it is submissions made by Busbridge to the IPO concerning his business relations with me. When what the truth is that I have not had any business relations with Busbridge over the past 18 years but I have pursued him for his stealing of my business and IP, something entirely different. What Busbridge has submitted to the IPO has been his litany of lies in order to consolidate his criminal acts of his stealing, by committing serial acts of perjury and forgery to do it. What I have submitted to the IPO (which Walters ignores, is my evidence against RB)

Then Walters says I allege that .Busbridge got me charged with perjury (and forgery) **and then he says it in such a way that I claim to be able to prove there was lies in RB's evidence, as if I was dreaming or something.** Of course I can show he lied and if he had read the whole dossier he would have seen my evidence of his lies and the proof *and Martins affidavit!*

3/ He then says my letter to Travers dated 6th June 2009 (it was sent in 2010 so that shows how unable to get anything right) shows that the IPO have an "Alternative Dispute Resolution" service and it had been tried but had failed! I wonder what Planet this man is on as I made no mention of any such body in the IPO or any mediation. The IPO have no such thing. (In my letter to Sgt Walters about this email, which he ignored, I asked him if he had been on hash when writing the email?) Maybe he is saying these things just to muddy the waters and give him excuses not to investigate.

He carries on in this fantasy world because he then says that there are a huge number of details around the history of events given by Busbridge that I dispute. You could not make this up, I swear.

He goes on to say that I am now attempting to make criminal allegations against RB. Now apart from the grammar of that sentence, I am NOT attempting, I AM making allegations, and providing the evidence to prove the allegations. Then he does the classic Cop thing, which is a cop out to actually investigate crime when it is reported…"Nuttin to do with us Guv, it's a civil matter… go to the High Court." Oh yes, thicko copper, if I could afford to do that we would not be here and I would have dealt with Conman Busbridge back in the early 90's!

4/ After waffling on about the High Court, he then again shows his ignorance by saying that in his view, what Busbridge told the IPO about his dealings with me did not amount to perjury. This when the evidence he had been shown, is that RB had no dealings with me after 1991 except when I was pursuing him for ripping me off. The evidence showed overwhelmingly that "his accounts" contained massive amounts of perjury in order to pervert the course of events and so he could gain control of the Viper trademark and then sell it to Chrysler. All that is evidenced and was in my dossier. Walters simply says that I disputed these "facts" and this shows bias towards RB as it appears that in his eyes what RB states are FACTS and not allegations. I am then brusquely told that this will not be recorded as an allegation of a crime. That is how the Police acts so many times today and it is a disgrace that is not dealt with. But then the police today regard themselves as "Untouchables" a law unto themselves that no politician or civil servant has the balls to sort out. They can get away with blowing people away with guns as evidenced only recently, *so they have no fear of lesser matters as they know they can get away with even murder!*

Hence why we see so many people run over or filled full of lead and no copper ever pays a price. In the paper of today as I write this, an arrogant cooper who is thankfully on trial, said to his victim who he had raped, "I am the law and untouchable." This is the face of Police today and this arrogant man Walters falls into that category.

5/ He finishes off by advising Dorset that it is up to them, yet they were (according to them) asking if the Met would take over the case as it happened on their patch. He tells them they may look at things re the charging of myself in 1999 and the lies RB told to get me charged. Of course they do not do that and made feeble lying excuses about it was up to the trial Judge to recommend he be charged with perjury or what ever, when that is a nonsense (as you will eventually see).

I replied to all that crap with a very strongly worded email pointing out all his mistakes and telling him that I was going to include him in my complaint I had already before Sir Paul. Of course no answer, just as he never answered my polite letter sent before I saw the email, asking why he had told Brimicombe that this was a civil ongoing case, which it is patently neither. I bet that this will end up before the IPCC. I will wait until the complaints department say what I think they will say.

I rang them up after they had not contacted me for 10 days as advised to do so, in the letter to me from Sir Paul's office. At least the guy answering sounded half decent. What is happening is that he had received my email about Sgt Walters and had sent that and the file to a person at Camden Police HQ. A person who deals with standards will contact me... eventually, but will it be excuses?

I eventually get an email from a Sgt Downs at Camden and I am told he is going to look into this and he will get back to me. I pre-empt things and send him an email outlining what my complaints are re being ignored by their online operatives and by Walters who I had sent an email asking why he had refused to reply about getting involved with investigating perjury. I then get another email asking for some details about me like my DOB and to give him a summary of the history of events between me and RB. (Does he want a 500 page book I wondered?) I send him an email back and I very briefly give him a run down.

Next thing is he rings me one day around 12. Sounds extremely easy going but I know from experience that you can never trust a copper, *nice cop-bad cop* and all that! We chat for about half an hour and I outline again a brief history of what I have had to suffer from conman Busbridge. He asks how I can prove what I am saying, so that means me explaining how. I make a point of telling him that *I do have plenty of irrefutable evidence*. He comes the old act of saying the story is complex as if this lets off the Police from investigating it, just like Brimicombe had and Walters. I put him straight by saying it is not at all complex, but in order to easily understand he needs to sit down with me, with the evidence I had made out for Dorset, and I go through with it line by line and by the end of that he *would understand easily what it entailed*.

I ask you, what is in these cops heads? Can they not understand anything that is more than a couple of paragraphs of evidence? Then he lets the cat out of the bag when he tells me that he will contact Walters and talk with him and he may very well end up agreeing with what he had said. I protested and said that all Walters had said was garbage and he obviously hadn't a clue as to his understanding of what my evidence had said. I wondered why he would need to talk with someone who had admitted he couldn't understand the evidence. Downs then tried to soften me up by saying he would have to look at everything before he could say whether they would investigate. He also dropped in the fact that he thought they may not even **be able to investigate, as it was down to a judge to decide that it needed investigating.** A tack Brimicombe tried on. Well Mr Downs I am getting a solicitor to answer some questions on that one. The way I read it, all they have to do is either go to the Attorney General and say they want to investigate and get his permission, or to a court. However I find that hard to believe and told him so, because how was it that only back in 1999 Busbridge just trots along to the Met and in 5 minutes they are investigating me. He had no answer to that which is no surprise. So that is were that ended and I awaited an answer.

I will make a prediction here and that is he will get back and that will be his excuse, we cannot investigate it for that last reason. If that is the case then how can the Police start any investigation, for I refuse to believe that in every case they have to ask a court or the Att/Gen? I will also ask my ex Met copper landlord. I now have to wait, once again. The way this is going I will have died of old age and nothing will have gone anywhere.

The day after I wrote the last paragraph I got an email off this Sgt Downs bloke. The outcome was as I suspected. "Don't want to know" However the excuse used was the other that had been used by Sgt Walters and that was it is a civil matter and go and get a solicitor! How these bastards get away with this blatant refusal to act on *criminal matters* and how they can be so blatantly hypocritical when they thought differently when they charged me for the exact same charges, but of course Busbridge is a conman and I am a law abiding person. We all know that the criminals in this country are treated better than law abiding folk, and of course Busbridge is an adept liar!

One thing that also annoyed the hell out of me is that here we have a situation where I complain to the Head Honcho of the Met and it ends back up being investigated by one of Sgt Walters cronies in the same police station. *How corrupt can that be?*

It also annoyed me that I had also complained about Busbridge forging letters and I said that I had further information of criminal matters which if I could be interviewed I would talk about.

These two points were completely ignored, so one has to take it that the Police these days also do not do forgery nor want to know about any criminal matters at all.

"They are all CIVIL; go away peasant and pay to pursue criminals yourself".

I have mentioned above that I had wanted to talk to the Met about another criminal matter to do with RB. Now is the time for me to bring this up for I was so pissed off at the lack of willingness to nail a crook, that information I had on criminal activities by RB in other ways that I had been informed about, I had held off bringing these into the arena for good reasons which at that moment I did not divulge in order to protect my source. However had I been treated properly by the Met and interviewed I could have discussed a way forward that would have given them even more for which they could nail him for his corrupt ways.

Because of my frustration at the Met and not being interviewed, I now will divulge what it was that I would have discussed at any meeting. During my course of conversations with Martin he eventually said that he had one over his brother if it had to come to it. Apparently Robert during the course of running the business had taken on work for people he either knew or had come to him, but more likely he knew them or they knew someone he knew, in order for an insurance scam to be perpetrated. He would take in vehicles that they wanted to 'disappear' and dismantle them. A claim for a 'stolen' vehicle would then be made. Three vehicles were lined up to be made to 'disappear' One a lorry was too big to get into the workshop, the other two were worked on. Maybe more were dismantled after Martin left the business. Martin said he did not know that a scam was being operated by his brother at that time and thought that it had been just work that had been taken on. For stripping some cars down to sell off as parts is common in the trade as selling them as parts brings in more money than selling as a full car.

It was not until after that he found out what the truth was and it was this that if it came to it, he could divulge.

As for me, it just shows what a little criminal this Robert Busbridge is and it just makes me more mad at how the IPO and Police have turned their face away from him as if he were an angel and I was the crook. No doubt now the Police would say it was too far back to investigate and they would once more get out of things by that excuse. Another thing that hacks me off is that Robert was aided at that time in the office by an ex Met copper called McCracken (Phil, maybe?) He had to be in on it and I wouldn't be surprised if he didn't set it up as he has remained good friends with RB ever since and has appeared as 'Moral Support' for the wimp Robert, at hearings. What did I say about Cops being crooks in uniform?

I am pretty sure Martin did not know what was going on, but who knows. Now I am afraid I have to waste time and go through the motions with the IPCC, and if their response is what I expect, and if that is yet another failure of a government entity (and bull to all that claptrap that they are independent).

Chapter Forty
Continuing Efforts to Get Justice

Talking about MP's, my wonderful MP Chris Chope has so far done nothing about the fact Ken Clarke has done nothing, after many many months, about my notifying him of the facts about the Judge Hobbs corruption issue and the cover up by OJC & JACO.

Also I will send copies of this book to as many IP lawyers as I can find and Professors of Law at various Uni's. See if there are any with a heart out there who are interested in Justice more than their pockets. Pigs might fly and I may win the Lottery.

Quite frankly I have given up on the British as I feel that the majority have become in my lifetime, a complete basket case and I am thus completely cynical that anyone out there either has the character or sympathy for others who have been wronged in some way, or have the willingness to try to help. The British general character of today, compared to what it was in the 40's & 50's is but a shadow.

Just maybe a judicial character may see that this story shows us just how low the British Judicial system and governance system, has sunk to. They may think it their duty to expose it.

Probono lawyers

One area that I thought I would try to see if I can find any kindly lawyers are those who advertise they do ProBono work. However I am again not confident as whilst in the States **many lawyers do this charity type work,** here in the UK it is my opinion that UK lawyers are more concerned with their pockets and don't give a fig for poor people, who now that there is virtually no legal aid for, cannot get justice over a whole host of legal areas.

I did see only one charity called Barprobono on the whole of the web, which tells you all. They require you to send in a form, outlining your poverty status and get that checked and verified by Citizens Advice, and you include the details of what advice/help you're after.

I did that and it soon became apparent that I was dealing with an organisation that was as difficult, unbending and unhelpful as any civil servant could be. Certainly their way of working and the rules they set down seem to me to show that their prime objective is to make it as difficult as possible for someone like me to actually get what they need.

In my case all I wanted was to get a series of questions answered on points of law. I would have thought that was immensely more easy than some barrister having to get to grips with the details of a past case or ongoing case and then giving advice on the 16 questions I posed along the lines of; "What does IP law/rules say about the question of"... Any barrister worth his salt could have answered all these questions within an hour.

Well I know now how lawyers and barristers minds work. If you ask any one of them what I think is a simple question, they refuse to answer it. They use excuses like "Well in what context is this question being asked? What are the details of the case to which it is involved with?" And so on. What they are, is petrified of is giving you an answer which you then use in a case, quoting them as the authority and it turns out that they are wrong because in this case the context is different, so a different answer should have been given. Then their name is mud and we can't have that, can we? Poor dears.

So they want to see all the paperwork in order that they can soak up all the facts of the case, etc, etc, and then give a considered answer. However there are questions that can be asked that even though they were part of a case long gone by, the person wishes to know if the authority who came to decisions over a point in that case, came to the right decision.

Example:- (This actually formed my first question) Back in 1992 I opposed Chryslers application as you know, to register a trademark that I owned (in common law terms). So did RB and he applied ***before me.*** Yet the IPO let me go first. Why was that, as when the IPO in taking away my trademark, said that IP Law says that, he by virtue of applying to register the same trademark ***before me,*** meant he had prior rights to me.

Now my question was simple. "What is the law on applications being submitted to the IPO in relation to who applies first. Is it the person who applies first who gets to have their application heard first?"

So why the hell cannot some egghead barrister simply answer that question? Really it is a trick carried out by lawyers so they can make what is a simple procedure into a seemingly incredible difficult one and then they can take much longer to answer your question and guess what? They can charge you much more because of that. Nice one Cyril!

What I got back at first from the Probono charity on all my questions, was that I had not submitted documents to support my questions, even though I told her (the woman I had to deal with) my questions did not apply to an ongoing case or past one in the true sense (as I wasn't appealing anything). No matter what I said in order to get through to this woman, made any difference. First she said they could not just give advice not related to a case. That excuse was blown out of the water when I sent her a copy of an email from one of her colleagues saying I could get advice on only questions.

I told her that whilst all the questions had a relationship to a series of 8 past hearings, I had 16 bulging files on each case and hundreds of documents. How was I supposed to know what document a barrister would want to see in relation to each of the questions, when answering the question did not need to have a connection to a case, in order to be answered? I mean, if I asked a barrister "What is the law on drink driving?" Would he refuse to give me an answer because I could not or would not give him documents relating to a case, because I merely wanted to know what the law said? Now I might have been charged with drink driving and I may have thought that the authorities dealt with the actual law in a way that did not smack as if it was a true representation of what they law actually said. So I merely wanted to know what the law did say and from the horses mouth. From a supposed expert.

Then if he told me something that did not gel with what had happened, in law in my case, I would know something was amiss and wrong on the part of the Police or CPS or the Courts.

Applying that simple analogy to myself and the first question, it is therefore quite straight forward. That is to me, but apparently not to the judicial eggheads. Anyway after several difficult emails she sent a reply which said she had indeed passed my questions onto 'Their own barrister, a QC'. (I wonder if it was Hobbs and I wonder what IP experience he had?) He had said that my questions could not be answered because:-

1/ *The questions are actually partly matters of law and partly matters of practice and or fact".* Now what the hell is all that supposed to mean to a layman? Why is it that all judiciary people speak with forked tongues? Of course they are matters of law and I said that was what I wanted to know. What was the law? What the hell has 'practice' got to do with a question that asks what is the law this. If there is a law he can says what it says. If there is no law and the judge or hearing officer makes it up as he goes along, then say that is what happens. If there is no hard and fast law and it relies on case history in similar cases etc etc , say so. Is he saying there is no law and it relies on what the facts were of that particular case and the judge would tailor the law as it were, then why couldn't he say so. So he could say that it depends on the cases and it could be down to three different factors. Then give three examples. "Simples!"

2/ Then he says *"He notes that the answers to all the questions could depend on the background circumstances"*.

Well that is the same as "facts" as above. But what intrigues me here is if that were the case, then what he is saying is that what a judge decides should be the outcome on all these legal points, are not down to what the laws on IP may say, but on how he sees the case and how he interprets the facts and that seems madness to me. If that were the case then you wouldn't need any laws and the 1994 trademarks Act could be scrapped, as could all the Rules that the IPO have brought out separately and all can all be ignored. I know that is not right too.

If it were right, I would then ask the question, why did the IPO categorically state an IP law of the 1994 TMA to back up their decision making on the last hearing re making my trademark invalid, on the basis that the law said he had prior rights due the the fact he applied before me? Yet if they had applied what this barrister says, they should have looked at all the circumstances surrounding the application of RB for the trademark registration and have taken note of what evidence we showed, that it had been got by fraud, forgery, perverting the course of justice, partnership law had been flouted (as per Landau) it had not been bonafide and so on. Yet the IPO stuck rigidly to *one fact*... the *IP law* said... I have long been saying that this is what they should have done as did my lawyer on that last case. So who is right and what is the law or is there no law? He could have answered all that very easily without having to know all about any of the cases or seeing any documents. What is up with these guys?

3/ He then says *"without knowledge of the background circumstances it is not possible to form a view"*.

Well that is a repeat of 1 & 2 and I end up with no answers which I feel he could have come up with had he wanted to. Also in their blurb on their website they do say that when the barrister to whom the whole questions are given to, he can ring you to clarify matters if he needs to. So why the hell couldn't that have been done in my case?

This means that a charity has completely let me down by being nit pickers and rigid in their approach to individual cases. Are they supposed to be helping people or being obstructive? Maybe this is their way of weeding out as many applicants as possible so they don't have to spend as much money. *Just like a bunch of civil servants*, and I did tell her early on, that I was getting the vibes that they were behaving like a bunch of civil servants in their being difficult.

So now I have to go to a firm of lawyers and spend a few hundred pounds on asking them to answer the questions, if they will that is. So that is my next step and I may see if they will take on suing the IPO as well.

Trying to find evidence to prove that the Hobbs hearing was indeed corrupt

I decided I must do this and I deduced that the first place I must visit would be to get a transcript of the Annand hearing. This because from memory she made several remarks about what evidence she could hear and that she could not revisit old hearings. Something that other hearings and especially Hobbs had ignored. So I wanted to see exactly what she said and compare the way she conducted an appeal hearing that had identical backgrounds with the Hobbs hearing. By that I mean both were appeals against the decision of an IPO hearing officers decision and heard by an Appointed Person.

I had to approach the T/Sol again and whilst I was at it I wanted to know what evidence statements had been put into the evidence for that hearing and what guidance notes or booklet did they have on appeals. So I sent them an email to their Mr Prior who I had dealt with over my complaint in 2009 about the behaviour of Hobbs. He took his time and eventually I had to ring him. Immediately he sounded very unhelpful which was much the same as he had been before.

He started by telling me he had sent the transcript off. I asked him what about my question about evidence statements and guidance notes. He told me in a very surely manner that he could not tell me about either questions. I remonstrated and told him that any statements were public knowledge and he couldn't refuse me. That if there were guidance notes I had to know. This to no avail.

Honestly these civil servants can be total ****** so this meant finding out who his boss was and an email was sent to him, a Mr Buttrill. Whether he was his boss is anyone's guess but it had the desired effect and eventually I was told that there were no evidence statements, only the statement of Grounds. The details of some places to look on the website of the IPO were given.

At the same time as all this I sent the IPO an email and asked for a copy of the Statement of Grounds by RB and this was sent me with no trouble. I also asked them about guidance notes/rules/laws. I was told that as the appeals were held by the T/Sol I was to ask them.

I got the distinct impressions that from both the IPO & the T/Sol there was a reluctance to own up to whether there were guidance rules for appeals. This because they would know what I was up to and they knew that if I got hold of these and found evidence that Hobbs never followed the rules, I had him. I was directed to the Civil Procedure Rules Act, but there I found nothing that actually covered appeals before a Tribunal, except a few lines that said that the hearing could only receive evidence that had already been in the original hearing and that an appeal could only be granted if the original hearing had manifestly been wrong or had suffered from wrong doing in the way it had been handled.

So this meant that in this appeal of Hobbs I could not see that any evidence had been put up for it to be considered and the S of G contained absolutely no evidence or relevant reasons to be able to appeal. Hence why Hobbs never discussed them and only briefly mentioned he had read them.

The real evidence of wrong doing was contained in the transcript of the Annand hearing. She had constantly referred to why she could not venture into old hearings not make comment about them, as |I have outlined above in Chapter 24. So it is clear that she was working to guidelines and within 'boundaries' and she had no jurisdiction in certain areas. To say those things means that there just must be written down rules or guidelines which she had to work to. And they obviously were not obeyed by Hobbs, at all.

Were the IPO and the T/Sol deliberately keeping those away from me? I wouldn't put that past any of them to do just that. I mulled all this over then realised that even though the IPO and the T/Sol was trying to play me off against the other, they were forgetting that there are two types of appeal. One that can be heard by an IPO officer, or if you were mad enough to believe you could get an **Independent** Appointed Person to hear it, basically both appeals would cover exactly the same grounds. Or at least they should do. So now I had to find out what guidelines the IPO had on their appeals. Get them and they would be the same as for AP's. Despite sending an email to Skilton asking him to tell me. I got no answer.

When I found that email from Hayward (of the IPO) to Brimicome, I was so mad I sent off an email and asked him why he had twice tried to pervert the course of justice by stopping me from getting the Police to investigate the perjury of RB by brainwashing them into thinking no perjury had been committed? I called all the IPO persons that I had to deal with "tossers" A few days later I get a reply from no less than James, he the "corrupt one", the absolute little hypocrite, saying that I had sent abusive emails (plural) and in future that I should only send him emails. He accused me of being not willing to accept the IPO hearing decisions. Too damn right I don't. I replied pointing out his sheer hypocrisy when he and his staff are indulging in having conversations about me with Dorset Police, slagging me off and trying to pervert the course of justice by stopping them from investigating perjury, by feeding them lies about what constitutes perjury etc. I also told him I had not forgotten his part in the corrupt Hobbs hearing and that I was after him personally for his actions. He will just love that. I am now contemplating complaining once more to the Parliamentary Ombudsman, however I very much doubt I will ever get anywhere with them either, even if I do.

Chapter Forty One
Showing How Incompetent/Corrupt All IPO Hearing Officers Are

I can now show that for every hearing I have been involved in many mistakes have been made in them over procedures, following the law and rules etc. I now list each hearing with their attendant mistakes that I can identify:- (as opposed to the general mistakes the IPO have made and I have already listed above).

1/ The Reynolds Hearing;

As early as page three he shows bias against me by saying that my perjury trial (which in actual fact was a forgery trial as perjury was dropped "may shed light on my credibility" Why is he visiting a judicial action that has nothing to do with this case of which he has no direct knowledge of? (Only to slag me off on a personal level and make it appear I have no credibility.

He makes a big deal over the fact that I did not advertise my own product and thus by not advertising and using the trademark Viper this goes against me. This despite it was obvious why, that is by my going into only wholesaling my product and leaving the retailing to RB as my agents. This is obviously sheer lunacy especially as it forms the main plank of why he found against me. The point being is that he does not state under what law he can justify those stupid observations and decision.

He refuses to believe that our agency document is anything but a forgery, just because RB says it is. Yet no evidence except the word of RB is ever put forward and he ignores the fact that I had been not guilty on the highest grounds of evidence required. He uses the feeble excuse that this being a lower court he can apply lower grounds of evidence required. Thus he completely ignores the fact that this hearing did not go through a complete appraisal of whether this document was a forgery and what was the credible evidence for that. He admits that had he viewed this document as a genuine one RB's case would have collapsed. (So we see here that is exactly what he does...he intimates it is a forgery as far as he is concerned and in one movement he has won the case for RB.) Yet he also ignores the fact that this document had TWO signatories and he was only seeing and hearing one. I view this part of his hearing as the most damming example of his mistakes, for using the balance of probabilities should have meant that he could not say for certain as he was only taking in one persons say so and even on the lower grounds of evidence this was not enough.

He makes a similar mistake further on over another document I put into evidence, that being the statement made by a customer for a fully built car who first came to me to have it built, but I was too busy. I told this man that RB as my agent could build it and that is what happened. This man had made an evidence statement for me for my forgery trial and that was put into evidence and accepted as such with no bother. Yet Reynolds says he cannot rely on it and gives ridiculous reasons for this. So here we have Reynolds applying rigid rules about it as if he were a higher court and this in direct contrast as to how he viewed the agency contract.

The point being here with these documents and the mistakes in law that Reynolds made is that BOTH these documents had the capacity to trash RB's case and Reynolds even says that. *It is obvious that Reynolds did not want me to win this case so he trashes the two most important pieces of evidence for my case… now I wonder why that was? And you have to wonder why the lower level of evidence that is required for civil cases, is not used to say that the balance of probabilities could say that taking into effect the fact that Busbridge had everything to gain and I had everything to lose, so it could have been Busbridge who had forged that document.*

Of course Reynolds never asked why Martin was not giving evidence for his brother and had he been present, the evidence he later gave in 2009 would have trashed the vacuous twitterings of this man Reynolds. For he would have shown that the agency document was real and he had signed it as had RB and that they had stolen my trademark and that the evidence document of the man over the car being built was stating the true facts. Also he would have confirmed that the advertising was controlled by me and half the costs were borne by me. In 2009 I got evidence from no less than RB himself that I paid out for advertising and marketing as outlined above.

Reynolds further made mistakes by harping on that there was little or no evidence that I traded with the mark, yet he also admits that all the kits and car parts I supplied to RB were Viper kits and parts. Thus contradicting himself.

Reynolds further shows a bias towards RB by saying that evidence given by him as to how he can claim the ownership of the mark, has to be tempered by the fact that RB is not an IP lawyer. Yet I too am not an IP lawyer, yet Reynolds gives me no such leeway in the way I presented my evidence.

Reynolds makes yet another mistake by stating that my adverts for 427 cobra parts did not mention the name, Viper. Yet he was told that these parts were universal **Cobra** parts and *not* Viper parts!

Another mistake is when he says that there was no evidence to suggest that at any point Mr Cook's or Classic Replicas name appeared in relation to the goods. Yet he had seen copies of all my invoices to RB for Viper kits and parts and the orders from RB for same, on which the name Viper did appear and he even admits this was the case. He does not quote any law which states that a manufacturer when advertising his product has to state the trademark when doing so each and every time.

However the greatest blunder I believe that Reynolds committed was by ignoring the rules for hearings by visiting areas outside his remit to visit. He spent much time talking about my history with the trademark during the time with my company Brightwheel Replicas and the cessation of that company in Sept 1989.

He completely ignores the fact that I had undergone a lengthy battle with Chrysler to prove my ownership of the mark and that hearing had agreed with my evidence and granted me registration. So here was Reynolds revisiting all that evidence and in effect retrying that hearing and coming to a different conclusion, which in effect said I did not have ownership of it. Not only was this gross in itself but it was outside his remit to do so. He should have taken the stance that I was the owner at the time that RB applied to register to mark, under common law and I had prior rights anyway.

Effectively I had fought Chrysler up to a date of January 1990 which was the date they had applied to register. My winning surely that then gives me rights to the mark from that date onwards. He also ignores the fact that the IPO had put RB's application on hold until my battle with Chrysler was over. Surely that can only have been so, as they knew that my evidence showed prior use to the evidence shown by RB in his application to register? Otherwise why suspend his application, especially as he made the application before me. Also that the Registry had told my agent that they viewed my evidence as showing I had prior use to RB.

2/ The Landau Hearing;

Landau conducted his hearing because I had objected to the alleged assignments that RB had put into evidence at the Reynolds hearing in order to show that the trademark had been assigned away from Cobretti his company, to yet another company and then at a convenient time, back to him (after his bankruptcy had finished).

I have no idea what remit Landau had been given as this hearing was not a normal hearing brought either by me or RB. Yet what happened was that Landau in effect actually re-heard the Reynolds hearing. He came to a completely *different* conclusion than Reynolds and one that was on my side, as it effectively would have taken the registration away from RB, had it ever been enacted. Which of course it never was, because as I say, the IPO did not want its conclusions enacted. To have done so would have opened the door for me to maybe sue the IPO for incompetence etc, etc. Something we all know that government departments definitely will do *anything* to avoid. Even to carrying out illegal acts.

My point here is why is it that *two hearings officers come to entirely different conclusions about one case?* The evidence seen in both cases was exactly the same.

3/ The Hobbs Hearing;

This case was brought about because RB appealed the Landau decision (obviously). Now straight away here I ask why was he allowed to appeal? In the Civil Procedures Rules it states that appeals can only be given if it can be said that the original decision was wrong, and or the case was unjust because of serious procedural irregularities.

The reasons that RB gave in his S of G's had nothing to do with either of those reasons and were in fact totally irrelevant to the case. The IPO failed to spot this as the Law Manual, Section 7.5 says that "on receipt of evidence the Registry will scrutinise the evidence for defects in their format" So I say they did this deliberately.

So the hearing went ahead and everything that went on in that hearing was corrupt; Civil Procedure rules state Section 52.11 (1) The hearing should have been limited to a review of the decision. It did no such thing. It discussed Case

Law which had nothing to do with the decision, it revisited old hearings like my Chrysler case and my copyright case against RB and so on.

CPR's state Section 52.11 (1)? The hearing will only receive evidence that was before the previous hearing. It did not as no evidence was ever produced and as already said, what little so called evidence of the case in the S of G's, was nothing to do with the previous hearing.

Judges Rules prohibit judges from being biased, they must not have any connection with the case in any way and their behaviour must be above reproach.

The Law Manual states, Section 2.1 Rules of the Registry; Those who represent the Registry and work in the Registry, particularly in the Tribunal Section must remain impartial at all times & are therefore unable to advise litigants on their cases. Yet in this Hobbs hearing Mr James the *head of the tribunal section* who was inexplicably present for what should have been a minor case, colluded with Hobbs to help RB, by giving him hints as to the legal position he was in, this by both of them discussing case law, which was not in their remit to do as what they discussed was not in the previous hearing. Then he again gives assurances to RB that the Registry will help him and not stand in his way if he follows the advice he is given. *totally illegal advice and actions.*

This unsavoury business is also against the advice given in the Trocadero case (B/L 0/440/99) when it was said by the A/P, "It is not for those arbitrating to become involved in debate", yet this is definitely what James and Hobbs did in this hearing between themselves and with RB.

On the behaviour issue of Judges, when Hobbs slagged me of and implied that I was involved in proceedings that were messy, and sordid etc, he was again breaking the rules under which he is supposed to work to, as he was visiting a case that was not relevant to this hearing and his behaviour should be above reproach and slagging off someone who is not even involved with the case does nothing for his behaviour.

Then Hobbs looks at the hearing of Landau, a case against which this appeal was, and he comes to yet another conclusion that was different to Landau. So what in effect we have here is that the original case which was my opposition to RB registering my trademark, is given one decision by Reynolds, a second completely different interpretation given by Landau and now a third, different interpretation by Hobbs. *What a incompetent state of affairs we have here!* How are we supposed to be able to have confidence in any of this?

3/ The Foley Hearing:

Well Foley makes many mistakes and in this case we have a Professor of IP Law saying so. First of all in his decision document he talks about the case coming under the TMA Sect 64 (1) when it should have been under 64(5) Prof Annand said that had it really proceeded under 64(1) it would have had to take a completely different avenue. Off to a good start then. However to my inexperienced mind, surely that means that his hearing was null & void? How can you have a hearing being undertaken under the wrong law? This would come under a technical fault, but then what am I and what do I know? This seen through IPO eyes!

He said that I had applied to rectify the Registry and that was why the Landau hearing was heard. This shows that Foley has not done his homework properly and it is a nonsense, as I did no such thing.

Another mistake Foley made was to say that he said there had been an error or omission in the Registry and that allowed RB to apply to Rectify. I had objected to this and had said there had been no error or omission. Prof Annand agreed that I was right.

He constantly revisits old hearings even when he actually states he shouldn't and when I point that out to Annand in my appeal against Foley, she agrees and finds it as strange as I do. But what it really means is he is incompetent and yet I have to bear the consequences of his incompetent hearing.

Foley makes many statements quoting the Hobbs hearing, yet this hearing is to Rectify the Registry so why is he talking about Hobbs? He does it so often that my suspicions are aroused and that was what prompted me to get hold of the transcript of the Hobbs hearing.

He makes a mistake when he says that there is no relevant legislation with regards to applicants going bankrupt. Yet there is as the IPO have said so on a number of occasions.

He then comes to conclusions about what the Insolvency Receiver knew or didn't know about RB's lies about the trademark. He had no evidence to come to the state the stupid statements he did.

He also makes a similar assumption as to what Martin would have accepted as an indemnity. This with absolutely no evidence to back up the conclusion he came to.

Once again, can one have faith in this bloke Foley and all that he said in his summing up and decision? I certainly didn't and neither did Annand if she had been 100% honest and not on an IPO mission to find against me, as it did not suit their agenda.

4/ The Annand Appeal Hearing;

She makes less mistakes than the previous three but she is not 100% mistake free. Firstly, why did she spend so much time going over my application to admit late evidence re the Insolvency Service and how they had acted over his bankruptcy and had then given RB a letter saying they had never been interested in the trademark. Yet to me they had said they couldn't comment on any aspect of his bankruptcy including the veracity of their letter, because they had destroyed all the files on his case.

I had only gone down this road because Foley had made a big deal out of all this in his decision. She then tells me that whatever Foley had said it was all irrelevant. It takes her no less than 24 pages to waste time on all that, before she gets to the chase.

Then despite saying she has no remit to visit other cases, like Foley she does just that by visiting Hobbs and Landau. They are priceless these IPO people, even if she is only indirectly part of them.

When she states that she found it entirely reasonable that Foley removed Martins name off the Registry and this after I had made strong representations that Martin had not been consulted about any of this. She obviously thinks it fine that we can all take the word of a liar that he doesn't know where his brother is.

She makes comments that she feels for RB and all the hearings he has had to endure and the irregularities in them (cockups). This is totally mad and out of order to side with anyone that is part of a hearing. After all, all these hearings were totally down to him and his criminal actions and not mine.

She in revisiting Hobbs to quote him at length is against the rules and she has previously said at the hearing she could not revisit other hearings. In doing so she is agreeing with what Hobbs said about how he thinks RB was able to say he was able to take over his brothers assets. Yet this hearing is about my appeal against Rectification not about the matter Hobbs was hearing.

After spending many pages waffling on about a hearing she has previously said she has no remit to comment on she is siding with what Hobbs says. You couldn't make it up, especially as she ignores everything I objected to about what Hobbs had said.

5/ The Invalidity Hearing by Salthouse;

As soon as I clapped eyes on this man Salthouse, I knew we were dealing with yet another asshole this time a hand picked one. I say this as he was obviously picked by the IPO for this case hearing because he was a large man who oozed 'Rottweiler' and his decision document shows this.

He makes a good start as per usual for IPO hearing officers, by getting his facts wrong by stating MB said in his evidence that when Cobretti were taken on as agents by BRL (me) it was to enable them to build fully built cars that BRL had gained orders for. This is not what MB said and it is not fact.

Then he says that MB stated that once I had left for Switzerland he and his brother changed the advertising which had hitherto been controlled by me, to now read that they were "under new management" Mistake as it read "now under new ownership".

Now he implies that a signature of RB on the agreement to split up the partnership is "considerably" different to the signature of him on our agency agreement. This is implying that it is a forgery and this is not only outrageous as Salthouse is supposed to be dealing with an application to make my registration invalid. Yet here he seems to be conducting a forgery trial and making aspersions so as to muddy the waters and make either me or MB appear as forgers. Yet if you look at all the signatures of RB over the years they are not all *exactly* the same, as indeed neither are mine... the duplicitous bastard!

Now he tries to again cast aspersions on both me and MB because MB had said that we both had a common goal against RB due to his deceptions. What he is craftily doing here is intimating that we will both say anything to nobble RB.

It was also along these lines that he now ***deliberately*** manipulated the evidence given, that was to do with what the consequences of the breakdown of the business and the partnership. MB had rightly complained that whilst he lost his house, RB did not. This was the absolute truth, yet Salthouse manipulated this to read that this was not the case and RB had (poor boy) also lost his house. All the evidence, had Salthouse ever read it and he should have, said that RB had a lien put on his house **one year after the breakdown** of the partnership, **and for reasons that were nothing to do with MB or the breakdown.** So this was a deliberate attempt to try and show sympathy for RB in that he too was a victim and had also found himself without a house.

It was also a deliberate attempt to show that MB was lying when he said he was the only person to lose his house over the breakdown of the partnership. When the truth was that RB if he ever did have his house subjected to a lien by the Insolvency Service, it was entirely his own fault. His bankruptcy had nothing to do with MB and it was RB's manipulation of events after the breakdown were he deliberately moved the assets of the Cobretti business away from it and conveniently into a limited company run by his wife when he knew that the Cobretti business was really bankrupt at the point of the partnership breaking down in mid 1992. He deliberately ran Cobretti for another year before throwing in the towel and going bankrupt (or someone forcing him into it) and no doubt getting the most out of his creditors before bankruptcy. Then he just carries on with this new limited company as if nothing had happened. Now Salthouse knew all this, as it was in my evidence and MB alluded to it as well. So it is as I say, a cynical and deliberate ploy by Salthouse to misrepresent the true facts in order to besmirch Martin. This has to be illegal and is most certainly corrupt.

Continuing his agenda to besmirch MB and his evidence he goes on the quote four paragraphs of one of his evidence statements. This by saying he found them to be "of interest" but note he does not say what that interest actually is. Again another intimation that they are all dubious or not to be believed, or for some other reason.

Firstly MB just says the partnership broke up because it would be financial suicide to continue. Nothing wrong in that, I say. MB says that the partnership broke up but that he had not given his brother his rights to his share of the assets. What is wrong about that?

MB admits he had not played a part in the business since 1992. Again what is wrong in stating that?

In the last paragraph he is merely stating that his brother (RB) had coerced their Mother to write him (MB) out of her will. Quite why Salthouse finds that he has to bring this up as it is evidence that has no bearing on these two cases. This is outside his remit to visit. But it is quite easy to see why the duplicitous bastard has done this... to say in effect that MB was out to get his brother... so we cannot believe anything he says.

Salthouse now turns his attention to me and my statements and immediately he plunges into making his first mistake about them. For he states I made a statement dated 18th Feb 2009, when no such statement was ever made! Then he says I claimed that I was the owner of the trademark Viper. It is said in such a *way as to imply to the reader that I was lying!* As I had registration then I am entitled to say I am the owner of the trademark. End of story.

Now he tries to imply I am a liar by saying that when I pointed out that the copy of the registration certificate that RB had put onto his website to show he was now the owner of the registration of the mark, this showed what a liar he was, yet it is implied I am the liar. This because the IPO in their usual incompetent way had issued him with and incorrectly made out registration certificate because Reynolds had said it had to be in the name of both Robert & Martin trading as Cobretti Engineering. This is what I *clearly* stated in my evidence, only to have that misrepresented. After I had complained to the IPO he was reissued with the correct registration certificate. I have all the paperwork to prove that, yet here is this asshole Salthouse, twisting the facts to make me out to be a liar.

He then goes onto more sticking his knife into me by saying that when I claimed what were the facts of my opposition to Chrysler, I was being "selective" in what I had said. Yet this duplicitous bastard goes onto being highly selective in what he says throughout the following paragraph, number 20 where he goes through all of my evidence exhibits. I will not go through everything he says because they have been already covered above in my breakdown of that Invalidity Hearing.

My point in saying what I have said immediately above is that this Salthouse, goon of the IPO, has behaved in the same way as all the hearing officers have, from day one. I will cover that at the end of this piece about his mistakes.

What he has done by being highly selective in what he selected out of what both I and MB had said and showed in documents, and by continually implying that both I and MB were lying or indulged in forgery or being selective ourselves, is showing he is biased against us. This is strictly against all the rules. For throughout all of his paragraph 20 he continually makes snide remarks whenever he thinks he can. What is illuminating is that although he lists each and in many cases, inaccurately describes what each is, he does not make any comment on their worthiness or validity.

This in absolute stark contrast to how he deals with the applicants (RB) statements and exhibits.

Salthouse spends two pages over Martins evidence and 5 pages over mine and only one and a half pages over Roberts evidence. This again shows Salthouse's bias against me and MB and bias for RB, for it was up to RB to PROVE his accusations as it was he who brought the action against ME. Therefore the onus is on him to prove conclusively that I had no claim to the trademark. He did not do this at all and Salthouse acts as if he did. It is outrageous and corrupt.

Contrast the amount of evidence in statements and exhibits that RB put in, absolute reams of the stuff and yet Salthouse only refers to the statements he could find that gave him the chance to rubbish Martin and intimate he had an agenda against his brother over family matters. The family matters were of absolutely no relevance to this case, so why did he mention them? So as to slag off Martin and say he was only after his brother for revenge over family matters. Where is the truth and relevance of this? This is a prime example of IPO bias as you can get. Whenever RB has slagged me off over and over again the IPO have remained silent. The minute Martin tries to show the IPO what a crook his brother is, not only over what he has done to me but also recently what he has done to his own brother, the IPO jump down on him to accuse him of only saying what he did, as being the actions of someone out to get RB. They make me sick, the biased, utterly crooked bastards.

To compound his bias again, against me this time, Salthouse waffles on about the alleged forged agency agreement. Everything Salthouse quotes from what RB said about it being a forgery is unfounded and unchecked, lies and conjecture by RB. Salthouse had the ability to question me on these ridiculous claims by RB about when I started using my letter headings as if this proved that the agency agreement was a forgery. Yet he did not question me at all. Yet here he is quoting

RB as if what he was saying was the gospel truth, when it was all a fairy story made up to vainly try to make out how the agency agreement must be a forgery. No evidence, just wild stories that were a nonsense and had I been asked about them I could have shown what nonsense they were. It is sickening in its bias and unfairness and may I say corruptness, as it was a cynical ploy to rubbish me once again. That is not legal as IPO hearing officers are supposed to be *independent!*

Salthouse now deals with *only four* pieces of our documentary evidence as opposed to the dozens and dozens put in by RB. All are either irrelevant to this case and all are taken out of context, to show an untrue picture of the facts. This is again an example of Salhouse's manipulation of the evidence to paint as bad a picture of me as possible and again shows extreme bias towards and against me and my defence.

Salthouse shows that he is going to be biased for RB as he says openly in his preamble for this hearing that he and *the IPO want to wrap up this Viper case once and for all.* So we all knew what that meant and you have been able to see that he did just that in his corrupt decision and ignoring of all the glaring evidence that went against RB. Dust off his hands and think "Got you there you bastard Cook and you will not be able to do anything to alter that, so the end of you as we know you will not be able to afford to appeal or do anything to touch us, as we are too powerful for you!"

Another glaring mistake by Salthouse is that he ignored the IPO Rule for Invalidity that states that the person asking for Invalidity has to approach the holder of the registration with a view to coming to an agreement to buying the mark. Or vice versa with the holder doing the same. I complied with this to no effect, but Salthouse does not even make comment that RB failed to do this. Once again RB can flout the laws and rules and the IPO does nothing.

The next blatant piece of bias is when Salthouse talks about the allegation that RB lied when he gave on oath, Martins alleged Spanish address. The bias here is so pronounced that I believe Salthouse is guilty of open corruption, because what he is actually doing is excusing RB from committing blatant *perjury*. Are we to take it that IPO Judicial Officers side with people who are committing blatant acts of *perjury?* We can all see why Salthouse has done this as he is no more than a lackey of those in the IPO who want to brush this whole saga under the carpet... *get rid of it any way you can, for we are untouchable and can lie and perjure ourselves*

to get our own way and get rid of this pest Cook! Just as he said in his preamble!

Why I have listed the above, about what I see as the individual failings and all of the hearing officers with the exception of Landau, is to show you readers that the way the IPO works not only is incompetent but wholly corrupt, with hearings officers who do the bidding of the IPO hierarchy. These are the very people that anyone who creates IP and then has problems with crooks stealing their IP, you will not be able to rely on them to help you. As in my case, because of them, I have been put to 18 years of hell and expense and I end up ruined. My business ruined and my life and health.

I am accused by the IPO of being a liar, a forger, someone who's word is shit and cannot be believed. This not by openly stating that to my face but by innuendo and intimating it slyly and all the time.

The business I started was never mine, the IP in the designs of my product never belonged to me, the trademark was never thought of by me and I never owned it at any time. In other words my business history and what I created was all an illusion. Whatever I said was the ramblings of a person who not only was a liar, but a fantasist, someone who was bent on revenge against a poor little victim who was the true owner and instigator of the mark *Viper*, and who was the owner and designer of the product. (For any trademark has to apply to a product or otherwise what use is it?)

One has to ask what is the training and qualifications of all the IPO Hearing Officers? For they are akin to Judges and we all know what training Judges have to go through and we know that at least even if some Judges are raving dickheads, they are at least *independent* raving dickheads! (Or are supposed to be.) These HO's are not independent and just what training do they have? For what I have seen about the way they conduct hearings does in no way give me any confidence. They are all a shambles in the way they are conducted with many glaring and obvious mistakes being made which are shown in this book.

One puts in statements and documentary evidence to back up your case and what use is all that? Does it ever get taken into account? No is the answer, what they do is cherry pick what they want to and ignore all the rest even if it does prove your case. Accusations of law breaking are ignored wholesale (perjury for one). The Law Manual is ignored as are the Civil Procedure Rules, as are their own trademarks Rules or any other rule or law. Case Law is bandied around as if it were the be all and end all yet each IP case is entirely different and I fail to see how previous cases can all be exactly the same, so what was decided there... how can it apply to your case? But they are all thrown in like confetti to confuse the issues and show that the HO is a learned bloke who knows his stuff. In any case how do we the Public know what all these Case Laws cases that are thrown at you, actually mean as they are written in lawyers gobble-de-gook.

HO's make constant comments on what they think about certain facts yet never fully explain how they come to those conclusions. They quote their thoughts and decisions but never give the authority for those decisions. People want to know what Law or Rule entitles these decisions to be made, yet they are kept in the dark.

Contrast the way Criminal cases are conducted or maybe even Civil cases in the Crown and County Courts. These IPO slackers would never be allowed to get away with what they do in those courts. For a start most of the evidence that gets put into these IPO cases would never be allowed in as evidence, as they would either be irrelevant or hearsay or too personal and derogatory against the opponent. Etc.

Evidence that is left in would have to be ALL gone over with a fine toothcomb in a court, and people allowed to get over their points and fully explain what they meant. They would be asked questions by the Judge in order that he or she understood fully what was meant and or what the real facts actually were. Documentary evidence would not be able to be ignored, and I am certain if claims of perjury or forgery or perverting the course of Justice were made, it too would not be ignored.

In other words the way the IPO hold and conduct all hearings is incompetent and not fit for purpose. All they are doing is letting down the public and ruining lives in the process and allowing crooks like Robert Busbridge to get away with the wholesale crimes of stealing IP, passing off, forgery, perjury, perverting the course of justice.

Those who like me will not let it go without a fight are branded by the IPO as vexatious, litigious, liars, fantasists, out only for revenge, are nuisances, pests, wasting Public money, unable to accept IPO decisions or whatever sick name or handle they think they can stick on you. I would love to know what they have called me behind my back, especially to the police, in their efforts to stop me from getting justice.

For getting justice is all I am about. As I am not a weak person who will roll over and let it go and let them get away with it, they obviously hate me even more. I am thankful that I was born with a brain and intelligence that I can use to fight them back with and I hope one day I can win through. We will see!

Of course there will be many in the country on reading my story who will leap up and say that I should forget all this and get a life. My answer to that is until this happened I did have a life! For I find that these types of people these days, view anyone who complains about anything as being somehow "defective" in some way and they should shut up and let it all go. No doubt these uncaring and vacuous people when confronted with some sort of wrong doing heaped upon them, will be the first to scream and shout. You see these loathsome creatures shouting their vile mouths off on any blog or forum, usually with appalling grammar and many swear words, every other word.

Then there are people in government departments like the Police, who will throw their hands up on seeing the reams and reams of this case history and will say the story is too complex and long and somehow this is a cop out for them to not do anything. These very same people will also show a lack of empathy or sympathy for you as a victim. In fact they they do not even see you as a victim but somehow you are responsible yourself for your own misfortunes.

If you dare to protect and defend your case with vigour and intensity because you believe passionately that you are in the right, then you will be subjected to the taunts that we saw Salthouse heap upon me in his decision document where he accuses me of indulging in invective when there was no such thing. You are damned because you dare to stand up against the stifling hand of the establishment who only want to make you lie down and let them suffocate you, so they can get rid of you.

Others will as I have said, see you as just a nuisance or a fantasist, or someone who just wants to make a fast buck by suing for some huge amount of money.

These are all symptoms of a sad and sick society that I have had to put up and with this coming from the various entities I have been forced to go to for help in gaining some form of justice and *to stop this conman from carrying on conning other people.*

It never seems to occur to any of these people that I may just be right and surely they should investigate if I am. This is the World we live in, that law abiding people like me have to endure. There is an absolute culture in this country to make the criminal or instigator of any type of strife, to be the victim of society or some other imagined malady and the real victim is nothing more than some mental case who deserves the problems they have had pushed onto them. These facts are amply outlined in the book *"A Land Fit For Criminals"* by David Fraser and my case fits that writers outline of Britain today and how the Establishment has ruined the areas of Law and Justice. Don't forget it is impossible to get legal aid these days as only illegal immigrants, terrorists and law breakers get this, thus making it an absolute impossibility if you are not rich, to get *justice.*

To quote from this book I give you some of the choicest statements of fact:-

"Whilst writing this book I was contacted by a number of people who had become desperate in their search for protection from criminals. All spoke of their total failure to get local politicians, MP's, criminal justice officials, police or indeed anyone to take notice of their desperate situation"—Doesn't that ring a bell for you? It certainly does for me.

"The rotting influence of this ever growing mountain of crimes which are never dealt with from psychological, legal or justice standpoints is fast undermining our faith in law and order and our belief in the justice system"—**dead right I say.**

"All governments from the 60's have gone out of their way to introduce policies that have encouraged criminals to become more criminal. Numerous obstacles have been put in the way of arresting and convicting them"—You can fit this into my case like a glove.

"When I started as a Police Prosecutor everyone wanted to prosecute, The Police wanted to prosecute, the courts wanted to deal with cases and the magistrates wanted to sentence. Now no one wants to do any of these things"—You can see this exactly in my experiences.

"Prosecutors must always think carefully about the interests of the victims of crimes when deciding whether or not to prosecute an offender. However in practice the grounds

on which they have to make this decision revolves so much around costs and the need to save money that the victims are rarely given a thought"—This guy must have known about my case when he wrote this as it fits it so closely.

Lastly I quote:-

"The purpose of the criminal justice system is to protect the public from crime and provide justice for those victimised by criminals."

When you look at how the Dorset and Met Police treated me, you would think I was the criminal and providing Justice was furthest from their minds! When someone like me who is educated, simply cannot get Justice no matter what I do, what chance has someone living on a sink estate who is a good person but not educated or articulate have of getting the absolute bastards to protect them from criminals and or Yobs, or get them justice?

"Over 90% of offences are going unpunished… the government determination 'to filter out' as many offenders as possible from the judicial system by whatever means possible in order to control expenditure, rather than bring them to justice". We are worse than a banana republic as we aught to know and do better than this. However the Establishment know they have in the British Public a truly soft, pliant and apathetic bunch of people, so they know they can get away with this.

Doesn't this make you feel proud to be British?

Chapter Forty Two
Conclusion

So now has come the time to wrap up this book otherwise I will still be writing up my vain efforts to get our utterly corrupt Establishment to admit they have shat on yet another member of the British Public. For as I have said *I am by no means the only one in this country that gets shat on by politicians, all public sector workers and by a Police Force* that is totally unfit to do the job they are there for. Not just by being corrupt but by being incompetent and duplicitous as well. And let us not forget our wonderful Judicial system and all those in it, especially our useless *judges* who couldn't judge a rabbit competition let alone properly and professionally judge important legal cases in their courts, without screwing up and giving out lenient sentences because they are mostly softies on criminals and others.

I believe this story shows just what a state this country has become in my lifetime. I have watched my country become a broken down basket case where nothing works. All aspects of government and government departments, councils and all Public Sector workers, in fact everyone that is paid by you and me, have dragged this country down to its fourth rate level that it is at today. Many have been able to escape it all, but because I have been brought to a level where I am now dependant on the state to survive, I am stuck here. Think about that. Had this not happened to me I would have retired well off enough to never have been a state dependant as I am. So these thicko's have refused to protect me from a rampant criminal and now the state has to pick up the tab and has to pay me Pensions Credit, Housing Benefit and Council Tax and they complain that the welfare bill is too high… they make me sick.

I have for years now got more and more sick of this country and I am at the stage now where I absolutely hate the place. Do the Brit politicians not realise how many people in this country hate the place as I do. I have travelled widely in Spain, Australia and NZ and spoken with hundreds of Brits who are there and all say as I do, that Britain today stinks and that is why they got away.

I hate all its institutions and all forms of government and I know that I am not alone in thinking this way. I hate the vacuous nature of the society we now have. You see it on TV every day with programme after programme that are so bad there is barely anything now to watch. If I were not so poor thanks to the IPO and Busbridge I would have buggered off long ago like those lucky Brits I have met on my travels.

Maybe one day the Brits that are left here will wake up at last and there will be an uprising of sorts. We should be more like the French, for if we were, it would have happened already. Mind you I blame your Mr Average Brit for all that has gone on in my lifetime because the Brits are now just a mob of lazy, apathetic shadows of the people that once made our nation **great**, or they are the educated but greedy members of the Establishment and upper classes, filling their pockets with their corrupt ways and merrily contributing to the down grading of UK PLC.

This to the point that in less than 50 years this place will be like a banana republic swilling in corruption and crime and ethnic Brits will be in the minority and downtrodden and probably Islam will rule. For we are all to soft to stop it, so what chance is there for me to get justice over this subject and story of mere intellectual theft, when the cretins who rule us cannot even rule our country properly let alone investigate crime and deal with criminals. When they put in charge of justice a fat, sloppy, looney oaf like Ken Clarke and the first thing he does is say he wants to send even less criminals to jail? They should sack him and make him spend all his retirement in the grottiest part of any big city, or better still in a jail. I have had another go at Chris Chope MP about Ken Clarke and why haven't I heard back? He replied that he had sent Ken a copy of my last letter when I tore apart his reply to my first letter, and I should just wait for his reply. So much for Chope putting himself out for me. I have written and asked him to meet with me and discuss how he can help me... what has he done... not even replied to it.

Today we hear that some conman forged several so called art products produced by that, super con woman Tracy Emin who makes so called art which my 3 year old grand daughter could do better at. He sells them on Ebay and what happens. We have the very same Met Police rushing round investigating this as if the Bank of England had been robbed, and some oafish so called top Met officer on TV saying how awful all this copying and forging is and it ***must*** be dealt with. The very same police force that deliberately will not investigate the forging of my artwork (for my designs of my cars that Busbridge stole, which were beautiful works of art as classic cars are). No, because the Tracy Emins of this World are well known and the Met know the press are onto them if they do not perform, they will be slated. Unknowns can get lost. Thus making me hate the Police even more than I already do.

Final points

These concern the answers to a number of questions that have been answered for me by a legal firm that specialise in IP. The questions covered specific points in the history of this saga to do with what IP law actually said. About half of the 20 questions concerned partnership and business law and the other half to do with IP.

I will state what the question was and their answer, then make my comments in bold print. However before that I had a conversation with an IP lawyer who is connected to the company that represented me at the very beginning when I was fighting Chrysler. I had wanted to clear up some comments made by that patent agent which related to what the IPO had told him about my application to register the mark.

What came out of that conversation is interesting because we were talking about suing the IPO and he told me that he had never heard of anyone ever winning in lawsuit against them and he told me many had tried. (I am damn sure there will have been many dissatisfied people just like me at their lies and arrogance and sheer incompetence.) This I think explains their supreme arrogance and the fact that the IPO have acted as they have towards me, obviously in the knowledge that they are untouchable. This is democracy at its finest, with the ratbags that we employ and pay, stitching us up like kippers and what can we do about it?

Questions answered by an IP lawyer on matters to do with this whole story re IP & partnership law and my comments are in italic:-

When two people want to register the same trademark for the same class, who would be allowed to proceed to registration first? The first to apply regardless of who first started to use on a first come first served basis or would the IPO look at who first used the mark?

The answer I got is that the first to apply would get the registration first. Fair *enough you can say, but that is **not** what happened as the IPO allowed me registration first and it even put the first application on hold whilst I tested my claim to registration against Chrysler. If you apply the same logic to who should also be allowed to oppose and application to register, the first or the second to apply, in this case Busbridge should have been the first to have an opposition heard when in fact I was allowed to oppose first even though RB applied to oppose first. There are comments elsewhere on the ramifications of this warped history of actions by the IPO on who was allowed what and when. So I will not repeat them here.*

I then asked a second question which was similar to the first one above, just to see if the answer given was consistent. It was; If a person were to apply to register a trademark first, then a second application was made later on by another party who had proven earlier use, who would the registration be given to and who would get to have their application dealt with first?

*As you can see here I have added the question of provable earlier use into the equation. The answers I got were pure waffle from the point of view the lawyer did not stick to what I had asked and answer it in **one sentence**! As she waffled on about registered marks etc and I had not said that either application went to registration quickly to the point in time that they were applied for.*

In a hypothetical case we have three companies who all want to register the same mark for the same class. Company A applies say in Jan 2000 but has not started to use it. Company B has been using the mark since 2001 but has not registered it. Company C has been using it since 1996 and also has not registered it.

Company B on hearing of Company A's application in mid 2002, rushes to apply to register the mark and also applies to oppose company A. Company C on hearing about A & B applying to register is more laid back as he knows he has prior use to both A & B. He opposes the FIRST application of A (after company B had) and knowing if he wins that he will also have proven use over B as well. He eventually puts in his own application to register in 2006.

Question 1 is; as company B put in an opposition first, would he have his opposition heard first?

Question 2 is; The IPO allowed company C's opposition against company A to go first, was this right and was it as they could show the earliest use?

Question 3 is; On winning Company C was given registration yet the application of company B which had been held on suspension whilst the case by C against A went ahead, was then allowed to go ahead. Surely this is wrong as it should have fallen away as it did not have earlier use to either A or C?

This question obviously was too difficult for this lawyer to grasp clearly and her answers were largely confusing. However she did say that Company C (Ken Cook) would have been allowed to be the one to oppose Company A's application first as they showed the earliest use. Also she said that Company B (RB) had no rights over A & C as he could not show earlier rights. Again this topic is discussed elsewhere and you can see what did happen, and it was not as the answers to the above questions. The answers coincide with what I feel should have happened. So if I and the lawyer are right, then the IPO have either cocked this up or they got it right by allowing me to oppose Chrysler first over RB and based on my earlier use which they now try to hide.

On the last question (3) the lawyer is confused but does say that I had earlier rights to RB but did not go so far as to answer with an opinion that it was wrong for RB to be allowed to go ahead with his application to register after I had won against Chrysler.

If in an IPO hearing the hearing officer was a faced with questions put in by the opponent that he would not answer and he said that another hearing would have to deal with that. The question is here, that the HO had all the time in the world to apply himself to that section of the evidence **before** the hearing or after and therefore be able to answer it himself so is it not unusual to order yet another hearing?

I got no coherent answer to this question as the lawyer seems utterly unable to understand what I was asking. Do not use this law firm for IP is my warning.

If after a hearing the appellant did not like the outcome and decision so he was allowed to appeal the rules state that in order to get an appeal you have to have absolutely good grounds to do so. The Judge/H.O erred in law on things like that. You cannot allow an appeal just because you don't like the outcome. The question is why does the IPO seem to allow appeals willy nilly?

Once again I got no coherent answer to this simple question as she went off into realms that I did not even ask about.

When the appellant at an appeal hearing then drops his appeal surely the decision of the hearing which he is appealing against has to be enacted?

Once again a simple question is not understood and the layer waffles on about appointed persons (who I did not even mention) and appealing to a higher court, when the question was: does the original decision get enacted if you drop an appeal (that appeal could be in front of Santa Claus for why does it matter who heard the appeal)? <u>If you drop it what happens?</u>

If the applicant to register a trademark, makes it knowing someone else owns it and the IPO are notified it is not bona-fide, then he becomes a bankrupt and again the IPO are notified and lastly the partnership that it is applied for in the name of, is dissolved and again the IPO are notified. Each time the IPO are asked to disqualify the application but it ignores this each time. The question being is what should the IPO have done?

Once again these questions were not understood or answered.

If a company who manufactures a product, decide to take on an agent to take over the retailing of the product in order that the manufacturer can concentrate only on manufacturing and they allow the agent to use their trademark under a contract and its conditions prevent the agent owning the mark, that surely cannot allow the agent to later on lay claim to the trademark for himself?

A simple enough question not entirely answered except it is said that the terms of the licence would have to be obeyed. However this is obvious and was not what I asked so the bit about would RB have been able to lay claim to the trademark is not answered.

In any IPO hearing would not the HO be obliged to take into consideration all the evidence that is put before him by the opponent. Show he has done this in his decision document and to actually say why he may discount some of the evidence, and certainly not to ignore great swathes of it as if it were never said or presented?

Another question which it is said is incredibly difficult to answer. Quite frankly it shows the low level of intelligence of a lot of lawyers we put our trust and money into.

I now dealt with partnership laws and asked the question about the break-up of Cobretti and would the application by Robert to register a trademark whilst the partnership was still together, but never told Martin he was doing this. So would that application not be null and void as it was not legally applied for under partnership laws which say any partner cannot undertake actions without the knowledge of the other partner?

We now are having these questions answered by another lawyer who is no better than the first one. He too makes a meal of every question and wanders off into the bush as if he is on a walkabout. He confused me with Martin and kept referring to me as if I were Martin when in a preamble I said quite clearly I was not even involved in this partnership.

So this simple question was never answered despite 8 paragraphs of waffle on subjects that were not even in the question.

I then talk about this indemnity that was talked about but never was done legally as Martin was advised not to accept one as Robert had no money to back it up. I ask how is it the IPO think that they can just say that as it was talked about and as Martin had left, it can then said to have been an 'implied indemnity'? Especially when RN knew full well where MB was at all times and when MB came back from Spain in 2009 he specifically said he was against the ruling as it had been done without his permission. Were the IPO right to do this in law?

Another non answer to this question.

I then covered the vexed question of perjury and how does the HO deal with it? I also say that it was reported to the hearing officers and others in the IPO and yet time and again it was ignored so what is the position when it is not acted on by the HO?

Here he gives half an answer by saying if a judge feels there is sufficient evidence of perjury he will pass it onto the CPS.

I ask what should an HO do when he is told that a document is a forgery yet there are two signatories and only one is present and saying it is a forgery and the person who has been said to have made the forgery has been found not guilty in a higher court.

Here he says that the judge must decide the case on the evidence before him. So once again he only half answers as my question of the fact that only one signatory is in front of him making accusations that could be false as they are not corroborated by the second signatory.

I ask if in an IPO situation where HO finds against the appellant can he just ask for an appeal without showing very strong grounds for an appeal as one would need to in a higher court?
Not answered as obviously did not understand the question.

I ask if when the appeal has been dropped would it not be the case that the original decision would be enacted?
Not answered as obviously did not understand the question.

I ask if I can report perjury to the Police or do I have to get permission from the HO's of the IPO to report it?
Answer: This is the only question I got an answer to and that was, write to the Attorney General about it.

So I was really no further forward after that fruitless exercise and £250 lighter in my pocket. What a rip off.

You wouldn't believe the amount of trouble I had to get a lawyer to answer those 20 lousy questions.

I approached four firms who I had used at one time or another over the last 10 years to either answer questions or to be involved with the Chrysler issues and who had earned much money from me. One after the other they refused to answer them. They all said the same thing and that was they needed to see all the documents so as to get acquainted with the evidence. Having seen all the above evidence, and that is actually in knocked down form for this book, can you imagine how much these blood-sucking people would have charged me to answer a few questions that any decent knowledgeable lawyer should be able to answer off the top of their heads or at least after looking up various law books etc.

They either can't be arsed with little jobs or they are stupid. Or they are frightened to death of putting their name to answers that they think there is probably a million different answers to the question and I may put their answers into the public arena and they will get rubbished. I know what the answers are.

Those companies that pissed me right off with all that, were; Lawdit in Southampton, Laytons in Guildford, Simon Chapman in London at, Humphreys in Bristol and to hell with all of them. However I needed answers so I thought I would try a local IP company, Humphries Kirk as a last resort. I contacted them and asked if they would answer some questions on IP law and partnership law and I sent an email with the questions. They said they would but started off on the same old tack of wanting to know all the history. I convinced them that I was not about to go into litigation (which I am not, even though I would like to) and that I was just researching.

To use the car and garage analogy; if they brought a car into my garage that had a problem that they needed answers on and I treated them the same way and charged them heaps and yet did not even do the job properly, they would be screaming their heads off. What did I say about lawyers, earlier on? ***they are mostly legalised highway robbers*** (although there ***must*** some that aren't). I think you can guess what I said and so at this stage I still do not have my important questions answered, even though I think I know the answers anyway, but I wanted expert (what a laugh) answers to back me up. (Experts like Daniel Wallens of Lester Aldridge in Bournemouth who cost me £6K and then yet wanting another £4K all for nothing.)

At this point I have certain outstanding requests with different bodies trying to eventually get justice. A vain hope I think but I am going ahead so I can show you just how the Establishment will shut up shop and will get together to make sure you will get absolutely nowhere.

I list here, those bodies:-
- The Independent Police Complaints Commission.
- The Information Commissioners Office
- The Parliamentary Ombudsman
- Ken Clarke. MP
- Dominic Grieve. MP

- Chris Chope, MP

I complained to the IPPC because the police forces of Dorset and The Met as both refused to act on the perjury and forgery that I asked them to investigate. I will keep this and the following descriptions brief, as you will be able to see my letters to all these bodies and their replies, on my blog. As I expected both these police forces refused to investigate Busbridge and they gave various incredible excuses, mostly what they had been fed by the IPO, in that perjury could not have been committed. They knew that they were lying and even when I sent a copy of the Perjury Act and CPS guidelines, they just ignored those.

I sent in a report to the IPPC in London about the Met, with my supporting evidence. However I will bet you they will like all the bodies do nothing and will lie and give excuses and will twist what I have said and my evidence, so as to suit their answers. For this is what all the civil service ***holes do as they do not want to have to show up brother civil servants. For if you think they are Independent your as mad as a hatter. Ask yourself this; how many coppers can you remember getting done by the IPPC for heinous crimes like murder and killing members of the Public with gay abandon? The answer is *none!* That says it all I think. For coppers are only yobs and criminals in uniform, they know they are untouchable and they know the IPPC are toothless. I just want to hammer home to you just how *impossible it is for any one in my position to get justice! Also how all these government bodies, supposed to be there to protect you, are nothing more than a sham!* They are full of cringing useless civil servants, earning packets of money, who *you* pay for and for what?

I have sent the Information Commissioner reports on the IPO refusing to give me *all* the documents relating to what the Police asked them and what they told them back. The IPO have given me as you can see in the documents attached to the blog, just a few documents which only tell me that as far back as 2004, the IPO was viewing me as a 'difficult' person and 'angry' and that was *before* they had even had carried out any hearings. So what they think about me now is anyone's guess.

Ken Clarke I know will not reply to my reply to the initial knock back about when I complained that Judge Hobbs had conducted a corrupt hearing.

Dominic Grieves office clerk has consistently refused to answer my question as to how is perjury supposed to be reported. This as the Police have used this as one of their many excuses not to investigate. By saying that perjury has to be reported by the A/Gen, which I think is rubbish. In February I sent yet another request for the Att/Gen to tell me how perjury and forgery is supposed to be reported, but in stronger terms and asking Mr Grieves to read the letter and reply in person rather than it only being seen and replied to by a pen pusher of his.

The Parliamentary Ombudsman is a complete and utter waste of time, a con on the Public, a sham that is just set up to give a bunch of civil servants jobs and to make it appear that if you have been wronged by any government department, you have an avenue to get things righted. What a sick joke, as they are nothing more than a disgrace. I knew all that but I decided to put in a complaint about the IPO, just to see what they would do or say this time round. To test them, so to speak, so you can see through this book what a bunch of corrupt, lying, ***holes they are and on a level with the IPO. This being the *third* time I had tried them.

I sent a three page letter outlining the complaint that the IPO deliberately lied to the Police about what constituted perjury and had told them it had not been committed when it clearly had been. I said that as the IPO seemed to not want the Police to investigate Busbridge and his perjury and forgery, thus that constituted them trying to stop my getting justice and this was therefore, perverting the course of Justice.

The first thing this bloke, O'Connell says in his reply to me is that I am in a lengthy trademarks dispute with Busbridge as if this is still ongoing, which of course it is not as the last hearing is now going on for a year ago and I am not going to waste any more time pursuing RB especially through the IPO. They then go on to making various statements which are all grossly wrong and they say I stated things which I did not. You get this all the time with civil servants as if they are incapable of getting their facts right. For instance in their third paragraph they said that I had accused the IPO of 'colluding' with RB, when what I had said is that I thought that they had sided with him, which is something different. For them to have 'colluded' would have meant that the two sides got together to work out a strategy, something entirely different to siding with someone or having your sympathies with them but it never going so far as to work together to arrive at a mutually satisfactory outcome.

Then he says I had accused the IPO of 'inertia' which again is grossly wrong as I never ever mentioned that word. This they said I had, and had also said it had deprived me of my right to a fair trial, and this is another gross lie as I never mentioned any of this as you can see on the blog, when you read my original letter to them in which I outline my complaint. Again this is the devious and corrupt way civil servants work, putting words into your mouth in order to paint a picture of you that is distorted'.

I had in an email between us, said that I had not therefore, because of the allowing of constant perjury, received a fair trial which is against the Human Rights Act. This shows an incapacity get their facts right on simple matters as to what did you actually say. If they cannot do this properly, how can you have faith that their decisions are credible?

Another way the P/O fail in their duty to the Public is that whatever you accuse the government department of and say they are guilty of maladministration by their actions or lack of actions, they will disagree and say the department is whiter than white. He says in this letter that they need to see indication of maladministration from me which has caused me unremedied injustice. Now I ask you, what do you think I have suffered in this instance, by the IPO failing time and again, going back to 2004 to deal with all the perjury by RB? Then lately when they have fed the Police with a load of utter lies over their saying that perjury wasn't committed, CPR rules ruled the reporting of it and so on. Thus giving the Police the excuses they are looking for not doing anything. On top of that you can bet your life that they have painted a black picture of me to the Police and will have told them that if RB was charged with perjury and forgery, this would be letting the side of the civil service down as they would be shown to have been either incompetent or biased towards RB and against me.

You can also bet your life on this having been said to the police, for you cannot tell me that the Police, whether it is Dorset or the Met do not have access to the lawyers of the CPS to ask all about perjury and forgery. On top of that, do not forget that back in 1999 the Police had no problems saying *I had committed perjury and forgery and charging me in double quick time!* One of the lies the IPO told the Police is that as all the hearings had never been carried out under 'oath' therefore perjury could not have been committed. Think about that, for firstly it is saying that before IPO hearings you can win your case by lying through your back teeth on a serial level and you are not committing perjury. Yet the minute you take an oath you are committing perjury. Their duplicity and lying never ceases to amaze me. Then you must go back to the hearing back in 1998 when I was fighting Chrysler and they were asking me if I had forged the agency document, and that hearing was not under oath either, yet that did not stop the Met from taking on a case and me getting charged with perjury. Again the hypocrisy of civil servants is staggering and they get away with it.

So if I haven't suffered and 'unremedied injustice I am a Monkeys Uncle and I do not know what it is I have suffered... maybe it is all in my mind and I am hallucinating?

O'Connell then goes on to saying that the P/O would need to be satisfied that an investigation would need to provide a worthwhile outcome' This is what makes me 'Raging mad' whenever I have to deal with these civil service, devious cretins, when they make comments like this. I ask all independent intelligent readers of this book to say that if I could see RB charged and to undergo a trial, that that would not be worthwhile for me. Of course I would also like to see all the ***holes in the IPO that I have had to deal with over the last 10 years be dealt with in some way. Of course if I had the money I would have sued the IPO long ago or at least at the very beginning of this nightmare in 2004, I would have appealed to the High Courts and would have no doubt trashed them. So I have no illusions that my chances of retribution against the IPO are almost zero, so getting some justice against RB would have to do and that is exactly what I had said in my letter.

Yet another cretinous statement is made just further on when the writer says it does not appear that the IPO have acted 'unreasonably'. Of course he would say that but it is so far removed from the truth that it is sickening.

I made a point of saying that my complaint was not about the outcome of all the hearings. So what did they say in reply, in a nutshell the IPO did not believe any of my allegations about anything and this despite the evidence I showed in all the hearings and especially at the last hearing in 2010. So I am a liar and Busbridge isn't, yet no evidence that I am a liar has ever been shown in any of the hearings.

It is then said that the IPO CEO explained that officers conducting hearings would consider my claims, (presumably about perjury) when the truth of this is their CEO never ever said any such thing. *In fact in 2009 when I was complaining about the perjury I was told that the CEO could not comment about a forthcoming hearing. So more lies.*

Another lie is that the writer says at each hearing I was given the opportunity to make my allegations of perjury and submit them. ***This again is simply not the case and the Reynolds, and Annand hearings which I was present at, no such things were ever said to me. Why do these civil servants lie so much?***

Hearing Officers do not say anything to you at hearings about what you can put forward in evidence, as all your evidence is put in months before the hearing and the ***IPO cannot tell you what you should say in your statements of evidence—full stop.*** Of course in the hearings where I was able to put in written evidence statements, I did constantly bring up the perjury and forgery, only to have all that evidence totally ignored. In total there were SIX hearings; Reynolds in 2004, Landau in 2005, Hobbs 2006, Foley in 2008, Annand in 2009 and lastly Salthouse in 2010. I was only able to be present at Reynolds, Annand, and Salthouse hearings. In the Landau and Hobbs hearings I was not even able to submit evidence, and the Foley hearing I could submit evidence but as I have said, bizarrely I was excluded from the actual hearing. It was only at the very end, in preparation for the Salthouse hearing, after my bitterly complaining about the perjury and forgery not being addressed, that it can be seen that I was told I could submit whatever comments and evidence I wanted about ***all*** the perjury committed since 2004 and only because RB submitted evidence statements he made for the 2004 hearing into the 2010 hearing, for a second time, thus repeating his perjury).

All this again amounts to the deviousness or the incompetence of this civil servant when he makes these totally inaccurate statements in his paragraph 7, about how the IPO reacted and behaved regards my complaints about perjury. What of course he omits to admit to, is that every statement and complaint I made about the perjury and forgery by RB from 2004-2010 where all ignored. In all the decision documents there were no comments whatsoever about my allegations of perjury or forgery.

The cap off all his lies and insults to me, the one that makes me puke is the; 'It appears, based on the IPO repeatedly finding against Mr Cook, that the IPO did not believe his allegations' You can bet he was told that in his undoubted conversations he would have had with someone in the IPO. In other words, every word Busbridge said in all his lying evidence statements, was believed. Many times with no evidence having been put forward by him to ***prove*** his lies, yet whatever I said in my defence or when I was making my points, backed with documentary evidence in most cases, I was disbelieved. Now why was that I wonder? How would this vacuous civil servant react if I showed him videos made by the BBC and ITV of me in my factory in 1988, making Vipers for export to Japan, or our promotional video for my company made by a BBC man in 1987? Or another video made in 1989 by an independent kitcar magazine which again show my business making cars and kits and openly stating that the Busbridges were my agents. Yet according to the IPO after 1989 this *crook* Busbridge was given carte blanche by them to steal all that off me and purely by lies. Yet it is I that is made out by the IPO to be the liar. I kick myself from not putting into evidence these videos, that showed I thought up the trademark, the designs of the car, and not Busbridge.

Also what you should take note of is that I put forward backing affidavits from Kunzli which clearly showed that two documents RB put into evidence in 2004 were forgeries. In the 2010 hearing Martin Busbridge put in one affidavit on oath and three statements under 'truth' which backed up many of my claims about RB's perjury. So what the IPO are really admitting to is that no matter whether it was me or others, when ever we showed that the evidence of RB was tainted by lies and forgery, *none of us was believed… why was that I ask and have been asking since day one?*

Even when RB tripped himself up by making a lie or lies in one statement then contradicting himself on the exact same subject in a later statement, because he had forgotten his earlier lie, they still would not accept he'd lied. It is as I have said many times, glaringly obvious that the IPO had an agenda and that meant allowing RB to lie so they could side with him and deny me my rights. Rights to a fair trial or rights to MY IP.

Then we get to the part where I had said that the IPO had lied to the Police about whether perjury had in fact been committed. We have the unedifying picture of this duplicitous oaf O'Connell saying that the Police had approached the IPO and that the IPO had told them that as they understood things it *was not possible for there to have been perjury committed at their hearings and referring them to civil procedure rules.* For there is absolutely nothing in CPR's that lays out how it can be determined that perjury has been committed. You have to read the perjury act for that and even here the IPO lied again by telling porkies to the

Police by misquoting the Act. Then again you have to ask why the Police go the very institution that I am complaining about… to get Legal Advice from. Don't you find that strange? When all they had to do is ask the CPS, who they must be in constant touch with on a daily basis. Of course this corrupt O'Connell accepts all that the IPO have said to him at face value, does not get his own legal advice, ignores my evidence that what the IPO have done re the Police, is all lies. All this is par for the course for the P/O, as they work in tandem with those departments you complain about and they think you are as thick as a plank and that you will not be able to see through them.

O'Connell states in paragraph 8 that the correspondence we have seen does not indicate that the IPO lied to the Police. Well he would say that in order to 'protect' the IPO. I sent him a copy of the email from Hayward to DC Brimicombe where he states "perjury can only be committed if affidavits are filed—and only witness statements were filed" I also sent O'Connell copies of the Perjury Act which clearly shows that perjury can be committed under statements of truth. So that is one lie which O'Connell despite my pointing this out to him, ignores.

Then O'Connell says that Hayward directed the Police to CPR Rules which they elucidate by showing what Rule 32.14 says. Immediately this shows that by making the above claim he has lied because he goes on to show under this rule perjury *is* committed under a statement of truth. Yet O'Connel **still says, no lies have been made to the police.** How corrupt can you get? Don't tell me that the IPO do not know when perjury is committed as they have their own lawyers. Lastly he repeats the lies again about me saying the IPO colluded with Busbridge.

Lastly 'Chope the Chump' who is supposedly, my MP. When I had to send him my complaint about the P/O through him, he did not pass onto them my supporting documents and when I wrote to him asking him why this was so… he ignored my letter! Not the first time this complete and utter ***hole has done this. I then wrote another 'nice' letter saying I wanted help over my efforts to get Justice and would he help me. He ignored that as well, so I will now stir it up for him and report him to the Conservative Chief Whip, who I am told is the only person you can complain to about MP's not doing their job, that is to represent their constituents. What a waste of time that will be too.

I would urge all the readers of this story, which is an example of Establishment

failings, corruptness and how they treat the Public, to consider what the Prosecuting Council QC said in the recent trial of Tommy Sheridan over perjury which was held in Scotland:-

"His acts which although had no victim, *had to be prosecuted to the full, because PERJURY IS A SERIOUS CRIME that CANNOT BE IGNORED as it cannot be allowed to become the normal behaviour of people"*

Apparently this fact which I wholeheartedly agree with is not known to the following entities:- *The IPO, The Dorset and Met Police and their Commanders, The Parliamentary Ombudsman, The OJC and JACO, my MP Mr Chope, Ken Clarke MP, and the Attorney General Dominic Grieve MP.* For they all seem to feel perjury in my case can be ignored for who the hell am I to be bothered about or whether my life and business has been wrecked by not only perjury but forgery as well...*What do you think?*

March 2001 Just before printing this book the outstanding actions I had as to whether the requests to the IPO, the Met Police, the Dorset Police and the Parliamentary Ombudsman for documents under the FOI Act which were turned down by all of them, was correct. Because of this I had to complain to the Information Commissioners Office and the first reply from them did not set me alight with hope that here at last I had found a quango that would actually do something honest for a change. So I was forced to ring the person who had written to me, a certain Mr B.McNally. He turned out to be a typical evasive and arrogant civil servant who belong to the huge army of quango civil servants pushing pieces of paper around all the offices that litter the country and are there supposedly to be the checks and balances that Politicians are always boasting we have to protect us from the excesses of politicians and civil servants. Of course it is all a sham, a lie to pull the wool over our eyes. For all these people do is take our money in wages etc and do nothing to protect us from the Establishment.

He had said that I had asked for the ICO to look at complaints under the Freedom of Information Act when it appeared to him that I was asking for release of papers about me personally and that would come under the Data Protection Act. In fact I had asked for papers under both acts. I asked hypothetically , if I were to re-submit a request under the DPA and it was found that I had had documents withheld, then what powers did the ICO have to force the Police or the IPO to release them? This is where he suddenly became evasive but under determined questioning he admitted that the ICO could ask that documents be released, but when I asked if those requests had any powers behind them, it became evident that *once again we have here a toothless quango with no powers!!*. For if anyone was found to have not complied with these acts, in his words " the ICO would not take action against any department unless there had been a history of non compliance and he knew of no cases where this had happened' What a sham for I simply do not believe that there are absolutely no government departments that have wilfully withheld documents form the Public-EVER! It is more like a concerted act of covering up by all, to make it appear that everyone was clean and to hell with getting justice for anyone!

So it is clear to me that to try and get any of those incriminating documents out of those four bastard departments will be through this useless mob, the ICO, will be yet another waste of my time. So *another blow for getting Justice for the People in situations like me!*

With the Parliamentary Ombudsman, whilst I have responded to their crass rejection letter of my complaint as outlined above, I know if they do reply I will still only get another rejection and more lies and excuses.

The IPCC have now replied with their entirely predictable rejection of all my complaints about the Met and have basically sided with all the Dorset Police and the Met have done and said and this despite my detailed history of what the Met had done and said was an abrogation of their duties etc, etc. I will not go into detail here as to what I said in my letter of complaint to them or their detailed reply as I will put all that on the blog.

I have also received from the Dorset Police, their eventual reply (they took no less than 5 months get this reply together) to my original complaints that they refused to investigate the forgery and perjury committed in Dorset. Guess what?.... a complete and utter rejection once again. Some of their excuses and lies and behaviour have to be seen to be believed, *but the thing that really sticks in my throat is that they have lowered themselves even more than they already are in my eyes (and many of the Public's eyes) by lying on a grand scale (they are as bad as Busbridge in every respect and even worse as they should be) and have resorted to denigrating my integrity and my alleged behaviour during that interview I forced them to have.* Par for the course for our wonderful Police Forces in the UK, you may say If they in a hole they lie their way out and denigrate those rubbish those who are seeking justice for their behaviour, by accusing you of swearing and shouting, talking over them (whatever that means) and being overbearing (because you refuse to let them ride roughshod over you). I should have recorded the interview with the gizmo I now have for this purpose should it ever eventuate again. Once again the relevant letters will be put onto my blog so you can see for yourself how coppers are crooks and liars just as much as the criminals we hope they put away for us.

Lastly I have found that there is quango person called "The Victims Commissioner" sounds wonderful doesn't it? This is a person called Louise Casey and I can explain to her the treatment I have had to endure, however she like all the others has no teeth or powers to do anything, so what's the use of her and her Commission? Shall I bother to contact her? Yet here we have yet another overpaid civil servant, sitting no doubt in a big office surrounded by any number of civil servants all pulling in huge wages and costs at our expense and for what?

So to repeat again… for those who want to know the final outcomes and all the letters thereof, you can read my blog which I started in 2008, in which I give a running commentary on how things have gone, as they happened. I will include reporting on all my ongoing efforts to get *justice* should there be more actions to see a criminal in jail where he belongs. That blog is not as comprehensive with all the facts, as is this book. By putting in *all* the paper evidence that I talk about in this book you will be able to see for yourself that I have been scrupulously honest in what I have recounted about the evidence I have said exists.

For those of you in business, I hope I have been able to show you how to take care in what you do with your IP and how to be very wary about the IPO, the whole of the Judiciary and lawyers in general, and not forgetting our totally useless money grasping politicians. Certainly those who are in partnerships and or take on agents or dealers, be extremely wary and careful. Get everything legally done and in writing. Learn to cover your backside every which way you can, otherwise you can end up like me at 70, completely broke money-wise and stuffed. (but not broken in spirit). I hope that I will have at least helped someone along the line, for that will be something. At least writing this book has helped keep me occupied for over a year and kept the old brainbox working and in fine fettle.

However this story is not really just about me and my particular problems with the Establishment but it is a facsimile of the horrendous problems that countless thousands of the long suffering members of the British Public also suffer from, at the hands of the British Establishment. Think about all those people who have suffered in countless ways at the hands of the NHS, the Education system, members of the armed forces, the Police, local councils, the judiciary and so on. The list is endless as is the suffering which really warrants a damn good revolution in my opinion. May be we should ask the Egyptians to show us how to do it, seeing as we have become an apathetic, spineless and supine lot.

The problem is as of now no one gives a shit and this is certainly so in our media, as the only ones in this mad country today who get looked after are the terrorists, criminals and illegal immigrants and the like.

WELCOME TO THE MAD HATTERS TEA PARTY IN BRITAIN, IN THE 21ST CENTURY!

My Blog is on: www.bewareincompetentcivilservants.blogspot.com

For comments or suggestions, please use the blog facility. Only comments from bona-fide people will be answered. If you need an answer, leave contact details.

Ken Cook
March 2011.

CONCLUSION